THE WARS OF THE ROSES

Also by Desmond Seward

The Monks of War
Eleanor of Aquitaine
The Hundred Years War
Richard III
Henry V
Sussex

THE WARS
OF THE ROSES

THROUGH THE LIVES OF
FIVE MEN AND WOMEN
OF THE FIFTEENTH CENTURY

DESMOND SEWARD

VIKING

VIKING
Published by the Penguin Group
Penguin Books USA Inc., 375 Hudson Street,
New York, New York 10014, U.S.A.
Penguin Books Ltd, 27 Wrights Lane,
London W8 5TZ, England
Penguin Books Australia Ltd, Ringwood,
Victoria, Australia
Penguin Books Canada Ltd, 10 Alcorn Avenue,
Toronto, Ontario, Canada M4V 3B2
Penguin Books (N.Z.) Ltd, 182–190 Wairau Road,
Auckland 10, New Zealand

Penguin Books Ltd, Registered Offices:
Harmondsworth, Middlesex, England

First American edition
Published in 1995 by Viking Penguin,
a division of Penguin Books USA Inc.

1 3 5 7 9 10 8 6 4 2

CIP data available
ISBN 0-670-84258-3

This book is printed on acid-free paper.
∞

Printed in the United States of America
Set in Monophoto Garamond

For
Susan Mountgarret

'People of the Middle Ages existed under mental, moral and physical circumstances so different from our own as to constitute almost a foreign civilisation. As a result, qualities of conduct that we recognize as familiar amid these alien surroundings are revealed as permanent in human nature.'

Barbara W. Tuchman,
A Distant Mirror

Contents

THE PRIME OF EDWARD IV, 1471–83

THE REIGN OF RICHARD III, 1483–85

THE END OF THE WARS, 1485–99

EPILOGUE: THE FOUR SURVIVORS

Illustrations

Acknowledgements

My first debt is to my editor in New York, Carolyn Carlson of Viking. The book owes a very great deal to her enthusiasm and constructive criticism.

I am also grateful to Susan, Viscountess Mountgarret for many useful suggestions and for taking me round the battlefield of Towton; to Peter Drummond-Murray of Mastrick, Slains Pursuivant of Arms, for advice on the Earl of Oxford's genealogy and on the significance of the earldom of Derby; and to the staffs of the British Library, the London Library, and the Guildhall Library for all their patient assistance.

I have benefited immeasurably from the work of scholars during recent years, work which has enormously increased our knowledge of the Wars of the Roses and especially of Richard III. I would like to instance in particular the biography of Margaret Beaufort, *The King's Mother*, by M.K. Jones and M.G. Underwood; the publications of Dr M.A. Hicks, whether books or articles in learned journals; and the contributions of numerous specialists to *The Ricardian*.

I must record a special debt of thanks to Michael Kadwell and David Plumtree of Holleyman & Treacher, Brighton, for their help in finding the black and white illustrations.

Chronology

1462		execution of the Earl of Oxford and his son
		Margaret of Anjou lands in Northumberland
	December	Lancastrian garrisons surrender in Northumberland
1464		the Duke of Somerset rebels against Edward IV
	May	Edward IV marries Elizabeth Woodville in secret
		defeat of last Lancastrian army at Hexham
1465	July	capture of Henry VI in Lancashire
1468		Lancastrian plots – arrest of Earl of Oxford
1469	June	Robin of Redesdale rebels
	July	the Duke of Clarence marries Warwick's daughter
		Yorkist defeat at Edgecote
	August	Edward IV confined at Middleham
	September	Edward IV regains his freedom
1470	March	Sir Robert Welles's rising in Lincolnshire
		rebels defeated by Edward IV at Losecote Field
	April	Warwick and Clarence flee to France
	July	Margaret of Anjou and Warwick are reconciled
	September	Warwick invades the West Country
		Edward IV flees to Burgundy
1471	March	Edward IV lands in Yorkshire
	April	Yorkist victory at Barnet – death of Warwick
	May	Yorkist victory at Tewkesbury
		the Bastard of Fauconberg besieges London
		murder of Henry VI
1473	September	the Earl of Oxford occupies St Michael's Mount
1474	February	the Earl of Oxford surrenders
1475	July	Edward IV invades France
	August	Edward IV makes peace with Louis XI at Picquigny
1478	February	death of the Duke of Clarence
1483	April	death of Edward IV
		Richard, Duke of Gloucester's first coup
	June	Gloucester's second coup – death of Lord Hastings
		Gloucester proclaimed King
		coronation of Richard III
	July?	murder of Edward V and the Duke of York
	October	the Duke of Buckingham's rebellion
1485	August	Henry Tudor lands at Milford Haven
		defeat and death of Richard III at Bosworth

1487	June	defeat of the last Yorkist army at Stoke
1489	April	rebellion in Yorkshire
	December	the Abbot of Abingdon's conspiracy
1491	autumn	Perkin Warbeck starts career as 'Richard IV'
1492	spring	Warbeck received in France by Charles VIII
	November	Warbeck received in Burgundy by Margaret of York
1493	November	Warbeck received in Austria by Maximilian I
1495	February	Sir William Stanley executed for conspiracy
	July	Warbeck lands in Kent and Waterford
	November	Warbeck received in Scotland by James IV
1496	September	Warbeck and the Scots invade Northumberland
1497	June	Cornish rebellion and Battle of Blackheath
	September	Warbeck lands in Cornwall to start a rising
	October	Warbeck surrenders in return for a pardon
1499	March	Ralph Wulford's 'conspiracy'
	November	Warbeck and the Earl of Warwick executed
1500	September	death of Cardinal Morton
1509	April	death of King Henry VII
	June	death of Lady Margaret Beaufort
1513	March	death of the Earl of Oxford
1527?		death of Jane Shore

'Who's Who' –
Persons in the text besides The Five

Beaumont, Viscount: William Beaumont (d. 1508), whose father John, Viscount Beaumont, was killed at Northampton in 1460. He fought at Towton, after which his estates were confiscated and given to Lord Hastings. He fought at Barnet in 1471 and occupied St Michael's Mount with Lord Oxford in 1473. Restored to his estates in 1485, he went mad two years later, spending the rest of his life as Oxford's guest. His widow (born Elizabeth Scrope) married Oxford as his second wife.

Bourchier, Cardinal Thomas (1404?–86): Archbishop of Canterbury 1454; Lord Chancellor 1455–56; officiated at the coronations of Edward IV, Richard III and Henry VII.

Buckingham, 1st Duke of, Humphrey Stafford (1402–60): created duke 1444; Lancastrian peacemaker; m. Anne Nevill, sister-in-law of the Duke of York; fought at the first Battle of St Albans and killed at the Battle of Northampton in 1460.

Buckingham, 2nd Duke of, Henry Stafford (1454?–83): grandson of above; Yorkist rebel; m. Catherine Woodville, sister of Queen Elizabeth Woodville; supported usurpation of Richard III, but turned against him and was executed in 1483.

Catesby, William (1450–85): of Ashby St Ledgers, lawyer and member of Lord Hastings' council; secret agent of the Protector during coup of June 1483; Chancellor of the Exchequer and Esquire of the Body to Richard III, 1483; MP for Northampton and Speaker of the House of Commons in the parliament of 1484; fought at the Battle of Bosworth, being captured and executed.

Charles VII, King of France 1422–61; potential ally of Henry VI and Margaret of Anjou – hoped to recover Calais.

Charles the Bold, Duke of Burgundy 1467–77; pro-Lancastrian since his aunt had married Henry VI's uncle, the Duke of Bedford, but married Edward IV's sister

Margaret of York and sheltered and aided Edward 1470–71; killed in battle against the Swiss.

Chastellain, Georges (1404–75): Burgundian chronicler and herald; member of Charles the Bold's council; killed in battle against the Swiss at the siege of Neuss.

Clarence, Duke of, George Plantagenet (1449–78); third son of the Duke of York; m. Isabel Nevill, daughter of the Earl of Warwick; plotted with Warwick against his brother, Edward IV, in 1469–70; rejoined Edward in 1471, fighting by his side at Barnet and Tewkesbury; plotted against Edward again during the mid-1470s; condemned to death and murdered.

Clifford, 13th Baron, John de Clifford (1435?–61): Lancastrian commander, whose father had been killed at the first Battle of St Albans; fought at Wakefield in 1460 and, according to tradition, butchered York's second son, the Earl of Rutland; killed at Ferrybridge in a skirmish before the Battle of Towton.

Commynes, Philippe de (1447?–1511): Burgundian statesman and chronicler; chamberlain to Charles the Bold but entered the service of Louis XI of France in 1472, working closely with the King; although surprisingly modern and invaluable for glimpses of Edward IV and Hastings, his memoirs are biased in favour of King Louis – he believed that the Wars of the Roses were divine retribution for the miseries inflicted by the English on the French during the Hundred Years' War.

Cook, Sir Thomas (d. 1478): victim of the Woodvilles; warden of the Drapers' Company, 1439; MP for London 1460–61 and 1470–71, Mayor, 1462; in 1468, although a staunch Yorkist, he was wrongfully accused of treason and despite his eventual acquittal his goods were seized by the Queen's father, Lord Rivers, while he was unjustly fined by Queen Elizabeth herself; in 1470 he turned Lancastrian, supporting the restored Henry VI.

Donne, Sir John (c. 1430–1503): Yorkist civil servant and diplomat. The son of a Welsh adventurer but born in France, he married Hastings' sister Anne. Fought at Tewkesbury, being knighted on the field of battle. He is best known as the patron of the Flemish painter Hans Memling.

Dorset, Marquess of, Thomas Grey (1451–1501): son of Queen Elizabeth Woodville by her first marriage; fought for his stepfather, Edward IV, at Tewkesbury and was created Earl of Huntingdon in 1471; Marquess of Dorset and Knight of the Garter, 1475; m. Cecily Harington, stepdaughter of his enemy, Lord Hastings – his rival in many love affairs, notably with Jane Shore. Fled from Richard III to join Henry Tudor in France but later intrigued with King Richard. Under suspicion of plotting with Yorkists in 1487.

Edward IV (1442–83): Earl of March, eldest son of the Duke of York and Cecily Nevill, Warwick's aunt. King of England 1461–70 and 1470–83.

Edward of Lancaster, Prince of Wales (1453–71): only son of Henry VI and Margaret of Anjou, he married Warwick's elder daughter and was killed at the Battle of Tewkesbury.

Egremont, Lord, Thomas Percy (1422–60): younger son of 2nd Earl of Northumberland, created Lord Egremont, 1445. A Lancastrian thug, killed at the Battle of Northampton.

Elizabeth of York (1466–1503): eldest daughter of Edward IV and Yorkist heir to the throne after the disappearance of the Princes in the Tower. Wooed by her uncle, Richard III, she married Henry VII in 1486.

Essex, 1st Earl of, Henry Bourchier (1404?–83): the son of a granddaughter of Edward III, he married the Duke of York's sister Isabel, while his brother was Cardinal Bourchier. A veteran of the French wars, where he had served under York as Lieutenant-general of France, he was appointed Lord Treasurer of England by Henry VI in 1455 but was dismissed the following year and fought on the Yorkist side at Northampton. He was created Earl of Essex in 1461 and again served as Treasurer from 1473–83, dying just before Edward IV.

Exeter, 3rd Duke of, Henry Holland (d. 1475): descended from John of Gaunt in the female line, he was Henry VI's closest legitimate cousin and married the Duke of York's eldest daughter, Anne – who later deserted him – but became an irreconcilable Lancastrian. Cruel and violent, he fought at Blore Heath, Wakefield, second St Albans, and Towton, then in the Welsh mountains. He became a beggar in Flanders, returning to fight at Barnet where he was severely wounded. After spending four years as a prisoner in the Tower, he was murdered.

Fabyan, Robert (1455–1513): draper and former apprentice to Sir Thomas Cook, he compiled *The New Chronicle of France and England* (1504) and *The Great Chronicle of London* (1511).

Fauconberg, Lord, William Nevill (d. 1463): a younger son of Ralph, 8th Earl of Westmorland, he became Baron Fauconberg in right of his wife Joan Fauconberg (an 'idiot from birth'). A veteran of the French wars, nicknamed 'Little Fauconberg', he commanded the Yorkist vanguard at Northampton and Towton.

Fauconberg, Bastard of, Thomas Nevill (d. 1471): son of the above. A 'rover' (pirate), in 1471 he raised the Kentishmen in Henry VI's name and attacked London. Surrendering in return for a pardon in May, he was hanged, drawn and quartered in September.

Fisher, Cardinal John (1461–1535): friend and confessor of Margaret Beaufort, Bishop of Rochester, 1504. A supporter of the Pope, he was beheaded in 1535 – and canonized in 1933.

FitzGerald, Sir Thomas, of Lackagh (d. 1487): Chancellor of Ireland and younger brother of the Earl of Kildare, Lord Deputy, he was killed at Stoke fighting for Lambert Simnel.

Fogge, Sir John, of Ashford in Kent (1425–90): MP for Kentish constituencies; Treasurer of the Household and Keeper of the Wardrobe 1461–68; m. Alice Haute, first cousin of Queen Elizabeth Woodville, and as a Woodville supporter took sanctuary in 1483. Pardoned by King Richard, he joined Buckingham's rebellion, but was pardoned again in 1484.

Fortescue, Sir John (1394?–1476): Lord Chief Justice of the King's Bench, 1442. Helped to draft the attainders at the Parliament of Devils in 1459. Fled to Scotland and then Lorraine with the Lancastrian court; returning to England in 1470, he was captured at Tewkesbury but pardoned by Edward IV, who made him a member of the council. Author of *De Laudibus Legum Angliae* and *On the Governance of the Kingdom of England.*

Gregory, William (d. 1467): a rich citizen and merchant of London, a member of the Skinners' Company and Mayor 1451–67, he was probably – though not definitely – the author of the chronicle generally known as *Gregory's Chronicle.*

Gruthuyse, Seigneur de, Louis de Bruges (1427–92): a Burgundian nobleman and diplomat, he was the governor of Holland who in 1470 sheltered the exiled Edward IV. Made a Knight of the Golden Fleece in 1461 by Philip of Burgundy, he was created Earl of Winchester in 1472 by King Edward.

Hall, Edward (d. 1547): author of *The Union of the Two Noble and Illustre Houses of Lancaster and York* (1548). Although this Tudor chronicler largely depends on Vergil and More, he gives details found nowhere else and had access to sources since lost.

Hastings, Sir Ralph (1440–95): younger brother of Lord Hastings. Esquire and then Knight of the Body to Edward IV, Richard III and Henry VII; Keeper of the King's Lions and Lionesses 1461–63; fought at Barnet and Tewkesbury, being knighted on the battlefield; Captain of Guisnes 1474–83 and 1484–85.

Hastings, Sir Richard (d. 1503): another younger brother of Lord Hastings. Knighted on the field at Tewkesbury; summoned to Parliament as Lord Welles in 1482, having m. Joan, daughter and heiress of Richard, Lord Welles, but later styled Lord Willoughby.

Henry VI: King of England 1422–61 and again 1470–71. Son of Henry V and head of the House of Lancaster; m. Margaret of Anjou, 1445; murdered at the Tower of London.

Henry VII: King of England 1485–1509. Son of Edmund Tudor, Earl of Richmond, and Lady Margaret Beaufort; m. Elizabeth of York, daughter of Edward IV.

Howard, Lord, John Howard (1430?–85): served in France; MP for Norfolk, 1455; fought for Yorkists at Towton and knighted, 1461; Lord Howard, 1469?; Duke of Norfolk and Earl Marshal, 1483. Richard III's most loyal supporter, he was killed at Bosworth.

Howard, Sir Thomas (d. 1524): son of the above, fought at Barnet and knighted, 1478; key man in Gloucester's coup against Lord Hastings; Earl of Surrey, 1483; fought at Bosworth and subsequently imprisoned; defeated Scots at Flodden, 1513, and made Duke of Norfolk; 'Guardian of the Kingdom', 1520.

King, Dr Oliver: King's Secretary to Edward IV 1480–83, to Edward V, 1483, and to Henry VII 1487–95; Bishop of Exeter, 1492, and Bishop of Bath and Wells, 1495. Accompanied John Morton to Rome in 1484–85.

Lincoln, Earl of, John de la Pole (1464–87): son of John de la Pole, Duke of Suffolk, and of Elizabeth Plantagenet, sister of Edward IV; President of the Council of the North, 1483; Lord-Lieutenant of Ireland and heir to the throne, 1484. The man behind Lambert Simnel's conspiracy, he was killed at Stoke.

Louis XI: King of France 1461–83, the 'Spider King'. Aided Lancastrians in order to weaken England; bought off Edward IV with a pension when he invaded France; outwitted Edward at the Treaty of Arras in 1482, allying with Maximilian of Austria, husband of the Duchess of Burgundy.

Lovell, 1st Viscount, Francis, 9th Baron Lovell (144?–87): one of Richard III's foremost servants, created Viscount, Lord Chamberlain and KG, 1483; fought at Bosworth but escaped; tried but failed to start a rebellion in Yorkshire against Henry VII in 1486; fought for Lambert Simnel at Stoke and disappeared, either drowned trying to ford the River Trent or starved to death in a cellar beneath his house, Minster Lovell.

Mancini, Domenico (1434?–1500): Roman scholar. A visitor to England from late 1482 or early 1483 to just before Richard III's coronation, he wrote an account in Latin of King Richard's usurpation which only became known to English historians when it was published in 1936.

March, Earl of – see Edward IV.

Margaret of Anjou, Queen of England: daughter of Réné, King of Naples and Duke of Bar; m. Henry VI, 1445; gave birth to Edward of Lancaster, Prince of Wales, in 1453, and became the real leader of the Lancastrian party in exile in Scotland, Flanders and Lorraine 1461–70; returned to England and captured at Tewkesbury, 1471; imprisoned in the Tower till 1475; lived in Anjou until her death in 1482.

Margaret of York, Duchess of Burgundy (1446–1503): sister of Edward IV and Richard III; m. Charles the Bold of Burgundy, 1467, widowed, 1477; after Richard

III's death financed Yorkish intrigues against Henry VII for the rest of her life.

Montagu, Marquess, John Nevill (d. 1471): brother of Earl of Warwick, fought at Blore Heath, captured at second Battle of St Albans, destroyed the last Lancastrian army at Hexham in 1464; Lord Montagu, 1461, KG, 1462, Earl of Northumberland 1464–69 and Marquess Montagu, 1470. Abandoned Edward IV in favour of Henry VI and killed at Barnet.

More, Sir Thomas (1478–1535): statesman, scholar, author and martyr. In Archbishop Morton's household 1491–92. Speaker of the House of Commons, 1523, Lord Chancellor 1529–32, imprisoned in Tower, 1534, and beheaded, 1535. Canonized by Catholic Church in 1933. His history of Richard III, probably written at various times between 1518 and the early 1530s, is sometimes claimed as the first English biography and provided the portrait for Shakespeare's Richard. Although often inventive and fanciful, it is basically accurate and contains details known from no other source.

Morton, Dr Robert: succeeded his uncle, John Morton, as Master of the Rolls, 1479; relieved of office by Richard III in 1483; accompanied his uncle to Rome 1484–85; Master of the Rolls again, 1485; Bishop of Worcester, 1487.

Norfolk, 3rd Duke of, John Mowbray (1415–61): nephew of Duke of York, fought for Yorkists at second St Albans and Towton – his troops' arrival won the battle.

Norfolk, 4th Duke of, John Mowbray (1444–76): the last Mowbray duke, his heir male was his first cousin, Lord Howard, but the title and estates went with his daughter when - aged five – she married the five-year-old Duke of York, Edward IV's son.

Northumberland, 2nd Earl of, Henry Percy (d. 1455): killed by Yorkists at first Battle of St Albans.

Northumberland, 3rd Earl of, Henry Percy (d. 1461): Lancastrian leader, fought at Wakefield and at second Battle of St Albans, killed at Towton.

Northumberland, 4th Earl of, Henry Percy (d. 1489): attainted and imprisoned in the Tower, 1461; released and restored to the earldom, 1469; did not fight at Barnet or Tewkesbury; brought troops to Bosworth but took no part in battle; imprisoned, 1485; Warden of the East March and Middlemarch, 1486; murdered by a Yorkshire mob when explaining need for new taxes, 1489.

Oxford, 12th Earl of, John de Vere (1408?–62): veteran of French wars and Lancastrian, arrived day too late for first Battle of St Albans; plotted against Edward IV in 1462 and beheaded.

Paston, Sir John (1442–79): Norfolk gentleman, courtier and letter writer; served under Hastings in Northumberland, 1462; knighted, 1463; fought for Warwick – probably under Oxford – at Barnet where he was wounded; employed at Calais by Hastings.

Paston, John: brother of the above though with the same Christian name; country gentleman and letter writer; often in contact with Lord Oxford after 1485; in Henry VII's army on Stoke campaign of 1487 and knighted after the battle.

Pembroke, Earl of, Jasper Tudor (1431–95): son of Owen Tudor and Catherine of France, widow of King Henry V; created Earl of Pembroke, 1452; fought at first St Albans, Mortimer's Cross and Towton; tried to relieve Harlech, 1468; fled to Brittany with his nephew, Henry Tudor, in 1471; probably landed with Henry at Milford Haven in 1485 and fought at Bosworth; Duke of Bedford, 1485; m. Catherine Woodville, widow of Henry, Duke of Buckingham.

Philip the Good, Duke of Burgundy 1419–67: cautious supporter of his nephew, Henry VI.

Richard III: King of England 1483–85; Duke of Gloucester and youngest son of Richard, Duke of York, and Cecily Nevill; fought at Barnet and Towton; m. Anne, younger daughter of the Earl of Warwick; defeated the Scots and occupied Edinburgh, 1482; Lord Protector, April–June 1483; usurped the throne, June 1483; defeated and killed at Bosworth.

Richmond, Earl of, Edmund Tudor (1430–56): son of Owen Tudor and Catherine of France, widow of Henry V; created Earl of Richmond, 1452; m. Margaret Beaufort, 1455, and father of Henry Tudor; died of the plague.

Rivers, 1st Earl, Richard Woodville (d. 1469): father of Queen Elizabeth Woodville; courtier son of a squire; made his fortune by marrying Jacquetta, widow of the Duke of Bedford; created Lord Rivers, 1448; fought on Lancastrian side at Towton; appointed Lord Treasurer and promoted to earl, 1466; captured by Warwick at Battle of Edgecote and beheaded 1469.

Rivers, 2nd Earl, Anthony (1442–83): eldest son of above; Lord Scales, 1460, in right of his wife; fought at Barnet and Tewkesbury; 'governor' of Edward, Prince of Wales, the future Edward V; seized by the Duke of Gloucester in coup, April 1483, and beheaded in June.

Rotherham, Dr Thomas (1423–1500): keeper of Privy Seal, 1463; Bishop of Ely, 1468; Bishop of Lincoln, 1471; Archbishop of York, 1480; Lord Chancellor 1474–83.

Russell, Dr John (d. 1494): churchman, statesman and probable author of the 'second continuation' of the *Croyland Chronicle.* Keeper of the Privy Seal 1474–83, Bishop of Rochester, 1476, Bishop of Lincoln, 1480, Lord Chancellor 1483–85, and Chancellor of Oxford University 1485–94.

Salisbury, Earl of, Richard Nevill (1400–60): son of Ralph, Earl of Westmorland, and father of the Earl of Warwick; m. heiress of the last Montagu Earl of Salisbury; Earl of Salisbury, 1429, in right of his wife; Lord Chancellor 1453–55;

fled from Ludlow to Calais with Warwick and March, 1459; defeated at Wakefield
and murdered next day.

Simnel, Lambert (d. 1525): son of an Oxford organ-builder; impersonated Earl of
Warwick 1486–87 and proclaimed 'Edward VI' at Dublin; captured after his followers were defeated at Stoke in 1487; pardoned, employed as scullion in the
royal kitchens and then as a falconer.

Somerset, 1st Duke of, John Beaufort (1403–44): elder brother of 2nd Duke and
father of Margaret Beaufort, his only child and heiress; Captain-General of
France and Guyenne, he led a disastrous campaign through Maine and Brittany
in 1443; suspected of committing suicide in the following year.

Somerset, 2nd Duke of, Edmund Beaufort (d. 1455): Lieutenant-General of France,
1447; favourite of Henry VI and leader of court party, rival of the Duke of York;
killed at the first Battle of St Albans.

Somerset, 3rd Duke of, Henry Beaufort (1436–64): eldest son of above, favourite of
Margaret of Anjou and Lancastrian leader; wounded at first St Albans; fought in
Battles of Blore Heath, Wakefield, second St Albans and Towton; attainted, 1461;
surrendered at Bamborough, 1462; pardoned, 1463, but rebelled; defeated and
killed at Hexham, 1464.

Somerset, 4th Duke of – de jure – Edmund Beaufort (1438–71): returned from exile,
1471; defeated at Tewkesbury and beheaded the day after the battle.

Stafford, Sir Henry (d. 1471): younger son of 1st Duke of Buckingham and third
husband of Margaret Beaufort; fought on Lancastrian side at Towton but pardoned by Edward IV; fought for Yorkists at Barnet and wounded – probably
dying from his wounds.

Stanley, 2nd Lord, Thomas Stanley (1435–1504): magnate in north-western
Midlands and fourth husband of Margaret Beaufort. An opportunist, who
usually avoided taking sides; one of the four pillars of Richard III's régime, he
intervened and destroyed him at Bosworth; created Earl of Derby, 1485.

Stanley, Sir William (d. 1495): younger brother of above and 'the richest commoner
in England'; went over to Henry Tudor before Bosworth and led the Stanley
affinity's charge to rescue him; plotted to put 'Richard IV' (Perkin Warbeck) on
the throne and attainted, 1495 – leaving £9,062 in cash and jewels alone.
Beheaded.

Suffolk, 1st Duke of, William de la Pole (1396–1450): fought in France, later unpopular favourite and chief minister of Henry VI; impeached, 1450, and beheaded at
sea.

Suffolk, 2nd Duke of, John de la Pole (1442–91): son of above; first husband of
Margaret Beaufort and father of John, Earl of Lincoln; m. Elizabeth Plantagenet,

sister of Edward IV; fought on Yorkist side at second St Albans but not in other battles.

Trollope, Sir Andrew (d. 1461): Master Porter of Calais and a famous veteran of the French wars; Yorkish turned Lancastrian; tricked the Duke of York and the Earl of Salisbury at Wakefield; fought at second St Albans; killed at Towton.

Urswick, Dr Christopher (1448–1522): secret agent, diplomat and churchman; confessor to Margaret Beaufort and Henry VII; Master, King's Hall, Cambridge 1485–88; Dean of Windsor 1495–1522.

Vere, Sir Aubrey de (d. 1462): elder brother of Lord Oxford; favourite of Queen Margaret of Anjou; plotted to restore Henry VI in 1462 – hanged, drawn and quartered.

Vergil, Polydore (1470–1555?): churchman, papal official and historian. Born in Urbino, he began his career as secretary to the Duke of Urbino. First came to England in 1502 and three years later was invited by Henry VII to write a history of the English, which he published in Latin in Basle in 1534. Archdeacon of Wells 1508–54, naturalized, 1510, but spent long periods abroad, eventually returning to Italy.

Warbeck, Perkin (1474–99): son of a bourgeois of Tournai; impersonated the younger of the Princes in the Tower and accepted as nephew by Margaret of York, 1492; recognized as 'Richard IV' by Emperor Maximilian, 1493; welcomed to Scotland by James IV, 1495; accompanied Scots raid on Northumberland, 1496, when he was proclaimed 'Richard IV'; landed in Cornwall, failed to take Exeter and captured, 1497; imprisoned in the Tower – hanged, but spared drawing and quartering, 1499.

Warkworth, Dr John (d. 1500): academic and chronicler; a Northumbrian from his name, he was a fellow of Merton College, Oxford, but moved to Cambridge where he became Master of Peterhouse in 1473.

Warwick, Earl of, Richard Nevill (1428–71): the 'kingmaker'; son of the Earl of Salisbury and nephew of the Duke of York; Earl of Warwick, 1449, in right of his wife; fought at first St Albans and Captain of Calais, 1455; retired to Calais after attempt to murder him, 1458; fled from Ludlow to Calais with his father and the Earl of March, 1459; victorious at Northampton, 1460; defeated at second St Albans and fought at Towton, 1461; confirmed in all his offices, 1461; withdrew from court, 1467; defeated Edward IV's troops at Edgecote, imprisoning but then releasing him, 1469; deposed Edward IV and restored Henry VI, 1470; killed at Barnet.

Warwick, Earl of, Edward Plantagenet (1475–99): only son of George, Duke of Clarence, ultimate Yorkist heir to the throne and last male Plantagenet; impris-

oned in the Tower for life, 1485; tricked into plotting against Henry VII –
beheaded.

Waurin, Sieur de, Jean, Bastard de Waurin, Sieur de Forestal (d. 1474): Burgundian
soldier and chronicler.

Wenlock, Lord (*c.* 1400–71): veteran of French wars; chamberlain to Queen
Margaret of Anjou; Speaker of the House of Commons, 1456; fought for
Yorkists at Mortimer's Cross and Towton; Lord Wenlock and KG, 1461;
Lieutenant of Calais; supports Warwick, 1470 – killed at Tewkesbury.

Woodville, Elizabeth (1437–92): daughter of the Lancastrian Richard, 1st Earl
Rivers, and widow of the Lancastrian Sir John Grey of Groby – mortally
wounded at the second Battle of St Albans – she married Edward IV secretly in
1464. Despite intriguing with Henry Tudor after the disappearance of her sons
in the Tower, she was formally reconciled to their murderer, Richard III, in 1484.
Suspected of intriguing with the Yorkists in 1487, she spent what was left of her
life in Bermondsey Abbey. A cold, grasping woman, her attempts to promote the
Woodville family fatally undermined the Yorkist dynasty.

Worcester, Earl of, John Tiptoft (d. 1470): the Yorkist 'Butcher's; Constable of
England 1462–67 and 1470 – beheaded 1470.

THE HOUSE OF YORK

d.   died
ex. executed
k.   killed
m   married

Edmund of Langley
DUKE OF YORK
(4th son of EDWARD III)
d.1402

Richard
EARL OF CAMBRIDGE
ex.1415
m
Anne Mortimer
(dau. of Roger EARL OF MARCH
grandson and heir of Lionel
DUKE OF CLARENCE
second son of Edward III)

Edward
DUKE OF YORK
k.1415

Cecily Neville   m   Richard
(dau. of Ralph   DUKE OF YORK
EARL OF WESTMORLAND   k.1460
d.1495)

Anne
d.1476
1. Henry Holand
DUKE OF EXETER
(divorced 1472)
2. Sir Thomas Leger
ex.1483

EDWARD IV
d.1483
m
Elizabeth Woodville
(dau. of Richard
Earl Rivers)
d.1495

Edmund
EARL OF RUTLAND
k.1460

Elizabeth
d.1504?
m
John de la Pole
DUKE OF SUFFOLK
d.1491

Margaret
d.1503
m
Charles
DUKE OF BURGUNDY
k.1477

George
DUKE OF CLARENCE
ex.1478
m
Isabel Nevill
(dau. of Richard
Earl of Warwick)

RICHARD III
k.1485
m
Ann Nevill
d.1485
(dau. of RICHARD
Earl of Warwick)

5 other children
d. in infancy

Margaret
COUNTESS
OF SALISBURY
d.1541
m
Sir Richard Pole

Edward
EARL OF WARWICK
ex.1499

Edward
PRINCE OF WALES
d.1484

Mary
d.1482

EDWARD V
k.1483

Margaret
d.1472

John
EARL OF LINCOLN
k.1487

Richard
DUKE OF YORK
k.1483

Edward
d.1485

Edmund
EARL OF SUFFOLK
ex.1513

George
d.1479

Anne
d.1511
m
Thomas Howard
DUKE OF NORFOLK

Humphrey
d.1513

Catherine
d.1527
m
William Courtenay
EARL OF DEVON

William
d.1539

Geoffrey
d.?

Bridget
d.1517

Richard
k.1525

Elizabeth
d.1503
m
HENRY VII

Cicely
d.1507
m
1. John Viscount Welles
2. Thomas Kymbe

HOUSES OF LANCASTER,
BEAUFORT AND TUDOR

d. died
ex. executed
k. killed
m married

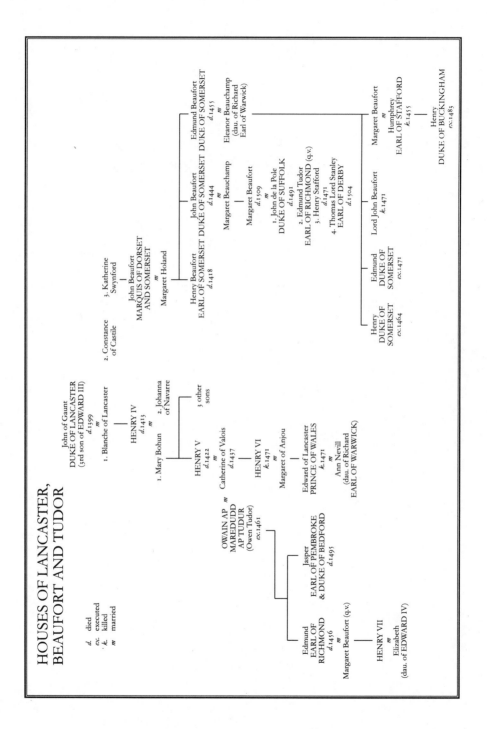

I

Introduction –
the Wars of the Roses

DURING the last years of the fifteenth century, on a morning in late summer, a small man stood alone by himself in a meadow in the English Midlands. His horse had become bogged down in some marshy ground so that he had been forced to dismount. All around him lay his dead or dying supporters, while others could be seen fleeing for their lives. In steel from head to foot, with a jewelled coronet on his helmet, he grasped a steel-handled battle-hammer. Although his sharp face was hidden by the helmet, he could nonetheless be heard shouting 'Treason! Treason!', over and over again. A growing mob of enemy soldiers was running towards him but, declining to mount a horse brought by a last faithful squire, he refused to leave the battlefield and waited grimly. He meant to fight to the death. Rank-and-file, men-at-arms, billmen or bowmen, they swarmed about him like so many hounds with a fox. Swinging that murderous little hammer to the very end, still screaming 'Treason!', finally he was mortally wounded by a Welshman's halberd and went down into the mud.[1] They ripped off the dead man's armour and felt under-clothing, kicking the body as it rolled in the dirt. At last his corpse, naked as the day he was born, smeared with mud and blood, a halter tied round its neck, was slung over a horse behind his pursuivant *Blanc Sanglier*, who was made to carry his banner of the White Boar in derision. When the two rode into Leicester, his dangling head smashed into a stone bridge, bruising the face still further. As he passed, men yelled insults and curses at what was left of Richard III.

According to tradition, Reginald Bray, an official in the household of Henry Tudor's mother, found the dead monarch's coronet in a hawthorn bush and at once took it to Lord Stanley, Henry's stepfather. Stanley, who had betrayed Richard by taking his troops over to the other side, placed the diadem on his stepson's head, shouting 'King Henry! King Henry!', a cry which was taken up joyfully by everyone present.

The Tudor Age had begun. In retrospect, the Battle of Bosworth would be seen as decisive, settling the fate of the English crown. It was almost – though not quite – the end of those thirty years of bloodshed known to history as 'The Wars of the Roses'.

The Wars of the Roses, that amazing fifteenth-century blood-bath in which partisans of the rival dynasties of York and Lancaster slaughtered each other for over three decades, are part of the English National Myth. However, they do not fill so honoured a place in it as the Hundred Years' War, when Englishmen fought Frenchmen at Crécy and Agincourt. Battles that cost the lives of so many fellow countrymen are as much cause for mourning as rejoicing. Some historians claim that the Wars of the Roses cannot stir the imagination like the Civil Wars of the seventeenth century between Royalists and Parliamentarians. Yet they certainly stirred Shakespeare's, prompting him to write his plays *Henry VI* and *Richard III*. Admittedly, visits to the National Theatre may not leave anyone much wiser about what really took place, since the Bard turned the conflict into a single bloodstained drama.

Plenty of academic ink has been spilt on showing that no contemporary would have recognized the term 'Wars of the Roses'. If York bore a white rose among its badges, and was sometimes styled the 'House of the White Rose', a red rose was never used by Lancaster. Only under Henry VII did the red rose become the Lancastrian badge, retrospectively; to facilitate the pretty conceit of the Tudor Rose – part red, part white, symbolizing the merciful union between the two dynasties which had brought peace to a distracted land. Nor do we know when the term came into fashion. David Hume is sometimes said to have been the first to use it, in his *History of England* (1762), though his actual words are 'the quarrel between the two roses'. It has also been suggested that Sir Walter Scott coined it, in his novel *Anne of Geierstein* (1829), but in fact he refers to 'the wars of the White and Red Roses'.

Nevertheless, although the term would not be immediately recognizable to men and women who lived through the Wars, the idea behind it must have been familiar enough to them. The late Professor Charles Ross quoted a line of verse in the *Croyland Chronicle*, written in 1486 and referring to Richard III's murder of the Princes in the Tower: 'And, to avenge the White, the Red Rose bloomed.' As Ross commented, only pedants could reject a name that has been in use for centuries.

Not only have there been many studies of the Wars, but they have inspired a flood of romantic novels. Most of the novelists subscribe to the strange cult of King Richard's innocence, which has mushroomed during recent years. (The Richard III Society numbers thousands and even has Japanese members.) Yet his short reign is only one episode towards the close of a very long story.

The Wars of the Roses lasted from the first Battle of St Albans in 1455 to the Battle of Stoke in 1487, and were fought to decide which branch of the English royal family should reign – Lancaster or York. Descended from a count of Anjou who had married William the Conqueror's granddaughter (and taking their name from the '*plant-genet*' or sprig of broom he wore in his helmet) the Plantagenets had ruled England since 1154. The dispute between the family's two branches stemmed from Henry IV's usurpation of the throne at the end of the fourteenth century, when he deposed and murdered Richard II to become the first Lancastrian sovereign. He was the son of John of Gaunt, Duke of Lancaster, who had been the third son of the great Edward III. For a long time Henry's Lancastrian dynasty seemed firmly established; his son Henry V ruled England from 1413 to 1422 and, as we know, led further spectacularly successful invasions of France. When he died young, his one-year-old son, another Henry, became king with general acceptance. Although a cousin, Richard, Duke of York (born in 1411), possessed a claim to the throne which was arguably superior – he descended from Edward III's fourth son in the male line but from his second son in the female line – no one challenged the Lancastrian succession.

The wars would never have broken out had it not been for Henry VI, who reached his majority in 1436 at the age of fifteen. Even his appearance failed to inspire respect. The only surviving portraits show a pitifully weak and worried face, while he was notorious for his drab clothes and clumsy shoes. As for his character, Pope Pius II described him as 'a man more timorous than a woman, utterly devoid of wit or spirit.' The son of the hero of Agincourt was the only monarch since the Norman Conquest to be incapable of leading an army in battle. He was easily dominated by his wife and his favourites, with disastrous consequences. Moreover, in his early thirties he began to suffer from fits of insanity.

During Henry's minority England had been governed by a council with considerable efficiency. The council had included the King's uncle, Humphrey, Duke of Gloucester and his great-uncle Henry Beaufort, Bishop of Winchester – a bastard but legitimized son of John of Gaunt. Across the Channel a third of all France, including Paris, was ruled by another uncle, the Duke of Bedford. For Henry was King of France as well as of England, being crowned in Paris in 1430, even if the vast majority of Frenchmen supported the Valois king. Everything changed for the worse when he began to govern in person.

In 1445 he married the fifteen-year-old Margaret of Anjou, a Valois princess, and adopted a policy of peace. At the start of 1449 the English still held Normandy and Gascony, but by August 1450 they did not hold a foot of Norman soil and by August 1451 not a foot of Gascon; an attempt to recover Bordeaux ended in disaster. England had finally lost the Hundred Years' War.

Much of the blame for the loss of English France lay with Henry's kinsman Edmund Beaufort, Duke of Somerset, who had replaced the Duke of York as the English commander. A 'dove', unlike York who was very much a 'hawk', Somerset was a spectacularly incompetent soldier. The explosive rivalry between Somerset and York – made Lord-Lieutenant of Ireland to keep him out of the way – began in France. In any case York felt increasingly threatened by the Duke of Somerset, who was bent on extracting as many lucrative offices as possible from the King.

There was trouble at home too. Looking back from the 1460s, an anonymous chronicler wrote of Henry VI's reign:

> The realm of England was out of all good governance, as it had been many days before, for the king was simple and led by covetous counsel and owed more than he was worth. His debts increased daily but payment was there none; all the possessions and lordships that pertained to the crown the king had given away, some to lords and some to other lesser persons, so that he had almost nothing left to own. And such impositions as were put on the people, as taxes and taillages, all that came from them was spent in vain, for he had no [great] household nor maintained any wars . . .

The legal system began to break down. Frequently judge and jury were intimidated by archers lounging menacingly at the back of a courtroom. Gang warfare erupted over law suits – generally about land or disputed wills – sometimes escalating into pitched battles, as magnates vied for supremacy. Banditry thrived. A poem from this time laments the premature death of Henry V, who had 'kept the law and peace' throughout England, ensuring good justice. Nowadays, people put on armour instead of going to the courts:

In every shire with jacks and sallets clean
Misrule does rise, and makes the neighbours war,
The weaker goes beneath, as oft is seen.

The king's lavish patronage of the Duke of Suffolk and other favourites created a greedy court party which battened on him. By 1450 the crown owed £400,000 and was still borrowing, £24,000 being spent on the royal household – out of a total revenue of £24,000.

Popular exasperation came to a head over the loss of France. In January 1450 William de la Pole, Duke of Suffolk, King Henry's avaricious first minister, was impeached by Parliament. Sent into exile in May by the King in order to save his life, he was waylaid at sea and executed with a rusty sword – news greeted with applause throughout England.

Jack Cade's rising during the summer of 1450 was no peasant's revolt, but an expression of widespread discontent. The rebels demanded that the King dismiss his favourites because 'his lords are lost, his merchandise is lost, his commons destroyed, the sea is lost, France is lost . . .' They urged him to govern with the advice of princes of the royal blood – notably the Duke of York.

However, Cade's rising was crushed, while Suffolk's place was taken by the Duke of Somerset – York's rival. There was little doubt that the years ahead would be troubled. Even so, no one can have anticipated civil war.

A brief résumé of the events of the next three decades is needed here, since the immediate aims of the combatants were constantly changing. When the first blood was shed in 1455 the issue was who should dominate Henry VI, though both sides were more than ready for violence. On one side was what would become known as the Yorkist party; Richard, Duke of York with his brother-in-law Richard Nevill, Earl of Salisbury, and the latter's son, Richard Nevill, Earl of Warwick. On the other side, the Lancastrian, were the ferocious French queen, Margaret of Anjou, and Somerset, with a strong court party. It was vital for York and for Somerset to control the royal purse strings; although the greatest landowner in England, the Duke of York faced ruin if he were not repaid the sums he had spent in France as lieutenant-general and in Ireland as lord-lieutenant – by contrast the Duke of Somerset, under-endowed with estates, depended largely on revenue from royal offices. As for the Nevills, father and son were old rivals of the Percy earls of Northumberland who supported the court, while Warwick was in dispute with Somerset over the rich lordship of Glamorgan.

The conflict was transformed into irreconcilable vendetta in 1455 when, after eleven years of childless marriage, Queen Margaret bore Henry a son and York ceased to be heir to the throne. The queen's troops forced York and the Nevills to flee abroad in 1459. They returned the following year, defeating the Lancastrian army at Northampton after which, driven by a mixture of ambition and self-preservation, the Duke of York browbeat a reluctant House of Lords into recognizing him as Henry VI's heir – and into disinheriting the infant Prince of Wales. In response Queen Margaret raised an army in the north of England, which defeated and killed York at Wakefield in December 1460.

York's son, the eighteen-year-old Earl of March, retaliated by occupying London and proclaiming himself King Edward IV early in 1461, after which he marched north to confront and annihilate the Lancastrians at Towton in the most terrible battle of the entire Wars. The new Yorkist king spent the next few years mopping up surviving pockets of Lancastrian resistance, crushing small risings in Yorkshire and Northumberland, a task which he had completed by 1464 with the total rout of the last tiny Lancastrian army at Hexham and the execution of its leaders.

But the Yorkists quarrelled with each other. Partly from resentment at the King's marriage to Elizabeth Woodville, an arrogant lady with greedy kindred, the Earl of Warwick – 'the Kingmaker' – plotted implacably to replace him. Outmanoeuvred, Edward fled to Burgundy in 1470 and Warwick brought back Henry VI, who had been a prisoner in the Tower of London.

Henry's second reign lasted only a few months. Edward IV returned with an army so small that a contemporary called his invasion 'coming in by the windows', yet, in two swift, savage campaigns, within a month he had destroyed the Earl of Warwick at Barnet and then the remaining Lancastrians at Tewkesbury; both Warwick and the Lancastrian Prince of Wales fell in battle, while the wretched Henry VI was murdered discreetly in the Tower. The prosperous years that followed were the Yorkist golden age.

When King Edward died unexpectedly in 1483, his brother the Duke of Gloucester seized power in two ruthless coups d'état. Swiftly deposing Edward's young son Edward V, who disappeared, he ascended the throne as Richard III. The new king was soon opposed by an alliance of outraged Yorkists and Lancastrian diehards, who found a rival candidate for the throne in Henry Tudor – through his Beaufort mother, the last heir of the Lancastrian dynasty. After an unsuccessful rebellion during the autumn of 1483, and much plotting, they succeeded in defeating and killing Richard at Bosworth Field in August 1485.

Two years later Henry Tudor, now King Henry VII, managed to beat off a final Yorkist challenge at Stoke in another fiercely fought engagement. It was the last real battle of the Wars of the Roses, although there would be Yorkish pretenders and plots until well into the next century.

This synopsis gives little idea of the appalling slaughter involved. In his memoirs Philippe de Commynes – a Burgundian statesman who served Louis XI of France and who had watched from across the Channel – writes of the Wars that 'there have been seven or eight memorable battles in England, and sixty or eighty princes and lords of the blood royal have died violently.' There were of course other less memorable battles while Commynes exaggerates only a little about the casualties if peers are included in his figures. Three kings, a Prince of Wales and eight royal (or semi-royal) dukes died by battle, murder or sudden death. Edward IV would order his troops to spare common soldiers but to 'kill the gentles' – there was no mercy for defeated leaders or their staffs. During the campaigns of 1460–61 alone twelve noblemen were killed and six beheaded – over a third of the English peerage. Entire noble families were exterminated; one Duke of Somerset fell in battle, two were beheaded, and their heir fell at Tewkesbury. The gentry suffered proportionately, though no exact figures are available; sixty knights and gentlemen (including twenty-five MPs) were attainted after Towton – one chronicler records the beheading of forty-two Lancastrian knights who had been taken prisoner during the battle.

The rest of Europe watched in amazement, even if the English were then regarded as the most violent and ferocious race in Christendom. 'Men of a haughty disposition, hot tempered and quickly moved to anger, difficult to pacify and bring to reason' was how the French chronicler Froissart had described the English at the beginning of the fifteenth century. 'They take delight in battles and slaughters.' Commynes too thought the English exceptionally 'choleric' (savage-tempered), especially those who had never been out of England.

Sudden death was not confined to the battlefield. A courtier could all too easily find himself on the scaffold. In a now-unfashionable book, *The Waning of the Middle Ages*,[2] the Dutch historian Johan Huizinga writes of 'that hell of hatred and persecution which was the English court.' He quotes the Flemish herald and chronicler Georges Chastellain, who had visited the English court and may well have had it in mind when telling his readers that 'princes are men, and their affairs are high and perilous, and their natures are subject to many passions, such as hatred and envy.' In a will made a few days after the battle of Bosworth, the

Yorkist Lord Mountjoy warned his sons 'to live right wisely and never to take the state of baron upon them if they may lay it from them, nor to desire to be about princes, for it is dangerous.'[3]

Commynes says with justice that 'the calamities and misfortunes of war fell only upon the soldiers, and especially upon the nobility.' The latter faced not just death in battle but, if they were on the losing side, the possibility of attainder. An attainder was an Act of Parliament, which only needed token approval by the House of Commons and the King's acceptance; the victim was condemned to be hanged, drawn and quartered while all his goods were confiscated and his heirs disinherited in perpetuity. It has been described as the legal death of a family.

Again and again, magnates and gentry were forced to choose sides – a nightmarish choice with very high stakes indeed. The former could not avoid taking part. They were too prominent politically and socially, while their 'affinities' or retinues amounted to private armies which were needed desperately by both sides. Out of 70 adult peers during this period, over 50 are known to have fought in battles they had to win if they wanted to stay alive. Holding office in a magnate's household or dependent on his influence, few English gentlemen had any option other than to fight for him.

The Wars shocked the gentry at the time, and not merely in retrospect. They saw them as a calamity that affected all their class. An unidentified government spokesman told the House of Commons in 1475 that 'none [of us] hath escaped', and clearly he was expressing a general opinion. The Duke of Buckingham claimed in a speech of 1483 that war was never 'in none earthly nation so deadly and so pestilent as when it happeneth among us . . . nor so cruel and so deadly foughten.' The Duke added that during Edward IV's reign alone 'the getting of the garland, keeping it, losing and winning again, it hath cost more English blood than hath twice the winning of France.' In other words, more Englishmen had been killed during Edward's struggle for the Crown than during the entire Hundred Years' War.

In many English churches one still finds brasses of long-haired knights and squires in fluted plate armour, with those of wasp-waisted wives in butterfly hats. Brief inscriptions, asking us to pray for their souls, tell us that they lived during these years but not much else. We know that they inhabited an England that was often a place of great beauty as well as cruelty, full of brilliant colour, that of Malory's *Morte d'Arthur* and the 'Ballad of the Nut Brown Maid', of fan-vaulted cathedrals and the polyphony of composers like John Dunstable. Yet, as we can see from the *Morte d'Arthur*, its inhabitants' mentality was immeasurably remote from our own, with fantastic values derived from chivalry and a ritualized code of courtly love. For us, Malory's knight errants, magicians and hermits, his enchantresses and damsels, come from an alien world – for the subjects of Edward IV or Richard III it was the ideal dream world, in which they felt completely at home. No doubt the Nut Brown Maid had a lyrical approach to love between the sexes:

> For I must to the greenwood go,
>   Alone a banished man . . .
>
> Make you ready, for so am I,
>   Although it were anon,
> For in my mind of all mankind
>   I love but you alone.

But cheerful romanticism of this sort was a rare enough phenomenon in the fifteenth century.

If we knew more about the men and women of Lancastrian or Yorkist England, we should think them rather gloomy people. Melancholy was much in fashion. 'I, man of sadness, born in an eclipse of darkness amid fogs of lamentation,' wrote Chastellain, emphasizing their pessimism. They were obsessed by death and the fleeting quality of life, an obsession to some extent understandable in a world frequently afflicted by plague or famine, where banditry, armed robbery, housebreaking and murder were commonplace, in which old age began at fifty. The *memento mori*, the reminder of death, was very popular. At Arundel the tomb of the seventh Earl of Arundel (who fell in battle against the French in 1435) has two effigies; above, he is in full armour with his helmet; below, he is a skeleton in a shroud.

The population numbered no more than three million at most. At the top of the social pile were a group of between fifty and sixty magnates, the peers or lords of Parliament, great landowners whose incomes might be in excess of £1,000 a year – a vast fortune. Below them came the richer knights, about 200 men with incomes of more than £100; then perhaps as many as a thousand lesser knights with over £40; and then at least 1,200 squires with over £20. Another 2,000 gentlemen had rather less.[4] According to Chief Justice Fortescue, thousands of yeomen (the more prosperous smallholders and tenant-farmers) lived well on £5 a year. While it is impossible to estimate the number of merchants, we know that a few were wealthier than the richest knights, who nonetheless looked down on them as tradesmen.

Since the population was so much smaller, the landscape was very different from today's, with much more forest, moor and heath – together with abandoned villages, especially in the Midlands, a legacy of the Black Death. In some areas, however, land was farmed very carefully. In 1466 a Bohemian party travelling through the south-east noted that 'peasants dig ditches round their fields and so fence them in that no one can pass on foot or on horseback except by the main roads.'[5] Towns were surrounded by small farms and allotments reaching to the town walls. There were comparatively few manor houses – in certain regions, such as the West Midlands, barely one village in ten had a resident squire. Frequently manors were moated, as were many farms, to protect livestock, and had ponds which provided fresh fish during Lent – a welcome alternative to salt-herring. Great houses often possessed deer parks to ensure a reliable supply of venison.

Towns and villages alike swarmed with beggars. Their numbers were swollen by refugees from Normandy and Maine after the fall of English France, former settlers who included churchmen, gentlemen and soldiers. Still more were on the road because of 'enclosures', which increased during the 1450s; landowners were converting arable ploughland into pasture for sheep, callously evicting villagers and pulling down their cottages: 'They must needs depart away, poor, silly, wretched souls, men, women, husbands, wives, fatherless children, widows, woeful mothers with their young babes, and their whole household small in substance and much in number' is Sir Thomas More's pitiful description in *Utopia*. 'Away they trudge, I say, out of their known and accustomed houses, finding no place to rest in.'

Corpses were a common enough sight by the roadside. A wet summer meant a bad harvest, with famine and starvation during the next year. Epidemics followed – bubonic or pneumonic plague. There were serious visitations in 1464, 1471, 1479 and 1485, with minor outbreaks in other years. The 'sweating sickness' was particularly vicious, sometimes killing its victims within two hours; its drenching sweat was accompanied by high fever, stomach pains, savage headache and dizziness, with occasionally a rash of black spots – and always a feeling of foreboding.

'The population of this island does not appear to me to bear any relation to her fertility and riches', commented a Venetian at the end of the century. He says there was no English innkeeper, however humble, who did not lay his table with silver dishes and drinking cups, that English abbeys were more like baronial palaces than monasteries. He thought the people strikingly handsome, both men and women, and extremely polite. 'In addition to their civil speeches, they have the incredible courtesy of remaining with their heads uncovered, with an admirable grace, whilst they talk to each other.' (Commynes records that when Edward IV met Louis XI in 1475 the English king 'raised his hat and bowed to within six inches of the ground.') Even so, the Venetian did not care for his hosts, whom he found extraordinarily cold. He never observed any one of them, 'either at court or among the lower orders', to be in love. He also remarked on their suspicion of foreigners, while 'neither have they any sincere and solid friendship amongst themselves, insomuch that they do not trust each other to discuss either public or private affairs.'

Another fifteenth-century Italian visitor, Domenico Mancini from Rome, commented on the Englishmen's powerful physique – 'their bodies are stronger than other peoples', for they seem to have hands and arms of iron.'

The Venetian was horrified by the lawlessness. He thought there was no country in the world with so many thieves and robbers as England – 'few venture to go alone in the countryside except in the middle of the day, and fewer still in the towns at night and least of all in London.'[6] He adds that 'people are taken up every day by dozens like birds in a covey, and especially in London, yet for all this they never cease to rob and murder in the streets.' This was written in the 1490s.

Life had been still more hazardous during Henry VI's reign and the early years of Edward IV's. In 1458 Margaret Paston wrote to her husband from Norfolk asking him to buy crossbows to protect their house whose windows were too low for longbow shooting; she also suggested buying poleaxes. The two heiresses of Wakehurst Place in Sussex omitted to take Mrs Paston's precautions and one day in 1463 two fortune hunters, the brothers Nicholas and Richard Culpeper, arrived at their house 'with force and arms, riotously against the king's peace, arrayed in manner of war' – in full armour. They abducted the girls, dragging them off to London where they married them, despite 'the said Margaret and Elizabeth at the time of their taking away making great and piteous lamentation and weeping.'[7]

For the workers in the fields who made up the bulk of the population – labourers, ploughmen, oxmen and shepherds, toiling for £3 a year if they were lucky – it was a time of mixed fortunes. Recurrent outbreaks of plague in the previous century had reduced the labour force, raising wages, but though serfdom was disappearing landowners were charging high rents for even the smallest farm. Much to Commynes' surprise, humble folk were left in peace by the Wars. 'England enjoyed this peculiar mercy above all other kingdoms, that neither the country nor the people, nor the houses, were wasted or destroyed', he comments. One reason was that hostilities amounted to a mere thirteen weeks of localized campaigning over a period of more than thirty years.

Cities and towns were almost unaffected by the Wars. There were no sieges, though more than once London was threatened by an army at its gates. Some citizens fought in the battles as men-at-arms or archers, while in London the richer lent money to both sides and aldermen squabbled over whom to support – since the greater London merchants were very close to the throne.

This book is an attempt to evoke the world of the Wars of the Roses, showing how they affected those who lived through them. I have built the book around the careers of men and women whose lives they spanned. Two at least saw the court of Henry VI and Margaret of Anjou, and survived to see that of Henry VIII and Catherine of Aragon. I have used contemporary sources as much as possible, particularly the 'histories' by Domenico Mancini, Polydore Vergil and Sir Thomas More – they had all spoken with men who actually fought in the Wars of the Roses, and who remembered vividly the Lancastrian and Yorkist kings. To a certain extent the structure of my book has been inspired by Barbara Tuchman's *A Distant Mirror*, but instead of a single shadowy figure I have used five reasonably well-documented personalities.

2

The Five

WILLIAM HASTINGS
JOHN DE VERE, EARL OF OXFORD
MARGARET BEAUFORT · DR JOHN MORTON
JANE SHORE

THIS chapter introduces the five, explaining who they were and why I have chosen them. They consist of a squire and a nobleman (both of whom fought in decisive battles), a great lady, a priest and a 'harlot'. I would have liked to have included someone from 'the wrong side of the tracks', but sadly the period has left too little documentation about common folk, so I have had to make do with the harlot.

The choice is far from arbitrary. All five of them were united in opposing Richard III and, as will be seen, the most dramatic events in each of their careers – in one case fatal – resulted from their opposition to him. All come most sharply into focus during his reign; at one stage or another King Richard publicly accused each of the five of plotting against him, while at least three played key roles in initiating the expedition that finally defeated and killed him at Bosworth. At the same time, however, these are also people who can only be understood within the wider context of the Wars of the Roses as a whole, the upheaval that shaped their lives.

If ever the Yorkists produced a hero, it was William Hastings (*c.* 1430–83). He began his career as a mere squire and a 'household man' of the Duke of York, but after Edward IV's triumphant seizure of the throne in 1461 he was swiftly transformed into a peer, a great landowner and Lord Chamberlain.

As King Edward's best friend, this brave and charming courtier-soldier soon became the most influential man in England, building up an enormous personal following. In his *History of King Richard the Third*, the Tudor statesman and saint Sir Thomas More gives us a portrait of William Hastings which resembles some knight errant out of the pages of the *Morte d'Arthur* – honourable and chivalrous, deeply admired by everyone who knew him, despite a private life verging on the dissolute. He had a notably distinguished military record. In 1461 his timely arrival with reinforcements ensured that the Battle of Mortimer's Cross was a Yorkist victory, while he was knighted on the field at Towton for his conduct; in 1471 he commanded the Yorkists' left wing at the Battle of Barnet and then their right wing at the Battle of Tewkesbury.

Hastings was the one man who might have saved the young Edward V in 1483 from the ambitions of his uncle Richard, Duke of Gloucester. Realizing that Hastings was incorruptible, Richard mounted a coup and ordered his immediate execution. He had been one of the most colourful figures to emerge during the entire Wars of the Roses.

His brother-in-law John de Vere, Earl of Oxford (1443–1513), was as unshakeably Lancastrian as Hastings was Yorkist. He was the head of England's most ancient noble family, a rare example of a great family that stayed loyal to the House of Lancaster throughout the Wars. He too was something of a hero, a fine soldier with a shrewd grasp of strategy and tactics.

Determined to avenge the deaths of his father and elder brother, who had been executed for plotting against the Yorkist regime, in 1469 Lord Oxford joined the Earl of Warwick's rebellion against Edward IV. Two years later, when commanding the Lancastrian right wing at Barnet, he routed Hastings, but as his men were returning from the pursuit their own side fired on them by mistake – an error that lost the battle. Fleeing abroad, Oxford turned pirate, and then in 1473 occupied St Michael's Mount on the Cornish coast. Surrendering, he was imprisoned for the next ten years at the Castle of Hammes near Calais; on one occasion he jumped from the battlements, trying to escape or to kill himself. During his imprisonment his wife had to support herself by sewing, while Gloucester bullied his aged mother into handing over everything she possessed.

Eventually Oxford succeeded in breaking free and was able to fight for Henry Tudor at Bosworth in 1485, where his tactics helped to defeat Richard III. Two years later, he commanded Henry VII's victorious army at Stoke, the final battle of the Wars. As Bacon puts it, the Earl of Oxford always remained the new Tudor king's 'principal servant for both war and peace.'

Save for the period's prejudice against women rulers, Lady Margaret Beaufort (1443–1509), half mystic and half dynast, might well have become Queen of England in her own right, as the last member of the Beaufort family (the bastard but legitimized branch of the House of Lancaster) with a claim to the throne which she passed on to her son Henry Tudor.

Marrying Edmund Tudor, Earl of Richmond, at the age of twelve, Margaret was still only thirteen when she gave birth to the future Henry VII. It was she who, with the aid of Dr Morton, forged the vital alliance between Lancastrians and Yorkists that eventually toppled Richard III. She helped to finance her son's invasions in 1483–85, while her fourth husband, Lord Stanley, betrayed Richard decisively at Bosworth. She then became the richest woman in England.

Most ladies were unable to play anything other than a passive role during the Wars of the Roses. Margaret Beaufort was one of the two magnificent exceptions – the other being Margaret of Anjou, Henry VI's tigress of a queen.

Although very few of the higher clergy were caught up in the Wars, generally prefering to stay prudently aloof, Dr John Morton (c. 1420–1500), the son of a Dorset squire, was a rare example of a political ecclesiastic – a loyal Lancastrian who turned loyal Yorkist. Ironically, the success of his clerical career owed a good deal to his secular activities.

As one of Henry VI's lawyer-bureaucrats, Morton was among those respons-ible for the murderous legislation at the Parliament of Devils in 1459 – designed to exterminate the Duke of York and his party. Captured by the Yorkists after the Battle of Towton, he was imprisoned in the Tower of London, but escaped to Flanders. Besieged in a Northumbrian clifftop castle in 1462, he survived to live as a penniless exile at Queen Margaret's little Lancastrian court in Lorraine. Returning to England in 1470, he was again taken prisoner by the Yorkists after Tewkesbury.

When it seemed that the Lancastrian cause was dead, Dr Morton transferred his allegiance to the Yorkists. He served Edward IV faithfully. Once more impris-oned in the Tower after Richard of Gloucester's coup, he was placed in the Duke of Buckingham's custody but persuaded the Duke to rebel against King Richard. When Buckingham's rebellion failed, Dr Morton hid in the Fens before escaping to Flanders, from where he was somehow able to warn Henry Tudor that the Bretons were planning to sell him to King Richard.

John Morton ended his long life as a cardinal, Archbishop of Canterbury, Chancellor of Oxford University and Henry VII's Lord Chancellor of England. In the writings of Thomas More, who was clearly devoted to the old man's memory, he is portrayed as an extremely formidable yet very likeable elder statesman.

Jane Shore (c. 1450–c. 1527), whose real name was Elizabeth Lambert,*[1] is the first ordinary Englishwoman recognizable as a human being from contemporary sources, from More's *King Richard*. (Sir Thomas knew her well by sight when she was an old woman and he may have spoken with her at length.) Since she does not come on to the scene until fairly late in the Wars, I have included the story of her father, John Lambert, a London alderman who was a staunch Yorkist and lent money to King Edward. Politically he was active enough for his brother-in-law to accuse him of having been seriously disloyal to Henry VI.

Although Richard III made Jane do public penance as a harlot and go barefoot through the City of London in her shift, for most of her life she was a thoroughly respectable married woman. However, as the mistress of Edward IV, then of his friend Hastings and then of his stepson the Marquess of Dorset, she knew intimately some of the most powerful men in England – at the cost of her reputation and of two spells in prison.

Ironically, she regained respectability by taking King Richard's solicitor Thomas Lynom for her second husband.

---

* Contemporaries refer merely to 'Shore's wife' or 'Mrs Shore', while the first mention of her as 'Jane' dates only from 1599. Yet it is by no means impossible that she used the name in preference to Elizabeth, so I have called her 'Jane' throughout – that is how she has gone down in history. I have also called her 'Mrs Shore' instead of 'Mistress' – just as I have used 'Mr' instead of 'Master' throughout – so as to avoid giving too archaic an impression.

THE WAY TO WAR,
1450–1460

3

Jack Cade's Revolt, 1450

JOHN LAMBERT (JANE SHORE'S FATHER)

P<small>ROBABLY</small> during the calamitous year of 1450 a baby girl was born in the City of London and christened 'Elizabeth'. Later she would be known as 'Jane' – perhaps a pet name or a name taken when beginning a new life. The birth must have been in some black-and-white timbered house, its eaves projecting over a narrow street not far from the Mercery in West Cheap. The Mercery was a long stone arcade divided into shops where her father plied his trade. Although the house was in no sense a shop, goods were stored in it and his apprentices ate and slept there. As he was a rich man, the house was furnished with what for the time was comfort, not to say luxury. London merchants and their wives drank from silver cups and had tall silver-salts standing on their tables, together with great pewter chargers and ewers; there were fine displays on their 'cup boards'. Jane is unlikely to have been born in a four-poster bed, since these were still rare, but it would have had a canopy with hangings of painted cloth.

Jane's father, Mr John Lambert, was a liveryman (or full member) of the Mercers' Company, one of the rich merchant companies that controlled the City. When he went out on business or to church – the nearest being St Mary le Bow – he wore an expensive 'livery' or uniform, a costly, gold-braided blue robe and hood, lined and edged with fur. He had become a man of standing in London, entitled to style himself 'Esquire', and one of the élite who elected the mercers' governing body, the wardens. Soon he himself would be one of the four wardens, who met at the Hospital of St Thomas of Acre to see that the company's statutes were observed. The wealthiest of all the 'mysteries' (companies), the mercers dominated not only the cloth trade but the merchant adventurers.

Formerly mercers had specialized in woollens. Nowadays, while still dealing in worsteds, they preferred imported textiles, rare and luxurious fabrics that were not yet manufactured in England, such as silks and velvets, though they might also deal in any commodity from wine to precious metals. No one could become a mercer without serving a long apprenticeship, which required an expensive premium, and then showing that he had a proper stock of goods. In 1503 the mercers would demand stock worth at least £100, though John Lambert may have begun with much less than this, perhaps worth as little as £40. He was also a merchant adventurer, with many contacts in the Netherlands.

John had been apprenticed in 1436 to a mercer named Thomas Onehand. Since apprentices were not admitted until they had reached the age of fourteen, and generally at seventeen, it is likely that John was born about the year 1419. His master was bound by the company ordinances to 'feed, clothe and teach [him] well and truly his art and craft.' John would have paid the company the enrolment fee of two shillings in silver pence or groats. Apprenticeship involved not only trade and the ways of the City, but buying and selling on behalf of Onehand, acting as his agent and travelling to fairs in the Low Countries as well as all over England, so that John may have acquired a smattering of French and Flemish.

He completed his apprenticeship in 1444, after less than eight years instead of the normal ten, and started his own business. We do not know how he found the money to do so. One possibility is that he had saved money from his wages and had been trading for himself; this was against the mercers' rules, so he would have had to hide his stock in a tavern or some other secret place. Another possibility is that he used the dowry from his marriage, for at some time during the 1440s he married Amy Marshall, his bride being the daughter of a rich London grocer who seems to have lived in Cripplegate parish. As a grocer, Robert Marshall belonged to another powerful livery company, controlling the lucrative spice trade in pepper, nutmeg and cinnamon, which were indispensable for making rotten meat and salt-fish edible during the winter months. Membership did not restrict Mr Marshall to dealing in spices – he may have traded in silks, like the great grocer Sir John Crosby, bringing him into contact with mercers.

There is evidence that later John Lambert was on bad terms with his brother-in-law Alexander, a dissipated young man. When Mr Marshall died in 1446 he left his son his estate on condition he abstained from 'riot and vices' – though he also bequeathed him a velvet doublet and a silver-mounted sword. Alexander did not reform and his sisters tried to prevent him from inheriting anything at all, alleg-

Jane Shore's father, John Lambert – 'citizen, mercer and alderman of London' – with her mother Amy, and their children. From a brass of 1487 at Hinxworth, Herts.

ing in the courts that he had had a loose woman in his room and had stolen a valuable salt cellar.

Both Jane's parents, therefore, came from well-to-do, largely self-made backgrounds. They were to have six children who survived infancy, four sons and two daughters, Jane (Elizabeth) being the elder of the girls. All of them had excellent prospects since John Lambert was an enterprising and no doubt ruthless businessman.

The Scots poet William Dunbar, who visited London half a century later, described it as 'Queen of cities all'. Its proud citizens had long known this to be beyond dispute. As England's largest city and the country's commercial and political capital, where the court resided – whether at the Tower or at the Palace of Westminster – its population may have been as high as 50,000. (That of York, its nearest rival, was only about 12,000; those of Bristol, Coventry and Norwich, accounted great cities, were as low as 5,000.) There were twenty-three monasteries and over a hundred churches within the walls, together with many imposing 'inns'. These were vast, rambling, semi-fortified mansions of brick and timber, built in the style which today we call 'black-and-white', housing noblemen, bishops or rich merchants. The greatest mansion of all was the grim Tower of London, a monstrous combination of fortress, prison and palace, tall, black and menacing despite its royal apartments and pleasure gardens. (Neighbouring Westminster upriver remained a separate city.) The countryside was only a very short walk away, just outside the walls, flat green fields filled with sheep and cattle before one reached the hills of Harrow and Hampstead with all their windmills. Downriver there were straggling suburbs on the north bank, faced by vegetable gardens and then marshes across the water.

The Thames was the main thoroughfare, barges and wherries taking the place of buses and cabs. There was a single massive bridge over the river, built of stone on great clumps of elmwood piles, which was crowded with houses four storeys high; the road across it went under archways and through courtyards, the arches adorned by the rotting heads of men who had been executed for treason. On the banks, amid a myriad of tall cranes, stood countless warehouses stuffed with gemstones, precious metals, silks and velvets, furs, sugar and spices, rare wines, and exotic fruits. 'The riches of England are greater than those in any other country in Europe', wrote a Venetian. Although he came from a city generally considered the most luxurious in Christendom, he was staggered by what he saw. In Cheapside (the smart shopping street) 'there are fifty-two goldsmiths' shops, so rich and full of silver vessels great and small, that in all the shops in Milan, Rome, Venice and Florence put together, I don't think there could be found so many as magnificent as those which are to be seen in London.'

Life in the bustling, opulent 'City' must have been pleasant for a prosperous young couple like the Lamberts, though the Venetian thought that Londoners had a peculiar way of enjoying themselves. 'Few people keep wine in their own houses, but buy it, for the most part at a tavern; and when they mean to drink a good deal they go to the tavern, and this is done not only by the men but by ladies of distinction.' However, Mr Lambert clearly spent more time at his shop in the Mercery than in the pubs.

Lit by rows of glass windows, and by a great fire in winter, his house would have been cheerful enough, with hangings of red, blue, green or tawny cloth, sometimes painted with saints or heraldic devices. There were also 'cloths of Arras' and tapestry, while coloured panelling was popular. Furniture was sparse – canopied beds, trestle tables, forms, stools and chests. Pewter services of plates, chargers and jugs, interspersed with silver cups and standing salts, stood on a 'cupboard'. There were wrought-iron fire-backs, brass and copper pots and pans.

The family spent a lot on clothes, a key element of status. A merchant like John aped the gentry, wearing gowns of silk and velvet, trimmed with beaver or marten fur, set off by silk belts and gold chains. 'A man would buy violet cloth for his wedding gown, with violet hose to match,' says Sylvia Thrupp in *The Merchant Class of Medieval London*.[1] 'Women seem to have had fewer gowns than their husbands, but their jewelry continued to be more elaborate. One widow had five gold rings, two "herts" of gold, a gold rose "powderid with perle", gold and coral beads, and four girdles with gold and silver fastenings . . . Women also needed stock of kerchieves for their headdresses.'

Even so, it was an anxious time for English merchants. The loss of Normandy was bad enough, but nothing compared to that of Gascony. Most of the vast quantities of wine consumed in England had come from south-western France. Wine has been described as almost a form of currency at this time, and cloth merchants such as John Lambert would often accept it in lieu of coin when trading abroad. No doubt he imported his own supplies from Gascony on board the fleet that sailed twice a year between Southampton and Bordeaux. However, in 1449–50 the fleet brought back a mere 207 tons compared with over a thousand during the previous year, while in 1450 there was no wine fleet. The price of wine in the taverns soared. Although the wine trade soon began to revive, it now had to cope with a new French government at Bordeaux and would not recover properly for another thirty years.

Trade across the North Sea was also upset by English pirates, who preyed on fellow countrymen as well as on foreigners. In particular they jeopardized relations with the Hanseatic merchants of Germany, already sour enough. In the summer of 1450 over 50 Hanseatic ships were seized in the Channel and their cargoes of salt sold in London. The Hanse retaliated by seizing the goods of all Englishmen who were trading in their towns – such as Cologne or Dantzig.

The fall of English France in 1449–51 began a slump that would continue for decades, harming merchants such as Mr Lambert. Not only the mercantile community was outraged by news of defeats across the Channel. During June 1450, led by an Irishman called Jack Cade, a host of armed petitioners from Kent and Sussex (including several gentlemen) stormed into London.[2] No doubt more than a few citizens like John Lambert agreed with the complaint in their petition to the king that 'his merchandise is lost', and much else too. What they did not want, however, was the sack of London. Cade's men occupied the Guildhall, freed the prisoners in the King's Bench and Marshalsea gaols, and looted private houses. A mob dragged the treasurer, Lord Saye, out of the Tower and beheaded him.

The angry Londoners rose to expel this 'multitude of riffraff' from the City. They spent an entire Sunday night 'ever fighting upon London Bridge, and many a man was slain and cast in [the River] Thames, harness, body and all.' One surmises that Mr Lambert was among the combatants; most well-to-do citizens owned 'harness' or plate armour. Early in July Cade was tricked by a false pardon into withdrawing from the City, and then hunted to his death.

While John may have despised 'riffraff', he can have been no mourner for the murdered Lord Saye. All his class disliked great lords who rode arrogantly through the streets to their inns, escorted by a menacing retinue of armed retainers, arousing fear and envy. No London inn of this sort has survived from the fifteenth century, though Crosby Hall (built of stone in 1466 and moved from the City to Chelsea in modern times) is the dining hall of one; a magnate ate in such a room, seated upon a dais and waited on by a miniature court of carvers and ushers. His retainers fed at long trestles, going to the fire in the kitchen at the end of the hall where whole sheep and oxen were revolving on spits and bringing back as much meat, 'sodden or roast', as they could carry on a dagger.

It is hard to exaggerate the gulf between the classes. For a peer, even for one of the upper gentry, men like Lambert were no less commoners than the toilers in the fields. Although a Burgundian, Georges Chastellain spoke for the English gentry when he wrote that nothing admirable could be expected of 'merchants and labourers' because both were 'servile'. There was little love between high and low. 'There are no more untrustworthy people under the sun than the middle classes in England', the snobbish Froissart had observed at the beginning of the century, adding that they would not let their betters have anything, even an egg or a chicken, without overcharging them.

Clearly, Mr Lambert must have had to meet both noblemen and gentlemen in the course of his business. They dressed according to their wealth – a great magnate might spend half a year's income on a doublet. Rare and costly fabrics were in demand, not just for apparel but for bedclothes, hangings, horse-trappings and pavilions. Mercers brought velvets, satins, brocades and damasks, cloth of gold or silver, shot silks or spotted taffetas, for these august customers to inspect. However, such contacts did not make for familiarity.

On the other hand, John had his social ambitions. As will be seen, it is obvious that he hoped to enter the lesser gentry, as had many other prosperous London citizens. He intended to acquire an estate and a manor house and found a landed family.

4

Margaret Beaufort
Is Married, 1455

THE great question of the early 1450s was who should succeed to the throne. King Henry was still without children when he reached the age of thirty in 1452, despite having been married for seven years; he was far from robust, and England remembered that his father had died at thirty-four. He dared not acknowledge the claims of his cousin, the Duke of York – to do so would bring into question his own right to the crown.

The problem was made worse by the power vacuum resulting from Henry's inadequacy. Everyone in the country was aware of it, even the humblest. In July 1450 two obscure Sussex farmers were in trouble with the local justices for saying openly at Brightling market that 'the king was a natural fool and would often hold a staff in his hands with a bird on the end, playing therwith as a fool, and that another king must be ordained to rule the land . . .' People must have sighed for a Henry V who could win back Normandy and Gascony.

Inevitably, the Duke of York and the Duke of Somerset clashed. Quite apart from blaming Somerset – who more or less controlled King Henry – for the Crown's refusal to pay its debts to him, York thought he was responsible for losing France. So did many others, with some justice. York could be blamed in no way for the disasters across the Channel, since he had been in Ireland. What he wanted to see in England would certainly have satisfied the more respectable of Cade's petitioners – a return to the government by council which had proved so effective during the 1420s and 1430s.

In 1451 Mr Thomas Yonge, MP, a Bristol lawyer employed by York, moved in

Parliament that because Henry VI had no offspring, it was necessary for the safety of the kingdom that it should be known openly who was heir apparent. Yonge then named the Duke, whereupon he was sent to the Tower. Privately, many (like the late Jack Cade) agreed with Mr Yonge, and wished that York governed the country instead of the Duke of Somerset and his rapacious friends. Early in 1452 York launched a coup d'état, not to seize the throne but to wrest power from Somerset. He issued manifestoes in which he claimed that Somerset was responsible for recent defeats in France, that he 'laboureth continually about the King's Highness for my undoing', and that 'the said duke ever prevaileth and ruleth about the king's person, that by this means the land is likely to be destroyed Raising troops, York marched to London, swearing 'he would have the duke of Somerset or die', according to a London chronicler. But only one other peer supported him. He was forced to submit, swearing an oath of allegiance to the King in a humiliating ceremony at St Paul's. Should York misbehave again, he would face the death penalty.

The court party tried desperately to find an alternative heir apparent to the throne. There were two candidates. One was the Duke of Exeter, descended from a daughter of John of Gaunt, but he was unstable and savage-tempered, a young man who made enemies rather than friends. The other was the wrong sex.

Although Somerset was the best-known Beaufort, strictly speaking the head of the family was a young girl, Lady Margaret Beaufort.[1] Born on St Petronilla's Day (31 May) 1443, she was the only child of his elder brother, the first Duke of Somerset. Her grandfather had been Henry IV's bastard half-brother, John of Gaunt's son by Catherine Swynford. Richard II had legitimized the Beauforts (named after the castle where they were born) after Gaunt married Catherine. Henry IV had confirmed their legitimacy by letters patent though he had added the words 'excepting the royal dignity' to exclude them from succeeding to the throne. However, because the clause had not received the authority of Parliament, it was deemed invalid by the present king. Since there were no other direct heirs of the House of Lancaster, Margaret's claims as a possible successor were therefore taken very seriously so long as Henry VI remained childless.

Her uncle, the Duke of Somerset, dared not aim at the throne himself. To have done so would have meant civil war. York was perfectly sincere when he accused Somerset of losing France. Not only did he blame him for the Crown's failure to reimburse his expenses as lord-lieutenant in both France and Ireland, but he genuinely believed that he was plotting his ruin. Although a Beaufort, Lady Margaret was not such a threat.

There was no precedent for a female monarch in England, and very few else-where in fifteenth-century Europe. The most recent had been Joanna II of Naples, whose reign had ended in anarchy in 1435; the Queen's father, Réné of Anjou, had tried and had failed to succeed her. Yet with a suitable consort the Lady Margaret might nonetheless wear the crown of England. No one had understood this better than the late Duke of Suffolk, who before she was seven married her to his son John, only a year older. (Either partner could dissolve such a marriage on reaching puberty, if he or she did not wish to consummate it.) Impeaching Suffolk, the House of Commons alleged that he had been plotting to make his son king, 'presuming and pretending her to be the next inheritable to the Crown.' Clearly, in 1450 most MPs were well aware of Margaret Beaufort's claim to the throne.

'Her father was John, duke of Somerset, her mother was called Margaret, right noble in manners as in blood', we are told by Cardinal Fisher, who knew both ladies. The duke, captain-general in Aquitaine and Normandy, had died in 1444, before Margaret was two years old; there were rumours that he had died by his own hand, from shame at mismanaging a campaign in France.[2] Her mother, daughter and heiress of Sir John Beauchamp of Bletsoe in Bedfordshire, had pre-viously been married to Sir Oliver St John, so that Margaret regarded her St John half-brothers and half-sisters as her closest kindred after spending her childhood with them, either at Bletsoe or at Maxey Castle in Northamptonshire. No trace survives of either house. Bletsoe is known to have been moated and crenellated; it vanished long ago, but Margaret would still feel at home in Bletsoe church. The Tudor antiquary John Leland visited Maxey, near Market Deeping and on the edge of the Fen country, where he saw 'a pretty turret called the Tower of the Moor. And thereby be made a fair great pond or lake bricked about.'

In 1447 the little girl acquired a stepfather when the Duchess took a third husband, Lionel, Lord Welles, who was a veteran of the French wars and an influ-ential member of the court party.

In February 1453 Margaret's mother was commanded to bring her daughter to court. On St George's Day, 23 April, they attended the Order of the Garter's annual ceremonies at Windsor. No new knights were installed that year, but Vespers and Mass were celebrated with the customary splendour. No one present can have guessed just how prophetic were some words in the Gospel for the feast: 'I came not to send peace but the sword . . . and a man's enemies shall be

Margaret Beaufort's parents, John, Duke of Somerset and his duchess,
Margaret Beauchamp. From a seventeenth century sketch of their tomb at
Wimborne Minster, Dorset.

they of his own household.' The Garter Knights' blue robes were a shade paler
than those worn today while the red mantles of the canons and Poor Knights
clashed with the blood-red gowns worn by the Queen and the great ladies of the
court. Such a display of chivalric ritual cannot have failed to impress the little girl,
a dazzling glimpse of a magic world of heroism and idealism.

Young though she was, Margaret Beaufort soon realized that there was a very
high place indeed for her in the hierarchy of England. On 12 May King Henry
ordered that 'our right dear and right well beloved cousin Margaret' be paid a
hundred marks (over £66) for raiment, a dress allowance that was four times the
income of a well-to-do squire. The King had given her as a ward to his half-
brother Edmund Tudor, telling him to marry her.

Edmund Tudor's father Owen Tudor had begun life as a humble Welsh
gentleman called Owain ap Maredudd Tudur, who had made his fortune by

secretly marrying Henry V's widow, Catherine of France. In 1452 their two sons, Edmund and Jasper – hitherto lowly, poverty-stricken hangers-on – had been transformed into great Lancastrian noblemen, being created earls with precedence over all other earls. It seems that Henry VI suddenly elevated his half-brothers in this way because he contemplated making Edmund his heir, basing his claim on Margaret's descent from John of Gaunt. (Presumably, had they succeeded to the throne, the couple would have reigned as joint king and queen like Philip and Mary in the next century.) Significantly, with Henry's approval, Edmund abandoned his Tudor coat of arms and adopted a version of the royal arms of England.

Many years later Margaret told her confessor, John Fisher, how she had worried desperately over whether to take Edmund or Suffolk – to whom she had been married at the age of seven.

> She, which as then was not fully nine years old, doubtful in her mind what she were best to do, asked counsel of an old gentlewoman whom she much loved and trusted, which did advise her to commend herself to St Nicholas the patron and helper of all true maidens . . . [and] as she lay in prayer calling upon St Nicholas, whether sleeping or waking she could not assure, but about four of the clock in the morning one appeared to her arrayed like a bishop and, naming unto her Edmund, bade [her] take him unto her husband.[3]

Her marriage to the boy Duke of Suffolk was dissolved. However, the wedding with Edmund was not to take place until 1455.

Any claim to the throne which Margaret and Edmund may have had was soon forgotten when the Queen bore King Henry a son in October 1453. Even so, it is clear from later events that Margaret always remained very conscious of the Beaufort claim. So would her son, who one day used it to overthrow the house of York.

In August 1453 Henry VI had gone mad from 'a sudden fright', losing all power of speech and unable to stand – a condition that may have been catatonic schizophrenia. He showed no reaction whatever to the good news that at last he had a son, Edward, Prince of Wales – generally known to history as 'Edward of Lancaster'. (Characteristically, when the King recovered he attributed the boy's paternity to the Holy Ghost.) Faced with Henry's total incapacity, the Lords

Lamphey in Pembrokeshire, Margaret Beaufort's first married home.

appointed the Duke of York to be Lord Protector of England in March 1454. No one wanted to be ruled by the French Queen. Even so, the Duke enjoyed only limited authority, being 'chief of the king's council' instead of a full-blown regent. He governed responsibly, consulting the broadly based council, but, inevitably, he ousted enemies and rewarded supporters. The Duke of Somerset had already been sent to the Tower by the council, largely for his own protection, and York took his post of Captain of Calais. He also appointed Somerset's enemy Richard Nevill, Earl of Salisbury, as Chancellor of England.

It is important to understand why the Nevills were to be such loyal Yorkists. In the first place, as Salisbury's brother-in-law, York was their best hope of triumphing over the Percies in the north, where a pitched battle had recently taken place between the two families. When they defeated the Percies in another battle in the autumn of 1454, York arranged for two of the latter's leaders – Lord Egremont and his brother Richard Percy – to be sent to Newgate gaol. There was also a quarrel between Salisbury's son, the Earl of Warwick, and the Duke of Somerset, the Earl being determined to occupy the rich lordship of Glamorgan although King Henry had granted it to Somerset.

It was a disaster for England when the King regained his senses on Christmas Day 1454. The Duke of York's protectorate came to an end in February 1455. He had tried to rule as fairly as he could in the circumstances. But Somerset was released from prison the same month and once again the country found itself governed by a selfish clique. Moreover, the Queen had developed an obsessive hatred for York.

Meanwhile, in the spring following King Henry's return to sanity, Margaret Beaufort had finally married Edmund Tudor, who was fourteen years older than she. He took her to live at Lamphey Court in Pembrokeshire, the westernmost corner of South Wales. The house was a former palace of the bishops of St David's. (Although in ruins, the chapel and much of the wings remain standing.) Margaret must have found the landscape windswept and treeless, with scattered white farmsteads amid strange black cattle. The Welsh must have seemed foreign too, speaking an alien tongue. Fifty years before, most of them had joined Owain Glyn Dŵr's national revolt and to some extent they were still a conquered race, resentful of the English, who distrusted them. The Marches of Wales did not become part of the kingdom of England until the next century and the King's writ did not run here, so that the region was in constant turmoil, local gentry feuding and stealing each other's cattle.

Shortly after their marriage, the quarrel between York and Somerset erupted into armed conflict at St Albans in May 1455. Although a very minor affair (see Chapter 5), it ensured a gradual descent into civil war in which the Tudors quickly found themselves involved. In August Margaret's husband Edmund, King Henry's lieutenant in South Wales, was captured by Yorkists in an obscure skirmish. Their leader, William Herbert, imprisoned him briefly at Caermarthen. Plague broke out in the town, and Edmund Tudor, Earl of Richmond, died of it two months later.

Although only thirteen and very small for her age – she would grow up to be a tiny little woman – Margaret was pregnant. Regardless of her childishness and pitiful size, Edmund had insisted on consummating the marriage, probably from

Margaret Beaufort's second husband, Edmund Tudor, Earl of Richmond. Father of her only son, the future King Henry VII, he died of the plague at Carmarthen in 1456. From a brass of *c* 1486 (restored in 1872–5) at St David's Cathedral, Pembs.

Pembroke Castle where Margaret Beaufort's only son, the future Henry VII, was born in January 1457.

avarice rather than brutality; if he could father a child on her, then by law he would be guaranteed a life interest in her estates. Her brother-in-law Jasper took the girl widow to Pembroke Castle for her confinement. The castle still stands, a massive fortress beside the Atlantic, on an arm of Milford Haven; from a rock a Norman keep ringed by high thirteenth-century curtain walls guards the little town lying beneath. It is hard to think of a harsher place in which to be pregnant during winter gales.

Long afterwards, she confided to John Fisher that she had been terrified that the child in her womb might be stricken by plague, but on 28 January 1457 she gave birth to a healthy son, Henry Tudor. The birth 'spoilt' her gynaecologically so that she could never again bear a child – indeed, given the period's obstetrics, she was lucky to survive. Understandably, she always remembered the day, St Agnes's Day, on which, as she wrote years afterwards, 'I did bring into this world my good and gracious prince, king and only son.'

5

The Earl of Oxford
Is Late at St Albans, 1455

THE EARL OF OXFORD (LORD OXFORD'S FATHER)

Aᴀꜰᴛᴇʀ the Duke of York's protectorate ended in February 1455 and the Duke of Somerset was released, the court party persuaded King Henry to call a great council of the realm, to meet at Leicester at the end of May. Probably Somerset intended that York should be censured during the council, perhaps summoned to be tried by his peers – or, at the very least, be forced to swear a humiliating oath of submission of the sort he had sworn after Dartford in 1452. The council was going to be at Leicester since Somerset was so much disliked in London. A chronicle known as 'Davies' (after its editor) says that the 'commons of this land hated this duke Edmund [of Somerset] and loved the duke of York, because he loved the commons . . .'

However, unlike the Londoners, at this date the magnates as a whole were steadfast in their loyalty to Henry VI. He was their crowned and anointed king to whom they had sworn fealty. They could be relied on to support him, just as they had after York's abortive rising three years earlier.

Should the council meet at Leicester there was every reason, therefore, to suppose that the Duke of York would suffer – and no doubt the Nevills too.

John de Vere, twelfth Earl of Oxford, was a typical establishment magnate of this sort. The de Veres were among the most illustrious families in England. 'No King in Christendom hath such a subject as Oxford,' Chief Justice Crewe told the House of Lords in 1623. 'He came in with the Conqueror, Earl of Guynes, shortly

after the Conquest made Great Chamberlain, above five hundred years ago by
Henry I, the Conqueror's son, brother to Rufus . . . no other Kingdom can
produce such a peer in one and the self-same name and person.' Even in 1455
the family was already deeply respected for its antiquity. It was also rich and influential, owning broad acres. If the de Veres had any ambition at all, it was to
recover the great chamberlainship of England, a ceremonial office of immense
prestige which it had lost during the previous century. The Earl's attitude towards
the Lancastrian monarchy and towards any sort of involvement in politics cannot
fail to have been strongly conditioned by hereditary memories. His own family
had suffered disastrously from playing too prominent a role in public life at the
end of the previous century. Robert de Vere, ninth Earl of Oxford, had become
the bosom friend and favourite of Richard II, who heaped honours upon that
unpleasant young man, making him Marquess of Dublin and then Duke of
Ireland. Eventually Robert's behaviour outraged the opposition to King Richard
known as the 'lords appellant'; in 1387 they proclaimed throughout the land that
the Duke was guilty of treason. His response had been to march on London with
a private army of several thousand men. However, when confronted by military
leaders who included the future Henry IV – founder of the House of Lancaster
– his troops deserted him and he had to escape abroad. He was attainted, forfeiting all his titles and property. When he died in exile in 1392 his uncle, Aubrey
de Vere (Earl John's grandfather), was re-created Earl of Oxford and recovered
the estates. But the attainder remained unreversed, breaking the continuity of an
earldom bestowed by Henry I, while the cherished office of Great Chamberlain
had not been restored to the family.

The present Lord Oxford was unshakeable in his loyalty to his crowned and
anointed king. Anyone as old as the Earl could remember the magnificent if terrifying figure of Henry V, who had instilled a veneration for the House of
Lancaster in the vast majority of Englishmen. At the same time, like most of his
fellow peers, Oxford was reluctant to become involved in the dangerous quarrel
between York and Somerset. Even so, he can never have suspected that their
quarrel was soon going to end in murder and ultimately in full-scale civil war.

He was an amiable, pleasant-mannered man who could laugh at himself,
judging from his letters to the Pastons. Although he sometimes visited London
– where he had a town house in the street called London Wall – going generally
on board a ship from Colchester rather than travel by road, his principal interests
lay in East Anglia. He was genuinely public-spirited, more than once expressing
concern for 'the public weal of all the shire'. He had five sons, the eldest, Sir
Aubrey de Vere, being by all accounts a most attractive personality. His second

son, John de Vere – who was only eight in 1455 – is one of the heroes of this book.

One chronicler claims that the Duke of York and his Nevill allies believed that Somerset ceaselessly 'provoked the king to their final destruction'. If this was the case, in order to survive they had at all costs to regain power, which meant obtaining control of the King's person, and eliminating Somerset. An armed coup was the obvious solution. In view of Somerset's notorious incompetence as a soldier, a small force was thought quite sufficient to ambush the royal party *en route* for Leicester, while it is far from inconceivable that murder featured in the Yorkist plan. What made the scheme so attractive to the Nevills was the presence in the party of the head of the Percies, the Earl of Northumberland, which would give them a chance of striking a decisive blow in their bitter feud. This was the origin of the first Battle of St Albans – the first in the Wars of the Roses.

On 21 May the King and Somerset set out from Westminster for St Albans where they were to be met by various magnates who would bring troops. (Lord Oxford was to be among them.) The Yorkists were waiting, 'having gathered privily a power of people and kept them covertly in villages about the town of St Albans.' Shortly after leaving Westminster, Henry received letters from York, Salisbury and Warwick, complaining that they had not been summoned to the council at Leicester because of 'the great defame and blasphemy thrown against us', and that they had had to assemble armed men to protect themselves. Nonetheless, the royal party – no more than 2,000 men at most, since it consisted only of the accompanying peers' households – continued on its way, quite unaware that it was walking straight into a trap.

When news came early on the morning of 22 May that Yorkist troops were in the vicinity, King Henry replaced Somerset as constable – commander of his little army – with the Duke of Buckingham, who was the brother-in-law of both York and Salisbury. The royal party reached St Albans at about 9 a.m. on 22 May. The Duke of York 'and with him, come in company, the earl of Salisbury, the earl of Warwick, with divers knights and squires', had been waiting since 7 a.m. in Key Field south-east of the broad St Peter's Street – the town's only large street. York had been well served by his spies and knew that the magnates whom the king was expecting would not arrive until the next day.

The Duke sprang the trap once the King and his party had marched into St Peter's Street. He and his men barred the street at both ends, then he sent a herald to demand that Henry hand over Somerset, 'the man disloyal to his country who ruined Normandy, whose negligence lost Gascony and who reduced the entire realm of England to a state of misery.' The King's answer (no doubt dictated by Somerset) was to tell the Yorkists to 'void the field' or 'I shall destroy them, every mother's son and they [shall] be hanged, drawn and quartered that may be taken afterward.'

The royal troops prepared to defend the town centre, erecting barricades across St Peter's Street. The King set up his banner in the street, halfway between the Abbey and the parish church, opposite the Castle Inn (on the site of the National Westminster Bank). Even so, Henry and the Duke of Buckingham, with many of their followers, thought that York was bluffing and did not bother to put on armour.

The aged Abbot of St Albans, John Whethamstede, was watching, apparently from the comparative safety of the Abbey gatehouse. (It is still there, having survived the Dissolution of the Monasteries.) The old man, who was horrified by what he saw, has left an eyewitness account.[1]

The Yorkists attacked the barricades between 11 a.m. and noon, but were beaten back. Then at the south-eastern end the Earl of Warwick with 600 northern 'marchmen' burst into Holywell Street, which led into St Peter's Street, breaking in opposite the Abbey gatehouse through the back gardens between two inns, the Keys and the Chequers. As they came on, the Earl's marchmen blew trumpets, shouting 'A Warwick! A Warwick! A Warwick!' Then at the northern end York's troops 'brake down violently houses and pales on the east side of the town, and entered into St Peter's Street, slaying all those that withstood them.'

Someone rang the curfew bell in the clock tower in the marketplace at the end of the street. (It too is still there.) Royalists who had not done so already now tried to put on their armour. There was a savage mêlée, first arrow fire, then hand-to-hand fighting. 'I saw a man fall with his brains beaten out, another with a broken arm, a third with his throat cut and a fourth with a stab wound in his chest, while the whole street was strewn with corpses,' writes Abbot Whethamstede. The King himself was wounded by an arrow in the neck; deserted, he took refuge in a tanner's cottage. The royal banner was left standing forlornly against a wall by its bearer. His men either fled into the surrounding fields or else begged for mercy.

Dan Robert Beauner, monk of St Alban's Abbey and a member of the community who witnessed the battle of St Albans in 1455. From a brass of 1470 at St Albans Abbey, Herts.

The Duke of Somerset, who had once had a fantastic dream that he should die under a castle, retreated inside the Castle Inn. When it was surrounded and the Yorkists began to batter at the doors, he came out fighting. He killed four of his opponents before being cut down with a poleaxe beneath the sign of the castle.

Among the 'lords of name' slain in the court party besides Somerset were Northumberland and Clifford, together with many courtiers, about seventy being killed in all. Buckingham's son, Lord Stafford (Margaret Beaufort's brother-in-law), had an arrow wound in the hand from which he later died, while Somerset's son, Lord Dorset, was so badly hurt that he had to be taken home in a cart, as was the Queen's chamberlain – 'and other divers knights and squires sore hurt.'[2]

Some royalists took refuge in the Abbey, including the Duke of Buckingham, who had been hit in the face by an arrow. He was joined by the standard-bearer, the Earl of Wiltshire, who was the Lord Treasurer and the most handsome man in the kingdom. As Gregory records, Wiltshire 'fought mainly with the heels, for he was frightened of losing his beauty'; prudently, he had taken off his armour and hidden it in a ditch, donning a monk's habit.

The Abbot says that as soon as the Yorkists knew they had won, they ran through the streets and started looting – '*Damnabilis detestabilisque depraedatio.*' He tells how the victorious troops, especially the northerners, broke into houses, stealing gold and silver plate, money and wine. At one moment the monks thought that they were about to sack the Abbey.

York and the two earls went to Henry VI's refuge in the tanner's cottage. Here they knelt before the wounded king, protesting their loyalty and insisting that they had never intended to do him any harm. Henry said he forgave them, asking that they stop the fighting. Then they escorted him to the Abbey where he spent the night. Next morning they took the King back to London where he was lodged in the Bishop's palace next to St Paul's. After this he had to suffer the further humiliation of attending a Mass of thanksgiving at the cathedral.

An anonymous contemporary notes that on the day after the battle the Duke of Norfolk arrived at 'Seynt Albons' with 6,000 men. He adds, 'And the earl of Oxenford also.'

No doubt the Earl received a very full account of what had happened from the Abbot and saw the damage done to the town, together with the corpses of the lords in the Abbey where they were awaiting burial. Judging from his subsequent record as a diehard Lancastrian, Oxford must have been deeply shocked.

A nobleman and his retainers. From the *Book of St Alban's*, 1496.

It was altogether too much of a coincidence that the only peers killed in the battle were Somerset, Northumberland and Clifford; the first being the enemy of York and the last two enemies of the Nevills. Murder had been done. Others, pillars of society, impeccably loyal to the Crown, men of Oxford's own rank and entitled to reverential respect in that hierarchical age, lay badly wounded. Scandalously, those of the King's party who survived had been robbed, 'despoiled of horse and harness.' In modern terms it was the behaviour of gangsters.

Most shamefully of all, King Henry had been wounded and insulted, his banner treated with contempt. To a fifteenth-century man with a conservative cast of mind such as Lord Oxford, that was sacrilege.

6

The Loveday at St Paul's, 1458

ELIZABETH LAMBERT (JANE SHORE)
MARGARET BEAUFORT

I~n~ London, news of the slaughter at St Albans, magnified by rumour, can only have alarmed prosperous merchants such as John Lambert. Although flourishing, and rising in the esteem of fellow citizens, like everyone else he must have been an increasingly worried man. From a respectful distance the City watched the hatred festering between the two factions – on the one side the young lords whose kindred had fallen at St Albans, and on the other those who had killed them – despite every attempt at reconciliation.[1]

During the summer of 1455 a nervous Parliament absolved the Duke of York and the Nevills from everything done at St Albans, putting any blame on the late Duke of Somerset and his friends – 'the which bill many a man grudged full sore . . .' Henry VI fell ill again in November, York becoming protector once more. Although the Duke's second protectorate lasted only until February 1456, he secured his hold on Calais, making Warwick's captaincy a reality by paying the garrison's arrears of pay. Now he controlled the Crown's only standing army.

Then the court party began to revive. Among its new leaders was young Harry Beaufort, Duke of Somerset – the late Duke's son. The foremost of those whose kindred and friends had fallen at St Albans, where he himself had been badly wounded, his charm and his ferocity impressed even enemies. During the summer of 1456, eager to avenge his father's murder, together with his cousin, the Duke of Exeter, he planned to ambush and kill the Earl of Warwick when the Earl rode to London; the plan entailed a minor pitched battle since like all men of rank Warwick always travelled with a large and heavily armed retinue. However, the Earl was warned and took a different road.

Queen Margaret, transformed by the birth of a son, started to assert herself. By the summer of 1456 York had recognized that she was his principal enemy; it was common knowledge in London that she and the Duke were waiting for each other to make the first move. In August 1456 she persuaded Henry to transfer the court from London to Kenilworth in Warwickshire. She then bullied him into appointing her nominees to key posts, such as Laurence Booth, who became Lord Privy Seal and Bishop of Durham. The situation continued to deteriorate throughout 1457, though it did not break into armed conflict.

In the City of London during the uneasy year of 1456 the mercers – or at any rate their apprentices – disgraced themselves by a vicious riot against the Italian community, particularly the rich traders who were competing for English business. The mercers were far from displeased by their apprentices' behaviour. A Tudor chronicler describes the Londoners at this date as 'sore abhoring the Italian nation for licking the fat from their beards and taking from them their accustomed living, by reason that the said strangers imported and transported into this realm all such merchandise, commodities and necessaries as the Englishmen only were accustomed to do . . .'[2] Houses belonging to merchants from Venice, Lucca and Florence were looted. Gregory says that during the mercers' 'wanton rule' (rioting) the 'Lombards' were treated so savagely that many left London for good, moving to Southampton or Winchester.

The mercers' riot typifies the xenophobia of fifteenth-century Englishmen of John Lambert's class. It also reveals the anger felt by many London businessmen at any preferential treatment given to foreign merchants by the King's ministers. Their resentment was fuelled by a commission set up to investigate the riots, chaired by the Dukes of Buckingham and Exeter. The latter had been appointed to the commission on the Queen's advice – an appointment that helped to alienate the mercers from the court party. A young man with royal blood, who was hereditary Admiral of England, Harry Holland, Duke of Exeter, had been imprisoned by his father-in-law York during his protectorate, for a foolish rebellion in 1453. He had an unpleasant reputation for violence and cruelty – the rack at the Tower (of which he was Constable) was known as 'The duke of Exeter's daughter' – though one day he would prove to the world that he was a brave and daring soldier. Queen Margaret had made a useful friend by showing that she forgave him for his rebellion.

Clearly Mr Lambert must have known most of the men who had taken part in the riot. It is very likely therefore that he attended the commission's sittings and watched 'my lord of Exeter', who no doubt wished to hang as many rioters as possible. The Duke's temper cannot have been improved by the commission being forced to postpone its enquiries after a warning that its members' lives were in danger. Its activities, such as sending apprentices to the gallows, made the court party still more unpopular in the City.

Regardless of Italian competitors or the Duke of Exeter's hangings, as usual Mr Lambert went on prospering quietly and steadily. In addition to his business as a mercer, he had become what would today be called a banker, lending money; given the rudimentary machinery for credit in fifteenth-century London, the recovery of loans and interest must have needed merciless tenacity. By now he was so highly thought of that in March 1457 he was one of ten financial experts appointed by the royal council to investigate ways of repaying the Crown's out-standing debts 'in good money of gold and silver', and instructed to submit a written report by 1 May 1458. In June 1457 he was to be among six mercers deputed by their company to confer with the King's French secretary, 'Master Gervys' (Gervace le Vulre), presumably about the same urgent problem of what should be done about the Crown's debts.[3]

So far the growing enmity between the Queen's supporters and those of the Duke of York did not affect comfortably-off London merchants such as Mr John Lambert. Nevertheless, they must surely have noticed that some very unsettling rumours were running through the City.

Even Henry VI recognized the danger. Apparently he took the advice of the Duke of Buckingham. The Duke, as rich and powerful a nobleman as York and with royal blood – his mother had been a granddaughter of Edward III – was very close to the King. Although never wavering in his loyalty to Henry, and though his elder son had been killed at St Albans, he always tried to keep on good terms with York, who was his brother-in-law.[4] Encouraged by Buckingham, the King made a genuine attempt to reconcile the Yorkists with the court party.

One gesture was to appoint the Earl of Warwick as Lord High Admiral in October 1457, in place of the Duke of Exeter. (The Duke had failed miserably to protect the Channel coast from French pirates, who had recently sacked the Kentish port of Sandwich.) It was no empty favour, Warwick being given £1,000 for expenses. The next step was to be a great council in London in February 1458, attended by relatives of those killed at St Albans and by York and the Nevills.

View of Maxtoke Castle in the County of Warwick.

The Duke of Buckingham surely took time off in January 1458 to attend the marriage of his son, Sir Henry Stafford, to the widowed Countess of Richmond, Margaret Beaufort. In the spring of 1457, accompanied by Jasper Tudor, she had met the Duke or his agents at his Monmouthshire manor of Greenfield to propose such a match. Clearly this remarkable thirteen-year-old wanted to remarry before a husband was chosen for her, and in worldly terms any son of the powerful Buckingham was a desirable bridegroom. It has been suggested that the wedding took place in the chapel of Maxstoke Castle in Warwickshire, the Duke's main residence. The castle, a great, square house of red sandstone with a tower at each corner, was to be largely rebuilt in Elizabethan times, yet she would recognize it even today.

From the scant evidence, it really does seem that the marriage of Margaret Beaufort and Henry Stafford was a happy one, perhaps the happiest time of her life. As a second son, he could expect only a small allowance from his father, but his wife's estates would enable him to live like a great nobleman.

At first the couple lived mainly at Bourne Castle in Lincolnshire on the edge of the Fens. It was near the great Benedictine abbey of Croyland, of whose confraternity they later became members. It was also close to Margaret's mother and stepfather, Lord Welles, at Maxey Castle, which they often visited, spending six weeks there on one occasion. (Her most recent biographers believe that Welles was a father figure to her.)

At the end of January 1458 the nobles of England rode into London escorted by their retinues, thousands of armed men clattering through the City streets. It was a matter for comment that York, who lodged at his inn of Baynards Castle beside the Thames, brought a mere 140. However, his Nevill brother-in-law of Salisbury, staying at his own inn (the Harbour on Dowgate Hill, on the site of Cannon Street Station), brought 400, eighty of whom were knights or squires. On the Lancastrian side, Somerset and Exeter each had 200 at their back while Lord Clifford and the Percy brothers, Lords Northumberland and Egremont, led a joint force of not less than 1,500 horsemen.

Londoners were fearful that mayhem and looting might break out. The Mayor policed the City and its suburbs with 5,000 citizens in full armour, riding daily through the streets, while 2,000 others under three aldermen kept the night watch until seven o'clock in the morning. (John Lambert may well have ridden on one of these patrols.) Tension mounted in February when the Earl of Warwick – widely blamed for the butchery at St Albans – rode in at the head of another large contingent.

King Henry and Queen Margaret arrived early in March, staying at the Bishop of London's palace near St Paul's. The council met sometimes at Blackfriars (where the station is now) and sometimes at Whitefriars in Fleet Street. Eventually Archbishop Bourchier coaxed it into a show of goodwill, York and the Nevills agreeing to pay compensation for St Albans. On 25 March there was a procession from the Bishop's palace to St Paul's with the King in his crown and robes of state; before him, arm in arm, marched the former enemies Somerset and Salisbury, Exeter and Warwick – behind him the Duke of York escorted Queen Margaret. Thousands of Londoners watched the 'loveday' procession, including, one may guess, the Lambert family.

Then, as now, St Paul's became the centre of the City of London on ceremonial occasions. Old St Paul's, later burnt down during the Great Fire of 1666, was even larger than the building that we know today. It was the best place in London for news, much important business being transacted in the cathedral precincts, while royal proclamations were read out at Paul's Cross – a lead-canopied pulpit just outside.

A Mass of reconciliation having been offered in thanksgiving, the celebrations continued with jousting at the Tower of London in the presence of Queen Margaret. In those days the Tower was not only a fortress but a luxurious palace as well, with long-vanished halls and chambers set among broad lawns and pleasure gardens. Tournaments were the spectator sport of the fifteenth century, watched enthusiastically even by those who, like the Lamberts, were not able to take part because of their class. Amid a solemn pageant of pavilions, banners, tabarded kings-of-arms and pursuivants, caparisoned and armoured gentlemen knocked each other out of the saddle with ponderous lances, or hammered away at one another on foot with blunted poleaxes. They fought beneath the admiring gaze of steeple-hatted ladies who sat in tapestried stands, with the Queen on a throne. The tournament was an Arthurian dream world enacted as well as a sport, a world of heroic knight errants and paladins, even if it was enlivened by an element of athletic competition – a poetic drama of heroism and love, and an escape into fantasy.

Yet even during the loveday of St Paul's there had been tensions. In February, while the meetings at Blackfriars or Whitefriars were trying to reconcile Yorkists and Lancastrians, it was reported from London that the Duke of Exeter was furious at having been replaced as Lord High Admiral by the Earl of Warwick –

'taketh a great displeasure that my lord Warwick occupieth his office.' It was no less widely known that the loveday had left undiminished the Duke of Somerset's bitter hatred of the Earl as the man whom he held personally responsible for his father's murder at St Albans three years before.

When Warwick attended a council meeting at Westminster in November 1458, fighting broke out between his men and the King's servants, who then attacked him. He had to cut his way through to the river and escape by barge. Instead of apologizing, Queen Margaret demanded that he be arrested. The Earl took refuge in Calais, insisting there had been a plot to murder him. There were also rumours that members of Somerset's household had planned to break into Warwick's London inn at night and kill him.

It was clear to most people in the City that civil war was not very far away. The Tudor chronicler Richard Grafton (who based his history on accounts by contemporary Londoners) observes of the end of 1458, 'Now again was renewed the cankered dissimulation which the last year was cloaked with, the name of agreement between the king and his lords.'

7

Dr Morton and the
Parliament of Devils, 1459

JOHN MORTON

A PRIEST who was also a lawyer scarcely sounds like a man of action. He was small too, and though John Lambert must often have passed him hurrying along Cheapside during the 1450s, on his way to his legal practice at the Court of Arches, Mr Lambert cannot have wasted a second glance on so insignificant a figure. Yet the little doctor was to prove one of the most formidable politicians to emerge throughout the entire Wars of the Roses.

If small in stature, nonetheless John Morton clearly impressed those who met him. He did so by sheer force of personality, though his 'countenance inspired respect rather than fear', says Sir Thomas More, who knew him well during his old age. Yet occasionally he could be alarming, and Francis Bacon (in his life of Henry VII) alleges that Morton was 'in his nature harsh and haughty.' However, More explains (in *Utopia*) that the doctor often adopted a caustic manner when talking to strangers, in order to see how they would react, but that normally he was 'lacking in no wise to win favour.'

A West Countryman, he had been born about 1420 in Dorset, either at Bere Regis or at Milburne St Andrew where his father was the squire. The Mortons came from a well-established family of minor gentry which had originated in Nottinghamshire. His uncle, who lived at Cerne Abbas, served as MP for Shaftesbury.[1] John was educated by the black monks of the Benedictine abbey at Cerne, beneath the great pagan god carved on the hill that overlooked them. Although the manor house of the Mortons at Milburne St Andrew has disappeared, John Morton would recognize the church of his childhood. There is much too that he would recognize were he to revisit the beautiful village of Cerne Abbas, such as the parish church, which was built during his lifetime, or the monks' gatehouse and guesthouse – not to mention the old giant on the hill. He went up to Oxford in 1446, to Balliol, eventually obtaining a doctorate in both civil and canon law. He then became a fellow of Peckwater Inn (now part of Christchurch, commemorated by Peckwater Quad), for which he was obliged to take holy orders.

Legal degrees have been described as the golden road to a mitre in fifteenth-century England, and diocesan administration as the sure way to preferment. After he was qualified, Dr Morton moved down to London to practise in the Court of Arches. Since this was in Cheapside, it really is quite likely that sometimes he passed John Lambert in the street. The Court sat in the crypt of the church of St Mary-le-Bow, hence its name. Under the direct jurisdiction of the Archbishop of Canterbury, it dealt mainly with errant clergymen, matrimonial troubles and disputed wills. A modern church stands on the site, since the medieval church perished during the Great Fire of London while Christopher Wren's successor was destroyed by the Blitz. (The City's curfew had been rung from the old church's tower, which is why it was said that a true Cockney must be born within the sound of Bow Bells.) However, the crypt where Morton practised, with its nave and two aisles, has been beautifully restored in recent years.

In February 1455 a new Archbishop of Canterbury was enthroned, Thomas Bourchier, who became Lord Chancellor of England in the following month. This shrewd, legally minded prelate at once recognized the little lawyer's calibre. Recommended by Bourchier, within a very short time he was recruited by the royal council and on 26 September 1457 'John Morton, clerk, doctor of the laws', was appointed chancellor of the household of the infant Prince of Wales. Soon he became one of Queen Margaret's most trusted advisers, and in consequence had to spend a good deal of time at Kenilworth Castle where the court was frequently in residence. Even so, he continued with his practice at the Court of Arches. Substantial preferment was beginning to come his way. Already principal of Peckwater Inn, subdean of Lincoln Cathedral and parson of Bloxworth in Dorset, he received the rich archdeaconry of Norwich; while drawing the income from these posts, it is unlikely that he ever visited any of them – save possibly Peckwater Inn for old times' sake.

Queen Margaret was badly in need of good advice. Enemies were circulating all sorts of unpleasant rumours about her, which the chronicles preserve; not only was she plundering the realm but the Prince of Wales was a bastard; some claimed that his true father had been either the Duke of Somerset or the Earl of

Wiltshire. There were stories too that she was secretly building up a private army of her own in Cheshire, to make her son king in place of his supposed parent, and that she had invited the French to sack Sandwich and was planning to hand over northern England to the Scots in return for armed assistance against the Duke of York.

Yet, whatever gossip might claim, most peers and gentry were loyal to Henry VI. Apart from Salisbury and Warwick, only one or two lesser magnates supported York. Emboldened by this knowledge, the Queen refused to contemplate any solution that might have satisfied the Duke and his friends. She meant to destroy them and they knew it. Nor did they underestimate her – 'a great and strong laboured woman, for she spareth no pain' is how a contemporary described her to Sir John Fastolf.

Margaret of Anjou, Shakespeare's 'proud insulting queen', was among the most formidable tragic heroines of English history.

> Her tears will pierce into a marble heart;
> The tiger will be mild, whiles she doth mourn

Clearly, she was influenced by her background. Her father, 'King Réné', of Anjou, was a Valois prince, a great grandson of John II of France who had been taken prisoner at Poitiers. Inheriting huge tracts of French territory which included all Provence, he had also been bequeathed the kingdom of Naples, together with shadowy claims to the thrones of Hungary, Majorca and Jerusalem. Although a mirror of chivalry and a lavish patron of the arts, his real fame lay in being one of the most spectacular royal losers in fifteenth-century Europe – outside England. He had had a good chance of becoming not only King of Naples but Duke of Lorraine too, and he had lost both. It would be very surprising if King Réné's failures had not been noticed by his daughter.[2]

Queen Margaret had come to England in 1445 when she was fifteen, to find herself detested as a Frenchwoman and blamed for the English reverses in France. She was also identified with her husband's greedy hangers-on. The birth of a son transformed her into a fiercely determined politician, leader of the court party and then of the Lancastrians; England must not be lost in the way in which her father had lost his inheritance. For seventeen years she would fight to save the throne for her son, Edward of Lancaster. The only convincing contemporary likeness of her is the profile on a medal by Pietro de Milano. It shows a handsome, slightly full French face with a sensual mouth.

By early 1459 she was preparing for armed confrontation. In May the royal council started to stockpile weaponry at the Tower of London, ordering bows and sheaves of arrows by the thousand. Magnates loyal to King Henry told their 'well-wishers' to join them at midsummer.

A magnate recruited his well-wishers from the neighbouring gentry. They signed indentures binding them to ride at his side when summoned, usually to local assemblies or to Parliament, receiving wages and protection in return. Although these 'affinities' of well-wishers were not private armies, if necessary they were ready to fight for their magnates.[3]

Having convinced Henry VI that the Duke of York was plotting to replace him on the throne, the Queen hoped to provoke York and the Nevills into disobeying her husband. They were therefore summoned to a Great Council which would meet at Coventry towards the end of June. She knew very well that they would not dare walk into the lioness's den and, by staying away, would give her the pretext she was seeking to destroy them.

Someone with a knowledge of the law had explained to her that she might crush the Yorkists once and for all by legal means – by attainting them. She decided that a bill of this sort should be introduced against York and his adherents in a parliament at Coventry in the autumn of 1459.

Such a bill needed the most careful drafting, while further legislation would be needed when it was passed. Morton joined a group entrusted with the task of drawing up the bill and planning tactics. The group included Sir John Fortescue (Chief Justice of the King's Bench and the greatest English lawyer of the fifteenth century), Dr Aleyn, John Heydon and Thomas Thorpe – the latter a former speaker of the House of Commons.

Obviously Morton and his friends were nervous about the scheme. Later in the year Aleyn was reported as saying that if King Henry retained power, they 'should be made for ever; and if it turned to contrary wise, it should grow to their final confusion and utter destruction.' (In 1461 Thorpe would be lynched by a Yorkist mob in London, beheaded in Haringay Park.)

York and the Nevills had to reach Henry if the process were to be stopped, but he was inaccessible at Kenilworth Castle – 'The Queen's Bower', as some called it sardonically – where he was firmly under his wife's control. The only way to reach him was to fight their way into his presence.

The Earl of Salisbury marched down from Yorkshire while his son Warwick sailed over from Calais, both intending to join the Duke of York at his stronghold in Ludlow in Shropshire. A small royal army intercepted Salisbury at Blore Heath in September. However, despite a fierce little battle with heavy casualties on both sides, they failed to stop him.

In October the Duke and the two earls occupied Worcester, where they publicly swore an oath in the cathedral to respect the King's authority. They retreated at the approach of Henry's main army, continuing to retreat until they were back at Ludlow. Here, however, they decided to make a stand. At Ludford Bridge nearby, they 'fortified their chosen ground, their carts with guns set before their battles [divisions] . . .' But the reinforcements they were expecting failed to arrive. Then Andrew Trollope (who commanded their vanguard and knew all their plans) went over to Henry, taking the men from the Calais garrison with him. During the night, deserting their troops, York and the Nevills fled; the Duke to Dublin and the two earls to Calais – the latter accompanied by the Earl of March, York's eldest son. Next day their army surrendered and the King's troops marched into Ludlow.

Alarming reports reached London of disgraceful behaviour by Henry's triumphant followers. Gregory writes in his chronicle of 'the misrule of the king's gallants at Ludlow' – how drunken royal troops, 'wetshod in wine', had looted the town and 'defouled many women'. Another chronicler says that Ludlow was 'robbed to the bare walls.' Such reports would do Henry's cause irreparable harm.

Attended by half the English peerage, what would come to be called the 'Parliament of Devils' met at Coventry in November 1459. The name befits its savage legislation. Those present took a special oath of allegiance to the King and his son, swearing in addition to protect the Queen. York and over twenty of his supporters were accused of treason and attainted as planned.

The Act itself is, to say the least, a colourful and even an impassioned document.[4] Those who drafted it were clearly inspired by the same fury as the Queen. It insists that the Duke of York had secretly been in league with 'Jack Cade, your great Traitor', in 1450. The Duke had come 'out of Ireland with great bobance and inordinate people to your palace of Westminster into your presence, with great multitude of people harnessed and arrayed in manner of war', it reminds King Henry. The Act deplores 'the execrable and most detestable deed . . . done at St Albans', complaining of 'the most diabolic unkindness and wretched envy' displayed by the Duke and the earls. It describes their recent flight from Ludford Bridge with a gloating gusto that verges on exultation.

> Almighty God that seeth the hearts of peoples, to whom nothing is hid, smote the hearts of the said duke of York and earls suddenly from that most presumptuous pride to the most shameful fall of cowardice that could be

thought, so that about midnight then next [en]suing they stole away out of the Field, under colour they would have refreshed them awhile in the town of Ludlow, leaving their standards and banners . . .

According to Friar Brackley, a grey friar of Norwich and an enthusiastic Yorkist – his patron the duke of Norfolk being one of the very few peers who then favoured York – Dr Morton and his friends were responsible for a malicious conspiracy against innocent lords, knights, gentles and commons: 'the perilous writing and mischievous indicting was imagined, contrived and utterly concluded by their most vengeable labour.'

8

'They that were in the Tower cast wildfire into the City', 1460

JOHN LAMBERT (JANE SHORE'S FATHER)

A FTER the 'Parliament of Devils' the City of London was understandably apprehensive, full of rumours about the 'lords of Calais', by which was meant Salisbury, Warwick and York's son March. It was obvious that such men would not be content to stay in exile as outlaws and that soon they were going to return to England. Bloodshed was inevitable. While the Londoners as a whole tended to sympathize with the exiled Duke of York and his followers, they were uncomfortably aware that there was a strong royal garrison in the Tower which was commanded by a famous veteran of the French wars, the staunchly Lancastrian Lord Scales. Should the Yorkists try to enter the City, there was bound to be fighting.

All three lords were formidable. Richard Nevill, the old Earl of Salisbury – born in 1400, he was nearly sixty – may be a shadowy figure, but as warden of the West March of Scotland for many years he had clearly seen plenty of fighting and was an experienced soldier. A younger son of the first Earl of Westmorland, he had married the heiress of the last Montagu Earl of Salisbury, acquiring his own earldom through his wife. Like most Nevills he was a ruthless predator and an unforgiving enemy.

His son Warwick, born in 1428 and also called Richard Nevill, was one of the most colourful personalities in English history. He too had made his fortune by marriage, his wife Anne Beauchamp being the Duke of Warwick's heiress. No less rapacious than his father, he was constantly trying to add to already vast

estates. Arrogant even by fifteenth-century standards, at the same time he possessed the common touch and knew how to make himself popular. He was hero-
worshipped on the south coast for ridding the Channel of French privateers, yet
he was going to prove a disappointing commander on land – excitable to the
point of hysteria, and losing control of himself and of his troops. Nonetheless,
until his final defeat he would always be considered a very dangerous opponent.

The young Earl of March, the Duke of York's son and heir, would soon show
himself to be the most dangerous of them all. Edward Plantagenet had been born
in 1442 at Rouen when his father was Lieutenant-General of France, his mother
being Cecily Nevill; she was Salisbury's sister and a famous beauty who in her
youth had been known as 'The Rose of Raby' (though some called her 'Proud
Cis'). Her eldest surviving son had grown to be a very tall and strikingly handsome young man, fair-haired and ruddy-faced, whose brains and well-attested
charm matched his bodily strength. This was the future Edward IV, still only
seventeen.

There was also York himself, at Dublin. The Anglo-Irish lords were his enthusiastic supporters; not only did he refrain from meddling with their parliament
but unlike most Englishmen he obviously had a knack of getting on with the
Irish. A small, spare man, apparently he looked very like his youngest son, the
future Richard III, with sharp features and brown hair. If haughty, he was honourable and genuinely public-spirited. However, isolated in Ireland, he brooded
over his wrongs until privately he decided on a solution that was more extreme
than anything envisaged by the Nevills. As for his military gifts, despite years of
campaigning in France he was a poor soldier, as indecisive as he was rash; his
flight from Ludlow had been a disgrace while his rashness would eventually
destroy him. Even so, in 1459 the Duke seemed quite as menacing as any of the
lords of Calais.

The Yorkists held two very important cards. One was that the Earl of Warwick
was Captain of Calais, an impregnable military base and ideal for launching an
invasion. The other, less emphasized by historians, was their command of the sea.
They had the ships and they knew how to use them – on at least one voyage
Warwick took over the steering himself.

The little ships of the period – cogs, carracks or carvels of only a few hundred
tons at most – may not perhaps seem very impressive to modern eyes, but it
should never be forgotten that Columbus discovered America in a carvel.
Generally three-masted by now, they were part lateen-rigged – a lateen sail being

triangular, on a long yard set at an angle of 45 degrees to the mast – which enabled them to sail much closer to the wind. A ship's master not only possessed compass, astrolabe, cross-staff and lead-and-line, but could obtain 'rutters' (sailing manuals) with detailed instructions for navigating the coasts of England, Ireland and France.

In January 1460 the lords of Calais sent a small force under a reliable lieutenant, John Dynham, to raid the important port of Sandwich on the Kentish coast. The purpose of the raid was twofold: to disperse a fleet that King Henry's ministers had been assembling for an attack on Calais, and also to see if the port would make a suitable invasion point. Landing before dawn with 800 men, Dynham routed the Lancastrian garrison with ease, returning to Calais with the entire enemy fleet in tow and some distinguished prisoners. In addition, the Yorkists clearly acquired useful agents who were ready to help with a larger landing at some future date.

At the beginning of March the Earl of Warwick sailed from Calais, all the way round the south coast of England and then up the Irish Channel to Dublin, for a discussion with the Duke of York. The Earl was so confident that he took his mother back with him to Calais in May. (Lady Salisbury had had the privilege of being the only woman to be attainted at the Parliament of Devils.) Reinstated as Admiral of England, the Duke of Exeter tried to intercept the Earl on his return voyage, but the Duke's crews, already mutinous from lack of pay and victuals, refused to engage Warwick. The Earl's recent and extremely effective operations against French pirates had earned him a reputation in the Channel ports of being the finest fighting seaman of his day.

Early in June 1460 another Yorkist raiding force from Calais seized Sandwich for a second time, establishing a bridgehead under Lord Fauconberg, Salisbury's redoubtable brother. The three earls joined him there on 26 June, bringing about 2,000 men with them, and marched into Canterbury the same evening. Next day, gathering recruits as they went, they advanced on London.

The City of London was a thoroughly uneasy place in 1460. These were very bad times indeed for business. Because of the civil war, during the years 1459–62 exports of wool to Calais and of broadcloth to Flanders would drop to a mere third of what they had been in the 1440s, while because of the loss of Gascony, imports of wine were down to little more than 4,000 tuns compared to 11,000 ten years before.

Even so, it is evident that John Lambert was continuing to flourish, however difficult the economic climate may have been for others in London. During the first half of 1460 he became alderman for the ward of Faringdon Within, elected in a process firmly controlled by the other aldermen who retained the right of final selection. A candidate for an aldermanry had to show that he owned goods worth £1,000, a fortune. There were twenty-four of these aldermen, the richest men in the City, from whose ranks came the Mayor and sheriffs. *Ex officio* members of the Court of Common Council, they formed a small, exclusive and highly privileged oligarchy which virtually ran London, administering its day-to-day government. The Court of Aldermen and Court of Common Council supervised almost every aspect of London life. They regulated trade and the markets and traffic along the Thames, looked after the hospitals and poor relief, maintained roads, bridges, prisons and fortifications, organized street cleaning and the water supply, and levied taxes. They were also responsible for the defence of London in times of war.[1]

John had now been accepted as a member of the City's ruling aristocracy. Even in the street he wore a blood-red hood to mark him out from other mortals, while Amy was addressed as 'Lady Lambert' as though she were the wife of a knight. Responsible to the Mayor alone, John remained in office at his own pleasure; there was no fixed term. If the general watch (the City's defence force) had to be assembled, he would personally lead the citizens of his ward, flying a pennon that bore his own coat of arms – two lambs heads. He enjoyed pleasant little privileges such as free water, and could enrol his apprentices free. And he was assured of a prominent place at all official functions, at every thanksgiving in St Paul's or banquet in the Guildhall.

In addition, Mr Alderman Lambert (as he was now addressed) was chosen to be one of the two sheriffs of the City of London for 1460–61.[2] He was elected on Midsummer Day by the liverymen of the great City companies, riding robed in solemn procession to the Guildhall escorted by his fellow mercers, also mounted and robed, together with drummers and minstrels. The sheriffs, who held office for a year, were assisted by under-sheriffs, by sixteen serjeants (each with his own yeoman), and by a host of clerks, stewards and porters. The position of sheriff was one of very considerable dignity and importance. A handsome post, carved and gilded, stood opposite the door of each sheriff's house, for posting proclamations.

The sheriffs' duties included enforcing orders made by the Mayor's court, debt collection, and extracting fines for trying to evade the Customs. At the sheriffs' court they sentenced men to imprisonment in Ludgate, to stand in the pillory, to sit in the stocks inside the wooden cage at the Tun in Cornhill, to be whipped at the cart's tail for petty larceny or be dragged through the streets on a muddy hurdle; a short-weight baker would make the journey with a loaf tied around his neck. They saw to the serving of writs, summoned jurors, ran Ludgate gaol, and supervised the execution of those condemned to death – whether by hanging, beheading, drowning or burning, or in cases of treason by hanging, drawing and quartering. They also had a military role, mustering the citizenry under arms when necessary and posting guards. Every well-to-do Londoner owned a 'jack and sallet' (leather jerkin and steel helmet), while many possessed a full suit of plate armour, besides bills and bows, swords and daggers.

Such important positions were open only to men of substance. Although he would not be sworn in and take office as sheriff until Michaelmas, plainly Mr Alderman Lambert was already a big man in the City, a well-known figure in London life, who was constantly in and out of the Guildhall. Yet, as will be seen, it was an uncomfortable time in which to be prominent.

The lords of Calais reached London on 2 July. Their army had by now grown to many thousand men and included several peers, among whom was the Duke of Norfolk. After negotiating with 'twelve worshipful and discreet aldermen', they were allowed to enter the City. (Mr Lambert may well have been one of the nego-tiators since as sheriff elect he was a leading alderman.) They immediately went to St Paul's to give thanks and then billeted their troops near Smithfield. Two days later Warwick and March took their troops north, though not before the City had lent them £1,000. (Mr Lambert is likely to have been among the subscribers.) Basically, their plan of campaign was very simple: it was to find and defeat the royal army, and get possession of King Henry – to whom they publicly and repeatedly protested their allegiance.

Salisbury remained in London with 2,000 men, blockading the Tower, whose garrison included several peers loyal to Henry. The garrison commander, 'the good old lord Scales', was a brutal veteran of the wars in France, accustomed to cowing opponents by savagery. Convinced that the King's army would crush Warwick and March, and expecting to be relieved at any moment, he meant to show Salisbury that he would never surrender. For the first time in history, the Tower turned its guns on London. 'They that were within the Tower cast wildfire into the City, and shot in small guns, and burned and hurt men and women and children in the streets,' a chronicler records. 'Wildfire' was the period's napalm, clinging to its target and burning more fiercely if water was thrown on it. Understandably, most Londoners were only too eager to help Lord Salisbury with the siege.

'And then they skirmished together, and much harm was done daily,' records a chronicler. This was one occasion when townsmen were fully involved in the Wars of the Roses. The common council supplied bombards (heavy cannon), taken from a royal depot; they were mounted opposite the Tower, on the south bank of the Thames, and fired to such effect that part of the Tower's curtain walls came crashing down. The sheriffs and armed citizens helped Lord Cobham blockade it from the City. Another group, led by John Lambert's fellow mercer John Harowe, joined Sir John Wenlock in investing it from St Katherine's at the east. 'And the Tower was besieged by land and by water, that no victual might come to them that were within,' says a chronicle. Every alderman donated five pounds to pay the men helping Wenlock to stop provisions reaching the Tower. Three days later they each added another ten pounds, partly to pay the boatmen who were preventing anyone from getting in or out, and partly to pay the navvies working on fortifications. On 12 July all the aldermen gave a further ten pounds.

Scales and the noblemen inside sent an angry letter to the common council, asking why the King's subjects were making war on them. The council replied that it was the garrison which had started making war, that men, women and children had been killed, maimed or wounded by their gunfire.

Then news reached London that on 10 July Warwick, March and Lord Fauconberg had routed the King's army at Northampton. (Among the casualties was Margaret Beaufort's father-in-law, the Duke of Buckingham, cut down by an axe as he stood outside the royal tent.) Henry VI was brought back to London, a prisoner, but treated with all the respect due to a king of England. On 19 July 'they that were in the Tower of London, for lack of victuals yielded.' Lord Scales tried to escape down the Thames in a wherry but was recognized by a woman and lynched by a mob of boatmen – covered in stab wounds, his body was thrown naked into the churchyard of St Mary Overy. All London thanked God for the victory at Northampton.

As it was, on Michaelmas Eve (28 September) John was sworn in at the Guildhall as a sheriff, putting a great gold chain of office around his neck. The other sheriff was Richard Flemyng and the Mayor was Richard Lee. The year ahead was going to be one of the most stormy in the City's history but, in accordance with hallowed tradition, the Mayor gave a sumptuous banquet in the Guildhall. The Venetian visitor cited before attended a similar meal thirty years later. He says there were at least a thousand guests while the dinner lasted for four hours. He adds:

a no less magnificent banquet is given when two other officers named sheriffs are appointed . . . I observed the infinite profusion of victuals, and of plate which was for the most part gilt; and amongst other things I noticed how punctiliously they sat in their order, and the extraordinary silence of everyone.

Those present at the sheriffs' banquet must have been very worried men since they knew that the Duke of York was on his way to London. On 10 October, less than a fortnight later, he arrived in the City after a leisurely journey from Dublin. Ominously, he came in unmistakeably regal pomp and splendour, with a sword borne before him like a king.

To his supporters' consternation, alarming even Warwick and Salisbury, instead of demanding merely that the wrongs done him be redressed, York publicly claimed the throne by right of descent – 'for though right for a time rest and be put to silence, yet it rotteth not nor shall not perish,' he declared. At Westminster he deliberately sat on the throne in the presence of the House of Lords, as though he were King of England.

However, the country was not yet ready to change its sovereign. No doubt Henry VI had more than demonstrated his inadequacy, and with hindsight it may seem surprising that the magnates did not turn against him sooner. But the majority felt a certain reverence for that divinity which 'doth hedge a king' and they remembered the oaths they had sworn to him.

After the Duke of York had made his formal claim to the throne, the Earl of Warwick warned him bluntly 'how the lords and the people were ill content against him because he thus wished to strip the king of his crown.' Henry told the assembled peers, 'My father was king; his father was also king; I have worn the crown for forty years, from my cradle. You have all sworn fealty to me as your sovereign, and your fathers did the like to my fathers. How then can my right be disputed?'

A compromise was reached, the Act of Accord, by which Henry would keep the crown but agreed to recognize York as his heir – disinheriting his own son. In the meantime, the Duke was to rule England as protector of the realm.

In spite of the Act of Accord, the Queen could be relied on to fight for her son. All too many people were shocked by the disinheritance of the Prince of Wales and a Lancastrian army quickly assembled in Wales, with another in Yorkshire. Sending his own son March to deal with their Welsh opponents, and leaving

Warwick in command at London, accompanied by Salisbury the Duke of York went north with 6,000 followers.

On the last day of 1460 the Duke and Salisbury rode out from Sandal Castle to give battle. After spending Christmas at Sandal, on the south bank of the River Calder near Wakefield, they had suddenly found themselves besieged by a large Lancastrian force led by the Dukes of Somerset and Exeter, and also Sir Andrew Trollope, who had betrayed them at Ludlow. Since most of their troops were away foraging, York and Salisbury were heavily outnumbered. Sandal was impregnable; had they stayed inside, they could easily have held out until reinforcements reached it. No one knows why they decided to fight, but Waurin tells us they were tricked by the wily Trollope, who sent in a stream of feigned deserters carrying messages that he was going to change sides and come over to them.

When they emerged, the Yorkists were cut to pieces. Over 2,000 of them fell compared to only 200 Lancastrians. The Duke was killed, together with his second son, the Earl of Rutland. Old Salisbury was captured that evening and taken to Pontefract, to be dragged out by a mob and beheaded by the Duke of Exeter's bastard half-brother on the following day. The heads of the two fallen leaders were stuck up over the gates of York, the Duke's decorated with a paper crown in derision. Among other Yorkist casualties was 'John Harowe of London, captain of the foot' – as his friend and fellow mercer William Caxton recorded in the *Chronicles of England* twenty years later. John Harowe had taken a leading part in the siege of the Tower during the previous summer. He would have been well known to Mr Sheriff Lambert.

The Tudor chronicles include some very unpleasant stories about the Battle of Wakefield. One is of the Duke of York crowned with bulrushes by captors and made to stand on a molehill before being beheaded, after which his head was brought on a lance to the gloating Queen. Another is of the sixteen-year-old Earl of Rutland begging for mercy from Lord Clifford who, as he stabbed him with a dagger, shouted, 'By God's blood, thy father slew mine, and so will I do thee and all thy kin.' While such tales are without foundation, they almost certainly preserve rumours that were circulating in the City at the time – Londoners were prepared to believe anything of the Queen's supporters.

Plundering their way southwards, a Lancastrian host of northerners and Scots carved a swath of devastation thirty miles wide as they marched, sacking the towns of Grantham, Stamford and Northampton. Because they were unpaid, the northerners insisted that they had a right to loot once they had crossed the River

Micklegate Bar, on which were stuck the heads of the Duke of York and the Earl of Salisbury in January 1461.

Trent, if Abbot Whethamstede is to be believed; he says that not even beggars were safe. The angry Abbot composed a vituperative poem about these men of the north – '*Gens Boreae, gens perfidiae, gens prompta rapinae.*' 'Northern people, faithless people, people prompt to rob.'[3] No less eloquent, the Prior of Croyland described 'an execrable and abominable army' sweeping onwards as a whirlwind from the north, 'like so many locusts'.

Even at the best of times Londoners did not care for northerners, who spoke a barely comprehensible version of English – Whethamstede says that when they talked, they sounded like the Hound of Hell barking. (It must be remembered that English only became a truly national language after the introduction of the English Bible during the next century.) The Londoners feared the Scots still more. The news of the approach of the Queen's army filled them with dread. No doubt they took comfort in having the Earl of Warwick to defend the City. His troops were equipped with all sorts of impressive weaponry – wildfire, mantraps, nets, caltraps (steel starfish), and guns that fired giant arrows. Unfortunately, the Earl's military skills were overrated while the gadgets would prove useless.

The Lancastrians had much better commanders than Warwick and their leadership was going to be decisive. They included the Dukes of Somerset and Exeter, the Earl of Northumberland, Lord Clifford and Lord Welles – Margaret Beaufort's stepfather. Somerset seems to have been in overall command. The Queen rode with them, though not into battle. On 16 February Exeter drove in a Yorkist outpost at Dunstable and before dawn the following morning – Shrove Tuesday – the Lancastrians attacked the Yorkists who had occupied St Albans. There was long and confused fighting during which Warwick obviously lost control of his troops; according to one source Somerset led several thousand men-at-arms in a charge shortly after midday which went far towards deciding the outcome. Finally the Yorkists fled, the Earl of Warwick among them. They left behind King Henry who, so the Dauphin heard in France, had spent the entire battle laughing and singing to himself.

Henry VI was reunited with his wife and son in Lord Clifford's tent. The royal family then installed themselves in the Abbey as Abbot Whethamstede's guests. Despite the Abbot's entreaties, their presence saved neither his abbey nor the town from being plundered by the northerners. Two days later Queen Margaret arranged for Lord Bonvile and two other captured Yorkists to be tried and condemned to death by her seven-year-old son, mother and child watching the executions.

'On an Ash Wednesday we lived in mickle dread,' wrote an anonymous Yorkist poet, conveying the mood in the City when the news of Warwick's defeat arrived.

Everyone feared that, having sacked St Albans only twenty miles away, the Lancastrians were going to sack the capital too. Wearing full armour, John Lambert and his fellow sheriff summoned the Londoners to take up arms and defend the City. London was in uproar. John would have been worried about his wife Amy and his daughter Jane, not to mention his house and his shop.

Carlo Gigli, an Italian merchant's agent in London, reported to his employer that the capital's gates had been closed and were guarded; all the shops were shut, their owners staying at home. Some days later he wrote of alarming rumours: 60,000 Irish Yorkists were said to be on their way to London, together with 40,000 Welshmen. The Mayor and aldermen were negotiating with the royal army, prepared to admit the King and Queen and the court into the City, but not their troops. 'People have quietened down, and I see no weapons except on the mayor and the sheriffs, who are mounting guard with a large force,' observed Gigli. (It must be remembered that, after the Mayor, the two men most responsible for London's defence were the sheriffs.)

Londoners 'dreaded the menace and malice of the queen and the duke of Somerset and others,' says one chronicler, 'for as much as the queen with her council had granted and given leave to the Northmen for to spoil and rob the said City.' It was widely believed that she had done so because she was unable to pay them properly. The aldermen, among them Mr Sheriff Lambert, had everything to fear. Not only would they lose all the considerable sums of money which they had lent to the Yorkists since the previous July, including a loan of a thousand pounds to Warwick less than a week before, but some of their heads might well end up on Tower Bridge. Three great ladies were sent as envoys to the Queen with a message that the gates would be opened if there was a strict guarantee that there would be no looting. The Mayor also attempted to send out 'bread and victual' together with money, but a mob led by Sir John Wenlock's cook ambushed the carts as they were going through Newgate, sharing the food among themselves. As for the cash, 'I trow the purse stole the money,' explains Gregory.

After receiving assurances that the Lancastrian army would behave itself, the Mayor issued a proclamation ordering Londoners to stay in their homes when it marched in. Terrified, the Londoners began to riot. On the advice of Dr Morton (clearly regarded by the Yorkists as a dangerous *eminence grise*), the Queen sent small bodies of men to the gates of the City and Westminster, where they asked to be let in. They met with a refusal, whereupon fighting broke out, many of the Queen's troops being 'slain for their cursed language.' After this, 'the commons for the salvation of the City took the keys of the gates where they should have entered, and manly kept and defended it from their enemies, until the coming of Edward, the noble earl of March.'[5]

Anxious not to alienate her husband's capital, the Queen reluctantly decided that it would be wiser to go back to the north. She 'deemed that the Northern men would have been too cruel, if they had come to London,' is what Gregory heard – meaning that she knew she could not control her famished troops. King Henry had little say in the matter; Pope Pius II described him as 'utterly devoid of wit or spirit, [a man] who left everything in his wife's hands.' Yet Dr Morton may well have helped her to reach a decision; we know from Gregory that the doctor had been giving her advice on dealing with the Londoners. And to return to York, the northern capital, made strategic sense. The Lancastrian army was running short of food, demoralized by foraging in a severe winter. Once back across the Trent, it would be able to find all the food needed and could wait in comfort for a campaign in the spring. Even so, William Worcester was convinced that had the Lancastrians occupied the City, the Londoners would have submitted. In his view, their failure to do so 'was the ruin of King Henry and his queen.'

The Earls of March and Warwick rode into London at the head of their troops on 27 February, receiving a rapturous welcome. The City had not faced such danger for centuries. Gregory is almost lyrical in recalling how people thanked God and said, 'Let us walk in a new wine yard, and let us make us a gay garden in the month of March with this fair white rose and herb, the earl of March.' No one can have been more thankful than Mr Sheriff Lambert.

THE WHEEL OF FORTUNE,
1461–71

9

The Squire of Burton Hastings
Goes to War, 1461

WILLIAM HASTINGS

In January 1461 Edward, Earl of March set out for London with an army that he had been raising in the Welsh Marches. Having learnt of his father's death and that the Lancastrians were marching on the capital, he thought it high time to rejoin Warwick. Then news came that the Earls of Pembroke and Wiltshire had landed in Wales, bringing a force of Frenchmen, Bretons and Irishmen, and were recruiting Welsh Lancastrians. He turned back to confront this fresh danger. Suddenly an old friend, his kinsman William Hastings, arrived with every man he could persuade to come with him, servant, retainer or neighbour.

Aged about thirty, Mr Hastings was squire of Burton Hastings in Warwickshire and of Kirby Muxloe in Leicestershire – the latter in the dull, flat country popularly known as East Leicestershire Forest. He had been sheriff for both counties in 1455, the year in which his father Sir Leonard had died, and was somebody of no little standing in the Midlands.[1] A substantial landowner and of ancient lineage (he could trace his ancestry back to the Conqueror's reign and to a steward of King Henry I), he even had some royal blood in his veins.

William's immediate forebears had been men of action. His maternal grandfather, Lord Camoys, had commanded the left wing at Agincourt where his father had fought in the retinue of the then Earl of March. Afterwards Leonard Hastings had spent many years in France, defending the doomed Anglo-French régime and working closely with the Duke of York, who referred to him in documents as his 'beloved counsellor.'

William's mother Alice Camoys was very well related indeed, her own

Mortimer mother having been Edward III's granddaughter. In consequence William Hastings was the late Duke Richard's second cousin.

The Mortimer link dated from well before the marriage of William's parents. Not only had Sir Leonard Hastings served at Agincourt under Edmund Mortimer, Earl of March, but (according to the seventeenth-century historian William Dugdale) Leonard's eldest brother Ralph had been beheaded in 1410 for 'having taken part with Owen Glendour, as tis like.' Part of the Welsh leader's programme had been to replace the Lancastrian Henry IV on the throne with Lord March. No one can have been more aware of the Yorkist claim than Mr William Hastings.

Hastings had three brothers – Ralph, Richard and Thomas. The first two were going to share in his rise to fame and fortune. Of his three sisters, Anne, the eldest, had made a good marriage to Sir Thomas Ferrers of Tamworth Castle, a younger son of Lord Ferrers of Groby. The couple had two sons who would one day fight at their uncle's side.[2]

Like his father Sir Leonard before him, Mr Hastings was a household man of the Duke of York, besides being 'retained'. In a deed dated 23 April 1456 at Fotheringay Castle, the Duke, addressing William as his 'beloved servant', granted him an annuity of £10 'to the end that he should serve him above all others, and attend to him at all times, his allegiance to the king excepted.' He was not just a 'well-wisher' but a professional bureaucrat employed by the Duke.

Undoubtedly William had received the instruction of a young man of his class, in horsemanship, hunting and handling his weapons, in an elaborate etiquette and in the formal code of chivalry, besides acquiring a smattering of Latin and French. Possibly he took a species of business course, either at Oxford or Cambridge, or at an Inn of Court in London. There was no question of reading for a degree or for the bar. Instead, he would have paid for tuition from one of the many unofficial masters who specialized in teaching formal letter-writing and the art of drafting documents, together with basic civil law – useful, not to say invaluable, preparation for a life that might largely be spent in administration.[3]

As a gentleman bureaucrat, William spent part of his youth in estate management, negotiating leases – such as that in 1457 for a watermill at Ravenstone to Thomas Barnwell for eighteen years at a rent of 13s 4d – and fighting legal battles. If so, he may not have been too efficient. There is evidence that the Duke of York's estates were badly managed and that the richest man in England was not getting a proper return from his lands. However, judging from Hastings' later career, in all probability his job had more to do with organizing the Duke's 'affinity'. In normal times there was nothing sinister or warlike about this sort of bastard feudalism. Its purpose was not to create private armies but to provide the machinery for keeping law and order in the countryside.[4]

Clearly the Duke of York was well disposed towards his kinsman Mr Hastings. William's election as sheriff in 1455 was almost certainly due to the influence of the Duke, who in the following year appointed him ranger of the chase of Wyre in Shropshire. Soon afterwards, York extricated him from a potentially ruinous affair which might have ended in his imprisonment.

Robert Pierpoint from Holbeck-Wodehouse in Nottinghamshire had been murdered in a quarrel over a disputed manor by Thomas Hastings and Henry Ferrers, who were forcibly interrogated by Robert's brother Henry Pierpoint. William, who was obviously deeply involved, asked the Duke to arbitrate. Together with Thomas Hastings, Ferrers and Henry Pierpoint, he was bound over to keep the peace by York, and in October 1458 ordered to pay £40 in instalments over two years 'in recompense to all manner of offences and trespasses . . . done to the said Henry Pierpoint, his uncle and brothers.' (An unlucky family, the Pierpoints were no strangers to violence; early in 1457 Henry's father had been killed in an affray with the Plumptons of Yorkshire on Papplewick Moor.) William was lucky to emerge so cheaply from this unsavoury business.

We know from his later career that Mr Hastings was a first-rate soldier, brave, resourceful and totally dependable – 'a good knight' is what Sir Thomas More calls him. It looks as though the Duke of York made him a gentleman-in-waiting to his eldest son, the Earl of March (the future Edward IV), when the boy was still very young and he himself had not yet come into his inheritance. Afterwards King Edward wrote that William had never ceased to serve him 'from his early manhood', while in 1483 Domenico Mancini heard in London how 'Hastings had been from an early age a loyal companion of Edward.'

Nevertheless, William's first campaign, during the autumn of 1459, had ended in disaster at Ludlow. Apparently accompanied by his brothers Ralph and Thomas, he joined the main body of the Duke of York's troops on the Welsh border. Here they would have waited for the Earls of Salisbury and Warwick to bring reinforcements. It is more than likely that William had been on the retreat before King Henry's far larger army, by way of Worcester and Tewkesbury, and then back across the Severn to Ludlow. Here, it will be remembered, York and the Nevills had fled secretly at midnight, leaving their bewildered troops without leaders.

All Mr Hastings could do was throw himself on the mercy of King Henry –

A fifteenth century squire, portrayed by Wynkyn de Worde in his 1498 edition of
Chaucer's *Canterbury Tales*.

or, rather, on the mercy of Queen Margaret. As yet he was politically insignificant, and during the Parliament of Devils had escaped the dreaded penalty of
attainder. He was granted his life but forfeited his lands, although he was soon
allowed to redeem them. On 23 February 1460, with Ralph and Thomas he
received a royal pardon for all treasons, rebellions, felonies and so on committed
before 4 January. (Richard Hastings had not applied for such a pardon, indicat-
ing that he had not ridden to Ludlow with his brothers.) William did not join York
in Dublin nor March in Calais, staying quietly at home in the Midlands. Nor did
he go to meet the earls in London in the summer or the autumn.

So far, therefore, William Hastings had had no real experience of war apart, no
doubt, from hearing his father reminisce proudly about the famous old campaigns in France – Sir Leonard must have been eloquent about Henry V and
Agincourt. Yet like all Englishmen of his class and time, William would have been
trained in all the period's martial arts. Men of his rank learned how to use a heavy
lance which could knock an opponent out of the saddle, but since they nearly

always fought on foot their two indispensable weapons were the mace and the poleaxe.

Using every financial resource available to him, together with the contacts made during his year as sheriff, William assembled and equipped the force that would prove so useful to the Earl of March. Even though the majority of all save the poorest fifteenth-century Englishmen generally possessed arms and armour of a sort, deficiencies had to be made good, and horses provided. Later the Earl of March himself commented on how much it must have cost Hastings.

Those who could afford it wore plate armour, popularly known as 'harness'. A man of William's rank owned at least one suit of 'Dutch' plate, since German armourers were the best in Europe. It went to the wars with him on a pack-horse, together with a set of thick felt underclothes to reduce bruising. Neither heavy nor constricting, a fifteenth-century suit weighed less than the equipment of a First World War infantryman, while its weight was distributed all over the body. However, although plate was arrow-proof, it could be ripped open by poleaxes or smashed in by maces (causing bruises that turned gangrenous), and in defeat an armoured 'man-at-arms' had little hope of escaping on foot. Some gentlemen preferred to fight in brigandines; not unlike modern flak jackets, these were quilted coats strengthened by metal plates, often velvet-covered, and worn with sallets – light helmets resembling steel sou'westers. Both harness and brigandines were so hot that normally those wearing them could only fight for a few hours, but it was a different matter in cold winter weather.

The billmen who formed the bulk of the foot soldiers used a weapon combining billhook and half-pike. Besides their bows, archers often carried long-handed leaden 'mauls' or mallets, while mounted archers had light lances. Their arrows had a fighting range of over 150 yards, with a plate-armour-piercing range of about sixty. For protection, billmen and archers wore sallets and 'jacks' – soft leather jackets stuffed with tow or made from layers of deerskin.

Hastings' force probably joined Lord March at Shrewsbury early in January 1461 – he campaigned at too fast a pace for Hastings to have caught up with him afterwards.[5] Later William's services against '*Jasperem Pembrochie*' and '*Jacobum Wiltes*' were commended (see p. 108), and the only time the Earls of Pembroke and Wiltshire are known to have been on campaign together was on this occasion. With them were Pembroke's father Owen Tudor (Margaret Beaufort's father-in-law) and two veterans of the French wars, Sir John and Sir William Scudamore, though apart from foreign mercenaries most of their troops must have come from the local Welsh gentry. The Yorkists included that redoubtable Welsh magnate, Sir William Herbert.

The Welsh Lancastrians' weakness lay in their commanders. Jasper Tudor was brave enough but never managed to win a battle during the whole of his long career. The Earl of Wiltshire (the handsome treasurer) was primarily interested in his own survival as he had shown at St Albans in 1455. By contrast, March was already a superb leader.

The two armies faced each other at Mortimer's Cross, between Hereford and Leominster, in a wide meadow by the River Lugg. Professor Ross suggests that the combatants should be numbered in hundreds rather than thousands. It was the morning of Candlemas Day (2 February) 1461 – the feast of the Purification of the Blessed Virgin, a day when everyone at Mass held a candle during the Gospel reading. Suddenly, at about 10 a.m., three separate suns were seen shining in the sky and then merging into one. The Yorkists were aghast, but

> The noble Earl Edward them comforted and said 'Beeth of good comfort, and dreadeth not. This is a good sign, for these three suns betoken the Father, the Son and the Holy Ghost, and therefore let us have a good heart, and in the name of Almighty God go we against our enemies'.

No account of the engagement has survived but clearly the Yorkists went with a will against their enemies. (Some old locals say that on the battle's anniversary the faint sound of horses' hooves and of men shouting can still be heard at Mortimer's Cross.) The Lancastrians broke and fled. There was a merciless pursuit, one of March's specialities. The victors revenged themselves for Wakefield, continuing the murderous pattern of reprisals begun at St Albans in 1455.

Several of the enemy commanders were captured and executed immediately, though Jasper Tudor and Wiltshire – as was his wont – 'stole away privily disguised and fled out of the country.' The former's father was not so lucky, as Gregory records in a famous passage: 'Owen Tudor was y-take and brought into Haverfordwest, and he was beheaded in the market place, and his head set upon the highest grice of the market cross, and a mad woman combed his hair and washed away the blood off his face, and she got candles and set about him burning more than a hundred.' (Since it was Candlemas Day, the churches were full of discarded candles.)

> This Owen Tudor was father unto the earl of Pembroke, and had wedded

Queen Katherine, King Harry VI's mother, weening and trusting all away that he should not be headed till he saw the axe and the block, and when that he was in his doublet he trusted on pardon and grace till the collar of his red velvet doublet was ripped off. Then he said 'That head shall lie on the stock that was wont to lie on Queen Katherine's lap', and put his heart and mind wholly unto God, and full meekly took his death.

Owen could not grasp that he was dying precisely because he was King Henry's stepfather. Sir John Throckmorton and nine other Lancastrian gentlemen died with him.

Although he won many more victories, Edward of March never forgot Mortimer's Cross. It was his first successful battle – Warwick had been in command at Northampton – while the three suns were surely a sign of God's favour, comparable to that cross of light which the Roman Emperor Constantine had seen in the sky before his victory at the Milvian Bridge. Henceforward Edward used a golden sunburst (or 'sun-in-splendour') as his principal badge, placing it on the livery of his men-at-arms and archers.

We know from William Hastings' later career that he had a talent for raising troops. The number and quality of those whom he brought to Mortimer's Cross may well have tipped the odds in favour of the Yorkists. Afterwards Edward referred to 'a plentiful multitude' (*multitudine copiosa*), and implied that they were expensively equipped. It was the start of William's rise to fame and fortune.

However, a fortnight later all England was talking of the Lancastrian victory at the second Battle of St Albans. Gregory says that Edward was badly shaken ('full sore a-feared') by the news, following on that of Wakefield. Warwick met the Earl at Chipping Norton, reassuring him with accounts of 'the love and favour that the commons had unto him', and urging him to take the crown. Men continued to flock to his standard.

On Thursday, 27 February the two earls entered London, cheered by the crowds. With his good looks and magnificent bearing, Edward of March was well suited to be a popular idol. He went to his father's former town house, Baynard's Castle, while Warwick lodged at the Harbour. On Sunday, 1 March the Bishop of Salisbury (Warwick's brother, George Nevill) told a crowd of thousands in St George's Fields that the Earl of March should replace Henry VI as king.

On 4 March he was acclaimed in St Paul's Cathedral as 'King Edward IV of England and France, Lord of Ireland', after which he was enthroned – though not crowned – in Westminster Hall. Then he went in procession to the Abbey where *Te Deum* was sung. As one of the City fathers, Mr Sheriff Lambert was present at these ceremonies. 'From what we have heard since, he was chosen, so they say, on all sides as the new king by the princes and people at London,' reported the papal legate Coppini. 'London . . . is entirely inclined to side with the new king and Warwick, and as it is very rich and the most wealthy city of Christendom, this enormously increases the chances of the side that it favours,' was the opinion of a well-informed Milanese observer, Prospero di Camulio.

The same observer commented that one reason why King Edward postponed his coronation was that he wanted 'the vengeance due for the slaughter of his father and of so many knights and lords who have been slain of late.' On 6 March Edward issued a lengthy proclamation. Its tone may be gathered from this extract, complaining that in Henry VI's time 'not plenty, peace, justice, good governance, policy and virtuous conversation, but unrest, inward war and trouble, unrightwiseness, shedding and effusion of innocent blood, abusion of the laws, partiality, riot, extortion, murder, rape and vicious living, have been the guiders and leaders of the noble realm of England.' Among twenty-two persons whom the proclamation specifically excluded from pardon was 'John Morton, late parson of Bloxworth in the shire of Dorset, clerk.'

John Lambert was among those who had the privilege of funding a new royal household, the City aldermen giving almost £150. Hastings became Lord Chamberlain, responsible for running many of its departments. In addition, the Mayor and aldermen lent £4,000 for the forthcoming campaign against the Lancastrians, since Edward was desperately short of ready cash.

It was far from certain that Mr Lambert and his fellow aldermen would ever see their money again. As another Londoner, the draper Robert Fabyan, observed, Edward and the Earl of Warwick had come to the City with 'a great power of men but few of name.' (Hastings was still too obscure to be noticed.) Even Coppini, biased in favour of the Yorkists, commented that Queen Margaret was very clever. Some of his English friends thought that by remaining on the defensive she ought to be able to win people back after they had grown tired of all the senseless bloodshed – 'who, when they perceive that they are not on the road to peace, will easily be induced to change sides.'

As he rode north William Hastings was well aware that not only his new office of chamberlain but his life itself depended on the outcome of the battle that was about to take place.

10

Dr Morton Sees a Battle – Towton, 1461

JOHN MORTON

D URING the last days of February 1461 Dr Morton was riding north from St Albans with the Lancastrian army, no doubt muffled in furs against the bitter cold. We know it was a hard winter and a man as successful as John Morton could well afford a fur coat.

Only recently Morton had been celebrating a victory. Gregory's chronicle gives us a glimpse of him at St Albans which resembles a passage from the *Morte d'Arthur*. 'And at the night after the battle the king blessed his son the prince, and Dr Morton brought forth a book that was full of orisons, and there the book was opened, and blessed that young child . . . and made him knight.'

But now the capital had been snatched from the Queen's grasp. The Lancastrians were marching away on empty stomachs without the 'bread and victual' they had expected to find in London. They had no commissariat while it was difficult to live off the country in winter.

Even so, they had won a great battle at St Albans, and two-thirds of England's magnates were still loyal to Henry VI. Like Morton they were shocked by the legal chicanery in Parliament of the Act of Accord during October, when the Duke of York's claim to the succession had been forced through, disinheriting the Prince of Wales. A sound lawyer, the doctor agreed with the peers' initial response before they were overruled: Acts of Parliament counted for more than descent, and conferred on King Henry and on his son an inalienable right to occupy the throne of England – 'the which Acts be sufficient and reasonable to be laid again[st] the title of the said duke of York.'

An army's horses and carts made winter roads worse than usual. Since it was

Lent, the troops' staple diet was meant to be salt-herrings washed down by small beer – like 'mild' diluted with water. (The luxury tipple was strong ale or a pale, thin claret.) But after plundering their way south they found little food or drink of any sort on the way home.

To make matters even worse, the bridges had been broken down and the rivers were in spate. Although no records survive, one may guess that this was a wretched trek back to the north through drenching rain and snow.

Dr Morton must have been very glad indeed to reach the warmth and the fleshpots of York, the Lancastrian headquarters. The northern capital was a thriving metropolis with 12,000 inhabitants, rich from trade across the North Sea; its imposing walls sheltered not only the vast minster but sixty parish churches together with a Benedictine abbey and several other monasteries. The royal party installed themselves in the castle; only a shell keep remains today, Clifford's Tower, but in the fifteenth century the castle was a great walled complex which brooded over the city.

It had made strategic sense for Henry VI's army to retreat from London. Nearly all the great lords north of the River Trent and their affinities – virtually the entire northern gentry – were faithful to Lancaster. They would be able to fight on their own ground and they had formidable commanders. Meanwhile, reinforcements were flooding into York. According to Waurin, Queen Margaret spent everything she had on hiring troops, 'gold, silver, rings and jewels.'

News came of a proclamation sent by Edward on 6 March to all counties south of the River Trent. In it, he explained that he had taken the Crown to remedy the wrongs suffered by the people of England under 'our adversary, he that calleth himself King Henry the Sixth.' Inspired by the Devil, the Dukes of Somerset and Exeter and others were riding through the realm and destroying it; they were robbing, raping and murdering 'in such detestable wise and cruelness as hath not been heard done among the Saracens or Turks to any Christian men.' The proclamation forbade anyone to 'pass over the water of Trent' without a permit, and claimed that the Lancastrians were recruiting Frenchmen and Scots.

Margaret retaliated by circulating a rumour that 'our great traitor the late earl of March hath cried in his proclamation havoc upon our true liege people and subjects, their wives, children and goods.' This piece of counter-propaganda insinuated that the north was facing a southern invasion.

As one of the Queen's most valued advisers, Dr Morton must have helped to shape her diplomacy. Secret envoys were sent to Charles VII of France, begging for troops. One envoy took a message that was too dangerous to put on paper; the French King was warned to be careful about his letters to the

Queen, because if her plans were discovered her own supporters would kill her. (She was offering him Calais.) Although ready to help, Charles would be overtaken by events. Another envoy was dispatched to Pope Pius II, to complain of the encouragement that his legate Francesco Coppini had been giving to the Yorkists. Despite all the hard work, presumably Morton was grateful for the comfort of a royal palace after that march from St Albans, but he would not have long to enjoy it.

Edward IV had not been idle. His biographer, Charles Ross, says it is an exaggeration to call him 'the greatest general of his age', yet he never lost a battle, his outstanding qualities being swiftness on campaign and boldness in attack. Firmly in command though only nineteen, the new King was determined to find and destroy the Lancastrian army as quickly as possible, regardless of the terrible winter. On 5 March he sent the Duke of Norfolk to East Anglia to raise troops, Warwick going up to the Midlands on the same errand. On 11 March Lord Fauconberg (Warwick's uncle) rode out from London at the head of the billmen and bowmen, most of whom came from Kent or Wales. Two days later, King Edward himself led his men-at-arms northwards, leaving the City through Bishopsgate. The Londoners cheered his army as it marched off to war.

There are accounts in chronicles or letters of the campaign, and of the slaughter in which it culminated, but none by an eyewitness. However, the Sieur de Waurin, who speaks of '*ceste horrible bataille*', had obviously spoken with men who took part.[1] Edward Hall's *Union of the two Noble and Illustre families of Lancastre and York* contains details that are found nowhere else. It is treated with caution by historians since it was written eighty years later. Nevertheless, Hall was unusually well informed; his grandfather had been in the campaign, while he had access to sources that are now lost. There is enough evidence therefore to reconstruct what happened with a fair degree of accuracy.

Edward arrived at Pontefract on Friday the 27th or at about dawn on Saturday, 28 March, having sent an advance party ahead under Lord Fitzwalter to seize the crossing over the River Aire at Ferrybridge, which was swollen by snow and rain and supposedly unfordable. Early on Saturday morning, led by Lord Clifford, a party of Lancastrian mounted archers – these carried lances but dismounted to shoot – attacked, seizing the bridge. Thinking that the noise was a quarrel among his own men, Fitzwalter grabbed a poleaxe and rushed out from his billet without bothering to put on armour; he was cut down immediately, together with Warwick's half-brother, the bastard of Salisbury. Wounded by an arrow in the leg, the Earl of Warwick lost his head, killing his horse with his sword and shouting, 'Let him fly that will, for surely I will tarry with him that will tarry with me.'

Fortunately for the Yorkists, the King arrived to restore morale, ordering anyone afraid of fighting to leave the field but offering rewards to those who stayed – adding that there would be double pay for killing men who tried to desert during the engagement.

Clifford was formidable. Some Yorkists remembered him from Wakefield where 'for slaughter of men he was called the butcher.' He broke down the bridge across the Aire, but left a few timbers. 'Eventually our men forced their way over by the sword,' wrote Bishop Nevill, Warwick's brother. 'Finally the enemy took flight, and very many were slain.' Hall (whose testimony on this point is accepted by most historians) says that the fierce little Lord Fauconberg succeeded in crossing the river at Castleford four miles upstream, trapping the Lancastrian archers in a small valley, Dintingdale, and then wiping them out. Lord Clifford, 'either for heat or pain putting off his gorget', was shot in the throat by a stray arrow.

The main body of the Lancastrian army was now within sight of the Yorkists. It was positioned on a low plateau about a mile wide between the villages of Towton and Saxton, eight miles south-west of York; its right was guarded by the steep bluff of the Dintingdale valley at the bottom of which flowed the Cock Beck, a humble tributary of the River Wharfe. This is very flat country and Henry's commanders had been unable to find higher ground to defend; firepower meant arrow-power and a defensive position gave a slight advantage in battle – no doubt the Dintingdale bluff to their right decided them.

The Yorkists stationed themselves on a ridge opposite the plateau, only the gentlest of hollows separating the two armies. However, by now it was twilight and many of Edward's troops had not arrived. He would have to wait until the next day before attacking.

Both sides slept in their ranks, on the ground in the open. 'It was very cold, with snow and hail, so much so that men and horses were in a pitiable state,' Waurin tells us, 'and what made it worse was that there was no food, yet they stayed there all night nonetheless.'

Although a road runs through it, the battlefield is miraculously unchanged. The two ridges on which the opposing armies faced each other can still be seen, together with the gentle dip down which the Lancastrians were going to charge, as well as the road along which Yorkist reinforcements would march from Ferrybridge – to roll up their left flank. One can see too that the bluff was steep enough to make the Lancastrian flank impregnable, though the Cock Beck looks surprisingly shallow.

There are no reliable figures for the number of combatants. Gregory claims wildly that there were 200,000 'knights, squires and commons' on the Yorkist side alone. Hall (who may possibly have seen the muster rolls) is more convincing in stating that the Lancastrians had 60,000 men and the Yorkists 48,650 – 'they that knew it, and paid the wages, affirm.' Charles Ross thinks that 50,000 took part in the battle, a plausible estimate if camp followers are included. We only know for certain that the Lancastrians outnumbered the Yorkists, and that over twenty peers were there with their affinities.

Why were all these men going to fight? There is ample evidence to show that most of the noblemen (more than a third of the English peerage) and gentry who were at Towton had been most reluctant to take up arms. A few may have been at each other's throats, like the Nevills and the Percies, but not enough for the country's entire ruling class to plunge into a civil war. Not until 1460 had anyone taken the Duke of York's claim to the throne seriously, not even the Nevills. No historian has been able to explain why so many magnates decided to support him in the months that followed the Parliament of Devils; presumably they were convinced that chaos would continue unless Henry VI was replaced or, more cynically, that York and his son were going to win. Some Lancastrians must have been there from simple loyalty and others from conservatism, a reluctance to overthrow the established order.

No doubt there was an element of regional hostility. Abbot Whethamstede writes that 'the realm of the North had risen against the realm of the South', and Gregory of how 'the king [Edward] met with the lords of the North.' As has been seen, there was no liking between those living on different sides of the Trent.[2] Yet even though some areas tended to be for York and others for Lancaster, what really held each army together was a patchwork of personal loyalties; whether retainers, levies or volunteers, men had come to fight on one side or the other because their local magnate had done so. There was nothing that can be remotely described as a political motive for most of these troops. Nonetheless, English stubbornness ensured that those present would go on killing each other all day long.

Next day was 29 March, Palm Sunday. Edward IV's men approached within bowshot of their enemy on the plateau. The Lancastrian commander who led from the centre was the Duke of Somerset, supported by the Duke of Exeter; his wings were under the Earl of Northumberland and Lord Dacre of Gillesland. The Yorkist commanders were King Edward himself, Lord Fauconberg, and the

Sir John Howard, Duke of Norfolk, a staunch supporter of his patron
Richard III. From a window once at Tendring Hall, Suffolk.

Earl of Warwick. The battle did not start for some hours. The Yorkists stood waiting in the icy cold for the arrival of their East Anglian contingent, which had been delayed by the Duke of Norfolk falling sick at Pontefract. Meanwhile the Lancastrians saw no reason to abandon the plateau which gave them a marginal advantage.

Judging from John Morton's behaviour after the battle, it is more than likely that he was present. Understandably, he wanted to learn the result as soon as possible and, since Towton was so near York, he could have ridden over with ease. A man of the cloth, no doubt he kept well away from the fighting, but he was able to watch the most savage battle in English history.

This is what he saw. At about 11 a.m., after it had begun to snow, King Edward told his men to engage the enemy, giving orders that no quarter be given or taken. The nobleman commanding his advance guard knew just what to do. A contemporary ballad calls him 'little Fauconberg, a knight of great reverence', meaning that he had a name for being a fine soldier, while Hall says he was 'a man of great policy and of much experience in martial feats.' He brought his archers within range of the plateau, ordering them to shoot one arrow each and then to withdraw out of bowshot. The wind blew snow and arrows into the faces of the Lancastrians, who shot blindly till their quivers were empty, hitting no one – 'they came not near the southern men by forty tailors' yards.' Lord Fauconberg then marched his archers forward, to fill their quivers with the spent arrows, and also to leave some sticking point upward in the ground to impede any attack.

Led by Somerset and Sir Andrew Trollope (a veteran of the French wars with a fearsome reputation), the Lancastrian men-at-arms launched a mounted charge down the slope through the snow storm into Edward's horse, which broke. But a less determined attack by Northumberland on the other Yorkist wing was beaten back. The combat became a murderous melée of dismounted men-at-arms, billmen and bowmen, the Lancastrians shouting, 'King Henry! King Henry!' Hacking and hewing, neither side dared give ground, knowing that to do so meant being slaughtered. 'This battle was sore fought, for hope of life was set on side on every part and taking of prisoners was proclaimed a great offence.' Afterwards, survivors said they had felt as though they had been fighting with hangmen's nooses round their necks, 'the one part sometime flowing and sometime ebbing.'

But during the afternoon, commanded by Sir John Howard, the Duke of Norfolk's men began to arrive along the road from Ferrybridge, falling in beside their Yorkist comrades. Even so, the Lancastrians went on fighting till long after dark. 'And all the season it snew.' (Some locals still say 'snew' for 'snowed'.) As it was snowing there was no moon. In the pitch darkness it was almost impossible for the commanders to see just what was happening. But whenever he appeared through the gloom, Edward IV was an inspiration to the Yorkists, a giant in gilt armour with a jewelled coronet on his helmet – in contrast to Henry VI who, according to plausible legend, spent the battle in prayer. Fighting like a lion, Edward still found time to help his wounded.

Enough of the Duke of Norfolk's men came up for Edward to outflank and then overwhelm his opponents' left wing. The Lancastrian army gave ground increasingly, until at about 10 p.m. it disintegrated. Its remnants fled west, towards Tadcaster. Many drowned trying to ford the Cock Beck, which ran red with blood; muddy banks are hard to climb for men in armour and Yorkist bills and axes hacked at them from above. The pursuit continued all night and most of the next day; occasionally fugitives turned and fought, with further slaughter. Some sources say 28,000 men died, though the real figure was probably nearer 20,000.[3] An area of bloodstained snow six miles long and three miles wide was covered in corpses, among them those of the Earl of Northumberland, Lord Egremont and Sir Andrew Trollope.

Dr Morton realized Lancaster had been defeated when he saw men stumbling back in the dark. Cut off from York and from the royal family – many were killed trying to reach the city – he rode away through the West Riding into Westmorland and then into Cumberland. He was with a party of fugitives who were making for the great Percy stronghold of Cockermouth.

Here, as its members were trying desperately to find a boat to take them to Scotland, the party was arrested by the Sheriff of Cumberland, Richard Salkeld. Besides Morton, it included that seasoned fugitive, the Earl of Wiltshire, Sir William Plumpton, and Morton's colleague, Dr Ralph Mackerell (parson of Risby in Suffolk). All were taken to King Edward at Newcastle. He had already executed 42 captured Lancastrian knights on the battlefield at Towton and gave orders for Wiltshire to be beheaded, the Earl's luck having finally run out, but Plumpton managed to buy a pardon. On 10 May a commission under 'William Hastynges, knight' was appointed to investigate 'treasons' committed by Dr Morton at York. He was sent with Dr Mackerell under guard to London where they were imprisoned in the dungeons at the Tower.

Meanwhile, the wondering Paston family in Suffolk – whose letters so often preserve contemporary rumour – heard how 'King Harry, the queen, the prince, duke of Somerset, duke of Exeter, Lord Roos, be fled into Scotland, and they be chased and followed.'

Although no eyewitness description of the flight of Henry VI and Margaret of Anjou, with their son and accompanied by their court, has survived, there is quite enough evidence with which to reconstruct one of the most dramatic scenes in English history. Within two hours of the Lancastrian army's defeat at Towton, they had hastily ridden out from York at midnight by the light of flaming torches – their wardrobes, jewel-boxes and money-bags, their seals and documents, strapped on to pack-horses – a panic-stricken, shivering party of bewildered gentlemen, ladies, clergy and servants nearly a thousand strong, which galloped north into the snowy darkness. They had left the city at midnight, when King Edward IV's victorious troops were already storming into it from the south.

Conflicting rumours ensued. The Milanese envoy to France was told that the royal party had been caught and Somerset beheaded; the Duke of Exeter had been spared because he was King Edward's brother-in-law, but 'since he is fierce and cruel, it is thought they will put him to an honourable death.' However, they had succeeded in crossing the Scots border safely. 'And King Henry lost all,' says a chronicler.

Dr Morton's time at the Tower cannot have been pleasant. A man who went to a fifteenth-century gaol 'seeth many prisoners sore punished', we are told by the doctor's near-contemporary, John Fisher. They are 'set in a stinking dark dungeon, bound with fetters of iron and for lack of meat like to die for hunger, naked without clothes, in the sharp cold winter no fire to succour them.'[4]

Few men have ever escaped from the Tower of London. Nonetheless, 'he 'scaped away a long time after,' Gregory recorded, 'and is beyond sea with the Queen.' In fact, it is likely that Morton did so before the end of 1461.

John Morton might easily have made his peace with the new Yorkist régime. So able a man would soon have received preferment. When Bishop Booth of Durham, a long-standing friend of Queen Margaret, went over to Edward IV after Towton, he was rewarded by being made the King's 'bishop confessor' – the highest clerical appointment at court. But the doctor chose to forfeit all his fat livings and become a penniless exile. 'He had been fast upon the party of King Henry while that party was in wealth, and nevertheless left it not nor forsook it in woe' is Thomas More's comment.

11

The Coronation of King Edward IV, 1461

JANE SHORE · MARGARET BEAUFORT

LONDON was full of unaccustomed optimism in the spring of 1461, the chroniclers recording general joy on all sides at the sudden and unexpected prospect of lasting peace. John Lambert had reason to welcome the advent of a strong new king, whose firm rule might end the slump in trade. Scarlet-robed, his gold chain of office around his neck, Mr Alderman and Sheriff Lambert (his full title) rode with his fellow aldermen, accompanied by 400 common councilmen in green, to greet Edward IV at Lambeth when he arrived on 26 June to make his formal entry into his loyal capital. They escorted him through the cheering streets of Southwark and the City to his apartments in the Tower of London. His coronation was to take place at Westminster Abbey two days later – even though a crowned and anointed king of England might still lurk in Scotland.

The Mayor, the sheriffs, the aldermen and a dozen elected commoners presented themselves to the high steward of England, the twelve-year-old Duke of Clarence, who granted their petition to represent the City at the ceremonies. On Saturday, 27 June, the vigil, they joined the cavalcade in which the king and the peers, with 32 newly created knights of the Bath and accompanied by heralds, minstrels and drummers, rode from the Tower to the Palace of Westminster. They went along Tower Street, Mark Lane, Fenchurch Street and Gracechurch Street to Cornhill, along Cheapside, down Ludgate Hill, through Ludgate and up Fleet Street and through Temple Bar. Cleared of booths and stalls, swept and gravelled, the streets were lined by liverymen from every City company in their best liveries. There were bands of minstrels at the conduit in Cornhill – flowing with wine – and at the Eleanor Cross, while cloth of gold or silver or rich arras hung from every window along the route.

On Sunday, the day of the crowning, the Mayor, sheriffs and aldermen were rowed up the River Thames to Westminster, to walk in the coronation procession from the Palace to the Abbey. The fountain in the palace yard ran with wine and, as in the City, King Edward was acclaimed by cheering crowds.

By virtue of his office, Mr Sheriff Lambert attended the coronation banquet in Westminster Hall, after the crowning, where swan and peacock were served to the highest in the land. Sitting just below the Mayor, among the aldermen at the first table on the left of the hall – 'next to the cupboard' – he watched the King's champion, Sir Thomas Dymoke of Scrivelsby, ride into the hall in full armour and throw down his steel gauntlet as a challenge to anyone who dared dispute Edward IV's right to the throne. Two days later Mr Lambert was at a great High Mass in St Paul's, where the King wore his crown again and the crowd was larger than 'ever was seen afore in any days.'

The citizens' wives watched the godlike young king ride by, so different from the drab Henry VI. Although contemporary portraits may show a fat face with small eyes, Edward's good looks are well attested. Philippe de Commynes, who saw him on several occasions, thought the King handsomer than any prince he knew – 'I don't recall ever having seen such a fine looking man.' His magnificent physique and height (six feet three and a half inches) were invariably set off by splendid clothes, very unlike the puny King Henry in his habitually dismal garb.

Mr Lambert's daughter, perhaps by now Mrs Shore, must have been among the City ladies watching from the windows. Fifteenth-century girls married very young, their marriages consummated when they reached puberty.[1] There are many documented instances of London merchants' daughters being married at eleven, and Sir Thomas More says specifically that Jane and her husband 'were coupled ere she were well ripe.' A Latin manuscript of More's *History of King Richard the Third*, dating from about 1520, which describes her as '*nunc septuagenaria vetula*' – now an old woman in her seventies – suggests she was born towards 1450, in which case she might well have been married in 1461.

In those days women were very much second-class citizens, young girls being disposed of like heifers. John Aubrey has an account of Thomas More marrying off his own daughters. (It was given to Aubrey by 'my honoured friend old Mrs Tyndale, whose grandfather, Sir William Strafford, was an intimate friend of this Sir W. Roper, who told him the story.')

Sir William Roper, of Eltham in Kent, came one morning pretty early, to my

Lord [Chancellor More] with a proposal to marry one of his daughters. My
Lord's daughters were then both together abed in a truckle-bed in their
father's chamber asleep. He carries Sir William into the chamber and takes
the Sheete by the corner and suddenly whippes it off. They lay on their
Backs, and their smocks up as high as their arme-pitts. This awakened them,
and immediately they turned on their bellies. Quoth Roper, I have seen both
sides, and so gave a patt on the buttock, he made a choice of, sayeing, Thou
art mine. Here was all the trouble of the wooeing.[2]

What makes this account not implausible is More's statement in *Utopia* that every
couple should see each other stark naked before marrying. Poor Jane Lambert
may well have been displayed to her future husband.

Often marriages were 'arranged' in fifteenth-century England, and sometimes
a broker was employed to find a suitable spouse, receiving as much as twelve and
a half per cent of the dowry. Whoever secured Jane's husband appeared to have
found a really worthwhile catch. Not only (to quote More) was the bridegroom
'an honest citizen, young and goodly, and of good substance', but he was also a
London mercer.

William Shore, who came from Derby, had been apprenticed to John Rankyn,
mercer of London, in 1452, which means that he was born in about 1435–40. A
document of 1472 describes him as 'formerly yeoman of the city of Derby', and
it is likely that his father was a small landowner in comfortable circumstances.
Clearly the elder Shore must have been reasonably affluent to put up the £100
needed to apprentice his son. Having completed his apprenticeship, William was
admitted to the freedom of the company in 1459 and was sufficiently well
thought of by the wardens to be among the fifteen young mercers who were
chosen 'to ride in blue to meet the king' when Edward returned from the north
in March 1463.[3] He would become a liveryman in the following year, entitled to
wear the coveted blue robes trimmed with gold. An able businessman, he had
interests abroad, in Ghent, Utrecht and Zealand.

His child bride was most attractive. 'Proper she was and fair, nothing in her
body that you would have changed, but if you would have wished her somewhat
higher. Thus say they that knew her in youth.' So Thomas More tells us. More's
parents (his father was then a rising young barrister living in Milk Street near

Jane Shore (Elizabeth Lambert). From her parents' brass of 1487 at Hinxworth,
Herts.

Guildhall) could well have known her in her early, respectable days; More says she was 'worshipfully friended'. He continues, 'Yet delighted men not so much in her beauty as in her pleasant behaviour. For a proper wit she had, and could both read well and write, merry in company, ready and quick of answer, neither mute nor full of babble, sometimes taunting without displeasure and not without disport.'[4]

The couple may have begun their married life in a house rented by Mr Shore from a family called Constantine (which he is known to have left in 1472), at the south end of Bow Lane in the parishes of St Mary-le-Bow and Aldermary, and near Cheapside. But it was not a happy marriage. To a girl not yet in her teens a husband of twenty-six was an old man. More comments that 'as they were coupled ere she were well ripe, she not very fervently loved for whom she never longed.' Worst of all, as will appear, William Shore was impotent.

The new reign brought Jane's father into close contact with the monarch. According to Professor Ross, Edward IV 'courted, honoured and flattered and rewarded the London citizens more assiduously than any king before him.' Few citizens were more important than Mr Sheriff Lambert. King Edward needed cash urgently to run the country and mop up Lancastrian resistance, and John Lambert was a well-established money-lender. In April 1461 the Mayor and alderman, including John, subsidized Edward yet again, with over £1,300, while John gave the King a further £300 on his own account. He also contributed £11 'for the speed of th' earl of Warwick in the North.' Eventually, the loans to Edward would prove to be a richly rewarding investment.

Later in the year he was appointed a Collector of Customs at Southampton.[5] The Croyland chronicler says that collectors such as John were 'men of remarkable shrewdness but too hard upon the merchants, according to general report.' He was well equipped for the job, by experience in collecting City dues, and by his activities as a money-lender – pursuing evasive borrowers through the law courts and enforcing repayment.

When Parliament met at Westminster in November 1461 the mood of both peers and commons verged on hero worship. No doubt previous parliaments had addressed their monarchs as 'Most Christian King, right high and mighty

Jane Shore's first husband, the 'frigid and impotent' mercer William Shore. From an incised alabaster slab of 1495 at Scropton, Derbys.

lord, and our aller most dread sovereign and natural liege lord', but they had never told them how good-looking they were. This time the Speaker, Sir James Strangways – who had fought by the side of Edward's father, the Duke of York, at Wakefield and survived – referred warmly to 'the beauty of personage that it hath pleased Almighty God to send you.' Sir James also congratulated the King formally on his victory at Mortimer's Cross, on his having rescued London from the northerners, and on his glorious triumph at Towton.

Enthusiastically, Parliament endorsed King Edward IV's right to the throne. At the same time it attainted the former King – 'the said Henry, usurper' – together with 112 of his relatives and supporters. As a consequence of these attainders, Edward received a great windfall of confiscated estates. With so many broad acres at his disposal, he had no need to ask Parliament for any new taxes, his income being twice that of the former Henry VI – now a forlorn pensioner of the Scots – when the latter had been King.

During the address in which he prorogued (dismissed) Parliament, Edward thanked the Speaker and the commons in what was clearly an emotional and deeply felt speech. It should not be forgotten that this amazing young man was still only nineteen.

> James Strangways and ye that be comen for the Commons of this my land, for the true hearts and tender considerations that ye have had to my right and title that I and my ancestors have had unto the crown of this realm, the which from us have been long time withheld and now, thanked be Almighty God of Whose Grace groweth all victory, by your true hearts and great assistance I am restored . . . I thank you as heartily as I can.

The new King thanked them too for 'the tender and true hearts that ye have showed unto me, in that ye have tenderly had in remembrance the correction of the horrible murder and cruel death of my lord my father, my brother Rutland and my cousin of Salisbury and others.' He ended:

> I thank you with all my heart, and if I had any better good to reward you withal than my body you should have it, the which shall always be ready for your defence, never sparing nor letting for no jeopardy. Praying you all of your hearty assistance, as I shall be unto you your very rightwise and loving liege lord.[6]

Margaret Beaufort must have been horrified by Towton and by the attainders that

'Hath not thy rose a thorn, Plantagenet?'
Shakespeare's imagined confrontation in *King Henry VI*, by Henry Payne

Henry VI. A sixteenth-century copy of a lost portrait

Margaret Beaufort, portrait by Maynard Waynwyk before 1523

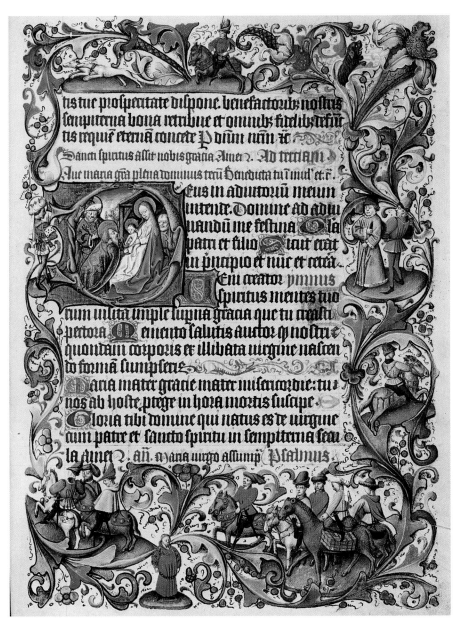

A great nobleman's 'riding household' c.1460

Edward IV. A sixteenth-century copy of a lost portrait

ELIZABETH VXOR
EDWARDVS IIII

Elizabeth Woodville, Edward IV's beautiful but greedy queen

Waurin presents his chronicles to Edward IV, probably at Bruges in 1471. The Garter Knight on the right may be Hastings, the Garter Knight on the left Gloucester

The battle of Barnet, Easter Sunday (14 April) 1471

outlawed her Lancaster and Beaufort cousins. She had had every reason to fear for her husband's life when he went off to fight for King Henry, having already lost her uncle Somerset and her brother-in-law Stafford at St Albans, her father-in-law Buckingham at Northampton, and her former father-in-law, Owen Tudor, at Mortimer's Cross. Indeed, her stepfather, Lionel, Lord Welles, fell at Towton. However, Henry Stafford not only survived the battle but secured a pardon on 25 June 1461 for 'all treasons, rebellions and felonies', which saved his estates. Edward IV was trying to win over Lancastrians.

Edward allowed Margaret to keep the lands bequeathed by her father and Edmund Tudor, and those given to her by Henry VI. Yet she was no longer a member of the royal family. Worse still, her little son Henry Tudor had been taken from her when Pembroke Castle surrendered to the Yorkists at the end of September 1461. His captor, Sir William Herbert – Edward's main henchman in South Wales, and notorious for greed – had bought his 'custody and marriage' from the King, intending to marry the boy to his own daughter. 'He himself told me', Philippe de Commynes records of Henry Tudor, 'that since the age of five he had been guarded like a fugitive or kept in prison.' No doubt he was brought up as a member of the Herbert household by Lady Herbert, but obviously he had unhappy memories of his time there. Margaret had good cause to dislike the new régime.

It was far from unthinkable that Margaret's cousin, Henry VI, might recover his throne. Despite the cheering and adulation, King Edward IV was very far from secure. The House of Lancaster still possessed many supporters, declared or undeclared; they remembered the oaths of loyalty they had sworn to a sovereign who had reigned for nearly forty years. Those who had lost relatives at Towton hoped to avenge them. At the same time, not enough magnates and gentry were wholeheartedly committed to King Edward. There had been a rebellion in support of Henry in the north-east two days before Edward's crowning, and William Hastings had to go up to Northumberland and lay siege to Alnwick Castle.

The Milanese envoy to the French court, Prospero di Camulio (who was kept well informed by the Lombard community in London), reported that unless Henry VI and his consort were captured further fighting was inevitable. 'Anyone who thinks of the queen's misery and the ruin of all those killed, together with the innate ferocity of this country and the victors' attitude, should – in my view – pray as much for the living as for the dead.'

In Camulio's opinion there was a threat to the Yorkist régime from another quarter, so far unrecognized but potentially even more dangerous. He prophesied that should Henry be made prisoner, then 'before long King Edward and Warwick will start to disagree and to quarrel, so that King Henry and the queen will triumph.'

I 2

'Lord Hastings of Hastings', 1461

WILLIAM HASTINGS

AMONG those determined that Edward IV should stay upon the throne was William Hastings, who owed his entire good fortune to being the King's best and most trusted friend. His life, which had begun to change after Mortimer's Cross, had been altered dramatically by Towton, where he was knighted on the field, one of only six gentlemen so honoured. A month after the coronation, he was created 'Lord Hastings of Hastings'. Although hitherto unconnected with Sussex, his rewards included one or two manors in that county together with Hastings Castle – hence his choice of title.[1]

The patent confirming his peerage, which was issued in the following year, is of the utmost interest. It reveals the King's deep esteem for him. Seldom has a document of this sort radiated such genuine affection:

> Calling to mind the honourable service, probity and valiant deeds of our dearly beloved knight William Hastynges, our chamberlain, we wish to raise him to the rank of baron and peer of our realm, as much for his martial exploits as for his good example and good counsel. We particularly single out how the said William with a large force of his servants, friends and well-wishers [*benivolorum*] did at heavy and burdensome cost and at manifold peril expose himself most courageously and shrewdly in our service in campaigns and battles against our arch-enemy the former pretended king of England, 'Henry the Sixth', with his accomplices and abettors, notably Jasper Pembroke and James Wiltshire, formerly earls, who together with other traitors and rebels waged war on us. From his early manhood he has never ceased to serve us . . .

William was appointed master of the king's monies, receiver-general for the duchy of Cornwall, and chamberlain of North Wales, as well as constable, steward or keeper of numerous royal castles, manors and forests – acquiring such arcane but lucrative dignities as those of parker of Brigstock Park and master-forester of Rockingham Forest. Each of these offices was accompanied by a substantial salary. As master of the king's monies he received a groat (4d) for every pound of gold or silver struck into coin of the realm at the London or Calais mints, while as forester of Rockingham he was paid 12d a day.

At the same time he was transformed into a great Midland magnate, being given most of the former lands of the Lancastrian Lords Beaumont, Roos and Wiltshire, 'for the better maintenance of his estate', as a grant puts it. As a rich peer, his 'estate' was most impressive. He had his own vast household, almost a court in miniature, which accompanied him from mansion to mansion, providing an escort of well over a hundred men. It included a comptroller, a steward, a receiver (of rents and revenues), a treasurer, a master of the horse, a groom of the hall, a groom of the chambers, a clerk of the kitchens, a librarian, a master of the wardrobe, a master of the fishponds, and a master of hounds, together with a carver, marshals and ushers, gentlemen and yeomen waiters, pages, chaplains, singing men and minstrels – not to mention cooks, larderers and cellarers. Pack-horses and mules carried not only clothing and provisions, but bedding, linen, and even furniture and windows – the latter being frames holding glass.

He also had his own baronial council, gentlemen servants from his household – his steward, his comptroller, his receiver, his chaplain, his treasurer or anyone else who had something useful to contribute. They advised him on estate management, legal and financial matters, on problems among the local community, sometimes even on political affairs. Occasionally men from outside the household were enlisted, experts such as feed lawyers. One day he would recruit a young neighbour with particularly valuable legal skills, a Northamptonshire squire called Mr William Catesby.

One of Lord Hastings' 'affinity', Nicholas Knyveton, Esq., Sheriff of Nottingham and Derby, who became his retainer in 1465. From a brass of 1475 at Mugginton, Derbys.

In July 1461 Hastings was made steward of the honour of Leicester, a vast network of royal manors in Leicestershire, Warwickshire, Northamptonshire and Nottinghamshire. The post's basic duties were administrative – looking after Crown estates and collecting revenues – but obviously gave the steward great influence throughout the region. For the appointment had a strategic purpose, William's job being to win support for the new régime in an area hitherto noted for its loyalty to Henry VI.

Clearly encouraged by King Edward, Lord Hastings began building up an affinity among the Midland gentry, retaining them by indentures. He recruited less than a dozen during the first decade, but eventually the affinity would number more than ninety.[2] In one indenture Sir Simon Montfort promised 'his full part and quarrel to take against all others' and 'to be ready at all times and places within this realm of England to attend upon the said lord [Hastings] . . . as well in time of peace as war, upon reasonable warning accompanied with such people as thereto shall be requisite'. Most of the retainers promised to come 'accompanied with as many persons defensibly arrayed as he may goodly make or assemble, at the cost of the same lord [Hastings].' They pledged themselves 'with him to ride and go within the ground of England at all such times as shall like his lorship.' In return William promised them 'good lorship', by which he meant that he would further their interests in every way he could. Undoubtedly the affinity was the biggest in England. It was also exceptional in owing its creation in large part to the King. The well-wishers were as much Edward's as they were William's – a subtle means of strengthening Yorkist authority in the Midlands.

These indentures would prove an invaluable political and military investment. The men whom he gathered into his affinity (and thus prevented from joining the affinities of other magnates) were the leaders of local society, and they enabled him to control the machinery that governed their respective counties. Over the next two decades at least ten would serve as MPs, another twenty as sheriffs, and no less than thirty-three as JPs. They also provided the captains who raised and officered the levies that composed the bulk of the King's armies.

Many of the affinity were the heads of families that continued to own substantial estates in the Midlands down to the present century, and in some cases still do. Among their names were those of Gresley, Eyre, Pole, Savile, Clifton, Chaworth, Harcourt and Fitzherbert. As people of substance, no fewer than six have left likenesses which survive today, since their sons could afford to commemorate them with brasses in their parish churches. Made from 'latten', an alloy of copper and zinc that was generally imported from Cologne and then engraved locally, such brasses were not cheap. Almost invariably, those depicted are shown wearing full armour so that no passer-by beholding them could fail to realize that they were gentlemen.

Even peers coveted William Hastings' good lordship, such as Lord Grey of Codnor, who became his well-wisher in 1464. Henry Grey was a former Lancastrian whose seat was the castle (now more or less demolished) at Codnor near Ripley in Derbyshire. An alchemist, he was engaged in the search for the philosopher's stone and the secret of how to change lead or iron into gold; in 1463 Edward IV licensed him to 'labour by the conning of philosophy the transmutation of metals at his own cost, but he should answer to the king if any profit grew.' However, the fantastic alchemist was also a most formidable soldier who took an energetic part in both local and national politics.

Although undeniably useful, such well-wishers could also be a source of grave worry to their 'good lords'. Like so many contemporary magnates, Grey was quarrelsome and violent. He waged a bitter feud against the Vernons of Haddon Hall, who were backed by another local magnate, the Earl of Shrewsbury. In November 1467 Grey's men clashed with a band of Shrewsbury's in a skirmish near Derby during which 'horrible murder' was done, the principal victim being Roger Vernon.[3] Lord Hastings, together with the Duke of Clarence and Earl Rivers, were sent to restore order at the beginning of 1468, but in the summer of the same year Grey on the one hand and the Vernons and Shrewsbury on the other had to be bound over to stop them intimidating jurors. In 1471 Grey would be accused of inciting dangerous riots in Nottingham against the Mayor and corporation. It is likely that Hastings had to intervene and save him. Grey's turbulent career highlights one of the problems faced by a great magnate with an affinity; often its members were at daggers drawn with each other – in 1471 Hastings would recruit none other than Henry Vernon, the son of the murdered Roger , while continuing to retain Lord Grey. Obviously, very considerable tact was needed if such mutually hostile well-wishers were going to ride side by side, let alone go into battle together.

Much of William's 'good lordship', the fifteenth-century term for influence, derived from his special position as chamberlain. According to the anonymous author of the *Black Book of the Household of Edward IV*, the chamberlain was 'chief head of rulers in the king's chamber.' In modern terms his job combined the duties of house and staff manager with those of private secretary. He ordered the King's meals and was responsible for arranging audiences – no one could meet

Edward IV unless they asked Hastings. A friend of the Pastons wrote with awe of 'what my said lord chamberlain may do with the king and with all the lords of England.'

Indeed, his good lordship was considered so valuable that he had no need to pay his retainers annual fees in cash, as was the normal practice. Everybody wanted William to be on their side. 'An impressive list of English lords and ladies, bishops, abbots and gentry paid him annuities or gave him profitable sinecures, and thought it money well spent to engage his influence with the king,' observes Professor Ross.

William's special position as chamberlain brought him nearer to the King than any other man. In 1436 Robert Russell, an official in the household of Humphrey, Duke of Gloucester, wrote *The Boke of Nurture*, which deals with the duties of staff in a royal household and describes a chamberlain's functions in some detail.[4] It was the chamberlain's task to ensure that fires were tended and candles lit in his lord's bedroom, that the bed was aired and the chamber pot emptied. After waking his lord in the early morning, he helped him to dress, first proffering him clean linen (warmed at a fire in cold weather) and then handing him well-brushed clothes. Later he aired the chamber, making sure to 'drive out dog or cat or else give them a good clout.' At night he helped his lord undress and go to bed. He also prepared his baths. This, according to Russell, entailed hanging linen sheets around a wooden tub and on a canopy over it, placing a large sponge in it for the lord to sit on, and personally washing him with a soft sponge, before finally sprinkling him with rose water. If necessary, he could provide a medicinal bath, using such herbs as hollyhock, mallow, fennel, camomile and scabious. Although he had pages to help him, and a deputy to take his place when he was away, presumably William performed all these intimate services for King Edward.

On St George's Day 1462 William was installed as a Knight of the Garter at Windsor. A page buckled the garter on his leg below the knee, before robing him in a purple surcoat and a blue mantle. Then two knights led him before their sovereign who received him into the order. Finally he dined with his knight companions, 'a very sumptuous and noble feast.' His helm, crest, sword, banner and

Another of Lord Hastings' affinity, Sir Thomas Stathum with his wives Elizabeth and Thomasine. In 1466 Sir Thomas was retained by Hastings 'with him to ride and go within the ground of England at all such times as shall like his lordship.' From a brass of 1470 at Morley, Derbys.

The garter-plate of Lord Hastings at St George's Chapel, Windsor.

garter-plate were set up over his stall in St George's Chapel. The plate is still there, with his crest of a bull's head.

Sometimes heraldry tells us a little about a man. Proud of his ancestry, William bore the Hastings arms of argent, a maunche sable – a black sleeve on silver – which he could never alter. However, his choice of bulls as supporters (shown on his seal but not on the garter-plate) may be a demonstration of loyalty to King Edward, who used a bull and a lion as supporters for the royal arms. More is revealed by William's badge, a 'manticore' or man-tiger. This may well express a womanizer's self-conscious virility. A drawing of the badge depicts a fantastic beast with exaggerated genitalia and with a satyr's grinning face, which must surely be a caricature of William.

The King reserved the Garter for foreign monarchs, for England's most powerful magnates and for his closest friends. He could have paid Hastings no greater compliment. Yet Edward IV's friendship was demanding. No doubt William shared his tastes for hunting and women; in Mancini's words, William was 'the accomplice and partner of his privy pleasures', and he may even have pimped for him. But that was only one side of his life. Besides the daily running of his department at court, he had countless other duties. 'The typical Yorkist courtier was no pleasure-loving favourite, no idle fop-about-town', Professor Ross reminds us. 'He was generally not only a courtier but also a councillor, administrator and king's servant.'[5] In addition, he had to be a good soldier as well as something very like a party boss in his own particular part of England.

William was ubiquitous and highly effective. Indispensable at the siege of Alnwick in 1462 – from where young John Paston wrote excitedly 'I am well acquainted with my Lord Hastings and my Lord Dacre, which now be greatest about the king's person' – William would play a key role in the negotiations with the Duke of Brittany in 1465, and in those with the Duke of Burgundy and the King of France in 1466. However, his most remarkable achievement would be to oversee the introduction of a new coinage.

Because of an increasing shortage of bullion, English coins were undervalued; a profit could be made from exchanging them abroad or melting them down, as Mr Alderman Lambert must have been very well aware. In consequence, not enough money was in circulation. The council that met at Reading in September 1464 agreed that there should be a reform of the coinage.

As master of the King's monies, Lord Hastings was nominally in charge of the operation. Technical details were handled by his deputy, Hugh Bryce,[6] a London goldsmith of Irish origin – from Dublin – who paid another goldsmith, Edmund Shaa, twenty pounds a year to strike the coins. William was responsible for security; although the mint was sited between the inner and outer walls of the Tower, so much bullion and cash was a temptation to criminals.

In the event, everything went well. New groats (4d), half-groats, pence, half-pence and farthings were issued, their silver content reduced by a fifth. A new rose noble or ryal of 10s replaced the old noble of 6s 8d, while a new coin of 6s 8d, the angel (one of the most beautiful in numismatic history), was introduced. All this involved calling in and recoining the previous currency.[7]

The Shores and Lamberts undoubtedly noticed the coins' decreased purchasing power. 'And they made new groats not so good as the old, but they were worth 4d,' says Gregory resentfully. As for the rose nobles and angels, 'at the beginning of this money men grudged passing sore, for they could not reckon that gold so quickly as they did the old gold. And men might go throughout a street or through a whole passage ere that he might change it. And some men said that the new gold was not so good as the old gold was, for it was alloyed.'

Despite initial hostility, the new coins were eventually accepted so that in just over two years the King made nearly £15,500 out of the reform. Men such as William Shore and his father-in-law profited too, if they had bought bullion early on. It was a triumph for Hastings, revealing a practical side to his character very different from the knight errant of tradition.

Since Lord Hastings had to spend so much time in attendance on King Edward, he needed a London home big enough to accommodate his retinue. This seems to have been the house near Paul's Wharf ('in the parish of St Bene'ts') which he leased for sixty years in June 1463 from the Austin canons of St Bartholomew the Great, Prior Reynold merely asking a token rent of a single red rose each year. Narrow but with two solars (forerunners of the drawing-room), the chamberlain's new residence was within walking distance of the Tower and the Cheap, conveniently close to the Thames along which a fast wherry could take him to Westminster or to Windsor.

Two of William's brothers shared in his good fortune. Ralph, who had fought by his side, was appointed an Esquire of the Body (a member of the King's bodyguard) in 1461 and given an estate.[8] He was made 'keeper of the king's lions, lionesses and leopards' at the Tower, for which he received 12d a day with 6d a day for their food.[9] He also became Edward's Master of the Horse. As a courtier but also a country gentleman, Ralph was, to quote Ross, among the men who formed 'one of the chief links between court and country'. Richard Hastings' rewards came later. Thomas, the youngest brother, was not so lucky. A former

William Hastyngs
Lord Hastyngs
ob 1463.

The face of William Hastings? The head of his 'man-tiger' emblem may well be a portrait. From a sketch of c 1466–70.

murder suspect, he may have been seen as the family's black sheep.

In 1462, or soon after, the Hastings brothers' youngest sister Elizabeth married a Welsh gentleman, John Donne. This was perhaps a little surprising since the English still regarded the Welsh as a conquered and, to some degree, a subject race.[10] (John's grandfather had risen against the English in Owain Glyn Dŵr's revolt.) However, during the last decades of the Hundred Years' War, his father, Gruffydd ap Maredudd Dŵn of Kidwelly, had served in the Duke of York's retinue in France, where John was born about 1430. John had entered the Duke's household, where he must have met William, and he had fought at Mortimer's Cross. In 1462 King Edward appointed him an usher of the chamber

– in which capacity he served under William – promoting him to an Esquire of the Body three years later.[11]

As for William's own marriage, the squire of Burton Hastings had risen so high that he was considered a good enough catch for the Earl of Warwick's fifth sister, Catherine, the widowed Lady Harington, who had a jointure of £400 a year. Her husband had fallen at Wakefield, leaving her with a posthumous daughter, Cecil, Baroness Harington and Bonville, who was the heiress to great estates and whose wardship provided her stepfather with further income. Catherine was to give William three sons and a daughter. The marriage, which took place some time before February 1462, made him not only brother-in-law to the 'Kingmaker' but first cousin to the King.

13

The Adventures of Dr Morton, 1462–63

JOHN MORTON

AFTER somehow escaping from the Tower of London, no mean feat, and reaching France, John Morton embarked on still more alarming adventures – to be 'continually tumbled and tossed in the waves of divers misfortunes and adversities', in the words of his friend Thomas More. 'And so by many and great dangers he learned the experience of the world.' Nothing could be more dangerous during the 1460s than to be a Lancastrian.

While Morton was in the Tower, the Lancastrians had not been idle. Henry VI and his queen received armed assistance on a large scale from the Scots and a substantial number of gentry south of the border stayed faithful to them, especially in Northumberland. In April 1461, in return for troops, the Queen ordered Berwick to surrender to the Scots, but in June Carlisle disobeyed a similar order. The Duke of Exeter joined Jasper Tudor in Wales and raised an army. However, they were defeated in October, John Paston hearing that every Welsh castle had surrendered to King Edward's men and that 'the duke of Exeter and the earl of Pembroke are flown and taken [to] the mountains and divers lords with great puissance are after them.' Nevertheless, Harlech held out for King Henry until 1468, while Exeter and Jasper got back safely to Scotland.

During early 1462 war seemed to threaten the Yorkist régime from every side. In February, under interrogation, a captured Lancastrian spy revealed a plot by the 'infirm' Earl of Oxford. When King Edward was travelling up to the border to join his army, escorted by only a handful of men, the Earl and his friends would attack him with 2,000. At the same time King Henry would invade from Scotland while Exeter and Jasper Tudor would land at Beaumaris and raise North Wales. In addition, according to one excited chronicler, 'Duke Harry of Calabria [the

Queen's brother], the Lord Hungerford, the Lord Morton [sic], the duke of Somerset, with 50,000 men of Spain, shall landen in the coast of Norfolk and Suffolk.' But all these threats came to nothing.

Undeterred, leaving her husband in Scotland, the Queen sailed to France in April 1462. Dr Morton, now 'Lord Privy Seal', was among her advisers during the negotiations with Louis XI at Tours in June; after she promised that Henry would hand over Calais to the French, when he had regained it, King Louis signed a treaty of alliance. He also gave her 2,000 francs and promised soldiers. However, when Edward IV retaliated by allying with Burgundy and Castile, Louis became less eager to help the House of Lancaster.

Nonetheless, in the autumn the Queen was able to sail from Honfleur with a fleet of forty-two ships which carried over a thousand French troops under a redoubtable French commander, Pierre de Brézé. The dauntless Dr Morton went with them. After putting in at a Scottish port and taking on board King Henry and the Duke of Somerset, together with a small Scots force, they landed at Bamburgh on the Northumbrian coast on 25 October. As a London chronicler wrote, the Queen 'came out of France into Scotland with a strength of people; and so entered England and made open war.' But although most of the Northumbrian gentry must have sympathized with his cause, there was no widespread rising in favour of Henry VI; too many remembered the kindred and friends who had died at Towton. Even so, the garrisons of the castles at Bamburgh, Dunstanburgh and Warkworth declared for Henry, while his troops quickly captured Alnwick. The Lancastrians now controlled half the Northumbrian seaboard – if the Scots sent enough reinforcements, the north might be persuaded to join them.

The indefatigable Queen set off for Scotland to find more troops, accompanied by her husband, Somerset and Brézé, but off Berwick their fleet ran into a storm. The royal party escaped only by abandoning ship and making for shore in a fishing boat. Their carvel foundered, taking with it most of the Queen's baggage, while three other vessels ran aground near Lindisfarne; marooned on Holy Island, most of the French troops who had been on board were soon killed or captured by men loyal to King Edward.

Meanwhile the Earl of Warwick was advancing on the castles. Edward, who fully appreciated the seriousness of the situation, brought an army even larger that that which he had commanded at Towton; it included two-thirds of the English peerage. When Edward was struck down by measles at Durham, Warwick took

Durham Castle in 1728, little changed since the Wars of the Roses.

charge of operations, using Warkworth – which had surrendered – as a base. Hunger was his weapon, since it would have been much too expensive to employ heavy artillery at all three castles.

We know that on 21 December the Lancastrian garrison inside Dunstanburgh numbered 120 men, under the command of the Duke of Somerset, Sir Richard Tunstall, and Sir Thomas Findherne. John Morton was with them, perhaps to stiffen morale. Eight miles north-east of Alnwick, on a promontory at the south side of Embleton Bay, Dunstanburgh stands on the crags of the Whin Sill. Its ruins still have a grim, not to say menacing, air. The curtain walls enclose eleven acres, dominated by a massive gatehouse. The central part was three storeys high, containing a great hall on the second floor, and was flanked by two D-shaped towers, each of five storeys. Although the castle's living quarters were here in the gatehouse, it was the first part to be assaulted by besiegers since it was the easiest to approach from the mainland. Morton may have lodged in the constable's house (which has not survived), but he would certainly have eaten in the great hall.

My Lord of Warwick 'rideth daily to all these castles for to oversee the sieges,' wrote John Paston, who was with the Duke of Norfolk's contingent. 'If they need victuals or anything else, he is ready to supply them.' Norfolk was at Newcastle, from where he sent Warwick a steady stream of provisions and ammunition. The castles were closely invested; anyone among the besieging troops who tried to go home could expect severe punishment.

Soon the Lancastrians were eating their horses in the great hall at Dunstanburgh, as they were at Bamburgh. Nothing bleaker can be imagined than these gaunt strongholds on the edge of the North Sea, and it was winter. There was no sign of a Scots army coming to their relief, although Paston heard on 11 December 'that as this day we had tidings that the Scots will come into England for to rescue these three castles.' Eventually there was no longer even horsemeat to eat in the great hall, and on Christmas Eve the garrisons of both Dunstanburgh and Bamburgh started to negotiate a surrender.

King Edward offered generous terms – a free pardon or a safe conduct abroad. Bamburgh surrendered on Boxing Day, Dunstanburgh on Monday, 27 December. There had been a reason for Edward's generosity; he knew that a Scots army under the Earl of Angus and Pierre de Brézé was on its way to relieve the castles. However, although he rescued the garrison of Alnwick, Angus would not risk a confrontation with Warwick and marched back to Scotland, leaving the Yorkists in possession of all three strongholds.

After the fall of Dunstanburgh Dr Morton rejoined the Queen on the other side of the border. That remarkable woman refused to give way to despair while her husband still possessed supporters, and during the summer of 1463 the three castles were again in Lancastrian hands. In July the Queen and Henry VI, together with Brézé (and no doubt Morton), accompanied little King James III of Scots and his army when they invaded England 'with great puissance' and laid siege to Norham Castle on the banks of the River Tweed. The siege was raised after only eighteen days by Warwick and his brother, Lord Montagu, who chased the Scots back over the border. The Queen herself had difficulty in escaping.

Waurin has a dramatic account of Queen Margaret's adventures after Norham, though he confuses them with her departure from Scotland later that month. It is worth giving in full, since he may well have heard it from the Queen's own lips.

> After hiding some of her best rings in her clothes, she and her son, young Edward, prince of Wales, mounted ponies and set off with guides, riding only by night, until they came to a very large and dense forest [still] in England. Here, she and her son were caught, captured by thieves and murderers who wanted to kill them, but a great argument broke out over whom was to have her rings and jewels. While it pleased God that these murder-

ers should be quarrelling with each other, taking her son in her arms she hid in the forest. Finally, overcome by hardship and exhaustion, she had no choice but to entrust her child to another brigand whom she encountered in the woods, saying to him 'Save your king's son.' Through this man she and her son escaped out of the hands of those robbers and murderers and got away . . .

She was able to reach Scotland safely – as was Dr Morton.

A flowery letter from 'W Hastings à Mr de Lannoy' (an influential Burgundian nobleman), dated 7 August 1463,[1] refers to 'the great enterprise of our ancient enemies of my said sovereign lord [Edward IV], those from Scotland, allied with those great traitors and rebels, Henry calling himself king and Margaret his wife, made on his castle of Norham by the king of Scotland with all the power of his land, furnished with its great ordnance . . .' William tells Lannoy with unconcealed triumph how Lords Warwick and Montagu, with only the men of the northern Marches, had chased the King of Scots and his army back to Scotland, pursuing them, plundering and laying waste a good part of their country, destroying several castles, killing many Scots and taking large numbers of them prisoner.

He continues that 'until the day of judgement they will repent of the favour and help they gave to Hery [sic] and Margaret and [I pray] that their repentance shall not be altogether forgotten. In short, I hope that it will leave such an effect and impression as to make them remember for ever the desolation and misery of the Scots nation through God's grace.' Even though the Scots may not have remembered for ever their rout at Norham, undoubtedly it discouraged them from giving any more help to Henry VI.

The purpose of Hastings' letter was to convince the Burgundian court that the cause of the House of Lancaster was now lost irretrievably. In the same letter he says that the defeat of the Scots had frightened Queen Margaret and 'her captain', Pierre de Brézé, into fleeing without further ado 'beyond sea'. He wrote in the knowledge that a peace conference would soon take place at St Omer, between England, France and Burgundy. As well as soldier and courtier, William was also a diplomat.

Margaret of Anjou had indeed crossed the sea, hoping against hope to persuade King Louis not to make peace with Edward IV. She had sailed from Scotland towards the end of July, immediately after her escape from the disaster at Norham, taking her son with her. They were accompanied by 200 followers, among whom were the Duke of Exeter, Sir John Fortescue and Doctors Morton and Mackerell. Gregory says the party made the voyage in four ballingers; these were small, shallow-draughted, oared sailing barges with flat bottoms – scarcely the most comfortable craft in which to cross the North Sea, especially when loaded to the gunnel.[2] Landing at Sluys, the party went to Bruges, where the White Friars gave them shelter in the Carmelite priory. The Queen realized that neither help nor refuge could any longer be expected from the cowed Scots, who were living in dread of an English invasion. Her last chance was King Louis. But, as she had feared, the French made peace with Edward in October 1463.

When the Scots too made peace with Edward in December, King Henry returned to Northumberland and installed himself at Bamborough, which was still holding out for him. His dwindling band of supporters waged a guerrilla war in the north for a few months longer, occasionally capturing one or two isolated castles. But in May 1464 their leaders were captured near Hexham and beheaded; among them died the Duke of Somerset (see p. 118) and Sir Thomas Findherne, who had been Morton's comrades at Dunstanburgh. One month later Warwick's cannon battered Bamburgh into submission. Henry VI's last bastion had fallen, though he continued to wander forlornly from hiding place to hiding place over the wild northern moors.

On 27 September 1464 Edward IV granted the revenues of Norwich archdeaconry to the Prior of Norwich Cathedral, for the repair and rebuilding of the cathedral church. They had been 'forfeited to the king because John Morton, clerk, archdeacon of Norwich, was attainted of high treason.'[3] If the little doctor was remembered in England at all, it was as an outlaw.

14

The Lord Chamberlain
and the Unwelcome Guest, 1463

WILLIAM HASTINGS

MORE than once during the year 1463 Lord Hastings must have had the privilege of seeing Henry, Duke of Somerset, in Edward IV's bed when, at first light, as was his duty as chamberlain, he drew the splendid bed curtains and woke the king. Somerset enjoyed the reputation of being the most ferocious of all the Lancastrian leaders, even fiercer than the brutal Duke of Exeter, and it is clear that many Yorkists were afraid he was going to murder their king. Indeed, it is far from impossible that Edward narrowly escaped death at his hands. Nonetheless, the King not only shared his bed with Somerset but made him captain of the royal bodyguard.

Eventually, the attempt to win over the Duke of Somerset to the cause of York failed in circumstances of some drama, and the episode is one of the more bizarre to emerge from the Wars of the Roses.[1] But nothing illustrates better Edward's political genius. Had he succeeded in detaching the Duke from Henry VI's cause, he would have deprived the Lancastrians of their most formidable leader, making them incapable of further military resistance in the north of England.

Edward's motives for trying to win over Somerset become clearer when one understands the King's dangerous isolation. Despite the Yorkists' overwhelming triumph at Towton, comparatively few magnates welcomed the new régime unreservedly, even if they and their affinities might ride with Edward on his campaigns. He knew very well that in the north, the West Country and throughout Wales support for Lancaster remained high. While Henry VI was scarcely a daunting opponent, his son – the grandson of the hero of Agincourt – might grow up to be a very different foe, and in the not too distant future.

The Duke of Somerset was unquestionably the ablest of the Lancastrian commanders, a brilliant soldier. Since commanding King Henry's army at Towton, he
had had an adventurous career. Admittedly, it was not quite as colourful as some
claimed; there was a rumour that, after Towton, Henry had been poisoned by
Queen Margaret who, it was said, intended to marry the Duke. What did happen
is that in the summer of 1461 Margaret sent Somerset over the North Sea from
Scotland to France, to beg for troops and money. Without a proper safe conduct,
the Duke was arrested but forced his way into the presence of the new French
King, Louis XI. Once there, his behaviour was scarcely prudent; he boasted that
he had slept with the Queen of Scots, Mary of Guelders. The King sent him back
to Scotland in a carvel, with nothing to show for his pains. Margaret may well
have given her paladin a cool reception before she herself set off for France.
Reports of Somerset's boast, apparently given wide circulation by the mischievous King Louis, reached Mary of Guelders, who was so furious that she tried to
persuade her real lover, the Master of Hailes, to murder him.

In September 1462 a correspondent of the Pastons reported a rumour in
London that Somerset was willing to change sides – 'it is said that my lord
Warwick had sent to the king and informed his Highness that the Lord Somerset
had written to him to come to grace.' However, in October the Duke was with
the Lancastrian forces that occupied the Northumbrian castles after these had
gone over to Queen Margaret and her French troops. He was at Dunstanburgh
just after Christmas, when the garrison accepted unusually generous terms and
surrendered to the Yorkists.

Instead of taking advantage of a safe conduct, like Dr Morton, and returning
to Scotland, Somerset chose to go to King Edward at Durham, where he and Sir
Ralph Percy (a brother of the Earl of Northumberland killed at Towton) formally
swore allegiance to him. This surprising conversion to the Yorkist cause was
taken at face value, and they were granted their lives and lands. The Duke was
immediately sent to help Warwick reduce Alnwick, still holding out, where he
made a useful contribution to the siege. When Alnwick too surrendered on 6
January 1463, Somerset accompanied the King to London. On 10 March he
received a general pardon. As soon as Parliament met, his attainder was reversed,
and he was restored to 'all estates, honours, dignities, styles and titles [and] his
name and fame.' The rolls of Parliament record that Edward's intention was 'that
thereby, of very gentleness and the noble honour that ought to be grounded in

every gentleman, he should have been [e]stablished in firm faith and truth unto his Highness.'[2] He was also given an annuity of £222 and a similar sum in cash for immediate expenses. His brother-in-law, Sir Henry Lewis, also had his attainder reversed, his mother, the dowager Duchess, received an annuity, and his brother Edmund was released from the Tower of London.

Edward was undeterred by the behaviour of Sir Ralph Percy. Placed in command of Bamburgh and Dunstanburgh in March, Sir Ralph betrayed his trust by immediately handing them over to a new Lancastrian force of French and Scots. Yet the King was convinced that Somerset was sincere and genuinely wanted a reconciliation.

If Lancastrians were horrified by the Duke deserting Henry VI, Yorkists were deeply alarmed by Edward's intimacy with him. Gregory records wonderingly in his chronicle:

> And the king made full much of him; in so much that he lodged with the king in his own bed many nights, and sometimes rode a hunting behind the king, the king having about him not passing six horse[men] at the most and yet three were the duke's men. The king loved him well, but the duke thought treason under fair cheer and words, as it appeared.

One should not read any hint of homosexuality into Somerset being 'lodged' in Edward's bed. Until the present century hospitable peasants in some parts of Europe would invite guests to share the family bed, and during the fifteenth century even monarchs owned very little furniture. The royal bed would have been distinguished for its size and rich materials – coverlets of silk and fur, down pillows – besides being swathed in elaborate curtains to keep out the draughts of winter. Indeed, it was such a precious object that Richard III took his with him on campaign, his money chest concealed underneath in a secret compartment.

At Whitsun King Edward staged a tournament at Westminster for Somerset, 'that he should see some manner sport of chivalry', during which the Duke impressed spectators by wearing a straw hat instead of a helmet.

During the months when the Duke of Somerset was the guest of Edward IV, Lord Hastings must have been closely involved in entertaining him. The nature of his post as chamberlain and proximity to the King would have brought him into contact with the Duke on many occasions. Presumably he watched him climbing into Edward's bed. Since he was responsible for organizing the royal amusements – to such an extent that he was later considered to be a bad influence – he had to arrange for this most important guest to take part in them too. No doubt he accompanied the King and the Duke on hunting parties, and probably on whoring parties too – Edward's favourite pastime. Undeniably, king, duke and chamberlain had a good deal in common, as virile soldiers who indulged a compulsive taste for wenching. (Somerset had an illegitimate son by a certain Joan Hill, from whom the Dukes of Beaufort descend.) Even so, William would have been less than human not to fear for the safety of his master; a swift dagger thrust from the Duke might only too easily put an end to King Edward IV.

Few at the Yorkist court can have forgotten Somerset's bloodstained record as the principal Lancastrian commander. His victory at Wakefield had been accompanied by a notoriously vicious slaughter, as had been that at the second Battle of St Albans – after his savage northern army's pillaging march south. Despite the material rewards, his new-found loyalty seemed barely credible to many contemporary observers, if the chroniclers can be believed, and we know now that the pull of the Duke's old allegiance to Henry VI was very strong indeed. Moreover, the chroniclers also make it clear that Somerset had a reputation for being revengeful, hot-tempered and violent. As one of Edward's bodyguard, Ralph Hastings must also have shared his brother's misgivings. But voicing them to the King, if either ever dared, can have made no difference.

When the King rode up to Yorkshire during the summer of 1463, 'to see and understand the disposition of the people of the North', according to Gregory, he 'took with him the duke of Somerset, and 200 of his men well horsed and well a-harnessed. And the said duke, Harry of Somerset, and his men were made the king's guard, for the king had that duke in much favour and trusted him well. But the guard of him was as men should put a lamb among wolves or malicious beasts; but Almighty God was the shepherd.' (Only Gregory could compare Edward IV to a lamb.)

Just how astonishing Edward's treatment of Somerset appeared to contemporaries may be seen from an incident during their journey to Yorkshire. When they reached Northampton on 25 July, uproar broke out. Locals had neither forgotten nor forgiven the town's sack by the Lancastrian army in 1460. Whatever the King might think, the men of Northampton and the country round about were furious when they saw that 'the false duke and traitor was so nigh the king's presence and was made his guard.' They tried to lynch him, apparently in the royal apartments at the castle, in front of Edward. He was saved by the King 'with fair speech and great difficulty.' Gregory comments, 'and that was pity, for the saving of his life at that time caused many men's deaths soon after, as ye shall hear.' Edward pacified the Northampton men with a cask of wine which he had placed in the marketplace, and smuggled Somerset out of the town and away to Chirk, a royal castle in Wales where he would be safe. The Duke's men were sent up to Newcastle, to reinforce the garrison.

The pull of dynastic loyalty was too much for Somerset. He could not forget that he was a Beaufort and therefore a member of the House of Lancaster, that his true sovereign was Henry VI. He chose to return to his old allegiance, even if he must have known that this meant danger and privation, and the almost certain prospect of a violent death. Perhaps the lynching party at Northampton had made up his mind for him.

According to Waurin, while in Wales the Duke contacted local Lancastrians and persuaded not less than seventeen leading Welsh landowners to rise for King Henry should the summons come. He also enlisted many gentlemen in southern England, especially in the West Country.

Gregory takes up the tale:

> And this same year [1463] about Christmas that false duke of Somerset, without any leave of the king, stole out of Wales with a privy mesnie towards Newcastle, for he and his men were confederated to have betrayed the said Newcastle. And in the way thitherwards he was espied and like to have been taken beside Durham in his bed. Notwithstanding, he escaped away in his shirt and barefoot, and two of his men were taken. And they took with them that false duke's casket and his harness. And when that his men knew that he was escaped, and his false treason espied, his men stole from Newcastle as very false traitors, and some of them were taken and lost their heads for their labour.

Nevertheless, Somerset succeeded in reaching the Lancastrian garrison at Bamborough where King Henry had now installed himself. The Duke assured Henry that his cause was far from lost. A very serious challenge to the Yorkist régime was being mounted; there were risings in Wales and in Cheshire, traditionally Lancastrian areas.

Although the Welsh and Cheshire revolts were put down with ease, operating from Bamborough the Lancastrians managed to capture several small castles in Northumberland and even in Yorkshire. However, the reinforcements they were expecting to come from France never arrived. Unable to put a proper army into the field, their commanders found themselves reduced to mere guerrilla warfare; Somerset's troops never amounted to more than 500 men-at-arms. Finally, in May 1464, the last Lancastrian fighting force was ambushed and routed near Hexham by Lord Montagu, the Duke being captured. In the words of Polydore Vergil, 'the duke of Somerset, for altering his mind, was beheaded out of hand.' This was at the express command of the King, enraged by his betrayal.

King Edward's bitterness is eloquently reflected in the wording of the Act of Parliament of the following year which posthumously attainted the Duke for a second time. He had acted 'against [the] nature of gentleness and all humanity, remaining secretly and fraudulently in his old insatiate and cruel malice.' One guesses that William Hastings had sympathized with the Northampton men who tried to lynch Somerset, was secretly relieved when he reverted to his Lancastrian allegiance, and rejoiced at the news of his execution. Both contemporary chroniclers and modern historians blame Edward IV for his foolishness in trusting the Duke of Somerset. Yet it is also possible to see his behaviour in another light. It can be argued that the King showed extraordinary imagination as well as magnanimity in his attempt to win over the Duke of Somerset. Where he erred was in underestimating the fierce loyalty of Lancastrians to the uninspiring Henry VI – despite every discouragement, loyalty to the death.[3]

15

King Edward Finds a Queen, 1464

JANE SHORE AND THE LAMBERTS
WILLIAM HASTINGS

At twenty-three, Edward IV was the most eligible bachelor in Europe, 'a man so vigorous and handsome that he might have been made for the pleasures of the flesh' in Commynes' opinion. Many princesses were considered. He rejected, among others, the King of Castile's sister, an insult that Isabella the Catholic never forgave. (Twenty years later her ambassador told Richard III that she 'had turned her heart from England' because of the rejection.) The Earl of Warwick had high hopes of a match with a French princess, having set his heart on an alliance with France. Instead, the King chose an English widow who was four years his senior, and who had two sons by her previous marriage. It was a fateful choice.

This is what Robert Fabyan heard:

> In most secret manner, upon the first day of May [1464], King Edward spoused Elizabeth, late the wife of Sir John Grey, knight, which before time was slain at Towton or York field, which spousals were solemnised early in the morning at a town named Grafton, near Stony Stratford; at which marriage was no persons present but the spouse, the spousess, the duchess of Bedford her mother, the priest, two gentlewomen and a young man to help the priest sing.

After hastily consummating the marriage, the King rejoined his entourage, pretending that he had gone hunting.

Lady Grey had been born in 1437, the eldest child of a courtier, Lord Rivers, and had married Sir John Grey in about 1452. Although he was the heir of Lord Ferrers of Groby, Sir John was comparatively poor and his young wife became one of Queen Margaret's four ladies-in-waiting. Fighting for Lancaster, he had been mortally wounded at the second Battle of St Albans (not at Towton, as Fabyan says), leaving not just a widow but an impecunious widow.

From her portrait at Queen's College, Cambridge, it is obvious that Elizabeth Woodville (her maiden name) was beautiful, despite her golden hair being shaved in front to give her a fashionably high forehead. She had refused to sleep with Edward even when he drew his dagger, telling him that while she might be too base to be a king's wife, she was too good to be his harlot. For months he concealed the marriage, sometimes spending a few days with Elizabeth at her parents' house at Grafton. 'In which season she nightly to his bed was brought, in so secret manner that almost none but her mother was of counsel,' says Fabyan.

During a Great Council held on Michaelmas Day (28 September) at Reading Abbey, according to Gregory the Lords begged the King to be 'wedded and to live under the law of God and the Church, and they would send into some strange land to inquire [for] a queen of good birth.' Edward then admitted that he was already married, presenting his wife to them. The Duke of Clarence and the Earl of Warwick led her into the Abbey chapel where she was acclaimed as Queen of England.

Although Edward IV's best friend might be William Hastings, the Earl of Warwick was still the most powerful man in the kingdom after the King. The Scots Bishop of St Andrews described him as 'governor of the realm of England beneath King Edward'. He was the Crown's richest subject, owning more than a hundred manors in twenty-one counties, and among his offices were those of Captain of Calais, Warden of the Cinque Ports, Warden of the Eastern Marches, and Admiral of England. Sometimes he took the King's place as commander in the field and often his indentures with retainers were unmistakeably 'indentures of war'. (In that which he signed in 1462 with Christopher Lencastre from Westmorland, for being 'well and conveniently horsed, armed and arrayed' and ready to ride with the Earl at all times, Lencastre was to receive five marks a year, while Warwick was to have 'the third of all winnings of war got by the said Christopher.'[1]) Even if the Earl was not called 'The Kingmaker' until Tudor times, he may well have seen himself as one. Certainly contemporaries did; in 1461 the Milanese Prospero di Camulio had reported that 'My lord of Warwick ... has made a new king of the duke of York's son.' The Earl had been lavishly rewarded. So too had his brothers – Lord Montagu was created Earl of

Northumberland and Bishop George Nevill was appointed Lord Chancellor of England.

The announcement at Reading Abbey humiliated the Earl of Warwick. Nothing could have demonstrated more publicly that he no longer enjoyed King Edward's full confidence. Only recently he had been in France negotiating in all good faith a marriage between his master and Louis XI's sister-in-law. His first instinct was to rebel, but he restrained himself.

Some attributed the King's marriage to spells cast by Elizabeth and her mother. In 1469 a neighbour in Northamptonshire, Thomas Wake of Blixworth, was to accuse Duchess Jacquetta of witchcraft. He produced two small leaden figures, supposedly representing the King and Queen, together with another of a 'man of arms' which had been broken in the middle and fastened with wire. So seriously was the charge regarded that Edward had to investigate it personally, assisted by members of the royal council. However, the witnesses whom Wake had brought from Northamptonshire refused to bear him out. Even so, during Richard III's reign it would be alleged in Parliament that the marriage had taken place because of witchcraft by Elizabeth and her mother.[2]

Contemporaries found it all too easy to credit accusations of this sort. The night before the wedding, that of 30 April, was notorious as one of the four sabbaths in the witches' year – the night the Germans called *Walpurgisnacht*. Local tradition said the king first met Elizabeth under an oak tree near Grafton, and everybody knew that witches always held their sabbaths beneath oak trees.

A not very plausible source claims that King Edward's mother, the Duchess of York, was so angry that she threatened to announce publicly that he had been a bastard. No doubt 'Proud Cis' was not exactly mollified by her son's cheerful reassurance that Elizabeth was sure to bear him children since she had some already, 'and by God's Blessed Lady, I am a bachelor and have some too; and so each of us hath a proof that neither of us is like to be barren.'[3] The Duchess argued that he was already betrothed to Elizabeth Lucy, the Earl of Shrewsbury's daughter, a betrothal that invalidated the marriage.

When sent for and questioned, Elizabeth Lucy confessed that she was pregnant by the king, explaining that 'his grace spoke so loving words unto her that she verily hoped he would have married her, and if it had not been for such kind words she would never have showed such kindness to him to let him so kindly get her with child.'

But she also admitted that there had been no betrothal.

Lord Wenlock confided to a Burgundian friend that the marriage had deeply displeased many great lords, together with the better part of the royal council. What they particularly disliked was Elizabeth Woodville's parvenu background, although her father might be Lord Rivers and her mother Jacquetta, Duchess of Bedford. When the Earl of Warwick had captured Rivers – then a Lancastrian – during a raid on Sandwich in 1460, he had reminded him scornfully that 'his father was but a squire', who had emerged from obscurity during Henry V's wars in France, and that he himself had become rich and a lord through a lucky marriage. William Paston, who reports the incident, adds (with considerable irony in the light of future events), 'And my lord of March [Edward] rated him likewise.' They had not been exaggerating.

A gentleman from Northamptonshire, Richard Woodville had begun his career as a servant of Henry VI while his father had been chamberlain to the Duke of Bedford. Reputedly the most handsome man of his time, the younger Woodville had then made his fortune by marrying Bedford's widow, much to the fury of her family, since Jacquetta was a daughter of one of the greatest noblemen in France, the Count of Saint-Pol.

Greedy and self-seeking, a courtier in the very worst sense, Woodville had been created a peer by Henry VI – not the best judge of character. His elevation was seen very differently from that of an amiable and much-liked hero such as William Hastings, who in any case was well connected and had a dash of royal blood. The new Lord Rivers (as he was now known) was generally regarded as an arrogant *arriviste* and blood-sucking parasite who lived shamelessly off his wife's dowry. He and his disagreeable duchess had five sons and seven daughters besides Elizabeth. They could be relied on to exploit their link with the throne.

Queen Elizabeth had inherited her father's avarice as well as his looks. A former lady of the bedchamber to Margaret of Anjou, she was accustomed to court intrigue and determined to secure rich pickings for her parents, for her brothers and sisters, and for her two sons by her first husband.

Very soon the Queen's father was using her influence with the King to offer magnates royal lands or offices in return for marrying one of his children. In September 1464, the same month during which Elizabeth was proclaimed Queen of England, her sister Margaret married the Earl of Arundel's heir. In January her twenty-year-old brother John married the dowager Duchess of Norfolk, who was well into her sixties but possessed a very rich jointure; the horrified author of the *Annales Rerum Anglicarum* called it 'a diabolical match'. By 1467 five more

Woodville sisters had made splendid marriages, their grooms being the Duke of Buckingham and four other peers.[4]

When Prior Botylle of St John's – head of the Knights of Rhodes in England – died in 1468, King Edward tried to bully the Knights into electing his youthful brother-in-law Richard Woodville as the new prior, although the boy was not even a member of their order. There was uproar ('*maxima turbatio*') in the priory at Clerkenwell. However, the brethren ignored the King's request and instead elected Fra' John Langstrother, one of the Earl of Warwick's affinity and henceforward no friend to Edward IV.

The *Annales* were only stating the obvious in recording that the marriages of the Queen's sisters were 'to the great displeasure of the earl of Warwick.' His own enormous family, the Nevills, owed its vast wealth and prestige to having married very rich heirs and heiresses methodically for two generations. Ironically, the Earl himself had no sons but two daughters. Now, because of the social ambitions of the Queen's kindred, it looked as if there would be no one of suitable rank left for them to wed – nor for his nephews and nieces – even though one day his girls were going to inherit the greatest estates in England. Moreover, King Edward stubbornly refused to let them have the most desirable husbands of all, his brothers the Dukes of Clarence and Gloucester.

Still more threatening for Warwick were the dynastic ambitions of Lord Herbert (Henry Tudor's guardian), who was another of Edward's protégés and his principal lieutenant in South Wales. The marriage of the Queen's sister, Mary Woodville, to Herbert's heir in 1466 meant the emergence of a Herbert–Woodville axis; now Lord Herbert could count on Woodville support in his feud with Warwick over lands in Glamorgan, and perhaps on the Queen intervening with King Edward. At the same time it was obvious that Herbert's ward Henry Percy, heir to the late Earl of Northumberland, was going to marry one of his daughters, in which case there was a strong possibility that Henry would be restored to his father's confiscated earldom and the Percy estates. If this happened, then the Nevills would lose a vast chunk of what they had gained in the north. Yet another of Herbert's son-in-laws, Lord Shrewsbury, even had a claim to the earldom of Warwick. The Earl could see a very menacing future indeed.

As an alderman, John Lambert must have attended Queen Elizabeth's coronation in Westminster Abbey at Whitsun 1465 and the ensuing banquet in Westminster Hall. The day before the coronation, she had been lodged in the Tower of London, being taken by horse litter to the Abbey on Sunday for her crowning, escorted by nearly fifty knights of the Bath, specially created for the occasion. (Among the latter were two of the Woodvilles.) Most significantly, the Earl of Warwick was absent from the ceremony. However, her mother's brother, Jacques de Luxembourg, Count of Richebourg, brought a delegation of Burgundian knights. Next day there was a tournament at Westminster in the presence of the Queen, Lord Stanley bearing away the prize – a ring with a ruby.

Jane Shore and her husband may well have been among the spectators since such entertainments were avidly attended by Londoners. There would be plenty of gossip about the upstart Queen with her arrogance and her greedy relations. There is no need to guess that the Shores and the Lamberts were delighted that five aldermen had been among the Knights of the Bath whom King Edward had created for her coronation, and that one of them, Hugh Wyche, was a mercer. Gregory comments proudly, 'it is a great worship unto all the City.' It must have aroused John Lambert's wildest ambitions, even though real gentlemen despised 'City Knights', however rich they might be.

In any case John was favourably inclined towards Edward IV for sound financial reasons. In May 1464 he had been granted £418 16s 2d from the Southampton Customs dues, in repayment of a loan. One is constantly surprised by his wealth and his skill at not just surviving but prospering during a severe recession.

Elizabeth Woodville had no reservations about her fitness to be Queen. In March 1466 the Lord Leo of Rozmital in Bohemia, brother-in-law to King George Podiebrad, visited the English court and was staggered by her hauteur. She dined publicly in silence and during the three-hour meal all the ladies in attendance – including her mother and King Edward's sister Margaret – remained kneeling, though the last two were allowed to rise to their feet after the first course. Then the court danced before her in silence, Margaret curtseying to the Queen from time to time. No doubt such silence was customary at the English court in the fifteenth century and previous consorts had been served in silence, but they had been kings' daughters. Everyone present was aware of the Queen's 'low extraction' and that she had been a woman of the bedchamber.

Not merely Elizabeth's brothers and sisters but her parents profited from her elevation. In 1466 her father was made Lord Treasurer of England and promoted to earl. Robert Fabyan, then an apprentice to the great draper Sir Thomas Cook, recalled long afterwards that in those days 'many murmerous tales ran in the City atween th'earl of Warwick and the queen's blood' – tales of growing hatred.

The Queen brought problems for Lord Hastings as well as for the Earl of Warwick. In More's words, 'women commonly not of malice but of nature, hate such as their husbands love.' Elizabeth resented William's influence over Edward, in particular his being 'secretly familiar with the king in wanton company' – a notorious boon companion in drinking and womanizing.

Moreover, when William knew Elizabeth before her marriage to Edward – as her neighbour in Leicestershire – he had not shown himself in his best light, even though he helped her do legal battle with a grasping mother-in-law over her sons' inheritance. Less than a month before the secret wedding, 'Dame Elizabeth Grey' (as she then was) and Hastings had signed an indenture that made financial provision for a marriage between her son Thomas Grey and any daughter born to William or to his brother Ralph Hastings within the next five years; should Thomas Grey die or if no daughters were born, Lord Hastings must be paid 500 marks (just over £232). Although the agreement was overtaken by events, one historian suggests that such tough bargaining may partly explain the Queen's dislike of William in future years.[5]

Only in retrospect would it be seen that the marriage of Edward IV and Elizabeth Woodville had undermined the entire structure of the Yorkist régime by creating a threat to the interests of the Earl of Warwick and the Nevill clan. Perhaps it was inevitable that the King and the Earl, his 'over mighty subject', would eventually fall out with each other, but Edward undoubtedly hastened the process by taking such a wife and by showing so much favour to her greedy relatives. However, despite the fragility of its foundations and the increasing dissension, the Yorkists still appeared to be totally in control of England. Across the Channel, Lancastrian exiles knew the meaning of despair.

16

Dr Morton in Exile, 1464

JOHN MORTON

'My lord', wrote Sir John Fortescue on 13 December 1464 to the Earl of Ormond, 'here beeth with the queen, the dukes of Exeter and Somerset, and his brother which – and also Sir John Courtenay – beeth descended from the House of Lancaster. Also here beeth my lord Privy Seal Dr John Morton . . .' Fortescue then names half a dozen knights, adding that there are many 'worshipful squires and also clerks.' Most of these had fled from Scotland across the North Sea in July, packed into little sailing barges.

They had found shelter in Lorraine at the château of Koeur-la-Petite near St Mihiel-sur-Bar, on the right bank of the Meuse not far from Commercy. The château belonged to Margaret of Anjou's father, the *'bon roi Réné'*, titular king of Naples, who gave her 6,000 French crowns a year, her sole income. 'We beeth all in great poverty, but yet the queen sustaineth us in meat and drink, so as we beeth not in extreme necessity,' Sir John told Lord Ormond. 'Her Highness may do no more to us than she doth.' He continued sadly, 'in all this country is no man that will or may lend you any money, have ye never so great need.' Koeur was the Lancastrian court in exile, a precursor of the Jacobite St Germain. Although the rightful king was still skulking amid the wild Cumbrian hills, a Prince of Wales 'over the water' lived here with his mother.

In 1465 Harry Holland, Duke of Exeter, grew bored with Koeur and went to Bruges, where Commynes saw him walking barefoot behind he Duke of Burgundy's train, and begging his bread from door to door without revealing who he was. The nobleman, who once had never ridden out with less than 200 horsemen, can have found little to eat if, as in English towns, from a quarter to a third of the inhabitants of Bruges were destitute. Meanwhile, at home his duchess Anne had obtained possession of all his estates and was living with her lover, Thomas St Leger, in the Duke's favourite manor of Dartington. Luckily for Exeter, he was recognized and given a small pension.

Exeter had followed Edmund Beaufort to Bruges. Edmund, who since the beheading of his brother at Hexham styled himself Duke of Somerset, had left England with his brother John Beaufort and come by way of Paris to Koeur, arriving in the autumn of 1464. He then joined the army of the future Duke Charles of Burgundy in the War of the Public Weal against King Louis, during the summer of 1465. He lived at Bruges briefly but soon attached himself to the Burgundian court. However, when Charles married Edward IV's sister, he told Somerset and Exeter to keep away from his court to avoid embarrassment; William Paston reported from the court at Bruges that Somerset had gone back 'to Queen Margaret that was, and shall no more come here again, nor be helpen by the duke.' In reality, Somerset and Exeter never returned to Koeur, though they always stayed in close contact with the Queen, while Charles continued to pay them pensions discreetly – he did not forget his close kinship with the House of Lancaster.

Depressing news from England had reached the exiles during the summer of 1465. King Henry had been captured in Lancashire after wandering for over a year from refuge to refuge in the wild fastnesses of northern England. Betrayed by a monk and chased from his dinner at the house of a sympathizer not far from Clitheroe, he was caught in a wood near a ford through the Ribble called Bungerly Hippingstones, deserted by all save two priests and a groom. In Sir John Fortescue's words, 'he fell into the bloody hands of his deadly enemies, his own subjects.' His feet tied to his stirrups beneath the belly of his horse, a battered straw hat on his head, the former King of England was paraded through Cheapside and Cornhill on his way to imprisonment in the Tower of London. He was led by Ralph Hastings, until recently Keeper of the Lions, an irony that is unlikely to have escaped the London crowds. He would spend the next five years in not uncomfortable captivity in the Tower, where he was even allowed visitors. Henry's life would be perfectly safe as long as his son stayed alive.

Despite being over seventy, a very great age in those days, the Lancastrian 'Lord Chancellor' Sir John Fortescue was Queen Margaret's chief adviser. He bombarded Louis XI with letters and memoranda, whose constant refrain was that Edward IV intended to invade France and that the only way to stop him was to put Henry VI back on the English throne. The Queen harped on the same tune, writing to Louis in 1465, in a burst of wishful thinking, that fighting had already broken out between Warwick and Edward. According to Milanese sources, her brother the Duke of Calabria, when dining with the French King early in 1467, told him that as he was so fond of the Earl of Warwick he ought to try to restore Margaret and be certain of peace with England.[1]

In addition, Fortescue – he describes himself as 'a certain ancient knight, being Chancellor to the King of England, who also in that miserable time did there remain in exile' – was educating the Prince of Wales. For the boy's benefit he wrote his famous book *De laudibus legum Angliae* which, while extolling the Common Law, is a nostalgic paean in praise of English life as a whole and of how fortunate its people are when compared with those of France. It is also a work of propaganda. 'During the cruel rage of the late mortal wars within the realm of England when the most virtuous and godly King Henry VI . . . was forced to fly the land' are its opening words.

Dr Morton, a colleague since the Parliament of Devils, no doubt collaborated with Sir John in diplomatic affairs and in writing the *De laudibus*. Fortescue recalls 'when I was abiding in Paris', and it is quite possible that Morton was there with him. Perhaps the pair used 'Law French', still a written language at home if full of archaicisms and English words, to communicate with the locals (As late as the 1730s a former Lord Chancellor said that some English law could only be understood by reading it in French.) In any case, both spoke Latin – the language of diplomacy.

A supporter even more aged than Fortescue arrived at Koeur in 1464 – George Ashby, who had been born in 1390 and was a former Keeper of the Signet to Henry VI and Queen Margaret. He had spent the previous year in the Fleet prison. He says he was

> Writing to their signet full forty year,
> As well beyond the sea as on this side

He wrote a poem, 'The Active Policy of a Prince' for Prince Edward's edification, exhorting him to live on his revenues when king – hinting that he must avoid his father's mistakes.

Other leading members of the circle at Koeur-la-Petite were Thomas Bird, formerly Bishop of St Aasaph, a shadowy figure whome Edward IV had deprived of his see, and three knights from the old Lancastrian court. These were Sir William Vaux, Sir Robert Whittingham, and Sir Edmund Hampden (the Prince's chamberlain). The first two had married ladies of the Queen's household in the days of her prosperity, while Hampden had been her carver. The exiled court's numbers never seem to have sunk below fifty.

Clearly Margaret of Anjou inspired deep loyalty. Her courage verged on the sublime. She had endured terrible defeats, had suffered storms and shipwreck, had fallen into the hands of brigands. She was so poor when she arrived in Flanders that she had to travel to the Burgundian court in a farm cart, dressed in rags – knowing that Yorkist agents were planning an ambush. But nothing could shake her determination to rescue her son's heritage.

Edward, Prince of Wales was handsome, intelligent and bloodthirsty. In 1467 the Duke of Milan was informed that 'This boy though still only thirteen years of age, talks of nothing but cutting off heads or making war.' He 'applied himself wholly to feats of arms, much delighting to ride upon wild and unbroken horses, not sparing with spurs to break their fierceness,' says Fortescue, who knew him well. 'He practised also sometimes with the pike, sometimes with the sword . . .' Sir John adds, a little apologetically, that it was only natural for him to give his sparring partners such savage blows. However, Edward of Lancaster was not always well and had been so dangerously ill during the previous year that after his recovery Queen Margaret had gone on pilgrimage to give thanks at the shrine near Nancy of St Nicholas de Port – the patron saint of Lorraine.

Sir John Fortescue regularly sent 'writings' to England, which depicted the cause of Lancaster as that of firm, honest and, above all, law-abiding government. He had realized that the Queen's policy of relying on foreign aid alone, for the French and Scots to restore her husband by force of arms, was simply not enough. The Yorkists had triumphed in 1460–61 after systematically exploiting discontent at both national and local level over a long period, and then turning it into organized rebellion under their leadership. The Lancastrians must learn to do the same.

Beyond question, by the end of the decade there was plenty of fresh discontent in England. Law and order were breaking down all over again, just as they had done under Henry VI; King Edward had failed to provide the reform he had promised and Yorkist magnates were exploiting their powers ruthlessly. In the eyes of many, the Woodvilles and their friends had inherited the mantle of King Henry's greedy court party. When Edward approved a programme to rebuild the City's walls in 1467 – Mr Alderman Lambert contributed 8s 4d – it undoubtedly reflected an atmosphere of growing uneasiness.

At the same time, more than a few observers must have seen the menacing implications for the future of that ever-widening rift between the Earl of Warwick and Edward IV. An increasing number of Englishmen – just how many will never be known – began to communicate with Queen Margaret and the Duke of Somerset, if only because they wanted to hedge their bets against a far from inconceivable change of régime. There were also those secret Lancastrian diehards who had never gone into exile, and some of them were among the very greatest in the land.

Meanwhile, there was mounting hope at Koeur-la-Petite. So shrewd a judge of human nature as John Morton must surely have listened with fascination to reports of the growing resentment of quite such an arrogant and over-mighty subject as the Earl of Warwick.

17

Lady Margaret
Entertains King Edward, 1468

MARGARET BEAUFORT

In 1466 Edward IV presented Henry Stafford and Margaret Beaufort with a palatial house in Surrey. Just outside the village of Woking and on the banks of the River Wey, this was to become their favourite residence. Once 'Woking Old Hall' had belonged to Margaret's grandmother, though in recent years it had been a manor of the turncoat Duke of Somerset. The King's generosity was much more than just a mark of favour to Stafford. The gift showed that Edward was prepared to forgive his bad taste in having married a Beaufort. Sir Henry and Lady Margaret moved into the house during the early spring of 1467.

Although so near London, fifteenth-century Surrey was in many ways a surprisingly remote county, much of it dense woodland or heath, while some areas were without roads. A good deal was left untilled because of sandy soil. However, Woking (nowadays known as Old Woking) was only a few hours' journey from the capital, being close to the Thames, down which the City could be reached by barge. The easiest way to the Thames from Old Woking, and the most comfortable, especially in wet weather when one could travel under an awning, was by boat along the little River Wey which flows into it.

Despite becoming a favourite palace of the Tudors, 'Woking Old Hall' was left to fall into decay during the seventeenth century, so that some overgrown rubble enclosed by a moat is all that remains of it today. The parish church, where Henry and Margaret occasionally heard Mass – normally they preferred to hear it in their chapel at the hall – survives. They may well have paid for the church's rebuilding since much of the fabric dates from their time. In the couple's day the house was unmistakeably the residence of great nobles. A big castellated manor built around a courtyard, it was entered across a drawbridge over a moat and through a gatehouse. A second, inner gatehouse led from the court into the main range which contained a dining hall, chapel and private chambers. There were orchards, gardens and a deer park, together with a hunting lodge at Brookwood nearby.[1]

'Her estate administration must rank as one of the most efficient of the entire middle ages' is the verdict of Margaret's recent biographers.[2] Clearly she spent much of her day checking accounts and leases – she was far too vigilant for any of them to dare to try cheating her. Religious observance occupied a good deal of her time. Rising at 5 a.m., she heard several Masses before breakfast, besides saying the Office (probably the Little Hours of the Virgin) during the day, as well as meditating and reading – aloud, as was the normal practice. She also looked after the local poor and sick, feeding them and changing their bandages, arranging for the children of needy mothers to be boarded out. She kept singing boys for her chapel and may have had a *schola cantorum* – she certainly maintained one in her later years. As for relaxation, she is known to have hunted and probably went in for hawking too.

The couple's life at Woking was conducted like that of a small court, a replica in miniature of the King's. Their household included a staff of nearly fifty servants, many of them 'gentlemen born', such as the receiver-general, Reginald Bray, a man whose family had come with the Normans. As a great noblewoman, Margaret ranked with her peers and was treated with due ceremony. Even when by herself she dined in splendour in her hall, at a high table on a raised dais, presiding over her household and retainers.

They entertained lavishly and kept a good table. Most of the food came from the neighbourhood; luxuries were ordered from London and brought up the Thames, though sometimes they were purchased at Guildford. The county town, Guildford, was very near Woking, and they visited it frequently. On one occasion Henry gave his kinsman Lord Berners lunch there.

The right relatives were a factor of vital importance. This was a very dangerous period indeed in which to be a Beaufort. The King's attempted reconciliation with the Duke of Somerset in 1462 had embraced the entire Beaufort family; although Margaret was not included in the general hand-out, she may well have received some gesture of esteem. But Somerset's defection had enraged Edward IV, and all Beauforts were in disgrace. The Duke's mother had her annuity taken away for a second time and was sent to prison. Margaret was lucky to escape scot free. It must have seemed as though she could scarcely hope for any favours from King Edward.

'She was no recluse but a veteran of bruising political battles', Margaret's biographers observe with some justice. She must have discussed the situation constantly with her husband. Both knew only too well that should he make the wrong decision he could lose his life, while she might forfeit her wealth and her liberty and find herself under house arrest in a convent.

After the King's marriage in 1464 they were protected to some extent by the Staffords' links with the Woodville family.[3] Lord Berners and his son acquired prominent posts in the Queen's household, the former becoming her chamberlain. Then in 1466 Henry's young nephew, the Duke of Buckingham, was married off to the Queen's sister, Katherine Woodville. Buckingham was the premier duke of England and among the richest landowners in the realm. Naturally his uncle was expected to come to court. This is almost certainly the reason why Edward granted Henry Stafford a residence that was so near to both London and Windsor. (Windsor could also be reached quickly from Woking by boat.)

The latest study of Margaret Beaufort argues convincingly that her marriage to Henry was a happy, harmonious one. Husband and wife had many interests in common, sharing their duties and their amusements. From their accounts it is clear that the couple worked together on the administration of their estates and on running their household. They also hunted regularly together, their quarry being generally fallow-buck, and they made sporting tours into Hampshire, where there were some famous deer parks. It is significant that they invariably celebrated their wedding anniversary, 3 January. A London poulterer supplied curlew, plover and larks for the anniversary of 1471.

Margaret's biographers emphasize her constant activity, whether in going to court or in touring her estates, and her skill at managing her property. She and Henry frequently visited the estates, as in 1467 when they toured her West Country manors from August to October, escorted by a small 'riding household' of forty retainers. The couple stayed at Curry Rivel and at Langport in Somerset, and then at Sampford Peverell in Devon, which was to become one of Margaret's favourite houses. The tour was a businesslike inspection of farms to check that they were being properly managed. Jones and Underwood (from whom these details are taken) point out that during the fifteenth century, even in the most harmonious marriages, 'it was unusual for the wife to travel so much with her husband rather than supervise affairs at home.'

Sir Henry and Lady Margaret also visited London and Windsor, no doubt very much aware that they had been given their fine house at Woking so that they would be able to come to court. In May 1468 the couple travelled down to the City by boat, staying at the Mitre Inn in Cheapside. Apparently this was because they wanted to be in London when King Edward made a public announcement of his intention to invade France – an invasion which, however, would be postponed for the time being. On at least one occasion (in May 1467) Sir Henry was summoned to a meeting of the royal council at Mortlake Palace. Yet, apart from the undeniably generous grant of Woking Old Hall, the King showed him comparatively little favour. It may well be that Edward felt he could never quite trust Henry Stafford because of that Beaufort wife with her Lancastrian cousins. There was still a Lancastrian party, even though its leaders might have fled abroad.

The couple's activities were to some extent limited by Henry's poor health. He was frequently unwell. It has been conjectured that his malady was 'St Anthony's Fire', erysipelas, which was then thought to be a form of leprosy. Revealingly, he joined the confraternity of the leper hospital at Burton Lazars in Leicestershire, while Margaret was noted for her devotion to St Anthony Abbot – the patron saint of those who were afflicted by skin diseases.

Margaret's son Henry Tudor remained in the household of his father's old enemy, William Herbert. As a zealous Yorkist, and Edward IV's most important and most trusted supporter in Wales, the latter had been created Lord Herbert – the first Welshman to become a peer. His own son had recently married one of the Queen's sisters, which therefore linked him to the Staffords through the Woodvilles. The connection ensured that Herbert was well disposed towards Sir Henry and his wife. During their West Country tour in 1467 they found time to visit young Henry Tudor, they and their household taking the ferry over the River Severn from Bristol to Chepstow in October. They spent a week at Lord Herberts' great castle of Raglan. This was Margaret's first meeting with the boy for several years, although it was not as if he were a prisoner; the children of magnates were often separated from the parents in this way since it was common practice to board them out in some noble household as part of their education. Moreover, despite his being landless and no longer an earl, because of his mother's wealth 'the lord Henry of Richmond' had been betrothed to Herbert's daughter Mary.

During the following year Margaret's former brother-in-law Jasper Tudor landed in North Wales and tried to relieve Harlech Castle, which had held out against the Yorkists for seven years. The last Lancastrian stronghold, its garrison's defiance was the inspiration for that magnificent Welsh song 'The March of the Men of Harlech'. But Jasper's little army was soon routed and on 14 August Dafydd ap Evan ap Einion, captain of Harlech, finally surrendered to Lord Herbert. It has been suggested that the eleven-year-old Henry Tudor accompanied his guardian on the campaign, witnessing the surrender, as there is evidence that his mother was worried about his safety.

A few months later Edward IV paid Sir Henry and Lady Margaret the ultimate compliment of a visit. On 20 December Stafford met the King and his retinue at Guildford, taking them to Woking for a hunt. What they hunted is unknown; while it is most likely to have been a fallow-buck, it could have been a stag, since some red deer were kept in the park, or even a wild boar – the latter were occasionally recorded in Surrey during the fifteenth century. The hunt would have been a far more stately business than in modern times, with much blowing of horns and ritual, the King being invited to dispatch the quarry with a sword.

Afterwards King Edward dined with his hosts in the hunting lodge at Brookwood. They ate in a tent of purple sarsenet, serenaded by the royal minstrels. Among the fish served on a new pewter dinner service (specially bought in London for the occasion) were conger eel, lampreys and 700 oysters. Margaret wore velvet, holland and brabant cloth.[4] Probably the couple tried to secure their guest's help in resisting a claim to their Westmorland estates, which had been made by Nevill supporters with the backing of the Earl of Warwick.

Although this was the first time Margaret Beaufort had met Edward IV, nothing could have demonstrated more clearly that she was still numbered among the great of the land than her hunting party at Woking.

18

'My lord of Oxford
is commit to the Tower', 1468

LORD OXFORD · JOHN LAMBERT

At least one peer had always remained staunchly Lancastrian and was ready to join in any rising against the House of York. As a younger son, John de Vere can never have expected to succeed to the earldom of Oxford. However, when his father, the twelfth Earl, and his elder brother Sir Aubrey were executed, Edward IV allowed him to inherit the title and the estates. But the King deceived himself in thinking that John's loyalty could be purchased so easily. The Veres were one of the only great magnate families that always remained consistently loyal to the House of Lancaster throughout the Wars of the Roses.

If they did not fight at Towton in 1461, spending the winter on their broad Essex acres, we know that the Veres were horrified by the defeat and ruin of Henry VI. They concealed their dismay, however, even when the coveted office of Great Chamberlain of England (hereditary in their family from Norman times until 1399) was given to Warwick. In 1460 old Lord Oxford had been excused from attending any parliaments or councils on account of 'infirmities', an excuse to avoid sitting in a House of Lords dominated by York. Even so, despite being 'far stricken in age' (he was in his fifties), he rallied sufficiently to go to London for Edward IV's first Parliament in the autumn of 1461, though he left before it had finished sitting. He went back to Essex with Aubrey to plan a rebellion.

Even before the end of 1461 there were rumours that Lord Oxford was behind a series of raids on the East Anglian coast, by Lancastrian privateers operating from French ports. Early in the following year, letters between Oxford, Sir Aubrey and Queen Margaret were intercepted, which revealed a conspiracy to overthrow Edward IV. Arrested on 12 February, the Veres were taken to the Tower, tried by the court of the Constable of England (John Tiptoft, Earl of Worcester) and executed without delay. One source says that Aubrey had accused his father of organizing a Lancastrian landing on the Essex coast, but such treachery conflicts with what is known of his character.

The Veres seem to have involved as many neighbours as possible. Three other East Anglian gentlemen, perhaps members of their affinity, were arrested and condemned with them: Sir Thomas Tuddenham of Oxburgh Hall in Norfolk, Sir William Tyrrell of Gipping in Suffolk, and John Montgomery of Faulkbourn in Essex. (Tuddenham had been treasurer of King Henry's household and keeper of the King's wardrobe.) The Abbot and monks of Bury St Edmund's were placed under arrest but escaped with a fine.

Sir Aubrey died first, on 20 February, drawn on a hurdle from Westminster to Tower Hill. On a scaffold eight feet high, specially built to give the crowd a better view, he suffered the statutory penalty for treason. Hanged until half choked, he was cut down to be disembowelled and castrated still alive, the remains being beheaded and cut in four; his entrails and offal were burnt on the executioner's fire but the head and quarters – boiled in salt and coated in pitch to stop the birds eating them – were stuck up on Tower Bridge and other places. Aubrey had been an attractive personality. In 1460 William Paston had observed of him 'he is great with the Queen', while years after, despite having remarried, his widow asked to be interred 'where the body of my dear heart and late husband resteth buried.' The East Anglian gentlemen were executed three days later.

Old Lord Oxford died on the same tall scaffold on 26 February. Waurin says he was tied to a chair in front of a great fire and had his entrails wound out of his body and burnt, after which he was castrated, what was left of him being thrown on the fire.[1] In fact the Earl's sentence would have been commuted to beheading, his privilege as a peer. Waurin's informant was probably a Burgundian unfamiliar with English customs, who had caught a glimpse of Sir Aubrey's execution.

Lady Oxford was punished too, being kept under house arrest until the late spring. However, Edward officially forgave her in a document dated 28 March in which, because of 'the humble, good and faithful disposition of Elizabeth, countess of Oxford, and the age, weakness and continued infirmity of body of the said Elizabeth, and the true faith which she bears us', he accepts her as his 'faithful subject' – permitting her release from any form of custody or surveillance.

The King began to build up the powers of other landowners in East Anglia, to diminish the standing of the Veres. The Archbishop of Canterbury's brother, Lord Bourchier – their neighbour at Little Easton, who had recently been created

Earl of Essex and given confiscated Lancastrian estates – was soon countering their influence throughout the region. Henry Bourchier, steward of the royal household from 1463 until 1471, was an old Yorkist workhorse, born at the beginning of the century. Although far more of an administrator than a soldier, he would cross John de Vere's path on at least one occasion.

Another rival whom King Edward transformed into a great East Anglian magnate was Lady Oxford's cousin, Sir John Howard, the squire of Stoke-by-Nayland in Suffolk. This brutally capable careerist and servant of the new dynasty would eventually become the first Howard Duke of Norfolk. He too was going to cross John's path.

Despite killing his father and brother, ill-treating his mother and favouring his rivals, Edward IV assumed somewhat optimistically that the young John de Vere would be loyal to the House of York. Since John's father had not been attainted but only condemned to death by the Constable's Court (which had no powers to confiscate a peerage), he was allowed to call himself Earl of Oxford. He was also able to inherit the family estates, though he had to wait until June 1464 before he was permitted to reoccupy Hedingham and Wivenhoe. During the parliament of that year he petitioned the King to reverse the attainder of his great-grandfather, the Duke of Ireland, which had been the work of 'Henry, Earl of Derby [Henry IV] acting against the law of God and of the Land, his faith and his allegiance.' No wording could have been more tactfully anti-Lancastrian, and the King granted his petition, restoring valuable estates to him.[2]

Marks of royal favour followed. At Queen Elizabeth's coronation in May 1465, Lord Oxford officiated not only as her chamberlain but, Warwick being absent, as Lord Great Chamberlain of England – that long-lost family dignity which was still coveted so desperately by the Veres. In addition the Earl was among the Knights of the Bath whom Edward created in honour of Elizabeth's crowning. He was even given a Nevill bride, Warwick's youngest sister, Margaret, becoming like Lord Hastings the King's first cousin by marriage.

Nevertheless, in retrospect it is quite obvious that young Lord Oxford nursed an abiding if well-concealed hatred for the entire House of York, and that he was an irreconcilable Lancastrian. He would have noticed with satisfaction the

A colleague of Lord Hastings, the Earl of Essex (in his robes as a Knight of the Garter) who was Treasurer of England. From a brass of 1483 at Little Easton, Essex.

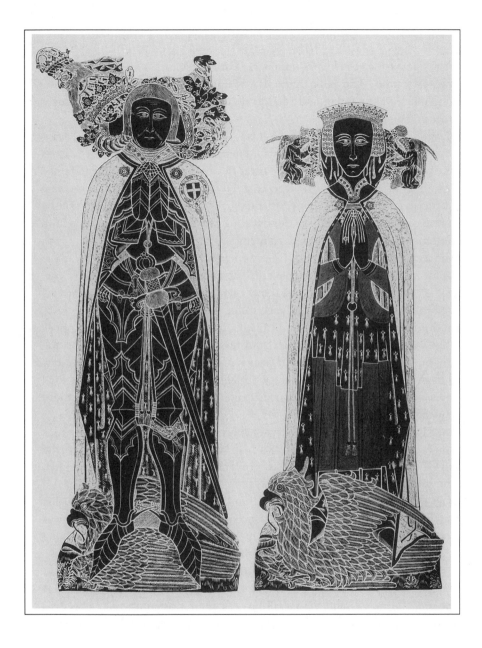

country's increasing restiveness under the Yorkist régime, not least because of Edward IV's taxes. The King himself was uncomfortably aware that he was growing much less popular, and tried to defuse the situation at the parliament that met in the spring of 1467.

Edward's attitude towards Parliament was simple enough. He used it to establish his legal right to the throne, to destroy enemies by attainder, and to raise extra income when money was needed for a war or putting down rebellions. He had men in the House of Commons who ensured its co-operation, MPs who were royal officials or retainers of trusted friends such as Hastings, and he always took very good care to treat it with the utmost courtesy. This time the Speaker whom the Commons elected was John Say, a member of his council.

'John Say and ye, Sirs, come to this my court of parliament for the commons of this my land, the cause why I have called and summoned this my present parliament is that I purpose to live upon my own and not to charge my subjects', Edward told them reassuringly. At face value, the words 'to live upon my own' meant that he would finance his government from his own revenues and impose no more new taxes. However, his handsome promise failed to soothe the Commons, who complained of increasing lawlessness throughout the land – murders and riots – and, by inference, of his failure to stop them. They demanded new measures to deal with piracy, Scottish raids and the emergence of even more anarchy than usual in Ireland.

Oxford must also have watched with increasing excitement the dangerous division between the King and the Earl of Warwick which had followed the Woodville marriage, observing their growing estrangement. In May 1467, without warning, Edward rode to Archbishop George Nevill's house at Charing Cross just outside the City and ordered him to surrender the great seal – dismissing him from his office of Lord Chancellor. Sacking Warwick's brother was a declaration of hostility so far as the Nevills were concerned, even if the King did not want an outright rupture with them.

In any case, by then Edward was showing a preference for Burgundy as England's principal ally, rejecting Warwick's advocacy of France. 'It is a question of who shall be master and who shall be servant,' reported one of Louis XI's ambassadors. If Edward should definitely choose Burgundy, it would be a bitter

Sir John Fogge, Hastings' colleague as Treasurer of the Household but his enemy as a Woodville kinsman. Later he plotted against Richard III. From the remains of a brass of 1499 at Ashford, Kent.

humiliation for the Earl. We know from the Croyland chronicler that Warwick hated Duke Charles of Burgundy 'with a most deadly hatred', though precisely why is not recorded. But in July 1468 King Edward's sister Margaret of York married the Duke of Burgundy. (John Paston, who was present at her wedding in Bruges, marvelled at the Burgundian court – 'I heard never of none like it, save King Arthur's court.') The marriage completed the rift between king and king-maker.

In June 1468 the authorities had arrested John Cornelius, a tailor, at the little port of Queenborough in Kent where he was about to board a ship to France. He was a servant of Sir Robert Whittingham, a well-known supporter of Queen Margaret, who was with the Lancastrian garrison of Harlech – still holding out, though at its last gasp. Apparently Cornelius was returning to Margaret after delivering letters to a Lancastrian cell in London. He was 'burnt in the feet' until he named them. They ranged from knights and squires to rich merchants.

Among the names was that of a servant of Lord Wenlock, John Hawkins. After being 'set upon the brake [rack] called the duke of Exeter's daughter', in his agony Hawkins accused a leading City alderman, Sir Thomas Cook, of treason. Cook, a draper and former mayor, was an old friend of the King, having lent him very large sums of money. Hawkins even hinted at the involvement of Lord Wenlock.

Queen Elizabeth's mother, the Duchess Jacquetta, coveted a wonderful tapes-try at Cook's house, 'wrought in most richest wise with gold of the whole story of the siege of Jerusalem' (which had cost him £800, according to his apprentice Fabyan), but he refused to let the Duchess have it 'at her pleasure and price.' She and her husband saw their chance of revenge when Cook was rearrested in 1468 after Jasper Tudor's raid and sent to the Tower.

Lord Rivers and his cousin Sir John Fogge, treasurer of the royal household, sent men to break into Cook's house and plunder it. They stole jewels, a great silver gilt salt and quantities of plate together with his tapestries – not just the Jerusalem arras but others too, depicting the Passion, Judgement Day and the lives of King Nebuchadnezzar and Alexander the Great. Very inconveniently, Hawkins then withdrew his allegations about Cook, the sole testimony against him. Even so, Chief Justice Markham was dismissed from the King's Bench when he declined to find Sir Thomas guilty of treason. Cook was deprived of his alder-manry on Edward's orders and, although pardoned, released only after paying the huge fine of £8,000.

Under an old law called 'Queen's Gold', Queen Elizabeth then demanded a hundred marks (£66) for every thousand pounds Sir Thomas had paid in fines, which he was forced to pay after a long and costly legal action. Nor did he ever recover the goods stolen by Rivers and Fogge. The King's jester joked that the rivers in England were so high that he was barely able to wade through them, meaning – Fabyan explains ponderously – 'the great rule which the Lord Rivers and his blood bare at that time . . . But this was an ill prognostication, as ye shall shortly hear after.'[3]

Meanwhile, two young gentlemen who had gone to Burgundy with the Duchess of Norfolk for Margaret of York's Arthurian wedding, John Poynings and Richard Alford, were arrested as soon as they returned to England at the end of July. The charge was that while in Burgundy they had had 'familiar communication with the duke of Somerset and his accomplices there, in the which they were both detected of treason.' Found guilty, the unlucky pair were executed on Tower Hill in November. They died the day after Richard Steeres, a member of the Skinners' Company who was 'one of the cunningest players of the tennis in England'; a former servant of the Duke of Exeter, he had been caught carrying letters from the exiled Queen Margaret. There was a further wave of arrests during the same month. This time the two principal suspects were West Countrymen, Sir Thomas Hungerford, who was Lord Hungerford's heir, and Mr Henry Courtenay, who was the heir to the confiscated earldom of Devon.

Soon after, according to Fabyan, the Earl of Oxford was 'taken by a surmise in jealousy of treason.' A servant of Sir William Plumpton wrote to his master that 'My Lord of Oxford is commit to the Tower, and it is said kept in irons, and that he has confessed much . . .'[4] It looks as though his confession doomed Hungerford and Courtenay, who were duly hanged, drawn and quartered. Yet Oxford was released, after a very short spell in prison, probably at Christmas 1468 and certainly before 7 January. He was extremely lucky to have escaped with his life. However, on 15 April 1469 King Edward granted a general pardon to 'John de Vere, knight, earl of Oxford, for all the offences committed by him before 14 April.' The influence of his brother-in-law, Warwick, may perhaps have contributed to his surprising survival.[5]

What was the attitude of Jane Shore's family to all these rumours of Lancastrian plots? Although they have not left any letters, we can nevertheless obtain some idea of what they were thinking from the London chronicles. King Edward IV seems to have been reasonably popular in the City; he made a point of flattering the leading merchants and their womenfolk, the latter perhaps a little too much. On the other hand, the Queen's kindred were widely disliked – for their rapacity and for being jumped-up folk of obscure origin. By contrast, so Fabyan tells

The seal of John de Vere, Earl of Oxford.

us, because of his hospitality the Earl of Warwick 'was ever had in great favour of the commons of this land'.

The Shores and Lamberts undoubtedly knew some of those arrested during the treason scares of 1468. Besides Cook they included Humphrey Hayford, one of the sheriffs, and Sir John Plummer, a rich grocer and fellow alderman, almost certainly Lancastrian sympathizers, though there was not enough evidence to convict them. The draper Piers Alfrey was found guilty but escaped the gallows, unlike the skinner Steeres. Commenting on Hayford's impeachment, Gregory says 'many more of the City lost much good for such matters'.

William Shore and his father-in-law must have been all too conscious that the recession showed no sign of ending. Foreign trade was seriously disrupted. Pirates continued to be a menace – a merchant could be ruined by the loss of a single cargo. If commercial relations were bad with France, they were even worse with Burgundy. Despite the repeal of the Act of Parliament that forbade the import of Burgundian goods into England, the Burgundians went on banning English cloth and yarn.

Even so, numerous City merchants had lent Edward IV large sums of money whose repayment depended on his survival. Before the end of 1469 John Lambert and Thomas Gay had jointly loaned him a further £95 8s, which they were not going to recover until 1477 at the earliest. For this reason if no other, Jane's menfolk wanted him to stay on the throne.

However, from at least 1467 the Earl of Warwick had been determined that if Edward was going to remain there, it should only be as his puppet. Dr Warkworth, an extremely shrewd and well-informed observer, tells us that after the King dismissed Warwick's brother Archbishop Nevill from the chancellorship during that year, 'the earl of Warwick took to him in fee as many knights, squires and gentlemen as he might, to be strong.' The word 'fee' is significant here – these were men who did not sign indentures but instead received a discreet down payment in return for a private promise to put on the Earl's livery when summoned and to fight by his side.

The struggle between Warwick and the King which ensued was a personal duel. They had so much in common. The Earl was a larger-than-life figure whose opulence and open-handed generosity won him many followers. Often arrogant and overbearing, fearsomely hot-tempered, at the same time he was genial and obviously possessed enormous charm. Yet he also had a strangely devious streak, with a sinister flair for concealing his real intentions. King Edward, no less of a swashbuckler, no less overbearing and no less charming, and equally ruthless, was by far the cleverer of the two. Clearly he was suspicious of Warwick, and Warkwork tells us that after dismissing George Nevill he 'did that he might to enfeeble the earl's power.' His weakness lay in his excessive self-confidence and optimism. His judgement was distorted by his own amazing success hitherto.

Even with hindsight, the events that followed remain obscure. The Earl moved with the utmost caution so that it was months before Edward, despite his natural wariness, began to feel suspicious. At first Warwick had only one unhesitating ally, his haughty brother George Nevill, the ex-chancellor. His other brother, John Nevill, Earl of Northumberland (soon to be Marquess Montagu), held back. However, Warwick quickly found another in the King's brother and heir presumptive, the eighteen-year-old Duke of Clarence, to whom in 1467 he offered the hand of his elder daughter, Isabel.

When Oxford became involved has not been recorded, for obvious reasons, but with his tragic family background he was a natural ally against Edward. As recent events had hinted, he possessed contacts among the Lancastrian exiles, and since his house lay on the shores of the North Sea it would be easy for him to communicate with the exiled court if necessary. But, to begin with, Warwick had no plans for a Lancastrian restoration.

In July, less than three months after his general pardon, the Earl of Oxford went down to Canterbury. Warwick was waiting for him, together with his daughter, Lady Isabel, Archbishop Nevill and Clarence. The party set sail for Calais where Warwick was Captain, and where Isabel and Clarence were to be married – although the King had expressly forbidden the match. The voyage set in motion a chain of events which, within a year, would bring about the flight of Edward IV and the return of Henry VI to the throne of England.

19

'Robin of Redesdale'
Invades the South Country, 1469

LORD OXFORD · WILLIAM HASTINGS

T HE sequence of events and the changes of fortune during the months from April 1469 to August 1470, when Edward IV lost his throne, are among the most complex and confusing in all English history.[1] Those who lived through them, even those who were directly involved, such as Lord Oxford, can have had surprisingly little understanding of just what was taking place. The confusion was very largely due to the Earl of Warwick – partly because of his carefully calculated dissimulation, and partly because he was constantly altering his political aims and adopting fresh plans.

First Warwick attempted to govern England by the hopelessly unrealistic expedient of putting King Edward under strict control and ruling through him (rather as the Duke of York had tried to rule through Henry VI). Then he contemplated replacing Edward with the Duke of Clarence. Finally, as a last resort, he decided to restore King Henry. The bewildering ramifications of the Earl's plotting extended all over the kingdom and across the sea to the exiled Lancastrian court in Lorraine. What makes all this even harder to unravel is the fact that Warwick's ultimate success was far from being a foregone conclusion.

The first signs of a revolt against Edward seemed to be no more than local disturbances, having no apparent connection with the Earl. Only with hindsight, and a very great deal of detective work by historians, does the involvement of Warwick, and also of Clarence and Oxford, become clear. In the spring of 1469 a mysterious leader called 'Robin of Redesdale' or 'Robin Amend-all' placed himself at the head of a band of North Country malcontents. (The name 'Amend-all' was borrowed by Robert Louis Stevenson for a character in a novel inspired by the Paston Letters, *The Black Arrow*.) According to the chronicle of Dr John Warkworth – the Master of Peterhouse College, Cambridge from 1473 until 1498, from whom much will be heard later – these dissatisfied northerners numbered 'divers knights squires and commoners'. Although Redesdale is in Northumberland, Robin seems to have been a Yorkshireman, either Sir John Conyers of Hornby or his brother, Sir William Conyers of Marske, cousins by marriage of Warwick, who was almost certainly behind the rising. Ironically, towards the end of April the rebels were dispersed by the Earl's brother, Lord Montagu, still a loyal Yorkist.

A second, unconnected rising by 'Robin of Holderness' in the East Rising, shortly after, muddied the water still further. What had provoked this new revolt was a tax on corn to subsidize an almshouse in York, but its members then demanded that Henry Percy should be restored to the earldom of Northumberland. As Montagu was in possession of the earldom, he had every incentive to put down the rebels, which he did swiftly, capturing Robin of Holderness and beheading him.

In June, Robin of Redesdale reappeared in Lancashire, this time with several thousand men, and began to march south. He issued a revealing manifesto, similar to Jack Cade's in 1450. The King had excluded the lords of the blood royal from his council and would listen only to 'the deceivable rule and guiding of certain seditious persons' – notably Earl Rivers and the Woodvilles.

Meanwhile, on 11 July, the Duke of Clarence and Isabel Nevill were married by Archbishop Nevill in the presence of Warwick, and probably of the Earl of Oxford as well. A marriage expressly forbidden by King Edward, it was a deliberate, carefully premeditated act of rebellion. From Calais they circulated an open letter to everyone who, as they put it, wished to heal England's ills; attaching Robin of Redesdale's manifesto, they asked them to come fully armed to Canterbury on 16 July.[2]

Just before the wedding in Calais, rumours began to reach Edward that Warwick and the Duke of Clarence were hatching a plot. At first he could scarcely credit it. On 9 July he wrote very friendly letters from Nottingham to the Earl, to Clarence and to Archbishop Nevill, telling Warwick that he did not believe he was 'of any such disposition towards us as the rumour here runneth.' However, when the King learnt of the wedding he at once realized that not only was there a very dangerous plot against him but that Robin of Redesdale was involved in

the plot too – and Robin was marching rapidly towards him with an unexpectedly large army. Edward made the mistake of staying a little too long in
Nottingham, waiting for reinforcements to reach him from Wales, despite the
news that Warwick, Clarence and Archbishop Nevill had landed in Kent.

Robin's manifesto referred to 'mischiefs that fell in this land in the days of
King Edward II, King Richard II and King Henry VI to the destruction of them,
and to the great hurt and impoverishing of this land' – these monarchs had
'estranged the great lords of their blood and [were] not advised by them, and
taking about them others not of their blood, and inclining only to their counsel,
rule and advise.' In recent years the Woodvilles, William Herbert, Henry Stafford
and others had played just the same role, said the manifesto, impoverishing the
King by obtaining from him possessions 'above their deserts and degrees.' They
were responsible for debasing the coinage, imposing extortionate taxes and
impeaching anyone they disliked, causing 'the utter impoverishment of us, his
true commons and subjects, and to the great enriching of themselves.'

The Earl of Warwick was a popular figure in Kent (for having swept the
English Channel free of French pirates), and he and Clarence had prepared their
Kentish rebellion no less carefully than their northern. Large numbers of sup-
porters rallied to them at once, and without wasting time they marched up to the
Midlands to reinforce Robin of Redesdale.

William Herbert (recently created Earl of Pembroke) tried to reach the King
at Nottingham but, separated from their archers, on 29 July he and his Welsh
men-at-arms were intercepted by Robin and cut to pieces at Edgecote in
Oxfordshire. Herbert was taken prisoner, to be beheaded the next day on
Warwick's orders. Shortly afterwards, the Queen's father, Earl Rivers, and her
brother, Sir John Woodville, were also beheaded, again without trial and on
Warwick's orders.

Many of King Edward's men fled when they heard the news of Edgecote
Field. The King tried to make his way south to London but was caught in
Buckinghamshire *en route* by the Archbishop of York. He was sent under guard
into strict if respectful confinement, first at Clarence's castle of Warwick and then
in Nevill country at Middleham Castle in the North Riding.

The Earl of Warwick's plan was to rule England in King Edward's name, just
as the Duke of York had ruled in King Henry's during the 1450s, and he hoped
to summon a compliant parliament at York. However, Edward IV was no weak-
minded simpleton like Henry VI, and the Earl soon began to realize that his
scheme was unworkable. Within a very short time, early in August, a very well-
informed Milanese observer in France had heard a plausible report that Warwick

intended to announce that Edward was a bastard and to replace him on the throne by his son-in-law, the Duke of Clarence. This plan too had little hope of success. Robin of Redesdale and his men had rebelled because they disliked the Woodvilles, not the King, and now they had eliminated the Woodvilles.

Edward IV's enforced absence from public affairs was generally seen as a complete breakdown in central government instead of a change of régime. A situation verging on anarchy ensued. Some magnates took advantage of a golden opportunity in which to revive private feuds and settle old scores, one or two of them fighting pitched battles with each other. There were riots and looting in London. In mid-August Sir Humphrey Nevill of Brancepeth, a Lancastrian diehard despite his name, emerged from his hiding place in the Lake District and once again raised the banner of King Henry VI.

Normally, Warwick would have had very little difficulty in putting down so puny a rising without delay, but this time the northerners declined to fight for him. Understandably, they were baffled by King Edward's disappearance. Eventually, the Earl – who, at this stage at any rate, had no wish to see a Lancastrian restoration – was forced to allow Edward to make public appearances at Pontefract and at York, in order to find the soldiers he needed, and, in response to the King's summons, troops flocked to Warwick's standard. Within a few days the Earl was able to hunt down and capture Sir Humphrey, who was executed at York in Edward's presence at the end of September.

Edward seized the chance to get away from his gaolers, calling on loyal magnates to join him – Lord Hastings among them. After seven weeks as a prisoner, the King rode back to London escorted by his friends. A chronicler commented that 'in a way which was almost miraculous and quite unexpected, he did not so much escape as find himself set free with the earl of Warwick's full agreement.'

Not only had Warwick and Clarence imprisoned the King but they had executed his father-in-law and brother-in-law and some of his most faithful followers. Astonishingly, Edward seemed willing to forgive them. He accepted George Clarence's marriage to Warwick's daughter while he betrothed his own eldest daughter to Warwick's nephew George Nevill, whom he created Duke of Bedford, hitherto a royal title. When he restored Henry Percy to the Percy earldom of Northumberland in March 1470, he compensated Warwick's brother John – who had been Earl of Northumberland for the last six years – with the Courtenay lands in Devon (though not Mr Lambert's) and made him Marquess Montagu. Even so, Warwick remained secretly determined to depose the King. If Edward would not reign as a puppet, then he would have to make way for the Duke of

Clarence, who was only too ready to take his brother's place on the throne.

For several months King Edward continued with the farce of pretending to forgive the plotters, ostentatiously inviting them to council meetings, though the atmosphere was fraught with tension. Sir John Paston wrote darkly to his mother in October 1469 that when Lord Oxford (Sir John's patron) and Archbishop Nevill had prepared to ride out and greet the King as he approached London, Edward had sent word that they were not to come near him unless summoned. 'I wot not to suppose therin,' comments the worried Paston. 'The king himself hath good language of the lords of Clarence and Warwick, and of my lords of York [and] Oxenford, saying they be his best friends, but his household men have other language.' However polite in public, Edward and the earl were intent on each other's destruction. Even the chronicler Waurin, who rather admired Warwick, was shocked by the 'great treacheries' (*grans faulsetez*) with which that almost insanely ambitious subject tried to bring down his sovereign lord.

An obscure affray in Lincolnshire turned into another plot against King Edward. Lord Welles (Margaret Beaufort's stepbrother) and his brothers-in-law, Sir Thomas de la Lande and Sir Thomas Dymoke – the King's Champion – had been feuding with Sir Thomas Burgh of Gainsborough, Master of the Horse. No doubt they were jealous of him as a 'new man', a favourite to whom the King had given confiscated estates, disliking him much as the old nobility disliked the Woodvilles. In February 1470 – almost certainly encouraged by Warwick and Clarence – they attacked his house at Gainsborough, demolishing it, stealing his goods and chasing him out of the county. This was exactly the sort of 'abusion of the laws' which Edward had sworn to stamp out, and the victim was a member of his own household. He announced that he would visit Lincolnshire as soon as possible in order to punish the rioters.

Warwick and Clarence sent secret messages to Lord Welles and his son Sir Robert, asking them to gather as many men as they could. Early in March 1470, calling himself 'captain of the commons of Lincolnshire', Sir Robert Welles summoned every man in the county to join him in resisting the King, who was coming to 'destroy the commons of the said shire'. Many responded to his summons since a fair number of Lincolnshire men had marched with Robin of Redesdale. Then Lord Welles and Dymoke lost their nerve. They went to court, hoping to defuse the situation, and were given a royal pardon, as was Sir Robert Welles.

When questioned by Edward, trusting in their pardons Lord Welles and Dymoke admitted that they were responsible for the rebellion, though they insisted that Warwick and Clarence were in no way involved. The King made

Welles write to Sir Robert, telling him that his father and his uncle Dymoke would be executed unless he surrendered at once. Instead, Sir Robert Welles marched as fast as he could to attack the royal army, in the vain hope of saving his father.

Regardless of their pardons, King Edward ordered the immediate beheading of Lord Welles and Sir Thomas Dymoke. On the same day, 12 March 1470, he crushed the Lincolnshire rebels near Stamford at 'Losecoat Field' – so called because they threw away their doublets in order to run faster. During the battle the rebels had shouted 'A Clarence! A Warwick!', and before his execution their leader, Sir Robert Welles, confessed that the real instigators of the rebellion were the Earl of Warwick and the Duke of Clarence and that its object had been to make Clarence King of England.[3]

Simultaneous risings had been planned to take place all over northern England, but they collapsed at the news of Losecoat Field. Although the Earl and the Duke rode through Derbyshire and Lancashire, hoping to find allies, no one would join them. Warwick may well have told his fellow peers that King Edward made 'more honourable account of new upstart gentlemen than of ancient houses of nobility' (if one may believe Polydore Vergil, writing a quarter of a century later), but for the time being this was no longer true. Very few men of substance wanted to risk their necks and their property by involving themselves in the Earl's quarrel with Edward. Still fewer can have wished to have the Duke of Clarence for their king.

On 2 April Edward IV issued a proclamation in which he publicly denounced Warwick and Clarence as 'rebels and traitors.' They fled south to Exeter, from where they took ship to Calais.

20

'Eleven days', 1470

JOHN LAMBERT · DR MORTON

No one can have expected that King Edward IV was going to lose his throne during the autumn of 1470. Save for Warwick's abortive coup, he had faced no serious challenge since that shattering victory at Towton, by then over nine years earlier. He was young, vigorous and impressive, still a magnificent figure of a man. His queen had already given birth to three fine daughters and there was every prospect of her bearing him a son and heir. In addition he had two brothers, so that the dynasty had every appearance of being solidly established. The Yorkist court was one of the most glittering and imposing in Europe, while among its courtiers were such loyal and able henchmen as William Hastings. Although the King was a realist, extremely shrewd and suspicious by nature, it is perhaps understandable that he had not realized how brittle were his régime's foundations.

Yet the Yorkist régime had forfeited most if not all of the heady popularity it had enjoyed at the beginning of the reign. Taxation had been too heavy, with too little to show for it. In fact Edward IV was proving to be a sad disappointment, so Dr Warkworth informs us. Everyone had hoped that he would 'amend all manner of things that was amiss, and bring the realm of England in great prosperity and rest.' Instead, there had been 'one battle after another, and much trouble, and great loss of goods among the common people . . . and King Edward had much blame for hurting merchandise.'

Many of the magnates who supported him were allowed to go on bullying neighbours and cowing juries just as they had under King Henry. 'They will not suffer the king's laws to be executed upon whom they owed favour unto,' the rebels had complained in their manifesto the previous year, 'by the which great murder, rapes, oppressions and extortions, as well by them, as by their great maintenances of their servants, to us daily be done and remain unpunished to the great hurt and grudge of all this land.' The countryside still swarmed with robbers. Merchants were worried by Edward's commercial policies, so much so that the City of London was no longer Yorkist to a man. Also, it is too easily forgotten that even if Warwick's coup had quickly collapsed, it had humiliated the King, seriously weakening his authority.

Even so, Jane's father had a very strong reason for wanting Edward IV to stay on the throne. On 17 January 1470 the King formally acknowledged that as a former Collector of the Customs at Southampton, John Lambert was owed the sum of £418 16s 2d, besides another £191 13s 4d which he had lent in 1469. The King therefore, in recompense and as repayment, granted 'the said John and his heirs' over 2,000 acres in the West Country. Much of this was good farmland, though a certain amount was moor or heath. It included three manors 'by Chittlehampton' near Molton in Devon, together with the manor of Puriton in Somerset and other lands in that county. There were houses and gardens in Exeter, one 'with shops, solars and cellars annexed in the parish of St Petroc, Exeter, in which Joan Quyk lately dwelt.'[1]

Every fifteenth-century merchant hoped to advance his family's social standing. Here was a glittering chance for Mr Lambert's descendants to rise in the world. Even though he himself would always remain a tradesman in the eyes of Devon and Somerset landowners, such an estate would enable his son to enter the ranks of the gentry and add the magic word 'gentleman' after his name; he might marry the daughter of some neighbouring squire. The snag was that the property had been confiscated from the Lancastrian Courtenays. Should Henry VI and the Courtenays come back, then Mr Lambert would lose it all.

Meanwhile there had been dramatic developments across the Channel. When the Earl of Warwick's ships arrived off Calais after his flight from Kent, far from welcoming the flotilla the Earl's lieutenant, Lord Wenlock, greeted it with cannon fire. Although the Duchess of Clarence was in labour with her first child on board Warwick's flagship, Wenlock refused to let the party land. In reality he was a secret supporter of the Earl and sent a messenger warning him not to enter what he called 'the mousetrap' where the garrison was still loyal to Edward. He advised Warwick to land at a French port instead.

After increasing his fleet by the simple expedient of piracy – seizing some sixty Dutch or Flemish ships whose crews would have been thrown overboard – the

Earl of Warwick put in at Honfleur at the end of April. King Louis XI saw at once that he could be used as a tool with which to restore the House of Lancaster; he could then forge an alliance with a suitably grateful English dynasty against the Duke of Burgundy. It did not take Warwick very long to agree with Louis. By now the Earl had obviously come to the conclusion that very few people in England wished to see the Duke of Clarence as their king in place of Edward IV.

Lord Oxford had already gone to see Queen Margaret. In July of the previous year he had brought his affinity to the aid of Warwick and Clarence, just before the Battle of Edgecote, having commissioned John Paston to buy him three sets of horse armour together with two banner staves; he had ended his letter to Paston 'I trust to God we shall do right well.' However, he had not been in Lincolnshire in March 1470, nor had he ridden with the Earl and the Duke on their recent disastrous campaign. He was nonetheless a marked man in King Edward's eyes and had prudently fled for his life. Instead of joining his friends, he crossed the North Sea discreetly from the Essex coast and went straight to the Lancastrian court. Since both his father and his brother had lost their lives because of their loyalty to the House of Lancaster, he was well suited to act as an envoy for Warwick.

The Earl of Warwick had figured in Lancastrian demonology ever since those ruthless murders at the first Battle of St Albans in 1455. From the very beginning of the Wars of the Roses, he had been the second man in the Yorkist camp, responsible not only for countless Lancastrian deaths on the battlefield or the scaffold but for the ruin of many families. Both he and Queen Margaret would have to swallow their pride in order to reach a political realignment. Clearly, it was an extremely painful process for each of them. Lord Oxford began the negotiations with the Queen, which went very badly at first.

Finally, in Angers at the end of July, Warwick – proudest, most arrogant of noblemen – was forced to kneel in front of Queen Margaret for a quarter of an hour and beg her to forgive him. Only with the utmost reluctance did she agree to do so, at the insistence of King Louis and of her father's household men.[2] (Born in 1408, the '*bon roi Réné*' was too old to take much interest in his daughter's affairs, devoting himself to books and music at his château in Anjou.) Another eloquent advocate of reconciliation was Dr Morton, who caught the eye of the French King – with whom he was going to do a great deal of business in future years. 'And after that, they pardoned th'earl of Oxford being with th'earl of Warwick; to whom the queen said that his pardon was easy to purchase, for she knew that he and his friends had suffered much thing for King Henry's quarrels.' So we are informed by an anonymous contemporary account.

Despite Queen Margaret's initial indignation at the very idea of the match, her son Edward of Lancaster – not yet seventeen – was betrothed to the Earl of Warwick's younger daughter, Lady Anne Nevill. 'That was a strange marriage', Commynes observes. 'Warwick had defeated and ruined the Prince's father, and now he made him marry his daughter.'

Then, on 1 August 1470 in Angers Cathedral, the Earl swore an oath on a fragment of the True Cross that he would 'hold the party and quarrel of King Henry.' The Queen also took an oath, promising she would never reproach Warwick for his past misdeeds and would always treat him as a true and faithful subject.

On the other side of the Channel, King Edward was well aware that Warwick's fleet lay off Barfleur, and that the Earl and Clarence were waiting at Valognes to launch an invasion. The King's ships, supported by a Burgundian flotilla under the Seigneur de Gruthuyse, patrolled the mouth of the Seine, ready to intercept them. Edward had sent out commissions of array in Kent and the West Country as early as 2 June. Lord FitzHugh, a brother-in-law of both Warwick and Oxford, rose in Yorkshire towards the end of July, as did Richard Salkeld (the Constable of Carlisle Castle who had arrested Morton in 1461) over in Cumberland. They must have expected the invasion to come at any moment, but it had been delayed by the Anglo-Burgundian blockade. Edward's lieutenants in the north, the Marquess Montagu and Henry Percy (the recently restored Earl of Northumberland), were quite capable of dealing with them, but the King insisted on going up to York where he stayed in case of further trouble. Although both rebellions quickly collapsed, it was a disastrous miscalculation on Edward's part. While FitzHugh and Salkeld had failed to raise the north against him, they had nonetheless ensured that he would be away from the south when Warwick and Clarence landed after a storm scattered the blockade, enabling their fleet to set sail.

From London during the first week in August John Paston informed his brother, 'it is said Courtenays be landed in Devonshire . . .' (Mr Alderman Lambert must have trembled for his West Country properties when he heard this particular rumour.) Sir John adds how it was also being said in London that 'the Lords Clarence and Warwick will assay to land in England every day, as folks fear.'

'We be credibly informed that our ancient enemies of France and our outward rebels and traitors be drawn together in accord and intend hastily to land in our county of Kent, or in the parts there adjoining, with great might and power of Frenchmen, utterly to destroy us and our true subjects,' Edward proclaimed from York at the beginning of September. When the invasion came at last on 13 September, however, it was not in Kent but in Devon, and there were no French troops. As expected, it was led by Warwick and Clarence, assisted by Oxford and Jasper Tudor. On Margaret's insistence, Edward of Lancaster was to stay in France until Warwick had conquered England.

Once again, there was panic in the City. Like every other Londoner, the Shores and the Lamberts had been thoroughly unsettled by the disturbances of the past year, which were very bad for business. Now, their worst fears were coming true. As soon as the Kentishmen heard that their old hero Warwick had landed, they came up from the Weald and began pillaging the London suburbs; the Duke of Burgundy was married to Edward's sister and a known enemy of the Earl, so his subjects were fair game – Dutch brewers of the new-fangled beer with hops suffering in particular. In response the aldermen mounted cannon at all gates and on London Bridge, while the City companies sent 3,000 armed men to the Guildhall.

Apparently John Lambert caused uproar at a meeting of the Mayor and aldermen at the Guildhall on 15 September. In consequence the Mayor 'exonerated' him – removed him from office as an alderman – besides fining him 200 marks for disobedience and contempt.[3] One can only speculate as to what he had said, though it must have concerned the political crisis. As a committed Yorkist, favoured by the King and with a stake in the régime, obviously he would have resisted any suggestions of compromise by his fellow aldermen – he would have no truck with the Earl of Warwick.

Mr Lambert paid dear for his loyalty. The loss of his 'cloak' was a crushing blow in terms of prestige and influence. No longer would he automatically fill a prominent place at all the City functions; no longer could his wife Amy call herselve 'Lady' Lambert. Just what the office had meant to John may be guessed from his describing himself as 'alderman of London' on his tomb.

Meanwhile, the invaders marched up to the Midlands, gathering support until it was claimed their numbers reached '30,000'. King Edward was coming south with 2,000 men, to confront them; *en route* he intended to join forces with Marquess Montagu, who was bringing another 6,000. But at Doncaster the King was woken during the night – presumably with the permission of his chamberlain, Hastings – by the sergeant of the minstrels, Alexander Carlisle, who warned him that his enemies were only a few miles away and 'coming for to take him.' They were led by Montagu. Angered at having his earldom of Northumberland removed and restored to Henry Percy – and at being given what he called 'a magpie's nest' in compensation – the Marquess had gone over to his brother Warwick. As a Nevill he was not prepared to accept the revival of the old Percy domination in the North Country.

King Edward realized at once that he was hopelessly outnumbered by Montagu's troops, and that in any case he had no chance of assembling a proper army before Warwick and Clarence joined forces with the Marquess. There is a tradition that Lord Hastings guarded the front door of the house at Doncaster in which his master had been staying while he escaped from the back. Followed by Hastings, Edward made for the Lincolnshire coast and then crossed the sands of the treacherous Wash estuary by night, some of his men being drowned during the crossing.

Reaching the port of King's Lynn on 28 September, he embarked hastily for the Low Countries with about 800 followers in a small English ship and in two 'hulks of Holland' – Burgundian merchantmen. There was not enough room on board for everyone, so Hastings told those who were left behind to make their peace with Warwick but to stay faithful to the King. (During the Wars of the Roses, unlike the gentry the rank and file were seldom imprisoned, let alone killed in cold blood when they were off the battlefield.)

The King and his party set sail just in time.

'Less than a fortnight before, he would have been astounded if anyone had said to him "The earl of Warwick will drive you out of England and make himself her master in eleven days".' This is the comment of Commynes – who had spoken with many of his courtiers – on the deposition of the former King Edward IV. The Burgundian adds, 'what excuse could he find after suffering this great loss through his own fault, except to say "I didn't think that such a thing could possibly happen?"'

21

The 'Readeption', 1470–71

JOHN MORTON · THE EARL OF OXFORD

On 3 October 1470 an agent of the Earl of Warwick, Sir Geoffrey Gate, secured the surrender of the Tower of London. On 5 October, having escaped from confinement, Archbishop Nevill entered the City and installed a new garrison loyal to his brother. The next day Warwick himself marched in. Dr Warkworth tells us the Earl

> went to the Tower of London where King Harry was in prison by King Edward's commandment, and there took him from his keepers, which was not worshipfully arrayed as a prince, and not so cleanly kept as should seem such a prince; they had him out, and new arrayed him, and did to him great reverence, and brought him to the palace of Westminster, and so he was restored to the crown again . . .

Henry VI was in no doubt as to whom he owed his restoration. He was grateful not only to Warwick and Clarence but also to Lord Oxford. A royal warrant stated that his return to the throne was 'by the favour and true acquittal of our right entirely and well beloved cousins, duke of Clarence, earls of Warwick and Oxenford.' Unlike the first two, Oxford was no renegade Yorkist but known to all as a Lancastrian diehard whose family had suffered tragically for its loyalty. He was appointed steward of the household and Constable of England.

Exactly a week after the arrival of the 'kingmaker' in London, Henry had the crown replaced on his meek head at St Paul's Cathedral. During the ceremony Lord Oxford bore the sword of state. The old King was reinstalled in the royal apartments at Westminster as though Towton had never been fought or lost. A

newly appointed master of the Mint (replacing William Hastings) struck an entire
new coinage of gold and silver with Henry's name. His restoration was officially
described as 'our readeption of our royal power' – a phrase that had surely been
coined by Sir John Fortescue, no doubt in consultation with his learned friend
Dr Morton. The power lay of course in the hands of the Earl of Warwick, who
styled himself 'Lieutenant to our sovereign lord, King Henry the Sixth.'

Dr Morton had accompanied Warwick from Angers, crossing the Channel with
his invasion fleet and landing at Dartmouth on 13 September. On hearing of the
flight of the former Edward IV, he hurried up to London with Fortescue; there
was a mass of business for them to prepare before Parliament met. When it did
so on 20 November, it was addressed by Archbishop Nevill, who had been reappointed Lord Chancellor. He took for his text a verse from Jeremiah: 'Return, O
ye revolting children, saith the Lord, for I am your husband: and I will take you,
one of a city, and two of a kindred, and will bring you into Sion.' Parliament then
reversed the attainders against Lancastrians, though it did not give them back
their estates – presumably much to the relief of Mr Lambert.

John Morton found an old friend in London, Dr Mackerell. Captured about a
year before, when on a secret mission to Norfolk, he had made his peace with
Edward IV a little too soon; on 27 November 1469 a pardon had been issued to
'Master Ralph Mackerell, clerk, doctor of either law.' He was forgiven this embarrassing error of judgement and appointed chancellor of Queen Margaret's household, soon receiving preferment – a prebendary's stall in the King's Chapel of St
Steven at Westminster and the living of Bottesford in Lincolnshire. The claims
of Dr Morton and Dr Mackerell were easy enough to satisfy, unlike those of the
exiled peers and gentry.

Despite his impressive offices of lieutenant and protector of the realm, and
Captain of Calais, Warwick was in a nightmarish situation. He was lieutenant only
until the arrival of the Lancastrian Prince of Wales, which might be at any
moment, while he knew very well that the Dukes of Somerset and Exeter hated
him; although now on the same side, they still had many old scores to settle. He
dared not restore confiscated estates to their former Lancastrian owners for fear
of antagonizing their new occupants. The Earl was also aware that Edward IV
was bound to fight for the Crown – his wife, in sanctuary at Westminster Abbey,
had just given birth to a Yorkist Prince of Wales.

In mid-February 1471, according to Warkworth, Somerset and Exeter 'with
many other knights and squires, gentlemen and yeomen came into England and

entered their lordships and lands.' But they can only have done so on a very limited scale since the sole lands available legally were those taken from King Edward and the Duke of Gloucester, though they may have seized some others by force. The Duke of Exeter, the former beggar of Bruges, reinstalled himself in his vast City mansion, the Coldharbour. He can scarcely have been overjoyed to learn that on 2 January Warwick had once again become Lord High Admiral of England – the post in which the Earl had replaced him so humiliatingly during the 1450s.

From being the King's brother, let alone a king in waiting, the Duke of Clarence was demoted into a distant, distrusted cousin of the restored royal family, who would have to surrender enormous tracts of territory to the returned exiles. He had his work cut out to regain his former office of Lord-Lieutenant of Ireland. No doubt he might have been recognized by Parliament as heir to the throne should Edward of Lancaster die childless, but even in the event of that unlikely contingency he knew that the Lancastrians would never accept him. Sooner or later they would bring about his destruction.[1]

When he had begun to plot with Warwick in 1468–69, Clarence can never have envisaged a Lancastrian restoration or such humiliation. Many of his kindred and friends were trying to reconcile him with Edward; among them were his mother, his three sisters (the Duchesses of Burgundy, Exeter and Suffolk), and Lord Hastings. Even when Clarence was at Calais, so Commynes reports, a lady-in-waiting came to his duchess with a secret message for him from Edward, begging the Duke not to ruin their family, warning that Warwick would never make him king after marrying his other daughter to the Lancastrian Prince of Wales. She was so persuasive – Commynes comments 'she was no fool' – that Clarence promised her that he would go over to his brother's side when he returned to England.

The Readeption had started inauspiciously in the City. When it was learnt that Edward had fled the country, uproar ensued. Prison gates were broken down, the inmates pouring out, while the Kentish men returned. They burst into such suburbs as Radcliffe, Limehouse and St Katherine's, setting fire to houses, plundering ale shops, raping and killing. (Down by the river and just outside the walls, the insalubrious area known as St Katherine's held a criminal population that was always ready to riot at times like these.) Armed citizens had had to patrol the streets until Warwick and his men arrived to restore order.

Although the Earl of Warwick kept London firmly under control, well-informed citizens such as John Lambert and William Shore did not have to be clairvoyant to guess that another vicious civil war was imminent. Despite his popularity, Warwick had too many enemies, while even if Henry VI was a symbol of legality, he was also one of dispiriting incapacity. It could only be a matter of time before the exiled king attempted to regain his throne. The sanctuaries were stuffed with his supporters, who took care to spread rumours neatly calculated to damage the Lancastrian régime. At the same time, Yorkist Londoners, of whom there were plenty, reminded all their friends how bad the situation was for business.

Since the Readeption's chances of success depended on reconciling former Yorkists with Lancastrians, of necessity there were very few reprisals. However, after moving with his retainers into William Hastings' London house on 15 October as Constable of England, Lord Oxford had the keen pleasure of sitting in judgement on the man who had condemned his father and brother to death eight years before. This was John Tiptoft, Earl of Worcester, that strange Italianate combination of scholarship and cruelty – an enthusiastic translator of Latin classics who introduced impaling into the English penal code. He was widely hated for having had the bodies of some of Warwick's supporters skewered on stakes after they had been hanged – Fabyan, echoing City gossip, relates that he was called 'the butcher of England'. Condemned to die by Oxford, at his own execution on Tower Hill, when the mob was baying for his blood, Tiptoft asked the headsmen to decapitate him with three strokes in honour of the Trinity.[2]

The Earl of Oxford had not forfeited his estates by attainder and he was soon able to make his presence felt throughout East Anglia, reinstalling himself at Castle Hedingham. In years to come he would be famous for the size of his affinity, so it is more than probable that he spent no less time on recruiting retainers than did William Hastings in the Midlands. Obviously Oxford's 'good lordship' was worth having, given his influence in local affairs and in law suits. None knew this better than the Pastons, whose contested legacy of Caistor Castle had been taken from them forcibly by the Duke of Norfolk.

On 12 October 1470 John Paston wrote excitedly to his mother:

> I trust that we shall do right well . . . for my lady of Norfolk hath promised to be ruled by my lord of Oxenford in all such matters as belong to my brother and to me; and as for my lord of Oxenford he is better lord to me, by my troth, than I can wish him . . . The duke and duchess sue to him as humbly as ever I did to them.

The Norman keep of Lord Oxford's ancestral seat, Castle Hedingham in Essex.
The mansion which he built next to it has vanished.

One of the architects of the Readeption and a pillar of the new régime, the Earl was in a position to dictate to John Mowbray, Duke of Norfolk, who had hitherto been all-powerful in the eastern counties, and also to his formidable duchess, Elizabeth – daughter of the Hundred Years' War hero 'Old Talbot'.

Paston continues, in the same hopeful vein, 'My master the earl of Oxenford biddeth me ask and have. I trow my brother Sir John shall have the constableship of Norwich Castle with £20 of fees.' The Constable of Norwich was Oxford's unloved cousin Lord Howard, very much a committed Yorkist who had been extremely lucky to escape arrest and whose son was in sanctuary at Colchester. The Duke of Norfolk was made to return Caistor to the Pastons in December 1470. Although nothing came of their hopes of the constableship, even the calculating, money-grubbing, unwarlike Pastons were ready to fight at the Earl's side.

Lord Oxford's affinity was not confined to Pastons, and must have numbered scores of retainers. No list of his indentures has survived (unlike those of William Hastings) but we can guess at the names of a few. Among the more substantial were Henry Spelman of Narborough in Norfolk,[3] and probably three other squires: Robert Harlyston of 'Shymplyng' in Suffolk, Robert Gibbon of Wingfield in the same county, and William Goodmanston of Bromley in Essex. Spelman was a former MP for Norwich (where he would later become recorder) while Goodmanston had been MP for Essex.

Unintentionally, Louis XI made further bloodshed inevitable in England, when he declared war on Burgundy in December and then insisted that Warwick do the same. English merchants were horrified by this threat to commercial interests in the Low Countries. The Earl found it very difficult to raise money for the war in the City.

Soon all England was once more in the grip of invasion fever. Oxford placed his brother Thomas de Vere in charge of coastal defence in East Anglia, where a Yorkist landing seemed most likely. On 14 March, writing from Hedingham, the Earl congratulated Thomas after receiving a letter from him about the measures he had taken – 'by which I understand the faithful guiding and disposition of the country, to my great comfort and pleasure.' He adds that he himself has collected all the troops he can in Essex, Suffolk and Cambridgeshire and is marching towards Norfolk, in case Edward with his company has arrived there, but that he will go to the north if he arrive northward . . . to follow and pursue him.'

Five days later we find Lord Oxford writing from Bury St Edmunds 'To my right trusty and well beloved Henry Spelman, Thos. Seyve, John Seyve, James Radcliff, John Brampton the older, and to each of them', that

I have credible tidings that the king's great enemies and rebels, accompanied with enemies strangers [foreigners] be now arrived and landed in the north parts of this his land . . . I straitly charge and command you, and in mine own behalf heartily desire and pray you, that all excuses laid apart, ye and each of you in your own persons defensibly arrayed, with as many men as ye may goodly make, be on Friday next coming at Lynn, and so forth to Newark . . .

Lord Hastings was busy sending similar letters to his own well-wishers, urging them to join him fully armed and with as many troops as they could bring.

Edward had indeed arrived.

22

William Hastings in Exile, 1470–71

WILLIAM HASTINGS

The normally cynical Philippe de Commynes was impressed that Lord Hastings should have remained faithful to his master despite being married to the Earl of Warwick's sister. Lord Oxford was his brother-in-law as well. However, William was much too loyal to contemplate changing sides, and in any case he was far too closely identified with Edward IV's régime.

When Edward's three little vessels sailed out from King's Lynn into the North Sea in September 1470, besides William they carried Richard Plantagenet, Duke of Gloucester, the King's eighteen-year-old brother, and the new Lord Rivers, who was the Queen's brother, together with knights and squires. Commynes, who met some of the party shortly after, says that they did not have a penny between them and had very little idea of where they were going. Chased by Hanseatic ships – Hansards hated Englishmen as pirates who seized their goods – they were lucky to reach the Frisian port of Alkmaar. Edward gave the skipper of his boat a coat lined with marten fur (the sable of fifteenth-century England), promising to pay him at a later date. 'There never was such a beggarly company,' observes Commynes. Their only clothes were those in which they had been campaigning.

Luckily for Edward IV, the Governor of Holland happened to be at Alkmaar. This was Louis de Bruges, Seigneur de Gruthuyse, who had been on embassies to England and had pleasant memories of the Yorkist court. He forbade the Hansards to attack the King, going on board his ship to welcome him. Gruthuyse then provided Edward with a wardrobe and money, before escorting him to suitably splendid accommodation in Bruges and The Hague.

Burgundy was the most opulent state in northern Europe. Belonging to a

Louis de Gruthuyse's mansion at Bruges (now the Gruuthuse Museum) where
the exiled Hastings spent several months in 1470–71

junior branch of the French royal family, its dukes derived their title from the
duchy and county of Burgundy in eastern France, but their wealth came from
what are now Belgium and the Netherlands. The magnificent Burgundian court
spent most of its time in Flanders, Brabant or Ghent.

Throughout the Wars of the Roses Burgundy played a vital role in English
affairs, both as a potential ally against France and as a source of support for York
or Lancaster. Moreover, commercial relations were of vital importance to
English merchants, who sold most of their wool and other goods in Flanders,
which was the source of many English luxuries.

The two Dukes of Burgundy during this period were Philip the Good, who
died in 1467, and his son Charles the Bold. Their attitude towards England was
practical enough. When Parliament had passed legislation in 1463 restricting
Burgundian imports, Duke Philip responded with a potentially ruinous embargo

on English cloth. The ensuing trade war ended in 1467 with a sensible commercial treaty, while Duke Charles married Edward's sister Margaret the following year. Hastings played a full part in the negotiations, as a member of several embassies.

Duke Charles was perplexed by the news that King Edward had arrived in his domains. Closely related to Henry VI, Charles had always been inclined to sympathize with the Lancastrians, paying pensions to the Dukes of Somerset and Exeter – who were still in Flanders at the end of 1470, pestering him to help Henry. On the other hand Edward was his brother-in-law and both belonged to each other's orders, the King wearing the Golden Fleece and the Duke the Garter. Charles did not know whom to support. He compromised, sending Commynes to Calais to offer congratulations on Henry VI's restoration while paying Edward a pension of 500 crowns a month. For the moment the Yorkist exiles had to kick their heels.

King Edward and his followers were able to maintain at least the semblance of a royal court. It seems that during their exile, Jean, Seigneur de Forestel, otherwise styled 'The Bastard of Waurin', presented the King with a copy of his rambling but surprisingly well-informed *Recueil des Croniques et Anchiennes Istories de la Grant Bretagne*. There is reason to think that Waurin's presentation took place in January or February 1471, when the King was staying with Gruthuyse. A miniature in a manuscript of the first volume of the *Recueil* dating from about this time shows Waurin kneeling before Edward in what appears to be a makeshift throne-room; the throne and its canopy look as if they have been improvised while a curtain hangs untidily over an open door. In addition to the King and Waurin, four courtiers are shown, two of whom are wearing the Garter; the nobleman in the left foreground with a sharp, sour face may be the Duke of Gloucester and the other on the right Lord Hastings. It is possible therefore that the miniature in the *Recueil* contains the only known contemporary likeness of William – apart, perhaps, from that grinning caricature in the sketch of his man-tiger.[1]

The exiled Yorkist court spent most of its time in Bruges or The Hague. The 'culture shock' for William Hastings would have been considerable. Although known to have visited St Omer in Artois on an embassy during the mid-1460s, he cannot previously have encountered Burgundian civilization at its most luxurious. Built on the banks of canals, Bruges (then the capital of Flanders) was a northern Venice, one of the richest and most cosmopolitan cities in Europe, a trading emporium and banking centre where Hanseatic merchants met their Italian counterparts. Fortunately, much of the city survives as it was in William's time, including the beautiful house at the far end of the Djiver canal, where he and his king stayed with the Seigneur de Gruthuyse – today the 'Gruthusmuseum'.

William Hastings must have seen truly wonderful pictures during his exile. The greatest of the painters then working in Bruges was the Flemish master Hans Memling, whose works could be viewed without difficulty in the city's churches or at the hospital of St John, impressing men by their dignified piety and their amazingly realistic detail. Indeed, William's brother-in-law, John Donne, thought so much of them that at some later date during the 1470s he would commission Memling to paint a tryptich of which the centre panel depicts not only the Virgin and Child but also the donor and his wife Elizabeth (*née* Hastings) with their little daughter Anne. A handsome couple, John and Elizabeth each wear a Yorkist collar of suns and roses from which hangs the white lion emblem of the Earls of March.[2]

The portrait of John Donne is the first realistic likeness of a Welshman to survive. We do not know if he was among the exiles who had fled to Flanders with the King but it is very likely, since he was a committed supporter of Edward IV and had been with him during the Lincolnshire campaign. Ross calls Donne a 'vigorous Yorkist civil servant', and after the death of Lord Pembroke (William Herbert) he had controlled the entire south-west of Wales as steward of all the main castles.

Lord Hastings also saw the illuminated manuscripts, which were a Burgundian speciality. Written on vellum, adorned with miniatures painted in brilliant colours and set off by gold leaf, these gem-like productions are among the most beautiful and attractive of all medieval art forms, seemingly more like jewels than books. They had reached their apogee in fifteenth-century Burgundy. King Edward began to collect them after his exile, William himself acquiring a fine book of hours.

Music was another Burgundian marvel, one celebrated musician in the ducal household being an Englishman, Robert Morton – no relation of the doctor, despite his name.

The spectacular Burgundian court was especially impressive. Financed by the riches of the Low Countries, it was the most dazzling in all Europe, famed for arrogant pomp and splendour. Amid a devout silence, the Duke took his meals with a ceremony verging on the liturgical, attended by courtiers who were dressed with breathtaking magnificence – though no one dared to be as magnificent as the Duke. Its banquets and entertainments were among the most fantastic known to history.[3] Sometimes the *Dance Macabre*, the Dance of the Dead, was enacted before the court by players dressed as skeletons. ('If we could form an idea of the effect produced by such a dance, with vague lights and shadows gliding over the moving figures, we should no doubt be better able to understand the horror,' comments Huizinga.)

As a Knight of the Garter William must have admired the Order of the Golden Fleece, described by one English historian as 'a kind of Burgundian Garter'. It was generally regarded as the most illustrious order of chivalry in Christendom and had been created with the specific purpose of outshining the Garter. Although William is unlikely to have attended its ceremonies, he certainly met its knights, 'belonging to the most ancient nobility', who wore its badge of a golden sheepskin around a fiery flintstone. Gruthuyse was among them.

Commynes tells us that Duke Charles had first been informed that Edward was dead, which 'did not disturb him greatly.' The King was a thoroughly unwelcome guest. Charles's priority was an alliance against France with whoever ruled England, and he began making diplomatic overtures to Warwick. Since he had been so hospitable to Somerset and Exeter, he assumed that it would not be too difficult to reach an agreement with the restored Lancastrian régime. Even though he paid Edward a pension, he refused to see him.

At first the Yorkists' position appeared desperate. Despite Warwick's difficulties, many in England welcomed the Readeption. If Henry VI was only a figurehead, he was an anointed king, while his seventeen-year-old son, Edward of Lancaster, could be expected to succeed him in the not too distant future. By all accounts the young man was a worthy grandson of Henry V, handsome, intelligent and warlike. It was therefore imperative for Edward of York to return to England as soon as he could. But it looked as though Charles would not allow him to leave Burgundy, let alone launch an invasion.

Fortunately for the Yorkists, the Earl of Warwick – who for some reason detested Duke Charles – stayed loyal to Louis XI and rebuffed the Burgundian overtures. What made this a disastrous decision was the French King's declaration of war on Burgundy early in December 1470. Determined to stop Warwick from sending English troops to Louis's aid, Charles invited Edward to meet him at Aire on 2 January 1471. A few days later they met again at St Pol-sur-Turnoise. Still hoping that Exeter would persuade the Readeption government not to support the French, in public Charles forbade his subjects from helping Edward. In private, however, he gave him £20,000 with four ships. The English merchant community in Bruges lent the King further sums, so that he was able to hire fourteen Hanseatic vessels while others were found at Bruges. At the same time, he warned his supporters at home to be ready to expect him.

William appears to have sent similar messages to all his well-wishers in the Midlands. Helped by Commynes, he had struck up a lasting friendship with Charles of Burgundy, which says a good deal for his tact, since the Duke was not the easiest of men. Charles gave him a pension and, according to Commynes, William continued to be a keen advocate of an Anglo-Burgundian alliance, both while Charles was alive and after his death.

The Yorkist invasion fleet assembled at Flushing, thirty-six vessels in all. They cannot have been very large since they had only to carry a force of about 1,200 troops. As chamberlain, Lord Hastings would have embarked with the King on board the *Antony* of Zeeland, lent by Gruthuyse's father-in-law.

Luckily for Edward IV, the Earl of Warwick's inability to raise money prevented him from blockading the port of Flushing, though the King was delayed there for nine days by unfavourable winds. He sailed out, bound for Norfolk, on 11 March 1471. His 'invasion' looked like a very forlorn hope indeed.

23

Who Will Win?, 1471

MARGARET BEAUFORT

For Lady Margaret Beaufort and her husband, Sir Henry Stafford, the Readeption and the months that preceded it were a time of what must have been almost unbearable strain. She had good reason to worry about the future of her son, Henry Tudor, even to fear for his life. Her stepfather and her stepbrother both died on the scaffold. Then, after the flight of Edward IV and throughout the Readeption, Henry Stafford was faced by having to make a nerve-racking and extremely difficult decision. For whom was he going to fight during the inevitable confrontation when Edward returned to England? The wrong choice meant a bloody death and family ruin.

Although Henry Tudor was still only twelve years old, his guardian, William Herbert, took the boy with him on his disastrous campaign against the Earl of Warwick in July 1469. As has been seen, Herbert was defeated at Edgecote and executed. Margaret made anxious enquiries about her son, who might easily have been killed during the battle. Then news came of how one of Herbert's followers, Sir Richard Corbet, had escaped from Edgecote with the boy and found a refuge in the house of Lord Ferrers of Chartley at Weobley on the Welsh border, 'where Lady Herbert had also sought shelter – Ferrers being her brother.'[1] Nearly forty years later, in an oration before Henry Tudor and his mother at Cambridge, Dr Fisher reminded them of their alarm when the boy had been in the charge of 'those caught up in constant warfare.' The Ferrers household at Weobley appears to have been kind to Henry; after his stay, two of the servants received presents of money from Lady Margaret.

During those weeks in the summer of 1469 when King Edward was Warwick's prisoner and the world seemed upside down, Margaret had attempted to improve the prospects of a son who had been deprived of both title and lands, but she made a bad mistake. In order to plead his case, in August she visited the Duke of Clarence at his mansion in London; he was briefly one of the two most power-ful men in England, as well as the holder of the Honour of Richmond which had formerly belonged to Henry. In consequence, when Edward regained his liberty, he was deeply suspicious of Lady Margaret and of her husband, Stafford.

Since Herbert (Lord Pembroke) was dead, besides being grimly determined to recover Henry Tudor's patrimony for him, Margaret wanted custody of the boy so that he could come and live with her. The invaluable Reginald Bray organized a search of the Exchequer and Chancery records, purchasing a copy of 'my lord Pembroke's patent for the ward[ship] and marriage of my lord of Richmond.' He sent a trusted servant down to Pembrokeshire, to see if he could find out any-thing useful which might serve as evidence. The very best legal advice was taken, Bray consulting a particularly distinguished lawyer, Master Humphrey Starkey, who was Recorder of London. In October 1469 Margaret and her husband, accompanied by 'their fellowship and learned council', met Lady Pembroke and her brother, Lord Ferrers of Chartley, who also brought their lawyers, in an attempt to reach a compromise over Henry Tudor's future. The meeting place was the Bell Inn in Fleet Street, where mutton, bread and cheese and ale were served to the party during the discussions. Although the details have not sur-vived, obviously some sort of agreement was reached since a new patent was obtained from the King shortly afterwards.[2]

Even if he was angry at Lady Margaret for calling on the Duke of Clarence during his own captivity in Yorkshire, King Edward had good reasons for wishing to remain on friendly terms with Henry Stafford, reasons that no doubt persuaded him to be helpful with the problems of his Tudor stepson. Not only was Sir Henry's brother, Sir John Stafford, a most valued supporter whom the King created Earl of Wiltshire, but so too was his stepfather, the former royal treasurer, Lord Mountjoy. And we know from Margaret's household accounts that the Stafford brothers were close; John visited Henry at Woking Old Hall, to hunt or to play cards. Moreover, their three Bourchier uncles were very power-ful men indeed – respectively Archbishop of Canterbury, Earl of Essex, and Lord Berners. For all her Lancastrian Beaufort blood, by marriage Margaret had some undeniably influential Yorkist relations.

Henry Stafford was present at Stamford in March 1470 when Margaret's step-brother, Lord Welles, was executed, and fought against Sir Robert at Losecote

Field. Since Stafford visited Maxey shortly after, he must have brought Margaret's mother, Lady Welles, the news of their executions. He had been summoned by the King and despite ill health had joined him hastily to prove his loyalty. Edward was a dangerous man to provoke. Sir Henry rode with the King in April when he tried to catch Warwick and Clarence as they fled to France.

In October 1470, immediately after King Edward's own flight, Sir Richard Corbet brought Henry Tudor to Hereford, handing the boy over to his uncle Jasper who had just arrived from France. Uncle and nephew travelled to London, to be met by Margaret and her husband. Apparently the family stayed in the City, since on 27 October all four – Margaret, Stafford, Henry and Jasper – went up the Thames to Westminster, where they were received by King Henry and dined at the palace.

Now that the House of Lancaster had returned, Lady Margaret Beaufort was once more part of the royal family. So too was her teenage son. The visit to Westminster was a moment of great dramatic significance in the life of the little family, and especially in that of Henry Tudor, who would eventually emerge as the ultimate winner in the entire bloodstained saga.

However modest they may have been, Henry VI had not lost all his wits, if one may believe a legend about his meeting with young Henry Tudor. According to Bernard André, writing thirty years later, he washed the boy's hands in a semi-liturgical gesture, prophesying that one day he would wear the crown. The scene is described in *King Henry the Sixth, Part III*:

> Come hither, England's hope: If secret powers
> Suggest but truth to my divining thoughts,
> This pretty lad will prove our country's bliss.
> His looks are full of peaceful majesty;
> His head by nature fram'd to wear a crown,
> His hand to wear a sceptre; and himself
> Likely, in time, to bless a regal throne.
> Make much of him, my lords; for this is he,
> Must help you more than you are hurt by me.

Henry Tudor then accompanied his mother to Woking Old Hall, but they were able to spend only a few days there together. On 11 November the boy left to go back to Wales with Jasper. Margaret would not see her son again for nearly fifteen years.

Part of the reason for Margaret Beaufort's visit to the King must have been to obtain the return of Henry Tudor's earldom, with the lands that Edward IV had granted to the Duke of Clarence. Between early October and early December Stafford saw the Duke half a dozen times, almost certainly trying to persuade him to give back at least some of them. But despite having been forced to disgorge the exiled queen's estates, Clarence was still in a position to refuse. Even so, Stafford never accepted the loss of his stepson's patrimony, referring to him pointedly in household accounts as 'Lord Richmond'.

As Margaret Beaufort's husband, Sir Henry Stafford could in theory become the first man in England. Should Prince Edward of Lancaster die, and he was far from healthy, Stafford might find himself lieutenant of the realm for the rest of Henry VI's lifetime, and then king consort. Clarence had been recognized as heir to the throne after Prince Edward, but too many Lancastrians held him in 'great suspicion, despite, disdain and hatred'.

The acknowledged leader of the Lancastrians was Edmund Beaufort, Duke of Somerset, who returned to England from Burgundy in February 1471. A dashing figure, thirty-one years old, like his elder brother Henry the Duke seems to have possessed charm and magnetism in abundance. No doubt too, like all exiles, he was intrigued by relatives who had stayed at home and prospered. The Duke called on his Beaufort first cousin, Margaret, at Woking early in March, to be entertained with a fine meal of fresh salmon, eel and tench, which had been specially purchased from a London fishmonger – such dishes made a pleasant contrast to salt-herrings, the staple diet during a fifteenth-century Lent.

On his way down to the West Country to meet Queen Margaret and raise troops for her, the Duke of Somerset again visited Woking Old Hall, where he spent four days, leaving on 28 March. He had an escort of forty men and tried to persuade Henry Stafford to ride with him, without success.

Nearly all historians of the Wars of the Roses emphasize Somerset's military experience. They cite how as a friend and favourite of Duke Charles he had accompanied the Burgundian army on campaign in 1465 and again in 1467. Yet there is no evidence that Somerset had ever held any sort of military command, while both of his Burgundian campaigns had been desultory and inconclusive affairs; reading the eyewitness account of them by Philippe de Commynes, one has the impression that they were unusually muddled and confused. Judging from his own tragically inept performance in the days that lay ahead, it seems very unlikely that the Duke of Somerset had learnt anything useful from them.

Sir Henry Stafford prevaricated, sending trusted retainers to Somerset's headquarters in Salisbury, with instructions to discuss matters for as long as possible and buy time. Edward IV's little invasion force had by now grown into a formidable army which was growing bigger every day, while its leader had a reputation for never having lost a battle. In an ideal world Stafford would have stayed at home; to fight on the losing side could mean death on the battlefield or on the scaffold, together with poverty for his wife. On the other hand, the victors might be infuriated by his failure to support them. What may appear to later generations as unprincipled self-seeking did not appear in such a light to contemporaries. There was no such thing as party in the fifteenth century, even though there might be faction. During the Wars of the Roses no one saw anything at all dishonourable in switching allegiance to whoever seemed to be the most likely winner.

Sir Henry found himself in London when King Edward and the increasingly impressive Yorkist army rode in on 12 April. He decided to join them, accompanied by the steward of his household, John Gilpyn, and other retainers. He was so unprepared that his 'harness' was incomplete; he had to send for the chain-mail gussets that reinforced his suit of plate. Something of his state of mind can be guessed from his making his will, evidently in haste. He appointed Margaret to be his principal executor, describing her as 'my most entirely beloved wife', and then instructed a reliable servant to take it home to her.

Stafford knew only too well that he might easily be killed in the fighting. He could remember countless friends and relations being slaughtered on that terrible day at Towton. Revealingly, he asked in his will to be buried 'where it shall best please God that I die.' No doubt King Edward was a gifted general but Warwick had an equally fearsome reputation. In case he should have to make his escape – as he had had to do after Towton – Sir Henry ordered ten of his men to wait for him at Kingston-upon-Thames; it was quite possible that he might find himself too hotly pursued to linger in London for a barge to take him back to Woking, and he wanted to make sure of being able to cross Kingston Bridge in safety.[3] One does not need much imagination to suspect that Margaret was a very worried woman indeed.

24

Lord Oxford Loses a Battle – Barnet, 1471

WILLIAM HASTINGS • LORD OXFORD

A MEMBER of Edward's household (probably Nicholas Harpisfield, clerk to the Signet) has left an account of the ensuing campaign, 'by a servant of the king's, that presently saw in effect a great part of his exploits, and the residue knew by true relation of them that were present at every time.' This is *The Historie of the Arrivall of King Edward IV in England and the Finall Recouerye of his Kingdomes from Henry VI. AD MCCCCLXXI.*[1] Although, naturally enough, biased in favour of the Yorkists, it is the testimony of an eyewitness – of someone who was actually there.

Apparently its author was on board when on the evening of 12 March 1471 King Edward's fleet dropped anchor off the Norfolk coast near Cromer. Two knights were sent ashore to spy out the land. When they reported to Edward that his friend the Duke of Norfolk was away in London and that 'those parts were right sore beset . . . especially by the earl of Oxford', he was so discouraged that he sailed north, into 'great storms, winds and tempests upon the sea', which scattered his little armada and drove it 'in great torment' into the Humber estuary.[2] Eventually his flagship, the *Antony*, reached Ravenspur, a port at the mouth of the Humber which has long since disappeared, where he decided to land, together with Lord Hastings and 500 picked men. The Duke of Gloucester disembarked with 300 further along the coast, while Lord Rivers did so with another 200 at Paull, fourteen miles up the Humber.

Edward spent the first night of his return 'lodged at a poor village two miles from his landing, with a few with him.' It was a dismal start to his campaign of reconquest and already there was much to discourage him. His first son, born in November, was still in sanctuary with the Queen at Westminster, in a capital that was occupied by his enemies. Everything depended on finding sufficient supporters who were prepared to fight for him, and so far there was very little sign of them. 'As for the folks of the country, there came but right few to him.' Weary of civil war, England did not welcome the prospect of yet another change of régime accompanied by more bloodshed. In Yorkshire the Percies dared not help him.

Undeterred, he marched towards York. He announced that he was coming merely to claim the Duchy of York and not the kingdom, ordering his men to shout 'King Henry!' as they went. Hull refused to let him inside its walls, and York did so only with the utmost reluctance. He continued marching southward, neatly avoiding a confrontation with the Marquess Montagu and his Nevill retainers. He began to pick up recruits, 600 men joining him at Nottingham. His 'scourers' (scouts) informed him that the Duke of Exeter and Lord Oxford were at Newark in some strength, but they fled when he advanced to attack them.

'At Leicester came to the king [Edward] right a fair fellowship of folks to the number of 3000 men well able for the wars, such as were verily to be trusted,' says the *Arrivall*, adding that they could be depended on to fight for him whatever should befall. They had been recruited by 'the Lord Hastings . . . the King's Chamberlain . . . stirred by his messages sent unto them, and by his servants, friends and lovers, such as were in the country.' (Among the foremost was the alchemist Lord Grey of Codnor, who brought a noticeably large contingent.) William must have ridden down to his 'country' – the Midlands – in order to collect them, after writing scores of eloquent letters. He was repeating the miracle he had worked during the Mortimer's Cross campaign on a bigger scale.

By now Edward had a formidable army, growing every day. On 29 March he invested Coventry, which was occupied by the Earl of Warwick with 'six or seven thousand men.' The Earl refused to come out and give battle; he was waiting for Clarence to reinforce him – the Duke was bringing 4,000 troops which he had collected in the West Country. Nor would he accept Edward's offer of peace. According to the *Arrivall* Lord Oxford and others, motivated by hatred of Edward, persuaded Warwick to refuse.

Throughout the campaign Edward used his well-attested charm to win over the other side, and on none more effectively than Clarence. The brothers met outside Banbury on about 3 April, and were formerly reconciled. The *Arrivall* gives much of the credit to 'My Lord of Hastings, the King's Chamberlain.' Together, they advanced on London.

The bewildered aldermen did not know whom to support, but they assembled a force of armed Londoners. According to Fabyan, Archbishop Nevill tried to arouse sympathy for King Henry by making him process through the City streets; his shabby, feeble-witted appearance only alienated support. Finally the aldermen decided that Edward would probably win. In any case, they were anxious about all those enormous loans which he had not yet repaid, while, if one may believe the drily amused Commynes, the 'wives of rich citizens with whom he had been closely and secretly acquainted, won over their husbands and relations to his cause.' They dispersed their troops, by ordering them to go home and have their dinner. Then, during the night, Yorkist agents seized the Tower – 'whereby he had a plain entry into the City,' observes the *Arrivall*.

Edward marched in on the morning of 12 April, being reunited with his queen who presented their son to him, 'to his heart's singular comfort and gladness.' Over 2,000 Yorkists poured out to greet him from the sanctuaries where they had been hiding, among them being nearly 400 esquires and gentlemen who were valuable men-at-arms. All the time more and more armed supporters were joining his army, such as Ralph Hastings.

The Earl of Warwick had been brilliantly outmanoeuvred, losing both his king and the capital to Edward. Even so, the Earl still possessed a much bigger army. Leaving Coventry, he advanced towards London, intent on winning a decisive victory before Queen Margaret reached England.

On the evening of Holy Saturday, 13 April, King Edward rode out to confront the Lancastrians, bringing the wretched King Henry with him. According to the *Arrivall* he had about 9,000 men and Warwick '30,000', though 15,000 is a much more likely figure for the Earl's army. Both sides were accompanied by artillery trains, cannon mounted on carts, while the Yorkist ranks included 300 Flemish handgunners who carried primitive matchlock arquebuses.

The Earl's 'afore-riders' (scouts) had penetrated the outskirts of London during the afternoon but had been speedily driven off after a skirmish in Haringay Park. The bulk of Warwick's army was approaching Barnet. Now a London suburb, in those days this was a market town called 'Chipping Barnet', eleven miles up the Great North Road. On the far side, about a mile from the town, the Lancastrians halted, waiting for the Yorkists along a ridge defended by a hedge – 'under an hedge-side.' King Edward made his men take up a position opposite the hedge, much nearer than he would had they been able to see properly, 'for it was right dark.' (Among his men-at-arms was Sir Henry Stafford.)

Edward gave his men strict orders to make as little noise as possible, and would not let his gunners fire at the enemy. Throughout the night Warwick's artillery pounded away, but 'always overshot the king's host, and hurted them nothing, and the cause was the king's host lay much nearer them than they deemed.'

Defensive tactics of this sort have not been unknown during the twentieth century.

Hastings commanded the Yorkist left, King Edward the centre, and the eighteen-year-old Duke of Gloucester the right. Opposite, Marquess Montagu led the Lancastrian centre, with Warwick in reserve behind him, Oxford the right, and Exeter the left. The fratricidal nature of the Wars was never more in evidence. Montagu and Warwick were the first cousins of the King and Gloucester, Exeter was the King's brother-in-law, while Hastings, Oxford and the Nevills were all brothers-in-law.

Regardless of a blanket of mist, King Edward ordered his men to attack at between four and five o'clock the next morning, Easter Sunday. There was a brief cannonade and then 'they joined and came to hand strokes.' The mist concealed the fact that the two opposing sides were not properly aligned. On the Lancastrian right Oxford outflanked Hastings while on the Yorkist right Gloucester outflanked Exeter. In consequence the battle soon swung round like a rugby scrum, pivoting at right angles. Taken from the side as well as from the front, Hastings' men broke, many of them fleeing to Barnet and to London – where it was believed that Lancaster had been victorious. Later, Robert Fabyan, a Lancastrian supporter as a loyal apprentice of Sir Thomas Cook, recorded proudly how 'the said earl of Oxford and his company quit them so manfully that he bare over that part of the field.'

Meanwhile the Yorkists had carried out precisely the same manoeuvre on their own right, overwhelming the Duke of Exeter, who was knocked unconscious, stripped of his armour and clothing, and left for dead on the field. (After the battle servants smuggled the Duke into sanctuary at Westminster, summoning a doctor.) In the centre the struggle remained in the balance for some time. Waurin was told – obviously by men who had taken part – that Edward fought magnificently, as did '*le seigneur de Hastingues*'. The Marquess Montagu also distinguished himself according to Waurin, 'slicing off heads and limbs from everyone whom he encountered.'

Ironically, Oxford's success lost the battle for Lancaster. 'But it happened so', Dr Warkworth tells us,

> that the earl of Oxford's men had upon them their lord's livery, both before and behind, which was a star with streams, which [was] much like King Edward's livery, the sun with streams; and the mist was so thick that a man

might not perfectly judge one thing from another; so the earl of Warwick's men shot and fought against the earl of Oxford's men, thinking and supposing that they had been King Edward's men; and anon the earl of Oxford and his men cried 'treason! treason!' and fled away from the field with 800 men.

Montagu was beaten to the ground and killed. In earlier battles Warwick had stayed on his horse, so that he could make an early escape if things went badly. However, on this occasion he had been persuaded by Montagu to dismount and send away his horse. He managed to find a new mount but was trapped in a wood 'where there was no way forth', according to Warkworth, 'and one of King Edward's men had espied him, and one came upon him and killed him and despoiled him.' It was not only the great who died. 'The slaughter was very heavy,' Commynes reports. 'When he left Flanders, King Edward made up his mind that he was not going to keep his old custom of shouting "Spare the commons and kill the gentles" as he had during earlier battles, because he had developed a deep hatred for ordinary English people on account of the earl of Warwick being so popular with them.' The battle had lasted about three hours.

King Edward rode back to London, where he was received as a conquering hero. He had the banners of Warwick and Montagu hung up at St Paul's in thanksgiving and their bodies displayed on the cathedral pavement for four days, naked in their coffins, so that no one could be in doubt that they were dead. The *Arrivall* explains grimly that this was to prevent 'new murmurs, insurrections and rebellions amongst indisposed people' of the sort who had supported Warwick, 'by means of the false, feigned fables and slanders that by his subtlety and malicious moving were wont to be seditiously sown and blown about the land.' It was a fitting epitaph.

Fleeing, Lord Oxford abandoned his own men when he discovered that the chaplain meant to betray him. He joined a party of northern fugitives and made for Scotland with them. A breathless letter which he wrote from some hiding place immediately after the battle has survived. It is to his wife Margaret, whom he addresses as 'Right, reverend and worshipful lady'.

'I am in great heaviness at the making of this letter but, thanked be to God, I am escaped myself.' He warns her about the chaplain, and asks her to reward the messenger because he himself has been unable to do so.

Also ye shall send me in all haste all the ready money that ye can make, and as many of my men as can come well horsed, and that they come in divers parcels. Also that my horse be sent, with my steel saddles, and bid the yeoman of the horse cover them with leather. Also ye shall send to my mother and let her wit of this letter and pray her of her blessing, and bid her send me my casket by this token – that she hath the key thereof but it is broken. And ye shall send to the prior of Thetford and bid him send me the sum of gold that he said I should have . . . Also, ye shall deliver the bringer of this letter an horse, saddle and bridle.

And ye shall be of good cheer and take no thought, for I shall bring my purpose about now by the grace of God, whom have you in keeping.[3]

The Earl's refusal to despair of Henry VI's cause is explained by a letter that his retainer John Paston sent to his mother, Margaret Paston, a fortnight later, after escaping from the battle with an arrow through his right arm – beneath the elbow. (He must have fought under Oxford with the Lancastrian right wing and may have been wounded by his own side.) Although in hiding, he reassures his mother it will not be long before 'my wrongs and other men's shall be redressed, for the world was never so like to be ours as it is now.' In the meantime, however, Mr Paston has run out of money and begs her

send me some in as hasty wise as is possible; for by my troth my leechcraft and physic, and rewards to them that have kept and conducted me to London hath cost me since Easter Day [the day of Barnet] more than £5, and now I have neither meat, drink, clothes, leechcraft nor money but upon borrowing; and I have assayed my friends so far, that they begin to fail now in my greatest need . . .

However, he ends his letter on a note of cheerful optimism.

I thank God I am whole of my sickness, and trust to be clean whole of all my hurts within a sennight at the furthest, by which time I trust to have other tidings; and those tidings once had, I trust not to be long out of Norfolk with God's grace.

Clearly Lord Oxford and John Paston were convinced that Queen Margaret and a new Lancastrian army should be able to restore the situation. As John's brother wrote from London to their mother:

> the world, I assure you, is right queasy, as ye shall know within this month; the people here feareth it sore. God hath showed Himself marvellously like Him that made all, and can undo again when Him list; and I can think that by all likelihood shall show himself as marvellous again, and that in short time.

The Yorkists were far from convinced that they had won. According to the *Arrivall*, they thought their opponents' cause 'never the feebler but rather the stronger' for Warwick's defeat at Barnet. Many Lancastrians who refused to fight for him had no reservations about joining an army led by the Duke of Somerset.

Yet, despite the hopes of Lord Oxford and his retainers, God had abandoned their party. In mourning for her brothers Warwick and Montagu, Lady Oxford would not see her husband again for fourteen years. However, John Paston would survive unscathed. As for the Earl, he would succeed in reaching Scotland.

25

Dr Morton Turns Yorkist – Tewkesbury, 1471

JOHN MORTON

Dr Morton had probably been in London with Archbishop Nevill, the Lancastrian chancellor, until only a few days before Barnet. However, when Edward IV entered the City on 11 April, the Archbishop hastily made his submission to the King and was promptly sent to the Tower. Either Morton rode off to meet Warwick advancing on London, in which case he saw the battle, or he went down to the West Country to join the Duke of Somerset and John Courtenay, Earl of Devon.

Those two Lancastrian veterans had left London on 8 April, intending to greet Queen Margaret and her son, who were expected at any moment, as well as to raise more troops. (Whatever Dr Warkworth says, Somerset did not fight at Barnet.) The doctor was certainly with them when they welcomed the Queen to England. Sailing from Honfleur in one of Warwick's ships, she had landed at Weymouth on the evening of Easter Sunday, 14 April – the same day as Barnet. The rendezvous on Monday was familiar to Morton – Cerne Abbey, where he had spent part of his boyhood.

At Cerne the Queen was given the bad news of Warwick's death, 'and was therefore right heavy and sorry', but her advisers assured her that they would all do better without the Earl. Going to Exeter, they soon raised 'the whole might of Cornwall and Devonshire', which were traditionally Lancastrian. They decided to march northward, linking up with supporters in Cheshire and Lancashire and above all in Wales, where Jasper Tudor was gathering an army.

In London Edward listened to his spies, trying to guess which way the

Lancastrian would go. In an angry proclamation the King denounced 'Margaret calling herself Queen, which is a Frenchwoman born and daughter to him that is extreme adversary and mortal enemy to all this our land.' Yorkists were far from confident. Sir John Paston's convalescent brother expected a Lancastrian victory, writing on 30 April, 'it shall not be long till my wrongs and other men's be redressed, for the world was never so like to be ours as it is now.'[1]

On 24 April Edward marched out from Windsor where, despite the crisis, he had found time to keep the feast of St George – William Hastings being among the Garter Knights present. Correctly, the King assumed that the Lancastrians were making for the Welsh Marches and he meant to intercept them before they reached the bridges over the Severn.

However, he failed to stop them entering Bristol, behind whose walls they found shelter and reinforcements. For a moment they seemed ready to give battle near Chipping Sodbury, but their commanders – the Duke of Somerset and Lords Wenlock and Devon – changed their minds at the last moment and made for Gloucester. However, Gloucester refused to open its gates to them. They marched on wearily to Tewkesbury, arriving there in the late afternoon of Friday 3 May; 'by that time they had travelled thirty-six long miles in a foul country, all in lanes and strong ways betwixt woods, without any good refreshing'. (This is the feeling testimony of the author of the *Arrivall*, who was with the pursuing Yorkist troops.) The Lancastrian foot could go no further, while even horses were dropping. 'They therefore determined to abide there the adventure that God would send them in the quarrel they had taken in hand. And for that intent they pitched them in a field, in a close even at the town's end; the town and the abbey at their backs.'

Many of the Yorkist troops, recovering from their exertions at Barnet, were no less fatigued. Over 3,000 of Edward's men were foot soldiers and they had marched 'that Friday, which was right an hot day, thirty mile and more; [during] which his people might not find in all the way horse meat nor man's meat, nor so much as drink for their horses save in one little brook, where was full little relief – it was so soon troubled with the carriages that had passed [through] it.' Moreover, they knew they were being watched from the woods by enemy scouts.

Learning that the Lancastrians had ground to a halt at Tewkesbury, the King rested his own troops briefly, feeding them with what provisions he had brought, before marching them up to a position about three miles from the enemy. This was towards dusk.

The next morning, Saturday, 4 May, Edward grouped his men in the customary three 'battles' (divisions). He himself commanded the centre, Gloucester the left, and Hastings the right. He also placed '200 spears' (picked cavalry) in a wood a quarter of a mile to the west. In all he had about 5,000 troops, about 2,000 of whom were armoured men-at-arms. Then the King 'displayed his banners, did blow up trumpets, committed his cause and quarrel to Almighty God, to Our Most Blessed Lady his mother, Virgin Mary, the glorious martyr St George and all the saints, and advanced directly upon his enemies.'

The Lancastrians were likewise in three battles, their centre under the septua-genarian Lord Wenlock (who had fought in France with Henry V), the right under the Duke of Somerset, and the left under the Earl of Devon. They too numbered about 5,000, but a greater proportion were unarmoured foot soldiers – probably raw levies. They were in a very strong position, 'full difficult to be assailed . . . In front of their field were so evil lanes and deep dykes, so many hedges, trees and bushes, that it was right hard to approach them near.'[2]

The Yorkists opened the engagement by shooting to such effect that Somerset's men soon began to show signs of stress; they 'were sore annoyed in the place where they were, as well with gun-shot as with shot of arrows, which they ne would nor durst abide.' The Duke responded by leading his men through a hidden lane up an unoccupied hillock on the west side and attacking Gloucester from the flank. Edward had anticipated just such a move. The lances concealed in the wood charged, routing the counter-attackers, who fled, many of them being killed.

Somerset succeeded in rejoining the Lancastrian centre. Here Wenlock, sens-ibly enough, had stayed in position to fight a defensive battle. Unfortunately, he had a well-known history of treachery. If Hall is to be believed, the overwrought Duke shouted that the old lord was a traitor and 'struck the brains out of his head' with a poleaxe. Meanwhile the Yorkists were pressing home their attack relent-lessly. The Lancastrian right had already collapsed and the inexperienced Prince Edward was quite incapable of rallying the leaderless centre. The entire Lancastrian army broke and ran. During the pursuit 'many of them were slain, and namely at a millpond in the meadow fast by the town were many drowned; many ran towards the town, many to the church, to the abbey and elsewhere as best they might . . . such as abode handstrokes were slain incontinent.' The *Arrivall* says that Prince Edward, the Earl of Devon and Lord John Beaufort were among those killed.

The *Arrivall* goes on to relate how the Duke of Somerset, the Prior of St John's (Fra' John Langstrother), and Sir Gervase Clifton, together with other knights and squires found in the Abbey, were tried by the Duke of Gloucester as Constable of England 'and beheaded every one'. Warkworth's account adds that when, sword in hand, King Edward entered the Abbey church where they had taken sanctuary, a priest bearing the Host made him swear to spare their lives, but they were executed two days later after drum-head trials. Another chronicler claims they were dragged out of the church after such a bloody resistance that it had to be reconsecrated.

Although the author of the *Arrivall* and Dr Warkworth state that Edward of Lancaster fell in battle,[3] Fabyan tells of the Prince being captured and brought to the King, who hit him in the face with a gauntlet, watching while Clarence, Gloucester, Hastings and Sir Thomas Grey cut him down. Polydore Vergil had heard a similar story. When asked by the King how he dared to come and make war in England, the Prince replied that he had come to claim his inheritance. King Edward 'gave no answer, only thrusting the young man from him with his hand whom forthwith those that were present . . . George, duke of Clarence, Richard, duke of Gloucester and William, Lord Hastings, cruelly murdered.'

While the story of Edward of Lancaster's murder is almost certainly untrue, the fact that contemporaries could find it plausible is helpful for a realistic assessment of William Hastings. He may have been 'a good knight and a gentle' (More's phrase), but he was also a ruthless courtier-politician. The end of the House of Lancaster guaranteed not only Edward IV's survival but that of Lord Hastings. In just over three weeks his master had regained his kingdom while he had recovered his estates. William did not wish to see them in jeopardy again.

Margaret of Anjou, who had taken shelter in a nearby convent together with the Prince's wife and the Countess of Devon, was brought to the King at Coventry. Not only were the Queen's son and the Beauforts dead, but so were even her faithful household men from Koeur – Hampden, Whittingham and Vaux.

Other prisoners included Sir John Fortescue and Dr Mackerell. There is no record of Dr Morton's capture; he was far too resourceful. Yet he must have known that it was time to surrender.

'From the time of Tewkesbury field,' boasts the *Arrivall* – written for popular consumption, in France and Burgundy as well as at home – 'in every part of England where any commotion was begun for King Henry's party, anon they were rebuked, so that it appeared to every man, at once, the said party was extinct and repressed for ever, without any manner hope of again quickening.'

But there was still commotion – in London.

The Lamberts and Shores found themselves threatened for the first time since 1460. *The Great Chronicle of London* tells us how 'a [sea] rover named the Bastard of Fauconberg having a multitude of rovers in his rule landed in Kent and there a-raised much idle people and after coasted towards London, and caused divers of his ships with ordnance to be brought into Thames.' He was no mere pirate but a natural son of the late Lord Fauconberg and Warwick's nephew, who commanded the Earl's navy. He had brought troops from the Calais garrison and hoped to rescue Henry VI from the Tower. Not only had he raised the Kentish men, who were led by the Mayor of Canterbury, but Essex men too who 'weaponed them with heavy and great clubs and long pitchforks and ashen staves.'

This was no peasant revolt. When Lord Rivers and the aldermen – stiffened by the knowledge of Tewkesbury and Prince Edward's death – refused to admit the Bastard on 9 May, he attacked London Bridge. He then set off for Kingston Bridge, ten miles upstream, intending to cross there so that he could return down the other bank and sack Westminster. Changing his mind, on 12 May he landed cannon from his ships in the river and 'loosed his guns into the City.' The aldermen's cannon fired back.

The Bastard had 5,000 men, armed with handguns as well as bows and bills, and they attacked London Bridge, Aldgate and Bishopsgate simultaneously, storming halfway across the bridge and burning sixty houses; they also set fire to the gates. The Mayor and aldermen with their citizens in harness held them off only with difficulty. Then Lord Rivers issued from the Tower through a postern with 500 men and drove them back over the Thames. Eventually they retreated, knowing that the King was on his way.

Later, Edward hunted them down. 'Such as were rich were hanged by the purse, and the others that were needy were hanged by the neck.' Despite a pardon, the heads of the Bastard and his friend the Mayor of Canterbury ended up on London Bridge – looking towards Kent.

Wealthy merchants like John Lambert and William Shore had had a bad fright. The Bastard's men had very nearly succeeded in capturing the City.[4] According to Warkworth, but for their burning the houses, the ordinary folk would have let them in regardless of Lord Rivers and the aldermen. Another chronicler says that many of the poorer Londoners would have been 'right glad of a common robbery so that they might get their hands deep into rich men's coffers.'

Jane's family must have been genuinely relieved to see King Edward ride into the City at the head of 30,000 men on 21 May. His entrance was almost a Roman triumph, with the wretched Margaret of Anjou displayed in a chariot on her way to imprisonment in the Tower. 'And thus,' states the *Arrivall*, 'with the help of Almighty God, the most glorious Virgin Mary his mother, and of St George and of the saints of Heaven, was begun, finished and terminated the re-entry and perfect recovery of the just title and right of our said Sovereign Lord, King Edward the Fourth, to his realm and crown of England within the space of eleven weeks.'

The *Arrivall* states blandly that because of the 'perfect recovery' the former Henry VI died 'of pure displeasure and melancholy.' Dr Warkworth is more specific, alleging that 'King Harry, being inward in prison in the Tower of London, was put to death the 21st day of May on a Tuesday night between eleven and twelve of the clock, being then at the Tower the duke of Gloucester, brother to King Edward, and many other.' The *Great Chronicle of London*, even blunter, says of Henry VI's demise, 'The most common fame then went that the duke of Gloucester was not all guiltless.'

The death of Henry VI and his son seemed to have extinguished the Lancastrian cause for ever. All its supporters in the north and in Wales hastened to submit when they heard the news of Tewkesbury. 'Whereby it appeareth . . . that peace and tranquility shall grow and multiply,' prophesied the smug *Arrivall*.

Margaret of Anjou was to languish in her former palace of the Tower for four years. In 1475 Louis XI would 'ransom' her for 50,000 crowns. In return she had to renounce all claims to any English dowry and surrender her rights to any part of her father King Réné's inheritance. Returning to France, she dragged out what by all accounts was a wretched existence at the château of Dampierre near Saumur, on a meagre pension from King Louis, until her death in 1482, when she did not leave enough to pay either her debts or her servants.

Always aware of talent, Edward IV was ready enough to pardon Queen Margaret's former advisers, such as Morton and Fortescue. Six weeks after Tewkesbury, the sharp little doctor made his own peace with the Yorkist King; on 3 July 1471 he received a general pardon for all offences committed by him before 17 June, together with remission of all fines and all forfeitures before that date. Fortescue had to wait till October for his pardon, besides having to repudiate 'the matters written in Scotland and elsewhere against the king's right and title.'

John Morton's new loyalty was wholehearted. Thanks to Sir Thomas More, we can see how he justified his decision to change sides, from Lancaster to York, from the very frank explanation he gave to the Duke of Buckingham in 1483:

Surely, my lord, folly were it for me to lie, for if I would swear the contrary your lordship would not, I ween, believe, but that if the world would have gone as I would have wished, King Henry's son had had the Crown and not King Edward. But after that God had ordered him to lose it, and King Edward to reign, I was never so mad that I would with a dead man strive against the quick.

THE PRIME OF EDWARD IV,

1471–83

26

William Hastings, Lieutenant of Calais, 1471

WILLIAM HASTINGS

THE Lord Hastings had become an even greater power in the land. No one had contributed more to the restoration of Edward IV. He had played a vital role in detaching Clarence from Warwick, he had brought his 3,000 troops to the King's aid at just the right moment, and he had led the right wing at Barnet and Tewkesbury. He was rewarded in full measure. Among his most important new offices were those of Constable of Nottingham Castle and Lieutenant of Calais. Even the Duke of Clarence rewarded him, with the stewardship of the honour of Tutbury and a string of Duchy of Lancaster manors in Staffordshire and Derbyshire; when the King 'resumed' (i.e. took back) the honour two years later, he reappointed William as steward for life. The Midland gentry flocked to his affinity.

William's family shared in his good fortune. His brothers Ralph and Richard Hastings, together with his nephews John and Henry Ferrers, and his brother-in-law John Donne, were knighted on the battlefield at Tewkesbury. 'Rauf' (as he called himself) was appointed Captain of Guisnes, one of the castles that guarded the marches of Calais, while Richard would eventually be summoned to Parliament as 'Lord Hastings of Welles' – by right of his wife Baroness Welles, who was Margaret Beaufort's stepniece.[1]

William had become a very rich man indeed. Besides the income from his wide estates, that from offices and pensions in England alone has been estimated at between £600 and £700 a year. This was supplemented by profits from grants and wardships of which no details survive. In addition, Charles of Burgundy was paying him a pension of £1,000, ostensibly in appreciation of his heroic conduct during the Readeption, though also, presumably, to further Burgundian interests at the English court. (We know from Commynes that William always remained a staunch friend of Burgundy, deeply hostile to France.)

In Lord Hastings' capacity as chamberlain, it was his pleasant duty to supervise the entertainment of Louis de Gruthuyse, the Burgundian nobleman who had been so kind to King Edward during his exile, when he visited the English court as an honoured guest in the autumn of 1472. Bluemantle Pursuivant, who accompanied Gruthuyse, has left us a detailed account of the visit, in particular of his stay at Windsor.

When the Seigneur de Gruthuyse and his son arrived at the castle, they were met by William, who brought them to King Edward and the Queen, before taking them to three richly hung chambers where they and their gentlemen were to sleep. That evening, with Edward they watched the Queen's ladies dance in her bedchamber – the King dancing with his six-year-old daughter Elizabeth. After mass next morning, Edward gave Gruthuyse a gold cup set with a piece of unicorn's horn. He was presented to the Prince of Wales (not yet two) by the Prince's chamberlain. Later the Gruthuyses and the King went shooting with crossbows and then, having dined at about 10 a.m., buck-hunting with hounds. After supper, they strolled through the castle gardens with Edward, visiting the 'vineyard of pleasure', and hearing Vespers sung in St George's Chapel before retiring.

The highlight of the second day was dinner in Queen Elizabeth's bedchamber. The Gruthuyses sat with the royal couple at the main table, together with the young Duke and Duchess of Buckingham, the Duchess of Exeter (the King's sister), and Princess Elizabeth. Courtiers and Gruthuyse's gentlemen sat at two other tables. The meal was followed by dancing, Buckingham partnering Princess Elizabeth. Gruthuyse and his son were then taken to new and still more sumptuously furnished chambers, hung with white silk and with carpets on the floors.[2]

Before going to their luxurious beds – one with a cloth-of-gold quilt lined with ermine – the Gruthuyses had a bath, Hastings bathing with them. (The baths were wooden tubs under white canopies, placed on a floor covered by warm towels, hot water being brought in ewers by a procession of servants.) The Lord Chamberlain said goodnight after the guests had been served with green ginger, comfits and spiced wine.

Calais, with its standing army of a thousand troops, was England's only permanent military establishment. Lord Hastings was appointed lieutenant in July 1471 (to the lasting resentment of its former lieutenant, Lord Rivers). When his fleet sailed into the roadstead in August with 1,700 men on board, the Lancastrian garrison commanders surrendered at once and were sent back to make their peace with King Edward.

William now had to spend a substantial part of each year at Calais. It needed manning by a large and extremely expensive garrison and the maintenance of strong walls and gatehouses, batteries of heavy cannon and a well-stocked arsenal, because the French were always on the alert for an opportunity to recapture it. Their eagerness was understandable, since the port was an English bridgehead on French soil from which an invasion force might pour forth at any moment, as in 1475. He must have been constantly inspecting its defences and checking security, and also those at the two castles that guarded the 'March of Calais', Hammes and Guisnes. Fortunately, the town itself was in a naturally strong position, defended on the landward side by marshes that could easily be flooded by the garrison in times of danger.

However, as lieutenant Lord Hastings was not merely commander of a permanently beleaguered outpost but the resident governor of a flourishing mercantile community, that of the staplers, who controlled the English wool trade since all exports of raw wool from England had to pass through the port. The 'woolmen', who dealt in wool, bought it from the sheep farmers at home across the Channel and then sold it to the staplers, who in turn sold it abroad – mostly in Flanders. Characteristically, William set about making himself popular with them, to the point of actually becoming a merchant of the Staple. No less typically, he appears to have done so with notable professionalism, reaping a fat profit. On a single day alone during 1478 he is known to have exported over 4,000 pells of wool from London. There was nothing to prevent a realistic knight errant from being a successful capitalist.[3]

In April 1473 Sir John Paston wrote from Dover to his brother in Norfolk that 'my lord chamberlain' (Hastings) had sent for his ward, Sir Thomas Hungerford's daughter, to join him at Calais, with his stepdaughter, little Lady Harrington (Cecily Bonville) and his young neighbour from the Midlands, Lord Zouche. 'Calais is a merry town,' adds Sir John with rare gaiety, though he does not know how long the party are going to stay. He says too, in coy allusion to their wealth, 'These be three great jewels'. But normally there can have been few amusements in this wet and windy outpost, apart from hawking over the surrounding marshland. William bought every goshawk he could procure, these being the best birds for hunting ducks.

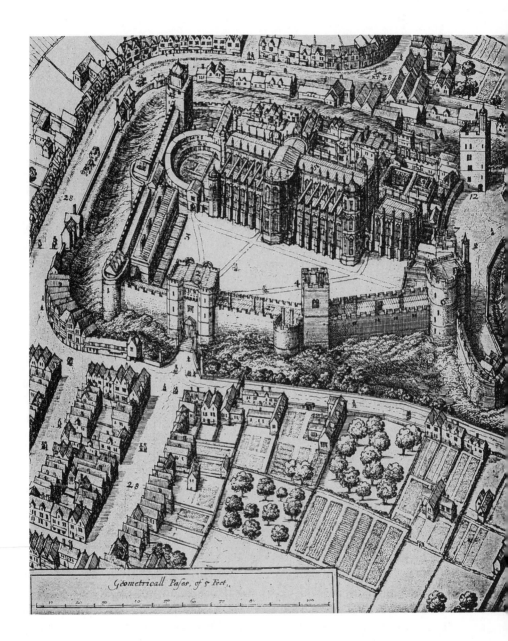

Geometricall Paſes, of 5 Feet.

Windsor Castle in 1673, still much as it was during the Wars of the Roses.

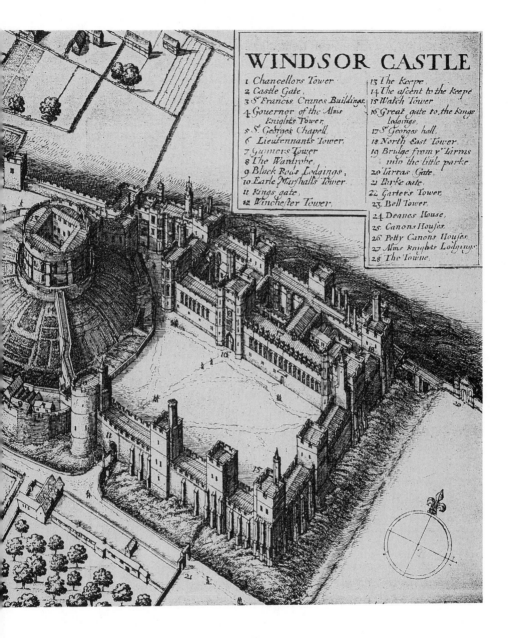

WINDSOR CASTLE

1 Chancellors Tower
2 Castle Gate
3 S.t Francis Cranes Buildings
4 Gouernor of the Alms
  Knights Tower
5 S.t Georges Chapell
6 Lieutennants Tower
7 Gunners Tower
8 The Wardrobe
9 Black Rods Lodgings
10 Earle Marshalls Tower
11 Kings gate
12 Winchester Tower

13 The Keepe
14 The ascent to the Keepe
15 Watch Tower
16 Great gate to the Kings
  Lodgings
17 S.t Georges hall
18 North East Tower
19 Brudge from y.e Tarras
  into the little parke
20 Tarras Gate
21 Parke gate
22 Garter's Tower
23 Bell Tower
24 Deanes House
25 Canons Houses
26 Petty Canons Houses
27 Alms Knights Lodgings
28 The Towne

However, he had very little time in which to grow bored, since he was always returning to England to perform his duties at court as chamberlain or to attend to his interests in the Midlands. He must have spent a considerable time on board a ship or on a horse. Then as now, the Dover–Calais crossing could be a truly horrible experience in stormy weather. During a fifteenth-century winter, the voyage might be a matter of days rather than hours, the tubby little sailing vessels of the period often being beaten back again and again by adverse winds, rolling and pitching amid the waves. Crossings of this sort seriously weakened the delicate Sir John Paston's health, contributing to his early death, though William seems to have survived them well enough.

Lord Hastings held another highly important military post, that of 'Constable of Nottingham Castle and Keeper of the Gate there.' For not only was that impressive stronghold the key to the entire Midlands but, being almost in the exact centre of the kingdom, it was a strategic strongpoint from which to control all England. As Constable of Nottingham, William would have had a suite of apartments in the castle. Similarly, as steward of the Honour of Tutbury, he must also have had apartments at Tutbury Castle in Staffordshire. This imposing fortress, much of which survives, also possessed considerable strategic importance. Undoubtedly, military considerations were very much in his mind and transformed his own homes.

In April 1474 William obtained licences to fortify his Leicestershire manor houses of Ashby-de-la-Zouch, Kirby Muxloe, Bagworth and Thornton, and also his Yorkshire manor of Slingsby. At Ashby he built a great square tower ninety feet high, which contained a chapel sixty feet long together with rooms on three floors. The new Kirby, to be begun in 1480 but never completed, was of red brick and clearly inspired by Tattershall Castle. It had a curtain wall, with an imposing gatehouse, and was surrounded by a moat.

While these manors remained country houses, to some degree they were also fortresses. At Ashby the tower had walls nine feet thick at ground level, with gunports covering the other buildings. They might not be able to stand up to heavy artillery but they could hold out for weeks against anything less. Moreover, there may have been a definite strategic purpose in fortifying four houses in a line that ran from south-east to north-west across Leicestershire.[4] (The ruins of Ashby-de-la-Zouch and Kirby Muxloe are well worth a visit.)

The Tudor antiquary John Leland has a story about William and the building of Ashby, which incidentally shows just how much law and order might still be flouted under Edward IV. Even a royal favourite could find himself defied at the sword-point. Belvoir, once the home of the Lancastrian Lord Roos, had been

Kirby Muxloe, another Leicestershire manor house fortified by Hastings. The gatehouse was still unfinished when he was beheaded in 1483.

given to William but 'coming thither upon a time to peruse the ground and to lie in the castle, [he] was suddenly repelled by Mr Harington, a man of power thereabouts and friend to the Lord Roos. Whereupon the Lord Hastings came thither another time with a strong power and upon a raging will spoiled the castle, defacing the roofs and taking the lead.' He used the lead for Ashby's roofs, leaving Belvoir to fall into ruin.[5]

The 'man of power' seems to have been Sir James Harrington of Hornby Castle in Lancashire. A well-known bully and lawbreaker, when his elder brother had died Sir James had seized his estates and castle, evicting his nieces, who were their rightful owners. Regardless of imprisonment and a determined siege by Lord Stanley, he had held on stubbornly to Hornby. Only personal intervention by the King and the Duke of Gloucester forced him to surrender. Nevertheless, he was appointed a Knight of the Body soon after his submission. The reason for Harrington's immunity was that he was a committed Yorkist, the man who had captured Henry VI in 1465.[6]

Ashby was the principal seat of Lord Hastings, and his favourite house. At the same time as the licence to crenellate, he obtained permission to enclose and

Lord Hastings' favourite country seat, Ashby de la Zouch in Leicestershire,
which he fortified with a ninety foot tower and cannon. From an eighteenth
century print.

empark 3,000 acres for a deer park in which to hunt fallow-buck. He rebuilt the
parish church next to the castle, repairing its roof and adding the clerestory and
the Hastings Chapel. (The chapel contains an effigy which may be his brother,
the failure Thomas.) Always at pains to be on good terms with neighbours, he
secured two new fairs for the little town of Ashby – one beginning at Whitsun
and the other on the eve of the feast of SS Simon and Jude (28 October).

It was now that Hastings acquired a really large affinity, enlarging it methodically, and not just in Leicester or Derbyshire. In 1472 he began to expand it to
Staffordshire, where it eventually numbered thirty-three, nearly all men of position and influence, whose families provided the county with sheriffs. At its
largest his total affinity amounted to over ninety persons, including two peers,
nine knights, fifty-eight esquires and twenty gentlemen.

Those 3,000 troops whom William had brought to fight for King Edward in
1471 had been recruited by the affinity. The King was only too well aware of its
value. Three weeks after Tewkesbury, he had ordered the Exchequer to pay Lord
Grey of Codnor £100 by way of reward for 'bringing unto us a great number of
men defensibly arrayed at his cost and charge.'

By the mid-1470s Hastings' 'well-wishers' could bring far more. Perhaps some
neighbours coveted his 'good lordship' and joined his affinity because he made
a point of being pleasant, signing his letters 'Your tru frend' or even 'Your felaw'.
But the main reason was that he had King Edward's ear.

He used every means of expanding his control over the Midlands. No magnate had a keener eye for a profitable marriage. In 1474 he secured the wardship of the fourteen-year-old George Talbot, fourth Earl of Shrewsbury, later marrying him to his daughter, Anne Hastings. During George's minority William administered the Talbot estates in the northern Midlands, strengthening his grip on the area and adding the stewardship of Derby to his offices.

He did not neglect his own family interests, marrying Mary Hungerford, heiress to three baronies – Hungerford, Botreaux and Moleyns – to his eldest son Edward. Born in 1466, during his father's lifetime Edward would be summoned to Parliament as Lord Hastings of Hungerford. However, William experienced one setback. In 1474, after pressure from the King, he gave the hand of his step-daughter, Cecily Harington, to the queen's son by her first marriage, Sir Thomas Grey. Created Marquess of Dorset the following year, he was to become his father-in-law's deadliest enemy.

Wherever he went, William wore a garter around his left leg, below the knee. (Fifteenth-century men did not need garters, their hose resembling the tights worn by women today.) It was the outward sign of his new, exalted rank, of his close friendship with the King. Often he took part in the Garter ceremonies. An account survives of the observance of the feast of St George at Windsor in 1476. Although William was absent, it is worth giving since he attended similar occasions in other years.

On Sunday, the actual day of the feast, the sovereign and the knights of the Order rode to Matins at St George's Chapel and then, after breakfasting with the Dean, processed into choir, to hear High Mass seated in their stalls. The Order's three royal ladies came on horseback to hear Mass with them, seated in the rood-loft and wearing 'murrey'-coloured (reddish-purple) gowns embroidered with garters; they were the Queen, the King's daughter, Elizabeth of York, and the King's sister, the Duchess of Suffolk. One of the three ladies who accompanied them, also mounted, was the wife of Sir Richard Hastings, William's sister-in-law, Dame Anne Hastings. Afterwards the sovereign dined in the great chamber of the castle with the Order's chancellor, Richard Beauchamp, Bishop of Salisbury, seated on his right, and the Dukes of Clarence and Suffolk on his left. The knights in their blue mantles sat at a long table down one side of the chamber, the Dean and canons of the order in murrey-coloured mantles at a long table down the other side.

The next day, the sovereign and the knights went in procession to the chapter

house and then, after a brief conference, into choir. The knights stood before their stalls while the sovereign offered a rich set of mass vestments and copes, received by the Dean, after which High Mass was sung. At the offertory the Marquess of Dorset and the Duke of Suffolk presented the sword of John, late Duke of Norfolk, then Lord Maltravers and Lord Howard presented his helmet, after which the knights – including the three-year-old Duke of York – made their own offerings at the chapel altar. Finally, having said the *De Profundis* for deceased knights, they processed back to the chapter house.[7]

The ritual expression of the highest brotherhood in the land, enshrining a sublime dream of chivalry, these ceremonies had a deep spiritual significance for those who took part. Too much has been made (by writers such as Huizinga) of the pagan origins of chivalry, too little of its Christian emphasis; until the Reformation, the Garter ranked as a religious order of the Catholic Church. William was genuinely devoted to it.

Three months later he attended the reburial of the King's father and brother. The Duke of York and the Earl of Rutland, slain at Wakefield, were disinterred from their previous resting place at Pontefract and brought in solemn procession to the burial place of the House of York at Fotheringhay. Escorted by peers and prelates, with sixty poor men bearing lighted torches, the Duke's funeral carriage was surmounted by a lifelike effigy dressed in purple velvet and ermine as if he had been a king – with an angel holding a royal crown behind its head, 'in token that he was king of right'. Each night the bodies rested on a catafalque at a church, the Office of the Dead being said in the evening and a requiem Mass sung in the morning.

When the procession reached Fotheringhay on 29 July, it was met at the church door by King Edward, wearing the same purple mourning as his father's effigy. A herald recorded that among the peers accompanying the King was '*le sire de Hastyngs, son chambellan*'. The next day, three High Masses were sung, the King and his lords presenting pieces of cloth of gold – arranged in a cross and offered to the bodies. This was one of the greatest spectacles of the Yorkist age, a magnificent public affirmation of the dynasty's right to the throne of England.

John Sacheverell of Snetterton and Hopwell, Derbyshire, who in 1478 promised Hastings that when summoned he 'with as many men as he may make, shall come to the said lord and take his part against all persons.' He died at Bosworth, fighting for King Richard. From a brass of 1525 at Morley, Derbs.

After the service there was a funeral banquet of staggering extravagance, at which over 1,500 guests were served in tents and pavilions. In addition, thousands of poor folk were fed from the royal bounty, so the herald tells us, 'and there was enough to drink and eat of wine and meat for everybody.' The King provided 40 pipes of wine (over 4,000 gallons) from the royal cellars, besides 31 tuns of ale. No less than 49 beef cattle, 90 calves, 200 piglets and 210 sheep were consumed, together with game, poultry and fish on a similar scale.[8]

Meanwhile Lord Hastings continued to be Master of the Mint, issuing another new gold coin. This was the angelet of 3s 4d, a smaller version of the angel, which remained part of the currency until the seventeenth century. Like the angel, it was used as a 'touch-piece', angelets being presented to those whom the king healed from scrofula (the 'king's evil', tuberculosis of the lymph glands) by touching them.

Clearly the partnership with Mr Brice, his goldsmith colleague at the Mint, was going smoothly. William was even associated with him in patronizing the pioneer printer, William Caxton.[9] Some time during 1481 Caxton published an illustrated book on popular science, *The Mirrour of the Worlde*, stating that he had done so

> at the request, desire, cost and dispense of the honourable and worshipful man Hugh Bryce, alderman and citizen of London, intending to present the same unto the most virtuous, noble and puissant lord, William Hastings, lord Chamberlain unto the most Christian king Edward the Fourth, and lieutenant for the same of the town of Calais and the Marches there.

William Hastings had risen so high that Thomas More, having met many people who remembered both, could speak of him in the same breath as the Duke of Buckingham. He describes them as 'men of honour and of great power, the one by long succession from his ancestors, the other by his offices and the king's favour.'[10] But in saying so More also puts a finger on William's weakness. His honour and his great power depended entirely upon Edward IV.

Sir Gervase Clifton, an Esquire of the Body to Edward IV, who in 1479 entered Lord Hastings's affinity, promising 'himself to be ready with as many men as he may goodly make, defensibly arrayed.' He fought for Richard III at Bosworth but survived. From a brass of 1491 at Clifton, Notts.

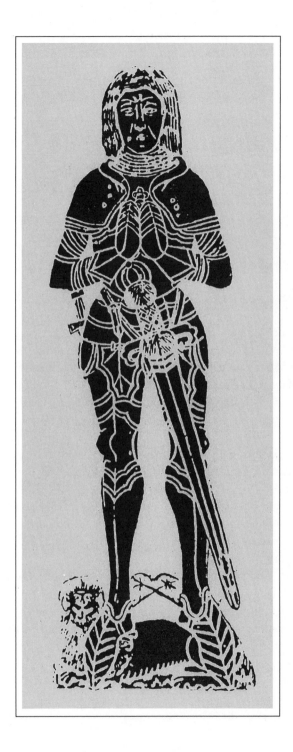

27

Lady Margaret Beaufort's Fourth Husband, 1472

MARGARET BEAUFORT • JOHN LAMBERT

O<small>N</small> 2 October 1471 the parson of Old Woking, Walter Baker, walked up from the priest's house to the Old Hall. One may still trace his route. No doubt 'Sir Walter' (as he would have been known in the village, after the custom of the time) was in a hurry. Henry Stafford, whose new will he had been summoned to witness, was clearly very ill indeed. Presumably the parson gave him the last sacraments, anointing him with the oil of extreme unction and administering the *viaticum*.

Sir Henry's premonition before Barnet had proved to be only too well justified. During the battle he was so badly wounded that there was no further need for him to prove his loyalty to York by riding with King Edward on the Tewkesbury campaign. Margaret had hurried up to London three days after the 'field' at Barnet, sending a mounted servant to search for him on the battlefield. Two days after the parson's visit, Henry died from the wounds he had received that spring.

In his will Henry Stafford did not forget the parish church of Old Woking, bequeathing ten shillings to make up for any tithes that might have been overlooked, together with another twenty shillings for repairs to the church's fabric. He left a set of velvet horse-trappings to his stepson, the Earl of Richmond, a bay courser to his brother, the Earl of Wiltshire, another horse ('grizzled') to his receiver-general, Reginald Bray, and £160 for a chantry priest to sing Masses for the repose of his soul. The rest of his estate went to 'my beloved wife, Margaret, countess of Richmond'.

Certainly, judging from the 'morning remembrance' preached after her own death by her admiring friend, the saintly Bishop Fisher, Margaret had many likeable qualities.

> She was also of singular easiness to be spoken unto, and full courteous answer she would make to all that came unto her. Of marvellous gentleness she was unto all folks but especially unto her own, whom she trusted and loved right tenderly. Unkind she would not be unto no creature, nor forgetful of any kindness or service done to her . . .

In addition, Fisher says that she was highly intelligent. 'A ready wit she had also to conceive all things, albeit they were right dark.'

Her husband was lucky to die in his bed. Because of his family's friendship with poor Henry VI – and that of his wife's family – he might well have fought for the Lancastrians at Barnet or Tewkesbury, to be killed or attainted. Fortunately for him and for Margaret, he had made the right choice.

As it was, Margaret had lost yet more kindred during the recent upheavals. Besides her Beaufort cousins, she mourned too for Edward of Lancaster and for the murdered King Henry. Historians of the Wars of the Roses cannot take into account the anguish of the bereaved women who waited for news from the battlefields, since no one thought it worthwhile to record their feelings.

By staying in Wales, Jasper Tudor had escaped both Barnet and Tewkesbury. If he wished to remain alive, his only chance was to flee overseas. Margaret shared his opinion, sending a warning to her son Henry that he must on no account trust King Edward and accept a pardon but should leave Britain at once – Edward had beheaded the Duke of Somerset after promising him a pardon.

On 2 June 1471, taking Henry Tudor with him, Jasper sailed from Tenby in Pembrokeshire on board a merchantman. Bound for France, their ship was blown off course and they landed in Brittany instead. The Duchy was almost an independent country, Duke Francis II being often at odds with King Louis. One can see with hindsight that the Tudors were lucky to have arrived in Brittany; the French would probably have sold them to Edward IV, who was eager to lay hands on Henry Tudor – 'the only imp now left of Henry VI's brood.' Even so, Duke Francis promised the English King that he would keep them under safe guard; they were separated, their servants being replaced by Bretons. Lady Margaret had little hope of ever seeing her son again.

It may be thought surprising that, after what had apparently been a happy marriage, Margaret should take a fourth husband within less than a year of Henry Stafford's death. Her most recent (1992) biographers find something unseemly about her remarrying in such haste. They point out that in fifteenth-century

England mourning was supposed to last for at least a year. However, so great a landowner as the Lady Margaret Beaufort, Countess of Richmond, was a special case; the King might well force someone uncongenial on her since she would never be allowed to stay single – if she wanted to choose her new partner, she had to move quickly.[1]

Accordingly, in June 1472 – still under 30 – she married Thomas, Lord Stanley, probably at his family seat of Knowsley in Lancashire. (One of the trustees of the complicated marriage settlement was Dr John Morton, the newly appointed Master of the Rolls.) Born in about 1435, a widower whose late wife had been yet another sister of the Earl of Warwick, he was the head of a recently established but very powerful family with vast estates and a large affinity in Cheshire and Lancashire. Subtle and ambitious, he was one of the Wars' most determined survivors, a champion trimmer who would one day become known as the 'wily fox'. For all his wiliness, he was nonetheless deeply respected by successive monarchs.

He had played an ambiguous, even a treacherous role in 1459–61 and again in 1470–71. The Pastons noted how, when Warwick and Clarence fled from King Edward, 'hoping to have had help and succour from the Lord Stanley . . . they had little favour.' Yet during the Readeption he had rallied with apparent enthusiasm to King Henry VI, vigorously besieging the Yorkist stronghold of Hornby. However, he had then been conspicuously absent from the battles at Barnet and Tewkesbury, although he controlled an affinity just as large as that of Lord Hastings – in 1481 he would bring 3,000 men to fight against the Scots.

Stanley's brother, Sir William, was still more slippery. He had been canny enough to join Edward at Nottingham in March 1471. William was always more of a gambler than brother Thomas. One day this tendency would prove his ruin.

Ignoring the family's somewhat tarnished reputation, Edward IV appointed Thomas Stanley to be the Lord Steward of his household, the august dignitary who was theoretically in charge of the dining hall, the kitchen and the pantry. These departments must be distinguished from those of the Lord Chamberlain, William Hastings, whose own jealously guarded responsibilities were the sleeping quarters. It was an office of very great prestige, and clearly much prized by a man quite so ambitious. In consequence Thomas Stanley was frequently at court and Margaret had to accompany him. As the Lord Steward's wife, she enjoyed the privilege of carrying Queen Elizabeth's train on state occasions. Since Thomas's son had married the Queen's niece, he was on excellent terms with the Woodvilles. In 1480 Lady Margaret was asked to carry King Edward's seventh daughter, Bridget, at her christening at Eltham Palace, which was a sure sign of the royal favour.

Although she spent some time at her new husband's houses – especially Knowsley, where her officials were given their own rooms – she kept Woking. She continued to visit the West Country, notably Sampford Peverell near Tiverton in Devon. Her residence here was the old Peverell Castle. Nothing is left of it, though she would recognize the church whose south aisle she rebuilt.

28

Lord Oxford Turns Pirate, 1473

LORD OXFORD

THE author of the *Arrivall of King Edward IV* tells his readers that in a short time the King 'shall appease his subjects through[out] all his realm; that peace and tranquility shall grow and multiply.' But, even though Henry VI and his son might be dead, opposition survived, led by the Earl of Oxford, who was inspired by hatred of Edward rather than devotion to the House of Lancaster. There are strong indications that its hopes centred on King Edward's brother George, Duke of Clarence.

Clarence had emerged unscathed from the events of 1469–71, for all his treachery. Astonishingly, honours were heaped upon him; he was restored to his old office of Lord-Lieutenant of Ireland, created Earl of Warwick and Salisbury, and appointed Great Chamberlain of England. Admittedly, after a long and vicious dispute, he had been forced to share his father-in-law's estates with his brother Gloucester, and the latter's marriage to the Earl's other daughter gave him a clear right to half of them. Nonetheless, he was still a power in the land. 'These three brothers, the king and the two dukes, were possessed of such surpassing talents that, if they had been able to live without dissensions, that such a three-fold cord could never have been broken without the utmost difficulty,' comments the Croyland chronicler.

However, so arrogant and unstable a man as George of Clarence could never rest content. In November 1473 Pietro Aliprando, the Papal envoy, observed that the English did not love their king and were convinced that another Earl of Warwick would come – Edward should take care that he was not overthrown by his brother, the Duke of Clarence.

The one Lancastrian leader who had not publicly submitted was Lord Oxford, who had succeeded in reaching Scotland safely after escaping from Barnet. From there he had gone on to France. The French were still at war with England and, financed by King Louis, during the spring of 1472, he led small raiding parties against Calais and the Pale.

The sole Nevill brother to survive was the Archbishop of York, who had made his peace with Edward when the King entered London just before Barnet. Although he had not been reappointed Lord Chancellor, he was undisturbed and allowed to enjoy his immense revenues in his own self-indulgent way. He visited the King at Windsor during the first months of 1472 and, according to Dr Warkworth, 'hunted, and had there right good cheer; and supposed that he stood in great favour with the king.' Edward told the Archbishop that he would come and hunt with him at his house, The Moor, near London.

But on the day the King was due to arrive, he summoned Archbishop Nevill to Windsor instead, where he ordered his arrest, accusing him of high treason – of helping the Earl of Oxford. 'My lord archbishop was brought to the Tower on Saturday at night, and on Monday at midnight he was conveyed to a ship, and so into the sea, and as yet I cannot understand whither he is sent,' John Paston informed his brother, Sir John, on 30 April. Dr Warkworth tells us that he was 'sent over the sea to Calais, and from thence to the castle of Hammes and there he was kept prisoner many a day.' He also says that King Edward appropriated his revenues and all his goods, using the jewels from his mitre to make himself a crown.

In his letter, John Paston mentions that 'The countess of Oxford is still in St Martins; I hear no word of her.' Nevertheless, her husband was undeterred by his wife having to remain in sanctuary. He was hoping to obtain a base in Scotland, since James III was in the process of negotiating an anti-English alliance with King Louis. Sir John Paston told his brother on 16 April that 'the earl of Oxenford was on Saturday at Dieppe and is purposed into Scotland with a dozen ships. I mistrust that work.' In addition, he had heard alarming rumours, though he does not say exactly what – 'there be in London many flying tales, saying that there should be a work, and yet they wot not how.' (By 'work' he means armed rebellion.)

Some sort of plot was afoot and, although never named, the Duke of Clarence must have been in the Pastons' mind. He was the only man capable of undoing the settlement imposed by Barnet and Tewkesbury. If there is no firm evidence, it is nonetheless almost certain that he was in touch with both Oxford and Louis XI – the latter desperately anxious to detach England from her alliance with Burgundy. The Duke had plotted against his brother before and, however unreasonably, he was outraged at being made to share his father-in-law's inheritance with Gloucester.

From London on 18 May Sir John Paston wrote, 'I heard say that a man was this day examined, and he confessed that he knew great treasure was sent to the earl of Oxford, whereof a £1,000 should be conveyed by a monk of Westminster, and some say by a monk of [the] Charterhouse.'[1] It was possible that the man would accuse a hundred gentlemen in Norfolk and Suffolk who had promised to help the Earl when he landed in their counties, 'which, as it is said, should be within eight days after St Dunstan [19 May], if wind and weather serve him – flying tales.'

Sure enough, on 3 June Sir John was writing, 'I trow ye have heard [on] your part how that the earl of Oxenford landed by St Osith's in Essex the 28th day of May, save he tarried not long.' Oxford had fled on learning that the Earl of Essex, together with Lords Dynham and Duras, was riding to intercept him. People were expecting some sort of trouble but did not know what – 'men buy harness fast.' He comments that London was full of household men of both the King and the Duke of Clarence, in large numbers, as if this were something strange. He adds, 'men say that the earl of Oxenford is about the Isle of Thanet hovering, some say with great company and some say with few.'

We know from a Milanese source that early in July Lord Oxford, asking for money to start 'the war', sent the King of France twenty-four 'seals of knights and lords and a duke' as proof of their determination to rise against Edward IV. However, the seals failed to convince King Louis, who gave the Earl no more money and little encouragement.

Oxford had been engaged in piracy since the spring of that year, 1473, and, so Warkworth informs us, had acquired plenty of booty and 'riches'. He had sold captured English and Burgundian ships with valuable cargoes in Scotland, but

Lord Beaumont, the Earl of Oxford's comrade at the battle of Barnet, in exile in Scotland and during the siege of St Michael's Mount. He spent the last twenty years of his life as Oxford's guest, after going mad in 1487. From a brass of 1507 at Wivenhoe, Essex.

after complaints from England the Scots refused to renew his safe conduct. His next move, totally unexpected, had no obvious explanation. On 30 September he seized St Michael's Mount on the Cornish coast. 'A strong place and a mighty, and cannot be got if it be well victualled with a few men to keep it, for twenty men may keep it against the world' is Dr Warkworth's comment. Oxford's garrison of 80 men included his three brothers, George, Thomas and Richard, and also Viscount Beaumont, who had escaped with him from Barnet.

Six years older than Oxford, William Beaumont was another Lancastrian diehard. His father had been killed at Northampton in 1460 and he himself taken prisoner at Towton. He had twice been attainted; most of his former estates in Leicestershire now belonged to Lord Hastings.

Warkworth was correct in thinking the Mount impregnable, the British Mont St Michel. The archangel had appeared here at the end of the fifth century and a fortified abbey was perched on the great crag rising out of the sea opposite Marazion, cut off from the mainland for twenty hours a day. It belonged to the nuns of Syon – history does not relate if any of them were in residence and, if so, how they got on with the garrison. Although it may look the same from a distance, the only building that remains from 1473 is the beautiful little chapel.

Warkworth says that when Lord Oxford arrived at the Mount, 'he and his men came down into [the] county of Cornwall and had right good cheer of the commons'. This welcome was largely due to Sir Henry Bodrugan of Bodrugan (otherwise known as Henry Trenowith), who has been described by a modern historian as 'the local party boss.' He was little more than a bandit; a petition to Parliament of this date complains of Bodrugan's 'Murders, robberies, as well as by water as by land, ravishments of women, extortions, oppressions, riots, unlawful assemblies, entries with force and wrongful imprisonments.' Because of his activities no foreign merchant dared to visit Cornwall, and no Cornish merchant put to sea so that 'merchandise in the said shire is utterly decayed and brought to nought.' Nevertheless, on 23 October Henry Bodrugan, together with Sir John Arundell and John Fortescue, Sheriff of Cornwall, were commissioned by the King to reduce St Michael's Mount. His employment of a pirate such as Bodrugan explains why Edward was not popular in some areas.[2]

What was Oxford hoping to achieve? If he meant to use the Mount as a base for piracy, it would soon be blockaded. The only feasible explanation is that he expected Louis XI to relieve it with an expeditionary force which was going to be joined by Clarence's supporters. On 6 November Sir John Paston reported to his brother from London that most of the men about the King were sending for their armour, that the Duke of Clarence was boasting of how he would deal with

St Michael's Mount on the Cornish coast, where the earl of Oxford, his brothers and his friend Lord Beaumont were besieged by Yorkist troops in 1473.

Gloucester, but that the King meant to force them to agree – '*and some men think that under this there should be some other thing intended, and some treason conspired*' [my italics]. Whatever the truth, there was neither invasion nor rising.[3]

Even so, Oxford continued to hold out. At first the Earl sometimes sallied forth to look for supplies, being wounded in the face by an arrow on one occasion, but soon there was no need. Warkworth (our main source of information) tells us that 'every day the earl of Oxford's men came down under truce to speak with Bodrugan and his men; and at the last the said earl lacked victuals and Bodrugan suffered him to be victualled.' Such a friendly relationship developed between besieged and besiegers that afterwards some of the garrison joined Bodrugan's bully boys and went plundering with them. The Cornishman's behaviour may well have been due to Oxford telling him that a rising was about to break out in favour of Clarence.

In November Richard de Vere, the Earl's brother, sailed to Normandy, asking King Louis for help. However, the French King had lost quite enough money backing Warwick, and in any case did not see Oxford as another kingmaker. He merely dispatched two boat-loads of supplies, neither of which seem to have got through. For a blockade began in December; commanded by Edward Fetherston in the *Caricou*, four ships with a complement of 600 men patrolled the sea below the Mount throughout the winter.[4]

Also in December, Edward put Fortescue in charge of the siege instead of Bodrugan – Arundell had died – and sent artillery. At first little progress was made, although 'for the most part every day each of them fought with the other, and the said earl's men killed divers of Fortescue's men; and sometimes when they had well there fought, they would take a truce for one day and a night, and sometimes for two or three days.'

But the King had given Fortescue most effective weapons – pardons in return for surrender, though Oxford and his brothers were promised no more than their lives. In consequence, 'the earl had not eight or nine men that would hold with him, the which was the undoing of the earl. For', adds Warkworth,

> there is a proverb and a saying, that a castle that speaketh and a woman that will hear, they be gained both . . . And so this proverb was proved true by the said earl of Oxford, which was fain to yield up the said mount and put himself in the king's grace – if he had not done so, his own men would have brought him out.

Although he had supplies to last until midsummer, Oxford surrendered on 15 February 1474. Together with Lord Beaumont and two of his brothers, he was taken prisoner to King Edward.

The Earl went off to imprisonment at Hammes, the period's maximum-security gaol, joining Archbishop Nevill. What happened to his brothers is unknown, though they were attainted with him in 1475, forfeiting their lands and goods. In any case the de Vere estates, including Hedingham and Wivenhoe, had been in the Duke of Gloucester's hands since 1471.

After being in sanctuary at St Martin's for nearly four years, the Earl's wife, Margaret, was given a pardon in 1475 though, if Robert Fabyan is to be believed, she was penniless and reduced to 'what she might get with her needle or other such cunning.' The Countess had lost even her dowry. However, in 1481 King Edward granted her an annuity of £100 during her husband's lifetime; when he died she would be allowed to recover her property.

Oxford's defenceless mother, 'Dame Elizabeth', the dowager Countess who had been born in 1410, suffered almost as much as her son. Not content with being granted all the Earl's lands, young Richard, Duke of Gloucester, was deter-mined to have those which the old lady held in her own right. According to a peti-tion that Oxford presented to Parliament many years later, 'in such time as the said John de Vere was not at liberty but in prison', the Duke, 'acting of his insatiable covetise', obtained her estates illegally 'by great threat and heinous menace of loss of life.' Because of her well-known loyalty to the late King Henry, Edward IV had had the dowager confined in a convent at Stratford-le-Bow – Bromley Priory, a small Benedictine house with less than a dozen nuns. Here, early in December 1472 – 'in the Christmas season' – Gloucester and his servants burst in on her. He announced that his brother the King had given him custody of her person and lands. At this 'the said lady wept and made great lamentation.' She was made to give the keys of her coffers to the Duke's men so that they could search them, and was then dragged off to Sir Thomas Vaughan's house at Stepney where Gloucester had installed his household. Ignoring the old woman's tears, he demanded that she make over all her estates to him – or else he would send her to Yorkshire and keep her a prisoner at Middleham. 'Wherefore the said lady, considering her great age, the great journey and the great cold which then was, of frost and snow, thought that she could not endure to be conveyed thither without great jeopardy of her life and [was] also sore fearing how she should be there entreated . . .' She gave in, crying, 'I thank God heartily . . . I have these lands which now shall save my life.' After being kept in a room in Vaughan's house until she had agreed to all the Duke's demands, she was taken on foot, by night through the snow, to a house at Walbrook where she was confined while the necessary documents were drawn up and duly signed and sealed. Her trustees and advisers were bullied into acquiescing – when her chaplain, Piers Baxter, protested, Lord Howard called him 'False priest and hypocrite!' Afterwards she was heard lamenting how bitterly she regretted having to disinherit her heirs.[5]

Although Lady Oxford had been born a Howard and was Lord Howard's first cousin, he too was in the plot. As an only daughter, she had inherited the Howard family estates which through her marriage had passed to the de Veres, and he saw a chance to recover some of them. This is the first recorded episode in his long and unholy alliance with the Duke of Gloucester.

Eventually, stripped of her possessions and her livelihood, the dowager was sent back into confinement at Stratford. Her former servant, John Power, visited her shortly after. She told him, 'I marvel greatly that ye durst come to see me, remembering the trouble I am in.' He asked how she was. 'Sore troubled,' answered the Countess.

> Nevertheless, I know well ye have loved me and all my blood, wherefore I trust you and pray you to show unto my son John, earl of Oxenford if ever ye speak with him, as I trust in God ye shall, that all such estates and

releases as I must make of my manors and lands to the duke of Gloucester
I do for great fear and for the salvation of my life, for if I make not the said
estates and re-leases [over to him] I am threatened to be had into the North
Country, where I am sure I should not live long . . .

John Power visited the dowager again a year later, just before Christmas 1473
when, although bedridden, she was still confined to the convent at Stratford.
From her bed she explained that she was very ill indeed, probably dying. The old
lady begged Power to keep in mind what she had told him and to tell her son,
'and also to say that she sent him God's blessing and hers.' She died eight days
afterwards. Always noted for piety, the Duke of Gloucester attended her funeral
at the Austin Friars' church in Broad Street, accompanied by Lord Howard.

Even before the Countess's death the Duke had been trying to sell her house
in London Wall, 'The earl of Oxenford's Place', offering it to Sir John Risley, who
was an Esquire of the Body to Edward IV. While hunting with the King in
Walthamstow Forest, Sir John asked him for his advice. Plainly embarrassed,
Edward replied, 'Risley, meddle not ye with the buying of the said place.' Perhaps
the title to the house was good enough for his brother or some powerful
magnate, yet 'might it well be dangerous to thee to buy it.' The King admitted
frankly that Gloucester had bullied the old lady into parting with her house.

Not only great lords but great ladies faced ruin in the Wars of the Roses. The
story of the dowager Countess of Oxford's despoliation is unusually well documented, because her son obtained official copies of the depositions that were
later made by witnesses. They cast a chilling light on the character of Richard,
Duke of Gloucester, when still only twenty.

At Hammes the Earl of Oxford had ample leisure in which to brood over the
wrongs done to his womenfolk by the Yorkists. He could also reflect on how very
foolish he had been in placing so many hopes in the Duke of Clarence – indeed,
any hopes at all. For while 'false, fleeting, perjur'd Clarence' may well have dreamt
of taking his brother's place on the throne, they were dreams which at most led
only to wild talk. The Duke lacked the political skill and the widespread popular
support which were prerequisites for challenging anyone quite so formidable as
Edward IV. At the end of his tether, Oxford had set far too much store by sensational rumours of the sort reported by Sir John Paston. He would have done
much better to have stuck to piracy than to have relied on a rising led by the Duke
of Clarence.

29

Edward IV Invades France, 1475

WILLIAM HASTINGS · JOHN MORTON

O N the Franco-Burgundian frontier, Calais was both a listening post for spies and a halfway house to the courts of the King of France and the Duke of Burgundy. A network of secret agents operated from the port, paid by the indefatigable Lord Hastings. In January 1473 he led yet another embassy to Duke Charles the Bold, who received them at Ghent. The English hoped to persuade him to help them reconquer France, but for the time being little progress was made. The negotiations were to be reopened by Dr Morton.

In March 1472 John Morton had been made Master of the Rolls, the third most important member of the judicature, second only to the Lord Chancellor in the Court of Chancery. He also became a privy counsellor, which in the fifteenth century was not the empty dignity it is today. Normally the royal council met in the Star Chamber at Westminster Palace, its function being not unlike that of a modern cabinet. (It must not be confused with the Great Council, to which every important personality in the realm, including all peers, was summoned.) The King's 'secret council' was the institution which, under King Edward, really governed the country. Here in the Star Chamber, as one of the most powerful men in England, Dr Morton would often have met and worked with Lord Hastings.

He was closely involved in Edward IV's foreign policy. The King hoped to revive the Hundred Years' War and recover the lost lands across the Channel. Not only did he call himself King of France, but he had been born in Rouen when it was an English city. He was only too well aware that one of the reasons for the ruin of the House of Lancaster had been losing Normandy and Bordeaux. But a war of reconquest was only possible in alliance with Burgundy and with sufficient funds to pay an army.

Before a firm Anglo-Burgundian pact against France came into being, an extraordinarily complex series of negotiations took place between England, France and Burgundy, with truces and counter-truces. Dr Morton played a crucial role in this diplomatic offensive. He and Lord Duras spent January to June 1474 negotiating with the Duke, finally returning with a treaty of alliance in which Charles agreed that Edward should be crowned King of France at Rheims. In December, together with Sir Thomas Montgomery and William Hatclyf (the King's physician), he went on a further embassy, dancing attendance on the Duke, who was besieging Neuss in the course of his war with the Swiss. The negotiations were not only about an offensive against France; a staple in Burgundy for Newcastle wool was proposed and there were also discussions about the Anglo-Burgundian exchange rate. They also tried, and failed, to secure a treaty with the Emperor Frederick III against France.

We catch glimpses of the little doctor in the Paston Letters; on 5 February 1475 Sir John Paston ends a missive from Calais with: 'As for tidings here, my masters th'ambassadors Sir T Montgomery and the Master of the Rolls come straight from the duke [of Burgundy] at his siege of Neuss, which will not yet be won.' By now, 'Our well beloved clerk Mr John Morton, Keeper of our Rolls in Chancery', was once again very much of a figure in English public life.

Raising money to pay for the war was far harder. Early in 1475 Paliament heard how some collectors were not levying taxes properly or else were pocketing them. The King therefore resorted to 'benevolences'. As many rich men as possible were summoned to audiences, each one being interviewed personally by Edward. A Milanese observer noted with amusement that he welcomed every victim as if he had known him all his life, and then asked just how much he was prepared to pay towards the French war. A notary stood by to write down the amount. However much the wretched man might offer, the King would then mention that someone far poorer had given a great deal more. Few dared resist his scowl. He also kissed the victims' wives. Edward went on progress through all England on a fund-raising tour of this sort, besides enlisting the help of mayors and sheriffs.

A glib royal spokesman told the House of Commons that war with France would reduce crime by shipping unruly elements abroad. He gave a fascinating glimpse not only of the impact of the Wars of the Roses on his hearers – 'every man of this land that is of reasonable age hath known what trouble this realm hath suffered . . . none hath escaped' – but on the country as a whole. Despite King Edward's happy victory, 'yet is there many a great sore, many a perilous

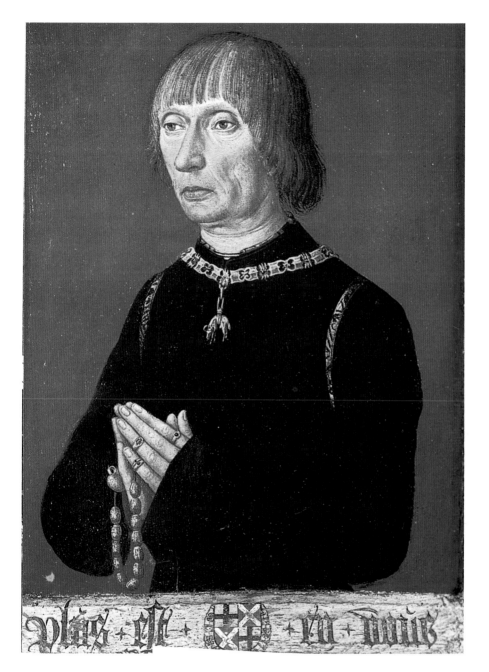

Louis de Gruuthuyse, the Burgundian nobleman
who sheltered Edward IV and Lord Hastings during their exile

A page from the Flemish Book of Hours
specially commissioned by Lord Hastings after his exile in Flanders

The Princes in the Tower, by John Millais

Altarpiece by Hans Memling, c.1477.
The kneeling donors are Sir John Donne and his wife, Hastings' sister Elizabeth

Richard III. A sixteenth-century copy of a lost portrait

Elizabeth of York, daughter of Edward IV and queen of Henry VII.
A sixteenth-century copy of a lost portrait

Henry VII. A copy of a lost portrait painted about 1500

wound left unhealed, the multitude of riotous people which have at all times kindled the fire of this great division is so spread over all and every coast of this realm, committing extortions, oppressions, robberies and other great mischiefs.'[1] What he tactfully omitted from his speech was the fact that some of the great mischiefs were due to the King's failure to control his magnates' affinities.

Margaret Paston gave vent to a taxpayer's exasperation in a letter to her son Sir John – 'the king goeth so near us in this country, both to poor and rich, that I wot not how we shall live but if the world amend,' she writes. She claims that the benevolences have impoverished all East Anglia.

An English invasion force of 11,500 men assembled in June 1475, much larger than any army commanded by Henry V. Yet though it included twenty-five peers, their troops were not of the highest quality. There were too many archers (even if a large number were mounted) and too few men-at-arms – where the ratio should have been one man-at-arms to every three bowmen, it was one to every seven. The ratio was still worse in Lord Hastings' contingent, though he brought forty men-at-arms and 300 archers, more than any other peer save the Duke of Clarence and the Earl of Northumberland. He was supported by John Donne and two other knights with 104 archers. Very few of these troops had had experience of warfare overseas. However, there was an impressive artillery train, said to be larger than the Duke of Burgundy's, while the King had brought a wagon-train of food in case the French should adopt scorched-earth tactics.[2]

The army began embarking in June. As Captain of Calais, Hastings – assisted by his lieutenant, Lord Howard – was responsible for problems of billeting, besides having to liaise with the Burgundians. King Edward crossed from Dover on 4 July, Dr Morton accompanying him. They found a good deal to dishearten them. The weather was atrocious, with heavy rain, and already it was almost too late in the year to begin a campaign. Moreover, a commander as experienced as Edward realized that his troops were not entirely satisfactory.

Commynes, who watched them, comments, 'I don't exaggerate when I say that Edward's men seemed very inexperienced and unused to active service, since they rode in such ragged order.' No doubt at home they were accustomed to dismounting and fighting on foot rather than on horseback. Even so, however fiercely they may have fought each other, the armies of late-fifteenth-century England were always amateurish and unprofessional. They must have been very difficult to command, not least the haughty, quarrelsome gentlemen who officered them.

Their leader had by now grown a little too fond of his comforts, while he was scarcely encouraged by the Duke of Burgundy's arrival at Calais without an army

– the Burgundian troops were busy campaigning elsewhere.

Nevertheless, King Louis was terrified out of his wits, as though Henry V had risen from the grave. If possible, he was determined to buy off the English. He had sent flattering letters to Lord Hastings at Calais, together with what Commynes calls 'a very big and handsome present' (presumably money), though in reply he had received only a polite letter of acknowledgement. But soon it became obvious that the campaign was not going very well for the English – at St Quentin their advance guard was routed by cannon-fire from the town walls, some men being killed or taken prisoner. Louis sent a message into Edward's camp. If the King of England wanted peace, then he would do his best to satisfy him. He apologized for having helped the Earl of Warwick, and emphasized how bad the weather was for July 'when winter was already approaching.'

King Edward held a council, attended by both Lord Hastings and Dr Morton. It decided to offer Louis terms; basically these would amount to an indemnity. On 13 August Lord Howard, Thomas St Leger, William Dudley and John Morton went to negotiate with the French at a village near Amiens – a few days later they saw Louis himself.

The terms were agreed. In return for leaving France, Edward was to receive a down payment of 75,000 crowns, together with a pension of 50,000 crowns to be paid yearly. In addition, the Dauphin was to marry one of the English King's daughters and there would be advantageous commercial clauses.

However, an agreement had not yet been signed, and Louis was anxious that the English should not change their minds. To make the settlement popular with everyone, he invited the entire English army to be his guests in the city of Amiens. If Philippe de Commynes is to be believed, what followed was the funniest episode in the whole history of Anglo–French relations.

The French King ordered two long tables to be placed on each side of the street that led into the city from its main gate. These were laden with all sorts of good dishes to accompany the wine, of which there was a very great deal and the best that France could produce. 'At both tables the king had sat five or six boon companions, fat and sleek noblemen, to welcome any Englishman who felt like having a cheerful glass ... nine or ten taverns were generously supplied with anything they wanted, where they could have whatever they ordered without paying for it, by command of the king of France who paid the entire cost of the entertainment which went on for three or four days.' At one tavern that Commynes entered, 111 bills had already been run up, though it was not yet nine o'clock in the morning. The house was crowded with Englishmen, 'some of whom were singing, others asleep and all of them very drunk.' King Edward was ashamed of his troops' behaviour, and had large numbers of them thrown out of the city.

Louis XI had thought of everything. He even seems to have provided whores, who took their own special revenge on the invaders. 'Many a man was lost that fell to the lust of women, who were burnt by them; and their members rotted away and they died,' claims one doleful English chronicler.

The two kings met on a bridge at Picquigny on 29 August 1475. Among those who accompanied Edward was William Hastings. 'The king of England wore a black velvet cap on his head, decorated with a large fleur-de-lys of precious stones,' Commynes recalls. 'He was a prince of noble and majestic appearance but somewhat running to fat.' Commynes adds that Edward did not look so handsome as when he had last seen him, during his flight from Warwick in 1471, but that he spoke to Louis in good French.

They had no hesitation in signing the treaty. To make certain that Edward's councellors would support it, Louis bribed them. Hastings got most, an annual pension of 2,000 gold crowns – to be supplemented over the next two years by 24,000 more in money and plate, including two dozen silver gilt bowls worth over £600. The French King was fully aware of the power and influence of the chamberlain, whom Commynes summed up as 'a man of sound sense, courage and authority.'

Commynes says it was not easy to persuade Hastings to accept the pension, as a loyal friend of the Burgundians who were already paying him a thousand crowns a year. King Louis sent an agent, Pierre Clairet, to England with the pensions and orders to obtain receipts so that the King could prove that Hastings and all the others were being paid by him. However, 'at a private conversation alone with the chamberlain in his room in London', William refused to sign for the money.

'I didn't ask for it,' he told Clairet. 'If you wish me to take it, then you can slip it in my pocket, but you're never going to get a letter of thanks or a receipt out of me. I don't want everybody saying "The lord chamberlain of England is in the king of France's pay."'

Commynes adds that Louis was so impressed by Lord Hastings' shrewdness that he went on paying the pension without asking for receipts, and felt more respect for him than for all the rest of Edward's counsellors put together.

Dr Morton was also recognized by King Louis as a man of power and influence. He received a pension of 600 crowns, though we do not know if he signed receipts for it.

Some people in England grumbled at the Treaty of Picquigny. After being told for three years that they were in honour bound to pay for waging war on 'our ancient enemies of France', besides suffering from 'benevolences', their king had returned ingloriously without conquering a foot of French soil; all the bright hopes of recovering Normandy and Bordeaux had vanished into thin air. Yet for Edward IV the settlement was a triumph of realism. He had seen that his brother-in-law of Burgundy could not be relied on, while he recognized that he himself was in no condition to undertake those exhausting campaigns of conquest that had destroyed Henry V's health. France was no longer the divided land of fifty years ago but ruled by one of her greatest kings. Instead of fighting a risky and ruinously expensive war, Edward had come home with a new source of income.

The King took the opportunity to attend to minor nuisances. Henry Holland, Duke of Exeter, did not come home. After the Lancastrian defeat at Barnet, Exeter had spent some time in sanctuary at Westminster Abbey before being moved to the Tower, where he had stayed until he either volunteered or was ordered to join the expedition. His wife Anne, King Edward's sister, had secured an annulment so that she could marry her lover, Sir Thomas St Leger – one of her brother's squires of the Body – with whom she was living on the Duke's former revenues. There was no place for the haughty Exeter in a Yorkist world. On the return voyage he drowned between Calais and Dover, 'but how he drowned, the certainty is not known,' says Fabyan. However, Giovanni Pannicharola, the Milanese envoy to the Burgundian court, was told by Duke Charles that the King of England had given specific orders for the sailors to throw his former brother-in-law overboard. It would not be the last of King Edward's convenient drownings.[3]

According to the same Milanese source, Duke Charles was so enraged when he heard the news of Picquigny that he ate his Garter, or at least tore it with his teeth. He had every reason to be angry, even though his lack of co-operation was partly responsible for the treaty. It weakened Burgundy enormously against France, in both military and diplomatic terms. There was no more hope of armed assistance on a really large scale from across the sea. Indeed, although English sovereigns might continue to call themselves 'Kings of France' until the nineteenth century, it was the end of the Hundred Years' War. Louis had won a great, bloodless victory. He boasted to Commynes: 'I kicked the English out of France much more easily than my father did – he had to do it by force of arms but I used venison pies and good wine.'

30

Mrs Shore's Divorce, 1476

JANE SHORE

Rɪᴅɪɴɢ home from Picquigny, King Louis told Philippe de Commynes with horror how, during their meeting, Edward IV had expressed a keen desire to visit Paris. Louis continued anxiously, 'He's a king, very handsome, and more than keen on the women. He might quite easily meet some cunning female in Paris who would know just what to say to make him want to come back.' Commynes comments that no man ever enjoyed his pleasures more than Edward, 'especially in ladies, feasting, banqueting and hunting.' After his return from France, he indulged them to the full. No doubt he spent more time with Jane Shore.

The prime of King Edward for both business and pleasure was during the years 1471–83, when he had eliminated his rivals so that there was no serious opposition. The French pension and his careful husbanding of his own revenues – he had a marked aptitude for accounts – stabilized the budget, while his commercial diplomacy established sound trading relations abroad and ended the economic depression. He understood exactly what merchants wanted, making sensible treaties with neighbours and eliminating piracy. Possessing genuine financial flair, he even engaged in commerce himself, the only English monarch to do so, shipping wool, tin and lead to Italy, while importing cargoes that ranged from wine and paper to sugar and oranges. He ruled much more firmly than during his first reign, putting down rioting, feuding and any attempts to cow juries. He was helped in this by his extraordinary memory, being able to recall the names and estates of all the gentlemen of England as though he were accustomed to seeing each one of them every day.

Yet at the same time the King was a glutton and a compulsive womanizer. Mancini says that he would purge his belly for the sheer pleasure of starting a meal all over again. His wenching was so well known that, in an attempt to discredit his memory during his brother Richard's reign, an Act of Parliament would allege in retrospect that no man in the kingdom had felt safe about his womenfolk because of Edward's lustfulness, and that every woman lived in fear of being raped by him. His combination of debauchery with sheer hard work astonished the Croyland chronicler.

What cannot be omitted from any assessment of Edward IV is the impact of his personality. Every contemporary source agrees that he had a magnificent appearance. 'Very tall . . . exceeding the stature of almost all others, of comely visage, pleasant in expression, broad chested' is what Polydore Vergil was told. 'He was of visage full faced and lovely, of body mighty, strong and clean made; with over liberal and wanton diet he waxed something corpulent and burly, but nevertheless not uncomely,' says More, who as a very small boy may himself have seen the King.

His manner was so friendly and lacking in pomposity that Vergil thought it a little undignified – 'he would use himself more familiarly among private persons than the honour of his majesty required.'

'Frequently he called to his side complete strangers, when he thought they had come with the intention of talking to him or having a close look at him,' Mancini noted.

> He was so genial in his greeting that, when he saw a newcomer bewildered by his regal appearance and royal pomp, he would give him courage to speak by laying a kindly hand on his shoulder. He listened very willingly to plaintiffs or to anyone who complained to him about some injustice – charges against himself he would disarm by an excuse even though he might not put the matter right.

His popularity was enhanced by a general sense of relief that the fighting had ended. In retrospect it is easy to forget that with the death of Henry VI and his son it really did seem that the Wars of the Roses were over. Before that venerable ex-Lancastrian Sir John Fortescue died in 1479, he wrote of Edward:

> He hath done more for us than ever did king of England, or might have done before him. The harms that hath fallen in getting of his realm be now by him turned into the good and profit of all of us. We shall now more enjoy

our own goods, and live under justice, which we have not done of long time, God knoweth.

Admittedly, no one could deny that Edward IV had his faults. 'He was licentious in the extreme', Mancini comments primly, adding:

> It was said that he behaved very badly towards numerous women after seducing them because, as soon as he grew tired with the affair, much against their will he would pass the ladies on to other courtiers. He pursued indiscriminately married and unmarried, noble and low-born, though he never raped them. He overcame them all by money and promises and then, having had them, he got rid of them.

Mancini may paint too kind a picture. He himself mentions how Edward threatened Elizabeth Woodville with a dagger when she resisted him before their marriage, while Vergil implies that he tried to rape a kinswoman of Warwick in the Earl's own house – 'the king was a man who would readily cast an eye upon young ladies and love them inordinately.'

Among the favoured courtiers to whom Edward passed on his discarded mistresses were William Hastings and the Queen's elder son by her previous marriage, Thomas Grey, whom the King had created Marquess of Dorset, and who was known by everybody as 'The Marquess'. Hastings had a feud with him, Mancini informs us, 'because of the mistresses whom they had abducted or had tried to entice away from each other.'

We know the names of surprisingly few of King Edward's women. He had two children by Lady Elizabeth Lucy, while after his death it was alleged that he had seduced a daughter of the Earl of Salisbury with a promise of marriage. More is tantalizingly unspecific in his account of the king's loves:

> King Edward would say that he had three concubines which in three divers properties diversely excelled, one the merriest, another the wisest, the third the holiest harlot in his realm, as one whom no man could get out of the church lightly to any place but it were to his bed.

The last two seem to have been ladies of the court, and were probably Elizabeth Lucy and Eleanor Butler. 'But the merriest was this Shore's wife', More tells us. 'For many he had but her he loved.'[1]

Meanwhile, in the City of London, the second reign of Edward IV was turning out to be a sunny period of peace and prosperity. However, poor John Lambert's aldermanship was not restored to him. Only a week after his 'exoneration' in 1470, his place had been filled by a fellow mercer, John Brown, and there would not be another vacancy for nearly twenty years. There is evidence from the second half of 1471 which confirms that Mr Lambert had been removed from office because of his political sympathies. In the course of a law-suit against his brother-in-law, Alexander Marshall (over his father-in-law's bequest of houses in the parish of St Antelyn's and gardens in St Giles without Cripplegate), John Lambert complained of Alexander's behaviour. His brother-in-law had 'openly noised him that he was a false traitor to Henry late called "King Henry the Sixth".[2] Obviously, during the recent Readeption, Alexander had put it about that John was an irreconcilable Yorkist.

In the following year, 1472, Mr Lambert was involved in another law-suit, with the Goldsmiths' Company, from whom he had rented a furnished house in Wood Street. The Goldsmiths took him to the Mayor's Court, alleging that when his tenancy came to an end he had taken away eight window panes from the parlour, the iron bars from over the shop counter, and twenty-seven shutters, together with the chapel panelling and a great pewter laver 'standing by the hall to wash men's hands' which he had sold to Edmund Shaa – a rich goldsmith and future Mayor of London. In 1474 judgement was given against him. He was made to return the fittings and pay for the repairs, while Mr Shaa had to give the laver back to the Goldsmiths' Company.[3]

This distressing episode does not appear to have harmed John's reputation. He was elected one of the four wardens of the 'holy fellowship of the Mercers' Company' for a second time in 1475, and in the same year, 'having livelihood of £51 by the year or above', was one of those unlucky mercers chosen by the company to present themselves to the King and give a benevolence for the French war. (He is listed as living in Cordwainer Street.) What he was wheedled or bullied into paying is not recorded, though it must have been a substantial sum.

William Shore was prospering as mercer and merchant adventurer. Although he did not become a warden of the company, let alone an alderman, clearly he was well respected. He had been taking apprentices since 1463, some of whom came from rich backgrounds – at least one being the son of a wealthy mercer. His sister had married into the Derbyshire gentry, her husband being John Agard of Foston on the Staffordshire border.[4] Agard's standing may be gauged from the fact that Lord Hastings thought him worth including in his affinity, retaining him by indenture in April 1474. The Agards had been employed for decades as officials of the Honour of Tutbury (part of the Duchy of Lancaster), of which Hastings had been appointed steward two years previously.

The principal information we possess about Mrs Shore is simply that she was childless and that she had been admitted as a Freewoman of the City of London. The latter was no mean dignity, being restricted to daughters born to London Freemen *after* their election, who must have reached the age of twenty-one. She too had a respected position in society, as a prosperous and well-connected City lady.

Although we have so few firm details, we can nonetheless guess a good deal about Mrs Shore's way of life. A very widespread impression exists that all medieval women were downtrodden slaves, apart from a few great ladies, but this was true only up to a point. It was certainly not the case with well-to-do females of Jane's class, especially if they had a strong character. Middle-class girls usually received some sort of formal education, even if they could not attend the grammar schools. They at least went to elementary schools or else were given private tuition, being taught to read and write, together with a little Latin and French, and perhaps a smattering of English Law. (We know from Thomas More that Jane could read and write.) A woman might take an active part in trade if she wished, acquiring the legal status of '*femme sole*', which enabled her to do business on her own account, and even to take apprentices; there were women brewers, women corn-merchants and, above all, women silk-weavers. However, they were the exception rather than the rule, their activities generally stemming from surplus energy rather than any need to supplement the family budget.

There is no record of Jane Shore ever having been in business. Presumably she supported her husband to the extent of dressing as richly as any court lady in order to advertise his prosperity. (Again, we know from More that she was fond of smart clothes.) After all, as a Freewoman of the City, she had a position to keep up. 'In the merchant class it is probable that they followed the custom of gentlewomen in the City, learning to hunt and going freely to taverns', says Sylvia Thrupp in her *Merchant Class of Medieval London*. Hunting included riding with the buckhounds – sitting side-saddle, a custom that had come in towards the end of the previous century – hare coursing, and hawking. No doubt many women preferred to treat these entertainments as spectator sports, merely going to a meet of the hounds or watching the hawks being flown from a convenient rooftop.

Other amusements were chess, backgammon and draughts, all of which could be played for money.

The first historical evidence that not all was well with the Shores' marriage dates from 1474. On 30 November William Shore made a gift of his goods and chattels to five friends, two of whom were mercers. This was a common legal device for protecting one's possessions, often adopted when leaving the country to travel abroad.[5] Mr Shore may have been considering emigration because of his wife's affair with the King.

Edward kept in touch with most of the richer London merchants and must have been told all the racier City gossip. So too would William Hastings, with his own mercantile activities and vast acquaintance. One can guess that both roared with laughter on hearing that a beautiful young woman was seeking to have her marriage annulled by the Church on the grounds of her husband's impotence. It could well be that it was their bizarre law-case which first aroused the King's interest in Mrs Shore.

Jane had been trying to obtain an annulment for several years. Her lawyers had taken her case more than once to the Court of Arches (Dr Morton's old stamping ground), but the Dean of Arches – the 'official principal' – had proved thoroughly unsympathetic. Why? Admittedly the grounds were most unusual; normally an annulment was granted because the marriage had been within a forbidden degree of affinity (of cousinhood, which was too close) or because there was evidence of coercion. Impotence was a very rare plea indeed, and the case was apparently unique in fifteenth-century England. Did the Dean suspect that poor Mr Shore's lack of virility was a convenient fiction? On the other hand, one can understand Shore's reluctance to appear before the court if he really was afflicted in this embarrassing way.[6]

Only the richest in the land could afford to go to Rome over the head of the Dean of Arches. Even a loving father anxious for grandchildren would have baulked at the vast sums involved. However, the money came from somewhere. (Did the King pay?) On 1 March 1476 Pope Sixtus IV dispatched a mandate from Rome to the Bishops of Hereford, Sidon and Ross in London, which empowered them to hear Jane's petition.

The papal mandate reads as follows:

> The recent petition of Elizabeth Lambert alias Schore [sic], *mulier*, of London states that she continued in her marriage, *per verba legitimi de presenti*,

to William Schore, layman of the diocese of London, and cohabited with him for the lawful time, but that he is so frigid and impotent that she, desirous of being a mother and having offspring, requested over and over again the [principal] official of London [the Dean of Arches] to cite the said William before him to answer her concerning the foregoing and the nullity of the said marriage and that, seeing the said official refused to do so, she appealed to the Apostolic See . . .

Jane's petition was granted and her marriage annulled. While there is no reason to suppose that she was lying about the wretched Mr Shore's inadequacy, the composition of the tribunal may have had something to do with its verdict. Although little is known of the Bishops of Sidon and Ross, 'my lord of Hereford' was a prominent figure at court and a close friend of the King. He was Dr Thomas Millyngton, a former Abbot of Westminster, who had played a most important part in the life of the royal family.[7] When the pregnant Queen and her daughters had gone into sanctuary at Westminster during the Readeption of 1470–71, as Abbot Dr Millyngton had housed them in his magnificent 'lodging', where Queen Elizabeth gave birth to her first son. After Edward's restoration, the grateful King had insisted on Millyngton's appointment to the see of Hereford, making him a privy counsellor. He was at the very least aware of the judgement in this case which would be most welcome to his patron.

We know from Thomas More's account that King Edward was captivated by pretty Mrs Shore's good looks and cheerful, amusing personality. In More's view, the young lady's miserable marriage 'the more easily made her incline unto the king's appetite when he required her', while 'the respect of his royalty, the hope of gay apparel, ease, pleasure and other wanton wealth, was soon able to pierce a soft, tender heart.' He adds that as soon as the affair had begun – probably at some date before November 1474 – Mr Shore, 'not presuming to touch a king's concubine, left her up to him altogether.' Apparently More had not heard about Shore's impotence.

Admittedly, our knowledge of Jane Shore and of her relations with King Edward IV is very scanty indeed. She belonged to a class that has left very few personal records, and in any case the chroniclers thought that no woman other than a queen, a great heiress or a saint was worth mentioning. The first firm date for Jane's very existence is that of the divorce tribunal's appointment in 1476; she is not heard of again for another seven years. We are totally dependent on Thomas More for any details of her romance with the King. No doubt their first meeting was followed by the usual pattern of swift seduction and a torrid affair.

What made it so different from Edward's other love affairs was that it turned into a firm friendship which lasted for the rest of his life.

There are many lurid tales about Jane, mostly apocryphal. One example in the *Dictionary of National Biography* – which gives as its source the *Huntingdon Peerage* – is especially colourful:

> It is said that Lord Hastings, who may have met her owing to her father's business lying much at court, tried to induce her to become his mistress; and that he even schemed to carry her off by night, but was defeated in his design by the repentance of a maid who was his accomplice.

Sadly, this story is nowhere to be found in the *Huntingdon Peerage* (which in any case is hopelessly unreliable) and has no historical foundation. William Hastings kept away from her until after King Edward's death.

The spectacular story of Mrs Shore's later fall from riches to rags (to be recounted further on in this book) appealed to the popular imagination. During the sixteenth and seventeenth centuries, plays and ballads would be written about her:

> Long time I lived in the courte,
> With lords and ladies of greate sorte;
> And when I smil'd all men were glad,
> But when I frown'd my prince grewe sad

However, all that was really known about Jane until 1972, when she was identified as John Lambert's daughter, came from the Tudor chroniclers whose only sources were Thomas More, a few lines in *The Great Chronicle of London*, and some references to her by Richard III.

William Shore left the City. On 4 December 1476 he was given letters of protection under the great seal for his lands, goods, servants and possessions, no more being heard of him in London records till the next reign. He moved to East Anglia or Flanders, or alternated between them, having close links with

Jane Shore's 'gay apparel' – how fashionable ladies dressed in Edward IV's reign. The material of the one on the left is similar to that of doublets worn by the king and his brother Richard in portraits painted about 1482.

Colchester and Antwerp. There he concentrated on his business as a merchant adventurer, exporting cloth and importing wine, trading as far afield as Iceland. Understandably, he did not marry again.[8]

'Shore's wife' was one mistress whom Edward IV did not care to pass on to his courtiers. More informs us that Lord Hastings fell deeply in love with her – 'on whom he somewhat doted' – but far from attempting to kidnap her, did not press his suit out of 'reverence towards his king, or else of a kind of fidelity to his friend.' His competitor, the Marquess of Dorset, who was no less attracted by her, also seems to have kept away from Jane until after his stepfather's death.

Like all medieval men and women, the King and his mistress rose early, their day beginning at 5.30 a.m. They sat down to dinner at nine or ten o'clock – somewhat later on fast days. By all accounts, Edward is unlikely to have enjoyed fasting. A fair number of his banquets seem to have been picnics during hunting parties, in 'lodges' made of green boughs, around the old royal palace of the Bower in Waltham Forest at Havering in Essex.

As with every fifteenth-century sport, where women were concerned the hunt was often a spectator sport. Jane watched it set off with due pageantry, waiting in the lodge until it returned with a boar, stag, buck or hares, whereupon the morning's sport was symbolically re-enacted before the women, after which everyone sat down to dine. The King also went in for angling parties, and perhaps tennis parties as well – what is now called 'real tennis' was fashionable. Much more enjoyable, probably, from Jane's point of view, was dancing.

This usually meant the 'Bace Dance', the slow, stately *Basse Danse* of the Burgundian court, which was very different from the hopping and skipping of country jigs. Writing in 1521, when it can have changed little, Robert Coplande explains, 'for to dance any Bace Dance there behoveth four paces, that is to wit: single, double, reprise and braule [*branle*]. And ye ought first to make reverence toward the lady . . .'

Each couple stood side by side, the lady on the man's right, giving him her left hand to hold at shoulder level. Gentle and undulating, this courtly dance consisted of grave advances and retreats, punctuated by the *branle* – a sideways step, swaying from left foot to right and back again. It was customary for the court to dance it before the King, and presumably Jane did so on many occasions in her most seductive apparel.

Clearly King Edward enjoyed her company very much indeed, appreciating the sweet nature for which she was so renowned. According to More, 'in his latter days, he left all wild dalliance and fell to gravity', yet he always remained good friends with Mrs Shore. 'Where the king took displeasure, she would mitigate and appease his mind; where men were out of favour, she would bring them into his grace.'

There is a tradition at Eton that she saved the college from destruction, when Edward contemplated transferring its endowments to St George's, Windsor. He had little reason to favour a foundation of Henry VI. It is said that Jane persuaded him to change his mind at the request of her confessor, Henry Bost, who was Provost of Eton. Unfortunately there is no hard documentary evidence for this story.[9]

Even so, More insists that Jane Shore saved a substantial number of people from ruin out of the sheer kindness of her heart:

> For many that had highly offended, she obtained pardon. Of great forfeitures she got men remission. And, finally, in many weighty suits she stood many men in great stead, either for none or very small rewards and those rather gay than rich: either for that she was content with the deed [it]self well done, or for that she was delighted to be sued unto, and to show what she was able to do with the king, or for that wanton women and wealthy be not always covetous.

In his *History* he writes only of Hastings and Morton with such obvious liking as he does of Mrs Shore.

However, More has to admit that the Queen – a good hater – could not stand 'Shore's wife . . . whom of all women she most hated, as that concubine whom the king her husband most loved.' Queen Elizabeth had reason to feel competitive. Despite his womanizing, Edward still found time to share the marital bed, fathering ten children who survived infancy – the last being born as late as 1480. There were so many royal palaces near London (his favourites being Windsor, Eltham and Greenwich), and he was so often on progress, that it was very easy for him to meet Jane without the Queen knowing, unless informed by spiteful gossips. Quite apart from his palaces, Mrs Shore had a comfortable house of her own in London, either in some smart street in the City off Cheapside or in a fashionable suburb such as Stepney. But if the bond with Jane was cheerful companionship rather than sexuality, this did not placate Elizabeth Woodville if she ever believed it.

The royal favour did not extend to Mrs Shore's family, save for the 'protection' given to her ex-husband. Edward IV was certainly not going to waste time on patronizing such a fool as Mr Lambert, who had lost his aldermanry. John must have reached sixty by the late 1470s and was therefore growing very old indeed. There are fewer and fewer references to him in the records. One of the last is in 1477, when he made a small contribution towards repairing the City walls, after an appeal by the King and the Mayor.

31

Lord Oxford
Tries to Drown Himself, 1478

LORD OXFORD · LORD HASTINGS

THE Duke of Clarence, no further to achieving his vague, ill-thought-out ambition of supplanting Edward on the throne, and still bitterly resentful at having to share the Warwick inheritance with Gloucester, had grown even more discontented. From the King's point of view Clarence had become an unmitigated nuisance. Most brothers would never have forgiven him for the part he had played during the Readeption, yet he was wholly without gratitude for Edward's magnanimity.

While beginning to grow popular, the King was aware that in some quarters there was a certain irreducible amount of dissatisfaction with his rule, though no open opposition. Many people disliked his uncomfortably efficient ways in financial matters, but they were unavoidable. Anxious to avoid stirring up discontent by direct taxation, he was determined to 'live of his own' – on Crown revenues.

The Croyland chronicler describes Edward's methods:

> Having called Parliament together, he resumed possession of nearly all the royal estates [those Crown lands given to favourites] without regard to those to whom they had been granted, and applied the whole thereof to support the expenses of the Crown . . . He also examined the register and rolls of Chancery and exacted heavy fines from those whom he found to have taken possession of estates without prosecuting their rights in form required by law.

The King was rigorous in enforcing the irksome dues on wardships and marriages, while he levied Customs duties with such harshness that there was considerable grumbling from the merchant community.

Fortunately for Edward, there was no one to challenge him. His only possible rival was the Duke of Clarence, whose character and record did not exactly encourage potential supporters. But then the Duke's nuisance value was exacerbated by totally unexpected problems overseas.

For a short time it really did seem that the inglorious expedition of 1475 meant lasting peace abroad. Determined to endear himself to the English court, Louis XI sent no less than 700,000 tuns of the best French wines procurable for Christmas 1476. However, news came in January that Duke Charles had been killed in battle by the Swiss, his successor being an only daughter by a previous marriage. It was the beginning of the end for Valois Burgundy, England's traditional ally against France.

Writing on 14 February from London to his brother in Norwich, Sir John Paston reported the general alarm:

> Yesterday began the great council, to which all the estates of the land shall come to, but it be for great and reasonable excuses; and I suppose the chief cause of this assembly is to commune what is best to do now upon the great change by the death of the duke of Burgundy, and for the keeping of Calais and the Marches, and for the preservation of the amities taken late, as well with France as now with the members of Flanders; whereto I doubt not there shall be in all haste both the dukes of Clarence and Gloucester . . . this day I hear great likelihood that my lord Hastings shall hastily go to Calais with great company . . . It seemeth that all the world is quavering.[1]

Hastings rushed across the Channel to Calais, which 'stood in great jeopardy and peril for sundry encounters and comings of our enemies thither and there about.' Even so, his great company consisted of a mere sixteen men-at-arms and 500 archers.

Then, for a moment, William fell victim to the machinations of Louis XI, who with his customary deviousness was trying to estrange Edward and his sister Margaret, the dowager Duchess of Burgundy, together with as many of the Plantagenets and their courtiers as possible. On his instructions the French ambassador, Olivier de Roux, insinuated that Margaret was scheming to marry her stepdaughter, Mary of Burgundy, to her favourite brother, George of Clarence, and that if the marriage took place Clarence was then going to use

Burgundian troops and treasure to make himself King of England. The Sieur de Roux further insinuated that the Lord Chamberlain of England, Lord Hastings, was closely involved in the plot. (Not for nothing has it been suggested that Louis was a model for Machiavelli's *Prince*.)[2]

For a time Margaret had indeed proposed such a marriage. Clarence was her favourite brother and recently widowed. But it would confront Edward with an expensive war on two fronts, since the Scots would join in on the side of the French, which might well destabilize the entire political situation in England. He was able to convince Margaret that the match was impossible, and Mary was betrothed to the Archduke Maximilian of Hapsburg. Clarence was bitterly disappointed. King Louis meant to profit from his dissatisfaction.

Briefly under suspicion, Hastings was summoned home to Windsor in June. Soon reassured, Edward sent him back to Calais, which expected to be attacked at any moment. 'And as it is said, if the French king cannot get St Omer that he intendeth to bring his army through these marches into Flanders, wherefore my lord [chamberlain] hath . . . broken all the passages except Newham bridge, which is watched, and the turnpike shut every night,' Edmund Bedingfeld reported in August. 'And the said French king within these three days railed greatly of my lord to Tiger Pursuivant, openly, before 200 of his folks; wherefore it is thought here that he would find a quarrel to set upon this town.' (Pursuivants were often employed as envoys.) Bedingfeld adds apprehensively, 'I fear me sore that Flanders will be lost, and if St Omer be won, all is gone.'[3] Although Burgundy survived for the time being and the situation settled down, it involved Hastings in a flurry of diplomatic activity. His lieutenancy of Calais was certainly no sinecure.

Meanwhile, since the spring rumours of plots had been circulating all over England. In June a rising broke out in East Anglia led by a man calling himself the Earl of Oxford. The impostor was speedily routed, but he had given the government a bad fright. (It did not make life any easier for the real Earl's countess – 'My lord of Oxenford is not comen into England that I can perceive, and so the good lady hath need of help and counsel how that she shall do,' commented Sir John Paston.)

What now befell the Duke of Clarence has to be set in the context of these rumours and of the false Lord Oxford's plot, and also of the French ambassador's insinuations. Recently the Duke's conduct had been eccentric, to put it mildly. In April that year, 1477, 80 of his men had abducted an elderly gentlewoman called

Ankarette Twynhoe from her house in Somerset, dragging her off to his town of Warwick. A former lady of the late Duchess, she was charged before a jury cowed by Clarence with having given her late mistress 'a venomous drink of ale mixed with poison', condemned and hanged forthwith. A John Thursby of Warwick was hanged with her, accused of having poisoned the Duke's son.

One thing at least is clear, that the Duke of Clarence was crazed by paranoia, to the point of insanity. He was convinced that his royal brother had been trying to murder him. He told his intimates that Edward employed magic to rule England, that the King 'wrought by necromancy and used [witch]craft to poison his subjects'. The Duke alleged that his own life was threatened by the King, who meant to 'consume him in likewise as a candle is consumed by burning.' Most unfortunately for the Duke, evidence then came to light which seemed to show that he himself had been enlisting the help of warlocks, with the worst possible intentions.

Shortly after the Ankarette Twynhoe incident, a fellow of Merton College at Oxford, Mr John Stacey, who specialized in the study of astronomy, was interrogated under torture. He had been charged with trying to kill Lord Beauchamp at the adulterous Lady Beauchamp's instigation, by melting a leaden image of the unloved peer. Mr Stacey broke down, confessing that he had had other and far more ambitious murders in mind, implicating not only a second member of his colleage, Mr Thomas Blake, but Thomas Burdet, Esquire, a substantial landowner and former MP for Worcestershire, who belonged to Clarence's household. As a result of Stacey's confession, all three were accused of 'imagining' the death of King Edward and the Prince of Wales by sorcery – by manipulating images of them so that they would be consumed. The three were additionally charged with circulating 'bills, rhymes and ballads' designed to alienate Edward IV from his subjects. Found guilty by a jury, Stacey and Burdet were hanged, drawn and quartered at Tyburn in May, protesting that they were innocent.

The allegations made against the Queen have already been mentioned. The fifteenth century believed implicitly in witchcraft. In 1484 Pope Innocent VIII was to commission two members of the German Inquisition to investigate the phenomenon, the result being the book entitled *Malleus Maleficarum*, the 'hammer of witches'. Accusations of casting spells were part of the standard political armoury. Edward IV was himself popularly rumoured to have enlisted the services of the celebrated necromancer Friar Bungay to shroud the battlefield of Barnet in mist and to stir up storms in the Channel to delay Queen Margaret's return in 1471.

Clarence responded to the execution of Burdet and Stacey by bursting into a session of the Privy Council in the Star Chamber at Westminster when Edward was absent. He had brought with him a friar, John Goddard, whom he ordered to read out the protests that the two men had produced at the foot of the gallows. The Duke was appealing against the King to the council. And Dr Goddard was a most unhappy choice – during the Readeption he had preached a sermon in Paul's Cross on Henry VI's right to the throne.

Edward IV finally lost patience with his brother. As Thomas More was to be warned of Edward's grandson Henry VIII, '*Indignatio principis mors est*' – 'the indignation of the prince is death.' Mancini says that though the King normally wore a cheerful expression, 'when he looked angry he could appear quite terrifying.' In July he summoned Clarence to Westminster, where in the presence of the Mayor and aldermen he rebuked him for conduct that devalued the law of the land and 'was most dangerous to judges and jurors throughout the kingdom' – an obvious reference to the hangings at Warwick. Then Edward ordered the Duke's arrest and his committal to the Tower.

In January 1478 a bill of attainder, signed by the King, was presented to Parliament. It was very carefully drafted – Dr Morton may well have had a hand in drawing it up. George, Duke of Clarence, was specifically accused of plotting to usurp the throne, and to destroy Edward and his children, 'a much higher, much more malicious, more unnatural and loathely treason than at any time heretofore hath been compassed, purposed and conspired.' He had attempted to alienate the King and his subjects, spreading rumours that Edward used necromancy and poison to control them. He had circulated a libel to the effect that Edward was a bastard. Finally, he had carefully kept a copy of an agreement between himself and Margaret of Anjou stating that 'if the said [King] Henry and Edward, his first begotten son, died without issue male of their body, that the said duke and his heirs should be king of this land.'

There was no difficulty in persuading the Commons to pass the bill since the House was packed, many of its members being royal servants or retainers of the Duke of Gloucester, of the Woodvilles or of others close to the King. Hastings' affinity may have supplied as many as ten MPs. Despite his former friendship with Clarence, William obeyed King Edward. The House of Lords was no less amenable, their spokesman, the Duke of Buckingham, formally pronouncing sentence of death. It is known that Clarence died at the Tower on 18 February 1478, though not precisely how. Nevertheless, Shakespeare is almost certainly correct in depicting his 'execution' by drowning in a butt of malmsey. Writing only five years afterwards, Mancini says that the Duke was 'plunged into a jar of sweet wine', while Philippe de Commynes says unequivocally that it was malmsey.

Was Clarence really guilty of treason? Mancini had heard that the Duke of Gloucester was so overcome with grief that he could not stop himself from promising publicly that one day he would avenge his brother's death. However, Richard Gloucester had attended all the meetings that must have decided Clarence's fate, while he himself benefited more than anyone else from the division of his estates – even before the trial he secured possession of Clarence's lordship of Ogmore.[4]

Contemporaries were bewildered. All Mancini could find out was that 'whether it was a fabricated plot or a real plot which had been discovered, the duke of Clarence was accused of plotting the king's death by means of spells and magicians.' Thomas More, equally uncertain, says 'were he faulty or were he faultless', and cannot decide whether Clarence had been maligned by the Queen and the Woodvilles; whether Richard of Gloucester had been active in 'helping forth his own brother of Clarence to his death, which thing in all appearance he resisted'; or whether it really was 'a proud appetite of the duke [of Clarence] himself intending to be king.'

Whoever else may have been involved, the man primarily responsible for killing Clarence was undeniably Edward IV, even if 'albeit he commanded it, when he wist it was done, piteously bewailed and sorrowfully repented.' For all his charm, there was a dark, sinister side to the King, as there was to most members of his family. Bacon was very near the mark in commenting, 'it was a race often dipped in their own blood.'

'Item, as for the pageant that men say that the earl of Oxford hath played at Hammes, I suppose ye have heard thereof?' Sir John Paston asked his brother sardonically in August 1478. 'He leapt the walls and went to the dyke, and into the dyke to the chin, to what intent I cannot tell. Some say to steal away, and some think he would have drowned himself.'[5]

Was Lord Oxford's 'pageant' at Hammes inspired by the news of Clarence's death? Was that why the Earl tried to drown himself? Certainly, it is a far from implausible explanation. Oxford had spent three wretched years in prison and must have been in despair at the prospect of spending the rest of his life behind bars. His occupation of St Michael's Mount was surely motivated by hope invested in the Duke, his very last hope – or so it seemed in 1478.

32

Dr John Morton,
Bishop of Ely, 1478

JOHN MORTON

EVERYONE knows the lines in Shakespeare's *Richard III*:

> My lord of Ely, when I was last in Holborn,
> I saw good strawberries in your garden there . . .

However, few appreciate just how imposing was the Bishop's palace there, with courts and gardens that covered many acres, or the sheer pride and pomp of a late medieval prelate.

John Morton was consecrated as Bishop of Ely by Cardinal Bourchier at Lambeth in January 1479, having been appointed to the see the previous August – nominally by Pope Sixtus IV but in reality by King Edward. Already the worthy doctor had been magnificently rewarded during a spectacular career as a pluralist. Between 1474 and 1478 he had held no less than seven archdeaconries simultaneously: Chester, Winchester, Chichester, Huntingdon, Berkshire, Norfolk and Leicester. It is unlikely that he ever visited any of them, merely drawing their substantial revenues.

Most fifteenth-century bishops were great royal servants rather than spiritual fathers. As a 'bureaucrat bishop', Dr Morton toiled away at the business of state, attending long meetings of the King's council almost every day. He simply did not have the time to leave London and visit his diocese other than on rare occasions, his duties there being performed by various clerical officials. Sometimes he was away from England on embassies abroad. He can have had very little knowledge of what was required from his parish clergy, let alone the incentive to supervise and help them.

The embassies were demanding enough in themselves, especially the negotiations with Louis XI of France and his ministers. Obviously Dr Morton had demonstrated to Edward's complete satisfaction his gifts as a diplomat at both Picquigny and the meetings that prepared the way for it. In 1477 we find him, accompanied by Sir John Donne, at Louis' court during the crisis that resulted from the death of the Duke of Burgundy, where they stressed King Edward's heartfelt desire to remain at peace with France and to adhere to the treaties signed at Picquigny. They also discussed such problems as ensuring free passage through France to Italian merchants who were travelling to England.

At the end of 1478 John Morton played a leading part in the negotiations in London with an envoy of Louis, the Bishop of Elne. The Bishop's opinion of Englishmen, 'cheats and liars', was to some extent justified on this occasion. The doctor, together with William Dudley, dragged him out of his lodgings and took him before a notary where they bullied him into signing a bond – which committed the French King and his successors to continue paying Edward 50,000 crowns a year for as long as the truce between the two countries should last. On returning to France, the unfortunate Bishop had to stand trial for negligence; before he left, King Edward joked to him unfeelingly that he might be going to lose his head when he got home.[1]

Dr Morton visited King Louis once again during the last months of 1481, apparently to reassure him about Edward's dealings with Archduke Maximilian, who now ruled in the Low Countries and in what was left of Burgundy.

Although a bachelor by necessity, it soon became evident that Bishop Morton was a man of strong family feeling. By the fifteenth century nepotism meant the advancement of all one's kindred and not just one's nephews, and was an accepted feature of life among the higher clergy. John had been the eldest of five brothers. The next eldest, Thomas, had also gone into the Church, and in 1479 John secured his appointment as Archdeacon of Ely. If Thomas does not appear to have been particularly effective, their nephew Robert (son of the fourth brother, William) was clearly a man of considerable ability, and the Bishop very soon obtained for him the archdeaconries of Winchester and Gloucester, together with a canonry at St George's, Windsor. Robert succeeded his uncle as

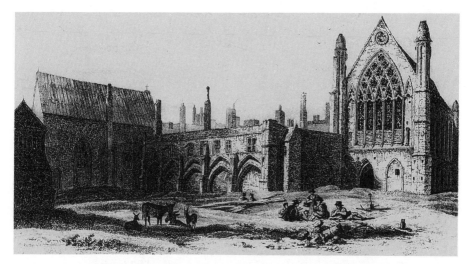

Ely Place, Dr Morton's London residence as Bishop of Ely.

Master of the Rolls.[2] The third brother, Richard Morton, who stayed a layman and became squire of Milburne St Andrew, rose modestly in the world, serving as sheriff for Dorset and Somerset.

The Bishop's London residence was the great palace at what is still called Ely Place in Holborn, a vast, rambling complex which was demolished in the 1770s. Morton's private chapel survives as the church of St Etheldreda. A tall, delicate building from the fourteenth century, it is one of the most beautiful Gothic churches in London, with a noble crypt and cloister.

Despite having little time to spare, the new Bishop took a keen interest in his diocese of Ely, though his activities do not seem to have had very much to do with the welfare of souls. No doubt he relished the independence resulting from its waterlogged landscape. Draining the fens did not start properly until well into the seventeenth century, and in Morton's day the Isle of Ely, an area forming about two-thirds of modern Cambridgeshire, was largely cut off from the outside world by marshes; these often made access difficult, especially when flooded during winter. Because of its isolation the Isle was a 'liberty'. In practice this meant that (like the Bishop of Durham) its bishop possessed powers of jurisdiction that elsewhere normally belonged to the King alone. Staffed by Benedictine monks instead of canons, Ely Cathedral was – and remains – one of the most

The western range of Hatfield Old Palace, built by Dr Morton when
Bishop of Ely

glorious cathedrals in Europe, a magnificent setting for a bishop's throne.

However, although Ely possessed a fine palace, Bishop Morton preferred
another town in the Isle, still more isolated but larger and more prosperous.
Wisbech was nearer the sea, a port with easy access to the Low Countries. The
Bishop used Wisbech Castle – pulled down during the seventeenth century – as
a diocesan palace. He also refurbished the church, where his arms may still be
seen on the tower.

In 1480 John Morton reached the advanced old age of sixty, but nonetheless
retained all his customary vigour of mind and body. In August that year, supported by the Bishop of Lincoln and other prelates who owned land in the
region, by the Abbots of Ramsey, Bury St Edmunds, Thorney, Peterburgh and
Crowland, by Sir Thomas Gray, Sir John Cheyne and a number of East Anglian
squires, he hopefully initiated an ambitious programme to drain the marshes
along the coast.[3] Not very much seems to have come of this scheme. He was
more successful in making access to Wisbech easier – though some blamed him
for interfering with the course of the River Nene – by having a dyke constructed,
forty feet across and twelve miles long, which took the river straight to Wisbech
and served as a canal. Even today the town benefits from 'Morton's Leam'.

However, Bishop Morton's favourite residence lay outside the Isle of Ely,
much nearer the capital. The Bishops of Ely had owned a house at Hatfield in

Hertfordshire since the early Middle Ages, and in about 1480 Dr Morton began to erect a new palace there, all in red brick. It was square in design, four wings around a courtyard, with an elegant castellated gatehouse. Three of the wings were demolished and rebuilt by the Earl of Salisbury in 1607, but fortunately one wing, the hall range, has survived together with the gate. (It was used as stables until the present century, when it was magnificently restored.) Some 230 feet long, the hall range contains a banqueting hall with a carved timber roof and a solar, together with a fine room below the hall – one feels very near its creator here. Late medieval English prelates were compulsive builders, but none of them can have built a more delightful bishop's palace than John Morton. With justice, Hatfield is often described as the finest example of medieval brickwork in England.

If Bishop Morton did not care to live in the episcopal palace at Ely, there could be no greater witness to his achievement in becoming such a pillar of the Yorkist realm than Ely Cathedral, whose wonderful octagon lantern can be seen from so many miles away. Twelve of the forty richest bishops in fifteenth-century Christendom lived in England, and clearly 'My lord of Ely' was among them. The hunted fugitive from Towton and Tewkesbury, the sodden refugee landing from the packed ballinger that had taken him across the North Sea, and the shabby, half-starved exile of Koeur-la-Petite had come a very long way indeed. However, there was no reason for him to suppose that he might one day lose his prosperity and eminence, or that he might aspire to even greater heights. No doubt he saw Hatfield Palace as a home for his ripe old age.

33

Hastings 'highly in the king's indignation', 1482–83

WILLIAM HASTINGS

In February 1478 William Hastings was appointed 'Lieutenant-General' of Calais for another ten years. He continued to enjoy Edward IV's favour, though as he grew older the King was becoming increasingly distrustful and suspicious of those closest to him. William had been made Master of the Mint for life during the previous year. Men went on joining his affinity, such as Lord Mountjoy in February 1480 (who, when dying, would warn his sons that it was dangerous to be a peer or wish to 'be great about princes'.) His influence remained paramount. The mercers record that in January 1480 he intervened with King Edward on behalf of the merchant adventurers. They also record how he warned the merchant adventurers not to boast that he was helping them – 'the lord chamberlain aviseth the fellowship to be more secret of their friends and that none avaunt be made [about] who is friendly and laboureth for us.'[1]

Yet, significantly, they thanked not just Lord Hastings but Earl Rivers and the Marquess of Dorset, who 'have been right friendly and laboured for us in our matter of subsidy. And [we] have prayed them of their good lordships.' More significant still, it was the Queen who finally persuaded Edward IV to grant the merchant adventurers' petition. The Woodvilles were keen rivals for the King's ear. William was uncomfortably aware that they were going do him all the harm they could. Above all, Earl Rivers coveted his lieutenancy of Calais.

Always under threat from the 'spider king', Louis XI, Calais was far from being a bed of roses. The town was Edward IV's listening post in the potentially disastrous (for England) struggle between France and Burgundy. Momentarily, English diplomacy seemed to prosper. In 1480 Edward signed a treaty of alliance with Mary of Burgundy and her husband, Archduke Maximilian, by which Edward's daughter Anne was to marry their heir, Philip. During the following year it was agreed that the Prince of Wales should marry Anne of Brittany, the heiress of the semi-independent duchy. However, Louis responded by encouraging the Scots to attack northern England. The Anglo-Scots war that ensued used up all Edward's resources, making it impossible for him to send adequate military aid to either Burgundy or Brittany.

Forgetting King Louis and the Scots, in the City the last years of Edward IV's reign appeared as a golden age. The economic depression had come to an end and business was booming. Thomas More recalls in wistful, elegiac tones an incident that took place in 1482. He may well have spoken to some of those present.

During the summer before King Edward died, he invited the Mayor and aldermen of London to join him at his hunting palace of the Bower in Waltham Forest, 'only to hunt and make pastime.' Here he gave them 'so familiar cheer, and sent also to their wives such plenty of venison that no one thing in many days before gat him either more hearts or more hearty favour among common people.' We know from a London chronicler that the King had given the Mayor's wife two harts and six bucks, together with a tun of wine, and that – her husband being a draper – she and the alderman's ladies then held their own party at the Drapers' Hall.[2]

While the citizens invited to the Bower were feasting in a lodge of green boughs on red and fallow deer, washed down by good Bordeaux wines, according to *The Great Chronicle of London* Lord Hasting visited them twice, 'to make them cheer.'[3] He had been sent by King Edward, who sat apart, to see that they were enjoying themselves. Although there was plenty to occupy him in Calais, William was often in England because he still had to perform his duties as chamberlain. He also had to report on the Burgundian situation and the threat from Louis.

Thomas More was born only in 1478, but obviously his parents had talked to him about the early years of their marriage. Living in the centre of the City, prosperous and well informed, they remembered Edward IV's reign as a time of political tranquility before 'the cruelty, mischief and trouble of the tempestuous world that followed.' He had made England rich and peaceful, free from any serious threat of invasion by French or Scots. His people supported him because they were genuinely loyal. He was always 'so benign, courteous and familiar' that he achieved real popularity.

King Edward stayed at peace with France, drawing his pension from Louis XI while allying with Burgundy and Brittany. A short war with Scotland was won in 1482 when Richard Gloucester briefly occupied Edinburgh in July and recovered Berwick in August. Edward 'had left off gathering money from his subjects, which is the only thing that draweth the hearts of Englishmen from their kings and princes,' wrote the Croyland chronicler. As for law and order, he had had much more success in reducing crimes of violence. England was better governed than at any time since Henry V's reign.

Although self-indulgent and grown fat, Edward looked healthy enough as he approached his forties. While thoughtful observers may have seen it as a bad sign that he did not lead his troops in person against the Scots, most people assumed that someone quite so tall and strong ought to reach fifty at least. In any case, the Yorkist succession looked secure. Not only did Edward have two sons, but Gloucester had one as well.

No king could have possessed a more reliable lieutenant than Edward's brother Richard, Duke of Gloucester, who made himself popular in the north of England by 'favours' and by ensuring that justice was done. 'Foreigners were deeply impressed by his reputation for clean living and his contribution to public life,' Mancini reports. 'He had such a name as a soldier that any serious threat to the realm was left to his discretion and his generalship.' Later the Duke of Buckingham would confidently refer to Gloucester's military prowess as common knowledge.

Mancini was impressed by the calibre of three of King Edward's ministers in particular. They were Archbishop Rotherham of York (the Lord Chancellor), Bishop Morton, and Lord Hastings. 'These men, mature in years and wise from long experience of affairs of state, helped more than any other members of the Council to shape royal policy and see that it was put into practice.' He notes, however, that not only was '*Astinco*' (Hastings) a policy-maker and someone who had shared every dangerous moment of Edward's life, but that the Lord Chamberlain aided and abetted Edward in his womanizing.[4]

The Italian then pinpoints a key factor in the troubles that were to follow Edward's death – the feud between William and the Woodvilles. Because of quarrels over women, he and the Marquess spread slanders about each other through informers who had been bribed – slanders so serious, according to Mancini, that they might have caused their execution. However, even more dangerous libels emanated from Lord Rivers.

Certainly William Hastings was very powerful indeed, and not just because he was an important minister. Polydore Vergil had been told by those who remembered William that 'amongst all the nobility [he] was for his bountifulness and liberality much beloved of the common people, bearing great sway among all sorts of men and persons of great reputation.' He enjoyed a long-standing friendship with the Duke of Gloucester – More believed the duke 'loved him well' – rejoicing at news of Gloucester's victory over the Scots. On 16 August 1482 the wool merchant William Cely wrote from Calais of the celebrations there at tidings of the occupation of Edinburgh, 'for the which my lord [chamberlain] commanded a general procession and at night bonfires to be made at every door as was at Midsummer's Night.' All the Calais cannon 'were shot for joy.'

Yet despite William's friendships with the King and Gloucester, he had a most formidable enemy in Anthony, Earl Rivers, the Queen's brother and head of the Woodville family. Elegant and well read, Rivers was a mystic, who wore a hair shirt, a man who could write a haunting poem while awaiting his execution – a 'death day ballad':

> Somewhat musing,
> And more mourning . . .

In many ways he comes down the centuries as rather an attractive figure. 'Lord Rivers was always considered a kind, serious and just man, and tested by every vicissitude of life', Mancini tells us. 'However much he prospered, he never harmed anyone, while doing good to many.' Even so, Rivers did his best to harm Lord Hastings and very nearly destroyed him.

Both men tried to ruin each other by accusations, at second hand, of plotting to sell Calais to Louis XI. It may have been Rivers who began the campaign. During the summer of 1482 rumours were circulating that 'my lord chamberlain' had had copies made of the town keys, to admit French troops secretly. Hastings blamed Robert Radcliffe, gentleman porter of Calais, for the rumours, ordering his servants to get out of the town at once – presumably he was unable to lay hands on Radcliffe himself. He retaliated in like kind. During the same month, interrogated at Westminster by the King and the council, a certain John Edward withdrew accusations he had made at Calais against Rivers and Dorset, saying that he had made them from 'his own false imagination' when in fear for his life and of being put in the 'brake' (i.e. the rack). In December John Edward and

Guillaume Vambard were hanged at Tyburn for libelling the Woodvilles. Everyone must have suspected, with justice, that Hastings had been behind the allegations.[5]

This smear campaign has to be set in context. It took place at a time when Edward IV's entire foreign policy was threatened with collapse. (In Ross's words, 'A foreign policy based upon the continuing good faith of Louis XI was always likely to end disastrously.') Mary of Burgundy had died unexpectedly in March 1482 from a riding accident, whereupon the Flemish, who disliked her widower, Archduke Maximilan, had opened negotiations with Louis XI. Crippled by the expenses of the Scots war, King Edward was unable to intervene. Hastings crossed and recrossed the Channel, reporting on the situation – on one occasion he was met at Dover by '500 men all in white gowns to bring him home', striking a joyful note at a most unjoyful time. By July the French were occupying the frontier towns. Maximilian finally despaired of help from England in September when Louis published a secret truce of non-aggression which Edward had signed with him the previous year, and began to negotiate with the French. Edward heard the news when Hastings came over to report to the council early in October. On 23 December Maximilian and Louis signed the Treaty of Arras; the former's daughter Mary was to marry the Dauphin and the counties of Artois and Burgundy were to go to France. There was no longer any need for King Louis to pay the English King a pension.

News of the Treaty of Arras reached Edward IV during the twelve days of Christmas. The Croyland chronicler, who spent Christmas at court, reports that the King 'thought of nothing but taking vengeance.' Regardless of expense or the lack of Burgundian allies, he began to plan another invasion of France. He may even have blamed the ruin of his foreign policy on the diplomatic shortcomings of Hastings, who had always taken the part of the Burgundians. If this really was the case, then King Edward would have been only too ready to credit charges of treachery.

There is some evidence that Hastings was sent to the Tower for a short period, where he daily expected his death warrant to arrive. 'I was never so sorry, nor never stood in so great danger in my life', More reports him as saying. Just when this occurred is not recorded, but it is significant that on 6 February 1483 William was replaced as Master of the Mint by Bartholomew Reed, a London goldsmith, although he had been granted the post for life.[6] Three months later, meeting his herald 'Tiger Pursuivant' on Tower Bridge, he reminded him that when they had met there previously, he 'had been accused to King Edward by the Lord Rivers, the queen's brother, insomuch that he was for a while, which lasted not long, highly in the king's indignation.'[7]

William was soon exonerated of any plot to hand over Calais to Louis XI, and of all blame for the Burgundian débâcle. However, the episode can scarcely have increased his affection for the Woodvilles. They were no less bitter. Lord Rivers had had copies made of John Edward's confession in August to show that he too had been the victim of a smear campaign.

What made the feud potentially so dangerous was the Woodvilles' combination of power and unpopularity. All too many thought that they were 'ignoble and new made men [*novi homines*], who were promoted above those who far excelled them in both breeding and ability', as Mancini puts it. Their lack of birth was exaggerated, but not the angry jealousy that many magnates and gentry felt for them. An opponent of the régime might decide to exploit the situation. Fortunately the régime had no serious opponents.

But at the end of March 1483 King Edward suddenly fell ill, struck down by a mysterious illness. Commynes believed it was an apoplexy brought on by news of the Treaty of Arras,[6] while Mancini thought the cause was a chill caught when the King was with a fishing party in a small boat on the Thames. Sir Winston Churchill – or one of his researchers – made a plausible guess in suggesting that it may have been an appendicitis.

Mancini records how on his deathbed, recognizing the seriousness of the Hastings–Woodville feud, the King 'who loved each of them' tried to reconcile William with his stepson, the Marquess of Dorset. Shakespeare's affecting scene is true enough:

Dorset, embrace him – Hastings, love lord marquess

But, as Mancini observes with considerable understatement, a latent hostility persisted between the pair. There was no attempt to reconcile William with Lord Rivers, probably because the Earl was away in Shropshire.

Comforted by Bishop Morton, Edward IV died at Westminster on 9 April, still only forty. He was buried with all the ritual pomp and magic that had not been seen since the interment of Henry V over sixty years before. After lying in state for eight days in St Steven's Chapel at Westminster, his embalmed corpse was borne on a bier into the Abbey by fifteen knights and squires of the Body in a procession that was led by ten bishops and two abbots. A life-sized effigy of the King, dressed in robes of state with the crown on his head, sceptre in one hand

and orb in the other, stood on top of the hearse in which he was laid. The image stayed on the hearse during the funeral progress to Windsor. At the offerings before Edward was finally laid to rest in his tomb in St George's Chapel, Lord Hastings and Lord Stanley carried his great gilded helmet.[9]

No doubt echoing what he had heard from his parents and from their friends, Sir Thomas More testifies to how popular Edward had become during his second reign, even among former Lancastrians:

> There never was any king in this realm attaining the crown by war and battle so heartily beloved with the substance of the people . . . At such time as he died, the displeasure of those that bare him a grudge for King Henry's sake, the Sixth whom he deposed, was well assuaged and in effect quenched.

As for his infamous womanizing, 'This fault not greatly grieved his people.'

Historians vary considerably in their estimate of Edward IV, but it has to be said that on balance he was colourful and impressive rather than truly great. Certainly he ended his life in unchallenged occupation of the throne, a fine fighting soldier who had defeated all his enemies, while his financial policy was so sound that he died solvent – something no English monarch had achieved for at least two centuries. On the other hand, he made disastrous mistakes. He was caught out by Warwick in 1469 and again in 1470. His foreign policy, dependent on the goodwill of the notoriously slippery Louis XI, ended in ruin. He failed to control retaining, through which affinities could so easily become private armies. Worst of all, by favouring the Woodvilles, he had made further strife inevitable.

John Skelton wrote dolefully in a funeral elegy for the king, 'I have played my pageant, now I am past.' But Edward's death was much more than the last act of a pageant. Skelton also wrote in his elegy, more truly than he realized, 'When death approacheth, then lost is the field.' The King's premature demise doomed the House of York, and the Race of Plantagenet itself.

Thomas More recalled a story his father had told him about the ominous behaviour of a neighbour, Mr Richard Pottyer. An attorney who worked for the Duke of Gloucester, he lived near the Mores' house in Milk Street. Before dawn on the morning after King Edward's death, a man called Mistlebrook knocked at Pottyer's door and gave him the news. '"By my troth, man" quoth Pottyer, "then will my master the duke of Gloucester be King."'

THE REIGN OF RICHARD III

1483–85

34

The End of William Hastings, 1483

WILLIAM HASTINGS · JOHN MORTON
JANE SHORE

THE late King's last surviving brother, the Duke of Gloucester, was still only thirty. He had an impressive military record. In January 1483 Parliament formally congratulated him on his victories over the Scots, while Mancini, Vergil and More all agree that he was a very fine soldier. Although little known in the south, since he had kept away from court and lived in Yorkshire, he was much liked in the north. Moreover, he had always been impeccably loyal to Edward IV.

Yet Richard Gloucester had also displayed a streak of vicious rapacity. When only nineteen, while squabbling with Clarence over Warwick's estates, he had refused to leave anything for the Earl's widow (his mother-in-law), imprisoning her at Middleham Castle for the rest of her life. How he bullied the old Countess of Oxford has been described. There were ugly rumours too about his part in the death of King Henry.

Gloucester was obviously a man of many talents, charming and persuasive when it was necessary, a man who knew exactly how to win support. Despite his unimpressive physique and normally somewhat acid expression, he undoubtedly possessed what is nowadays called 'charisma'. If he was ruthless and brutal, he was subtle too and, as will be seen, he was wonderfully adept at concealing his real aims beneath a cloak of urbane sincerity. He was also a brilliant propagandist, skilful at manipulating public opinion or at using a smear campaign with which to destroy an opponent's reputation. 'He was the master of the public statement and press conference, the open letter and manifesto, the inspired leak and innuendo, the personal appeal and the restatement of accepted values,' a

distinguished historian (Michael Hicks) has written recently. 'He understood
contemporary psychology as we cannot, knew what attracted and repelled, and
manipulated his audience accordingly. Thus he denounced his enemies as traitors, sorcerers, lechers, misers and evil councillors.'

At the same time, for all his very real abilities and subtlety, he was curiously
prone to wishful thinking and self-delusion, as we may judge with some degree
of certainty from the events about to take place.

However, none of these sinister qualities was generally attributed to Richard
of Gloucester in the early spring of 1483. Most people believed him when he
wrote to the council and assured them that he was going to be no less loyal to
Edward V than he had been to Edward IV. Should – 'God forbid' – the boy die
prematurely, then he would be equally faithful to the child next in line, even to a
girl. So Domenico Mancini tells us, recording that everyone in London thought
the Duke ought to be Protector, though he adds – and Mancini was not prone to
exaggeration – 'Some, however, who understood his ambition and deceit, always
suspected where his ambition and deceit might lead him.' But apparently Lord
Hastings had no reservations whatever about his old friend.

One consequence of King Edward's death was that William moved in with Mrs
Shore, 'with whom he lay nightly', according to More. The latter explains that
'When the king died, the Lord Hastings took her, which in the king's days, albeit
he was sore enamoured upon her, yet he forbare her, either for reverence or for
a certain friendly faithfulness.' Jane's house must have been comfortable enough
since Edward's presents had made her a very rich woman. Indeed, a modern historian has suggested ungallantly that Hastings and the Marquess of Dorset were
in love with her for her money.

Although he enjoyed Mrs Shore's favours, we know that William Hastings was
a very worried man. The new King was only twelve years old and clearly devoted
to his mother's family, and especially to his uncle, Lord Rivers, who had been
entrusted with his education. Should the Woodvilles gain control of Edward V,
they would not merely arrange for William's ruin but in all probability for his legal
murder as well. He grew seriously alarmed when the council rejected out of hand
the late King's wish that Gloucester should govern alone as Protector during his
son's minority. Instead, it decided that there should be a council of regency
presided over by the Duke. Mancini says that the Woodvilles and their followers
voted for this proposal because they were terrified of Gloucester.

Mancini's informants told him that 'the chamberlain Hastings' reported all the council's debates by letter and messenger to the Duke of Gloucester, because of their long-standing friendship and also because Hastings 'was hostile to the entire kin of the queen.' William advised Gloucester to come to London with troops as soon as he could to avenge the insult done him by the council – he would easily regain control of the situation if he secured possession of the young King and arrested any Woodville supporters in the royal entourage before they realized what was happening. He added that he himself was alone in the City and in considerable danger.

Richard of Gloucester was no less worried than Hastings by the Woodvilles, whom characteristically he later labelled as 'persons insolent, vicious and of inordinate avarice.' Clearly they smelt power. When the council fixed the date for the coronation, some members protested that they should wait until the Duke arrived before taking such a decision. The Marquess of Dorset retorted haughtily, 'We are quite important enough to take decisions without the king's uncle and see that they are enforced.' Sir Edward Woodville (Rivers' younger brother) took the royal fleet to sea, ready to block communications with Calais in case Hastings should send for its garrison. Dorset's head was so turned that he issued orders in his own name and in that of his uncle Rivers; they styled themselves 'Half-brother to the King' and 'Uncle to the King'. William could not contain his anger, shouting at a council meeting that their origin was too low and their blood too base for them to rule England.

The situation was made more explosive by lurid rumours which, it has recently been suggested, were circulated by Gloucester's agents. Among these was a story that the Queen, Sir Edward Woodville and Dorset had divided the late King's treasure among themselves. However, there was no treasure – Edward had left a mere £1,200 in money while his funeral had cost £1,496, so that his jewels were sold to pay for it.

Vergil believed that Gloucester only thought of making himself King when he heard of his brother's death. More suspected he might have had a contingency plan, since he had been expecting his brother to die young, 'but of all these points there is no certainty.' Professor Ross's view was that the Duke decided to seize power primarily for his own safety rather than from any deep-laid plan, let alone from the determination 'to prove a villain' attributed to him by Tudor tradition. The Woodvilles were quite capable of launching a coup and destroying him. On the other hand, if Gloucester eliminated them without taking the Crown, the young King might well avenge his favourite relations when he reached his majority in 1486 – fifteen being the age of royal majority.

Another factor in the Duke's calculations has recently been identified by

Michael Hicks. He had spent the last decade building up his power in northern England, where the nucleus of his estates consisted of the former Nevill lands of the Earl of Warwick and Marquess Montagu. The process appeared to be complete by early 1483, when Edward IV granted him the county of Cumberland as a semi-independent palatinate. Hicks suggests that the Duke may also have contemplated carving out a principality for himself in southern Scotland.[1] But at the beginning of May 1483, his entire position in the north was undermined by the death of his unmarried ward, George Nevill, Montagu's son and Warwick's nephew. As the heir of traitors, George, together with any children he might beget, had been deprived of his inheritance by an Act of Parliament that granted the Nevill lands to Gloucester. However, the Act had also stipulated that should George die childless, then the Duke could keep the lands only for his lifetime, after which they would revert to the Nevill family. In consequence, George's death weakened the Duke's authority throughout northern England, besides seriously diminishing his son's prospects.[2] Had Edward IV lived, he might have rescued Gloucester with further grants of land, but now the Duke was merely a member of the council, which would be most unlikely to help him in this way.

From the beginning, Gloucester had an ally in Henry, Duke of Buckingham, one of the richest and most powerful magnates in England. Through his descent from Edward III's youngest son, Thomas of Woodstock, 'Harry' Buckingham had Plantagenet blood in his veins and was the only man in England outside the House of York allowed to quarter the royal arms. Although married to the Queen's sister, he loathed his Woodville in-laws. Why he supported Gloucester's bid for the throne is not clear; hatred for the Woodvilles may have been the motive, or desire to secure the estates of his Bohun ancestors.

As soon as Edward IV died, Buckingham sent a servant north to Gloucester at York, where the latter was shedding 'plenteous tears' at his brother's requiem, with the message that he would support him in any plan, 'with a thousand good fellows if need were.' Bringing 300 men, he met Gloucester at Northampton.[3]

Dramatic news reached the City late at night on Thursday, 1 May. Gloucester and Buckingham had intercepted Edward V on his way to London. They had also arrested Lord Rivers, Richard Grey (the Marquess's brother), and the King's chamberlain, Sir Thomas Vaughan (apparently a Woodville ally), sending them under guard to Pontefract – where they would later be beheaded without trial. Queen Elizabeth fled into sanctuary at Westminster, taking her younger son with her. The Chancellor, Archbishop Rotherham, came before dawn the following morning to reassure her. He announced that he had just received a message from Lord Hastings to fear nothing – 'All should be well.' 'Ah, woe worth him,' the Queen burst out at the sound of the name Hastings, 'for he is one of them that labour to destroy me and my blood.'[4]

Both Mancini and More tell us that there were sinister rumours in the City to the effect that the Duke of Gloucester meant to seize the Crown. Some peers and gentlemen put on armour to defend the little King, but Hastings, 'whose truth toward the king no man doubted, nor needed to doubt', persuaded the lords of the council that the Duke could be trusted. He also convinced them that the Duke had arrested Rivers and his friends in self-defence. When Gloucester arrived with Edward V, his obsequious behaviour towards his nephew satisfied everyone, and at its next meeting the council had no hesitation in appointing him Protector of England. He at once altered the council's composition, replacing Archbishop Rotherham as Chancellor with Dr John Russell, Bishop of Lincoln, though retaining Dr Morton and Hastings. He also regained control of the fleet, Edward Woodville taking refuge in France. The Marquess went into sanctuary at Westminster.

The Croyland chronicler records how William was 'bursting with joy over this new world.' He was heard to say that the change of government from the Queen's kindred had taken place without any more bloodshed than that 'from a cut finger'. There is no need to disbelieve this account, even though Polydore Vergil claims that William was shocked by Gloucester's seizure of the King – he was only too relieved that such dangerous foes as the Woodvilles had been put out of harm's way.

Historians differ over what happened next. Gloucester's romantic apologist, Paul Murray Kendall, thinks that Hastings, Morton, Rotherham and Lord Stanley suddenly turned against the Duke, and contacted the Woodvilles with a plot to overthrow him. 'Such a reversal is a classical rhythm of politics,' observes Kendall solemnly. 'This policy was urged upon the Lord Chamberlain by more than reason. The bright voice of Jane Shore was in his ear . . . Once Hastings and his friends determined to join forces with the Woodvilles, Jane Shore was chosen to deliver their messages to the sanctuary.'

But Professor Ross, the author of what is so far the most scholarly biography of Gloucester, is convinced there was no plot against Richard. Admittedly, if anyone could have mounted a counter-coup, it was William. But he could never have trusted the Woodvilles, whose leader – now that Rivers was in prison – was the Marquess, by all accounts his most bitter enemy.

Certainly Mancini knew of no such plot. He merely reports that Gloucester

realized that Hastings, Morton and Rotherham stood in the way of his plans. He feared their combined ability and authority, says the Italian, since 'he had sounded out their loyalty through the duke of Buckingham, and learnt that they sometimes met in each other's houses.'

Nor does More mention a Hastings–Woodville plot. 'And of truth the protector and the duke of Buckingham made very good semblance unto the Lord Hastings and kept him much in company', Sir Thomas tells us. 'And undoubtedly the protector loved him well and loath was to have lost him.' Gloucester had shown his goodwill by restoring Hastings to his valuable post of Master of the Mint. He instructed his henchman Catesby to see if he could be won over, 'with some words cast out afar off.'[5]

According to More, William Catesby had his own reasons for wanting Hastings out of the way. A sinister figure who was to become one of Richard's principal advisers, unlike most of his master's confidants this unscrupulous squire turned lawyer was not a Northerner but a Midlander from Northamptonshire who worked closely with Hastings both in that county and in Leicestershire as a member of William's baronial council. More suspected that Catesby did not even raise the subject with him – 'whether he assayed him or not' – but pretended to Gloucester and Buckingham that he 'heard him speak so terrible words' that he dared not go on. More thought that Catesby deliberately 'procured the protector hastily to rid of him . . . for he trusted by his death to obtain much of the rule that the Lord Hastings bare in his country.' In other words, Mr Catesby was after William's jobs – he coveted all those extremely lucrative posts and offices in the Midlands.[6]

Whether or not Catesby was playing a double game, the Duke of Gloucester was quite shrewd enough to have guessed already that Hastings would always remain faithful to the oaths of loyalty he had sworn to Edward IV and his son. It is a testimony to Richard's liking for the man that he nonetheless bothered to sound him out.

What is beyond question is that Gloucester and Buckingham were planning a coup d'état. Fully convinced by now that William Hastings would never agree

William Catesby, a secret enemy who 'trusted by his death to obtain much of the rule which the Lord Hastings bare in his country'. Richard III's henchman, he was beheaded soon after Bosworth. From a brass of *c* 1500 at Ashby St Ledgers, Northants.

under any circumstances to their deposing Edward V, they knew they had to destroy him. Furthermore, they were going to take William completely by surprise – he could not see that he was in any danger.

More tells of a nightmare that terrified Lord Stanley early on the night of 12 June. He dreamt that a savage boar – the Protector's badge was a boar, as everyone knew – slashed both his own head and that of Hastings with its tusks, so that the blood ran down about their shoulders. Badly shaken, he at once sent a message to Hastings, although it was midnight, to tell him of the dream, suggesting that together they escape from the City. 'Tell him it is plain witchcraft to believe in such dreams,' was Hastings' response. 'If they were tokens of things to come, why thinketh he not that we might as likely make them true by our going?'

Stanley had already told Hastings that he was concerned at all the meetings the protector was holding at his house in Bishopsgate – Crosby Place. 'For while we', he said, 'talk of one matter in the one place, little wot we whereof they talk in the other place.' William told him not to worry. Someone who attended the meetings would see that anything hostile said about them 'should be in mine ears ere it were well out of their mouths.' More explains that William meant Catesby, 'whom he very familiarly used, and in his weighty matters put no man in so special trust', since 'there was no man to him so much beholden as was this Catesby, which was a man well learned in the laws of this land, and by the special favour of the lord chamberlain in good authority and much rule bare in all the county of Leicester where the lord chamberlain's power chiefly lay.'

More and Polydore Vergil give very similar accounts of the coup. Obviously each had spoken to an eyewitness. More had probably had access to a manuscript copy of Vergil's history, and his version is very much fuller.

There was to be a council meeting at the Tower on Friday, 13 June for a final discussion of the coronation arrangements. Fifteenth-century men and women rose much earlier than we do today, generally at dawn. Nevertheless, before William was up, and still in bed with Mrs Shore, Sir Thomas Howard arrived at Jane's house to accompany him to the Tower, 'as it were of courtesy.' Sir Thomas was the son of his old friend Lord Howard. With hindsight it is clear he had been sent by the Protector, to make sure that Hastings came to the Tower that morning.

On the way, William stopped to talk with a priest whom they met in Tower Street. 'What, my Lord, I pray you come on. Wherefore talk you so long with that priest? You have no need of a priest yet,' joked Howard, laughing. 'As though he would say, you shall have need of one soon,' comments More, adding that someone who actually overheard the conversation realized its significance before the day was over. He also says that Hastings was completely trusting and never merrier. When William encountered his own pursuivant on Tower Wharf, just before entering the Palace, he told him how cheerful he was feeling, referring indirectly to the imminent execution of Rivers at Pontefract – a prospect that gave him much pleasure.

Besides himself, those who came to the council at the Tower included Archbishop Rotherham, Bishop Morton, Lord Stanley, the Duke of Buckingham, and Lord Howard. It was a very small meeting because most of the council's other members had been invited to another discussion at Westminster, presided over by Dr Russell. Only Buckingham and Howard knew that the scene had been set for a meticulously planned coup.

The Protector joined the meeting briefly at about 9 a.m., in a most amiable mood. He asked Morton to send him strawberries from his garden in Holborn (More must surely have had this detail from Dr Morton) and then left. Returning at about 10.30 'with a sour and angry countenance', he demanded to know the penalty for planning 'the destruction of me, being so near of blood to the king, and Protector of this his royal realm?' Everyone was astonished. Hastings, 'who for the familiarity that was between them, thought he might be boldest with him', answered that they ought to be punished as traitors.

'See in what wise that sorceress [the Queen] and others of her counsel, as Shore's wife with her affinity, have by their sorcery and witchcraft thus washed my body?' said the Protector, rolling up his left sleeve to the elbow to show a deformed, withered arm. Every man present was fearful, realizing that some quarrel had inspired this outburst, More tells us. But with whom?

Then the Protector banged his fist on the table and armed men came running into the room. 'I arrest thee, traitor,' he shouted at Hastings. 'What, me, my Lord?' gasped William. 'Yea, thou traitor.' A man-at-arms aimed a blow at Lord Stanley, who dived under the table, blood running down his face, before being dragged off with Morton and Rotherham. Hastings was told to send for a priest and confess himself quickly. 'For by St Paul I will not dine until I see thy head off.' William was taken to the green outside and beheaded over a log.[7] (Mancini comments, 'Thus fell Hastings, killed not by those enemies he had always feared, but by a friend whom he had never doubted.')

Vergil supplies a few more details. He says that the Protector addressed Hastings as 'William', while the effects of the sorcery are specified: 'neither night nor day can I rest, drink nor eat; wherefore my blood by little and little decreaseth, my force faileth, my breath shorteneth and all the parts of my body do above measure as you see (and with that he showed them his arm) fall away, which mischief verily proceedeth in me from that sorceress Elizabeth the Queen.' There is no mention of Mrs Shore. In a manuscript version of his *English History*, he states that Sir Thomas Howard commanded the armed men who had been lying in wait next door.[8]

A herald was sent through the City with a proclamation. It said that Hastings had plotted to kill Gloucester and Buckingham and seize the King, adding that he had led the late King into debauchery, and that Mrs Shore 'was one of his secret counsel in this heinous treason, with whom he lay nightly, and namely the night past before his death' – so it was not surprising that 'ungracious living brought him to an unhappy end.'

Although no copy has survived, More's version of the proclamation is convincing, especially the odd, moralizing note, which would be heard again. It was not the last time Mrs Shore would feature in a document of this kind. More adds sarcastically, 'Now was this proclamation made within two hours after [Lord Hastings] was beheaded, and it was so curiously indicted, and so written in parchment in a fair, set hand, and therwith so large a process that every child might perceive that it was prepared before, and (as some men thought) by Catesby . . .'

Meanwhile, 'All men generally lamented the death of that man, in whom both they and the nobles who favoured King Edward's children had reposed their whole hope and confidence,' says Vergil, echoing the *Great Chronicle* – 'And thus was this noble man murdered for his troth and fidelity which he bare unto his master.' More's valediction is Arthurian.

> Thus ended this honourable man, a good knight and a gentle, of great authority with his prince, of living somewhat dissolute, plain and open to his enemy and secret to his friend, easy to beguile, as he that of good heart and courage forestudied no perils. A loving man and passing well beloved: very faithful and trusty enough, trusting too much was his destruction . . .

William Hastings had long made provision for his death and burial, in a will dated 27 June 1481, asking that he be interred near his master and greatest friend. 'I did write this clause and last article with mine own hand.' We can hear William's voice:

> And for as much as the King of his abundant grace for the true service that I have done, and at the least intended to have done, His Grace hath willed

and offered me to be buried in the college or chapel of St George at
Windsor in a place by his Grace assigned, in the which college His Highness
is disposed to be buried. I therefore bequeath my simple body to be buried
in the said chapel . . .

Otherwise, Hastings' will was conventional enough. He bequeathed sums of
money for almsgiving at St George's Chapel and to the Poor Knights of Windsor
– who deputized for the Knights of the Garter at its services. He also left 'a jewel
of gold to the value of £20' to the Dean and canons of the chapel 'there to remain
perpetually to the honour of God and for a memorial of me.' Another £20 a year
went to pay a priest 'to say daily Mass and divine service at the altar next to the
place where my body shall be buried in the said chapel . . . and there to pray daily
for the King's prosperous estate during his life and after his death for his soul.'
He exhorted his sons to be faithful to the King and to 'my lord prince' on penalty
of forfeiting his blessing – in his case more than a hackneyed gesture. Having
named his executors, William adds, 'And for the perfect and sure execution of
this my said last will and testament, I ordain and make the right reverend father
in God, John, bishop of Ely my good lord . . .' It was no mean compliment for
Dr Morton, the former Lancastrian, that he should have won the confidence of
such a man as Lord Hastings.[9]

A letter from one of Lord Chancellor Russell's servants, Canon Simon
Stallworth, who wrote from London to his friend Sir William Stonor soon after
the coup, says that all Hastings' affinity were transferring their allegiance. 'All the
lord chamberlain's men become my lord of Buckingham's men.'[10] They had to
think urgently about their survival in such a dangerous political climate and find
a new 'good lord' who could protect them. It was a question of self-preservation.
One of them, Sir Ralph Fitzherbert, affected to be a wholehearted supporter of
the Protector; he died later that year and on his alabaster effigy at Norbury
church in Derbyshire there hangs from his collar the white boar badge of the
Duke of Gloucester. But at least two of William Hastings' former well-wishers,
Humphrey Stanley and James Blount, were going to fight against Richard at
Bosworth.

The normal procedure would have been for the régime to attaint Lord
Hastings in due course, posthumously, as a 'traitor'. However, shortly after
becoming King, Gloucester presented his widow with an indenture in which he
promised her on oath that her husband would not be attainted, and by which he
allowed her to retain all his lands and goods, together with the valuable wardship
of her son-in-law, the Earl of Shrewsbury. He also took Lady Hastings formally

under his protection. Neither William's son, Lord Hungerford, nor his brothers suffered in any way from his fall; Ralph Hastings was briefly deprived of his captaincy of Guisnes, but he recovered it during the following year.[11] Such generosity bears out More's claim – that Richard had destroyed William Hastings only with the utmost reluctance.

35

Mrs Shore Does Penance, 1483

JANE SHORE

W E do not know Jane's reaction to the news of the death of a lover with whom she had spent the previous night. But we do know that she was in very serious trouble. On 21 June, eight days after the killing of Lord Hastings, Canon Simon Stallworth, prebendary of Crackpole St Mary in the diocese of Lincoln and a servant of the Lord Chancellor, wrote from London to a friend that Mrs Shore was in prison and he did not know what was going to happen to her.[1] Clearly, Richard was very angry with Jane. It can scarcely have been because of her 'sorcery and witchcraft.' Was there another reason for the Protector's hostility besides her friendship with Hastings?

Mancini may have given us the answer. He reports that about the time Hastings died 'the duke [of Gloucester] learnt from his agents that the marquess [of Dorset] had slipped out of sanctuary and, suspecting he was hiding in the area [Westminster], had its fields – already deep in standing corn – and its woods ringed by troops and dogs, trying to catch him by penning him in just as hunters do, but he was never found.'[2] The obvious person for the Marquess to run to was Mrs Shore; someone as kind as Jane would never turn him away. In any case, he was in love with her, and he had been without a woman at Westminster. It is quite possible, therefore, that she was arrested for sheltering Dorset. Undoubtedly they were together later that year, during the summer or in the early autumn.

The Great Chronicle of London says that shortly after the Protector's coronation as King Richard III on 6 July, a woman named Shore 'that before days, after the common fame, the lord Chamberlain held, contrary to his honour, [was] called to a reckoning for part of his goods and other things. In so much that all her moveables were attached by the sheriffs of London . . .'[3] This sounds like deliberate hounding on the authorities' part, since all her own goods had been stolen at the time of her arrest which, as we know from Canon Stallworth, took place some time between 13 and 21 June.

Describing the looting that accompanied her arrest, More emphasizes that Richard was punishing her in this way 'for anger, and not for covetousness.' He sent Sir Thomas Howard (who had seized Hastings in the council chamber) to take her to prison. Howard robbed her of everything she possessed, which was 'above the value of two to three thousand marks' – as much as a thousand pounds. This was no small sum since many comfortably-off squires had incomes of less than £20 a year.[4]

Mrs Shore was to enjoy star billing in the propaganda that followed. Already she had featured in the proclamation issued after William's death. (More could have seen both this and the sheriffs' order with his own eyes - as a lawyer and under-sheriff he had access to legal documents of the period.) She was going to be attacked publicly by Buckingham and she would also feature in a further proclamation. The régime was trying to make her the symbol of its opponents' 'vicious living'. But her liaison with Dorset is the most probable reason for her arrest.

Jane was able to avoid the worst gaols by insisting on her right as a Freewoman of London to choose the prison. Ludgate gaol was in the rooms over the gate at the bottom of Ludgate Hill, opposite St Martin's Church. Timber-framed on the side within the City but with a battlemented stone façade outside, it had a large window from which she could watch the crowd below passing in and out of the City, while friends were able to bring in food.[5]

Now that William Hastings was safely out of the way, Gloucester set about securing possession of the King's younger brother, the ten year-old Duke of York. On 16 July a party of the great and good, led by Buckingham, called on the Queen in sanctuary at Westminster; it included Archbishop Bourchier of Canterbury, Lord Chancellor Russell, and Lord Howard. Eventually they bullied her into parting with the boy, who joined his brother in the Tower. 'Farewell, mine own sweet son,' said the poor Queen. 'God send you good keeping. Let me kiss you once yet ere you go, for God knows when we shall kiss together again.'

Henceforward, according to *The Great Chronicle*, 'was the Prince and duke of York holden more strait and there was privy talk that the Protector should be king.' On Sunday, 22 June a sermon was preached at Paul's Cross next to the Cathedral, with the text 'Bastard slips should not take root'. The preacher claimed that Edward IV's marriage to Elizabeth Woodville had never been valid because at the time of the wedding he had been betrothed to Lady Eleanor Butler, the Earl of Shrewsbury's daughter, which precluded his marrying anyone else. Moreover, not only were the little King and his brother illegitimate, but Edward IV and Clarence had themselves been bastards. Only the Duke of Gloucester was his father's rightful son.

When the Duke of Buckingham made a very similar speech at the Guildhall two days later, he claimed that the late King had paid more attention to 'Shore's wife, a vile and abominable strumpet, than to all the lords in England except unto those that made her their protector.'

Buckingham's entire speech was part of a smear campaign, an attempt to discredit the memory of Edward IV.

> For no woman was there anywhere, young or old, poor or rich, whom he set his eye upon, whom he anything liked, either for person or beauty, speech, pace or countenance, but without any fear of God, or respect of his honour, murmur, or grudging of the world, he would importunately pursue his appetite and have her, to the great destruction of many a good woman . . .

Sir Thomas More is frequently accused of literary invention in the creation of his *History of King Richard the Third*, and Buckingham's oratory may seem like so much fantasy, something dreamt up by the author's imagination. Yet, as will be seen, there is every reason to suppose that the Duke really did make such a speech. The irony of this programme of sexual denigration – even now unique in English history – is that the Protector himself had sired at least two acknowledged bastards and probably a third as well.

On 25 June a delegation headed by the Duke of Buckingham, and composed of such magnates as Lord Howard, together with the Mayor and aldermen, formally asked Richard of Gloucester to assume the Crown. The peers and MPs who had come to London to attend Parliament – postponed for the time being – drew up a petition begging him to do so, a petition that would be embodied in an Act when they met the following year.

Echoing Buckingham's speech at the Guildhall, the petition alleged that during the late King Edward IV's reign this land was ruled by self-will and pleasure, fear and dread, all manner of equity and laws laid apart and despised. Whereof ensued many inconveniences and mischiefs – as murders, extortions and oppressions, namely of poor and impotent people, so that no man was sure of his life, land nor livelihood, ne of his wife, daughter ne servant, every good maiden and woman standing in dread to be ravished and defouled . . .

All this is very similar to the accusations made against Henry VI some twenty years before, save for the extraordinary sexual charges.

The 'pretensed marriage betwixt the above named King Edward and Elizabeth Grey was made of great presumption, without the knowing and assent of the lords of this land,' continues the petition, 'and also by sorcery and witchcraft committed by the said Elizabeth and her mother Jaquet, duchess of Bedford, as the common opinion of the people and the public voice and fame is through all this land.' Because of the pre-existing contract of betrothal ('troth plight') to Eleanor Butler, the marriage was invalid, so that 'all the issue and children of the said King Edward [have] been bastards and unable to inherit or claim anything.'

The petition is not a fabrication by 'Tudor propagandists' but a document that would later receive Richard's full, formal approval in Parliament as part of the Act *Titulus Regis*.[6]

On 26 June the Protector was proclaimed King of England. In the meantime 'Edward Bastard, late called King Edward V', as he was now known, and the Duke of York were seen less and less. After the elimination of Hastings, the former King's attendants were not allowed to visit him. 'He and his brother were taken into the inner rooms of the Tower itself and each day could be glimpsed more and more rarely until finally they ceased to appear at all,' Mancini tells us. Young Edward's physician, the last of his attendants to see him, reported that the boy spent his time in prayer since 'he believed that death was facing him.'

On 5 July Mancini watched Richard III processing from the Tower to Westminster, the day before his crowning, bowing from the saddle as the crowd cheered him. The route led down Ludgate Hill into Fleet Street, so Jane too must have watched the new monarch from her window as the coronation procession passed beneath her prison through the Ludgate. She saw a short, spare, wiry little man (with no outward sign of a hump or a crook-back), who wore a gown of purple velvet trimmed with ermine over a doublet of blue cloth-of-gold. His queen – Anne Nevill, Warwick's younger daughter – followed in a litter, flanked by five mounted ladies-in-waiting. They were escorted by most of the peers of England, some thirty-five. The spectacle can have done little to hearten poor Mrs Shore, who knew that the King had not finished with her. She was a key exhibit in his smear campaign.

Richard's charge 'that she went about to bewitch him and that she was of counsel with the lord chamberlain to destroy him' could not be proved and had to be dropped. Even so, the King hoped to use her reputation for loose living to discredit Edward IV, Hastings and Dorset. The *Great Chronicle* records that shortly after the coronation a woman named Shore was 'as a common harlot put to open penance for the life that she [had] led with the said Lord Hastings and other great estates' – 'other great estates' meaning King Edward and the Marquess of Dorset.

Everyone laughed at the authorities suddenly taking it so seriously that Jane had been free with her favours. 'And for this cause (as a goodly, continent prince, clean and faultless of himself, sent out of heaven into this vicious world for the amendment of men's manners) he [Richard] caused the bishop of London to put her to open penance' is More's sardonic comment.[7]

On a Sunday, Jane was made to walk barefoot in her kirtle through the City streets, carrying a lighted taper. She 'went so fair and lovely' and looked so comely, especially when she blushed, that many men cheered, 'more amorous of her body than curious of her soul.' Even those who disapproved of her way of life felt sorry for her, questioning the King's motives.

Soon after her penance, Mrs Shore was let out of prison. However, it would not be long before she returned to Ludgate gaol. For it seems that King Richard discovered that she had joined the Marquess of Dorset in his hiding place.

36

Lady Margaret Beaufort's Conspiracy, 1483

MARGARET BEAUFORT · JOHN MORTON

MARGARET Beaufort attended Richard III's coronation on 6 July 1483. As has been seen, her husband was steward of the household, first among the court dignitaries. Their presence at the crowning and anointing in Westminster Abbey and then at the banquet in Westminster Hall was therefore unavoidable.

Despite his arrest during the coup at the Tower, Lord Stanley had made his peace with Richard by agreeing to support him. In reward, he had been appointed High Constable of England, while later he would be made a Knight of the Garter. Together with the Duke of Buckingham, the Duke of Norfolk (formerly Lord Howard), and the Earl of Northumberland, he was one of the four magnates on whom the King depended, one of the props of the new régime. However, the wife of one of those props was determined to bring it crashing down.

Margaret Beaufort carried Queen Anne's train, taking precedence over all other peeresses, even over King Richard's sister. We know the gowns Margaret wore for the ceremonies: one was made from six yards of crimson velvet 'purfled' – bordered – with white cloth of gold, the other from six and half yards of blue velvet with crimson cloth of gold.[1] (Was John Lambert the mercer who supplied these rich materials?) In addition, she had been sent ten yards of scarlet cloth for her servants' livery, from the royal palace of the Wardrobe.

In the Abbey she watched the King and Queen stand naked from the waist up as they were anointed, the crowns placed on their heads by an unwilling Cardinal Bourchier, and then, during the banquet, saw them served with hypocras by the Mayor of London. She had an excellent opportunity to observe Richard at close quarters. Sharp-featured, he had 'a short and sour countenance' and bore a striking resemblance to his father, the late Duke of York.[2] As always he was very nervous, looking to left and right and behind him, fidgeting with one of the rings on his fingers or with the dagger at his belt. When thinking, he chewed his lower lip continually.

Like all England, she would have worried about the former King and his brother. Mancini says that he had met many Englishmen during his last few weeks in London who burst into tears whenever Edward V was mentioned. Even by the time Mancini left England, just before Richard's coronation in July, some people in the City suspected that the boys had already been murdered, although the horrified Italian adds that he was unable to obtain any definite information – the two children had literally disappeared into thin air.

In his *General Chronicle*, the Elizabethan antiquary John Stow – using sources long since lost – preserves a confused account of a plot to rescue them, otherwise unknown, which four humble men tried to organize during the month of July 1483. 'Robert Russe, sergeant of London, William Davy, Pardoner of Hounslow, John Smith, groom of King Edward's stirrup and Stephen Ireland, with many others . . . were purposed to have set fire on divers parts of London, which fire whilst men had been staunching, they would have stolen out of the Tower' – taking the little princes with them amid the confusion. Stowe also tells us that, when indicted, the four would-be rescuers were accused of having been in correspondence with Henry and Jasper Tudor; this suggests that their plot only came to light in October or even later, after the rebellion in which the two Tudors were involved. However, the four must have planned it in July when many Londoners thought that the boys might still be alive. Stowe's account continues, 'Robert Russe, William Davy, John Smith and Stephen Ireland were at Westminster judged to death and from there drawn [on hurdles] to the Tower Hill and there beheaded, and their heads were set on Tower Hill.'[3]

The Duke of Gloucester's well-attested popularity during his brother's lifetime, and while he was Protector, had blinded his normally shrewd judgement. Even though – taken by surprise – they were too frightened to resist his coup, most Englishmen could not possibly accept him as the rightful King of England. His glib pretext for setting aside his nephews was thoroughly unconvincing, the shallowest of bad law; invalid marriages and bastardy were not matters for Parliament to decide but for the Church, which had never been consulted at any stage.

Disinheriting a brother's children and stealing their property was shocking enough in itself. What made Richard's action so appalling was that the Crown was both hereditary and sacred; to steal it in this way was not just robbery but blasphemy as well. He was a criminal of the worst sort, however many great lords and proud prelates might outwardly acknowledge him to be their sovereign.

Most upsetting of all must have been the lurid rumours about how the children had died, in the presumption that they were dead. No doubt, if some refused to believe the rumours, many did. The absence of any firm information would have fuelled the general curiosity. 'What kind of death,' says Vergil, who had obviously made wide inquiries, 'is not certainly known.' Thomas More says they were smothered with a feather bed and then buried secretly at the Tower. Whoever wrote the *Great Chronicle* also believed that they had been smothered, between two feather beds.

John Rastell, in *The Pastime of People* – which he published in 1529 – had heard that they were killed in this way. His account of the murder is peculiarly horrible:

> the most common opinion was that they were smothered between two feather beds, and that in the doing the younger brother escaped from under the feather beds, and crept under the bedstead, and there lay naked awhile, till that they had smothered the young king so that he was surely dead. And after that one of them took his brother from under the bedstead and held his face down to the ground with his one hand, and with the other cut his throat bole with a dagger.

While Rastell was writing over forty years later, such a story may well have been in existence in 1483. Given the sensational circumstances of the boys' disappearance, and who they were, it is highly unlikely that rumours of this sort did not circulate. And although the fifteenth century was an age of the most savage violence and cruelty, it was not without pity. The folk tale of the Babes in the Wood and their wicked uncle is supposed to have emerged about this time, inspired by the events of 1483.

Probably Sir Thomas More's brilliant reconstruction is not too far from the truth, even if some of its details may be queried. According to More, the Constable of the Tower refused to kill the boys so King Richard entrusted the job to one of his household men, Sir James Tyrell. The Constable gave Tyrell the keys of the Tower for a night, the actual murder being committed by a professional thug called Miles Forest, 'a fellow fleshed in murder beforetime', and by Tyrell's 'horsekeeper', John Dighton.

Then all the others being removed from them, this Miles Forest and John

Dighton about midnight (the innocent children lying in their beds) came into the chamber and suddenly lapped them up among the clothes – so bewrapped them and entangled them, keeping down by force the feather-bed and pillows hard into their mouths, that within a while, smothered and stifled, their breath failing, they gave up to God their innocent souls into the joys of heaven, leaving to their tormentors their bodies dead in the bed.[4]

More adds that the boys were buried at the foot of a staircase. When a staircase to the White Tower was being demolished in 1674, workmen found a wooden chest containing the bones of two children of about the right age, though their identity has been questioned by Richard's modern partisans.

No one will ever know just how the 'Princes in the Tower' died. What is beyond dispute, however, is that by the autumn of 1483 a significant number of Englishmen firmly believed that the former Edward V and his brother, the Duke of York, were dead and buried. They were also convinced that Richard III had ordered their killing. It was a conviction which earned him a whole host of irreconcilable enemies. As *The Great Chronicle of London* (written by someone who had almost certainly lived in the City throughout these events) says of the new King, 'had he continued still Protector and suffered the childer to have prospered according to his allegiance and fidelity, he should have been honourably lauded over all, whereas now his fame is dirtied and dishonoured.'

Nothing else but an unshakeable belief that neither of the two boys would ever be seen again can possibly explain the subsequent behaviour of the Duke of Buckingham and of Henry Tudor, Earl of Richmond. Nor can anything else account for the uncompromising support given to Henry's two very risky bids for the throne by so many hitherto staunch Yorkists – a significant number of whom were former servants of Edward IV. They were prepared to venture their lives, their good and their families in a rebellion against an alarmingly formidable monarch, who was popularly considered to be one of the best military commanders of his day. By contrast, Henry Tudor was a totally unknown, untried and penniless adventurer.

The very knowledgeable and well informed author of the 'second continuation' of the *Chronicle of the Abbey of Croyland* (who has been plausibly if not conclusively identified as Richard's Lord Chancellor, Dr Russell) describes convincingly how the opposition to the new régime developed. At first, in order to deliver the princes from the Tower of London, 'the people of the southern and western parts of the country began to murmur greatly and to form meetings and confederacies.' Then, continues the writer, sinister rumours started to circulate widely, that the two boys had been murdered, rumours which were generally believed. He informs us that the thoughts of such people turned towards Henry Tudor, Earl of Richmond.

If Polydore Vergil is correct, Richard had himself spread the rumours that the boys were dead so that 'after the people understood no issue male of King Edward be now left alive, they might with better mind and good will bear and sustain his government.' The Croyland chronicler also seems to suggest that these rumours had emanated from the King. It was a disastrous blunder on Richard's part. He had left Henry Tudor out of his calculations; the elimination of the princes made Henry the only man who could reasonably challenge his right to the throne. Two people in particular had already reached this conclusion – Margaret Beaufort and John Morton.

For many years Henry Tudor had been a prisoner in Brittany, sometimes at the castle of Elven eleven miles north-east of Vannes – the Breton capital – and sometimes at Vannes itself. His uncle Jasper was kept away from him, in separate custody, either at Josselin or elsewhere at Vannes. Edward IV tried to obtain possession of Henry on more than one occasion. Bernard André records how in 1476 Margaret sent a warning to her son not to return to England, even though the King might offer him the hand of one of his daughters in marriage.

Vergil tells us that during the same year, 1476, 'seduced by money from honesty, faith and good dealing', Duke Francis II of Brittany agreed to hand over Henry to King Edward. Knowing that he was on his way to his death, when the English ambassadors took him to the port of St Malo to board a ship that was bound for England, he either fell ill 'through agony of mind' or else feigned illness. Luckily one of the Duke's advisers, Jean Chenlet, explained to Francis that Henry was going 'to be torn in pieces by bloody butchers' – to be hanged, drawn and quartered. The ducal treasurer, Pierre Landois, rushed to St Malo and had the young man taken into sanctuary at a church in the town, promising the ambassadors that he would be kept in confinement.

However, Margaret herself did not allow Edward to forget Henry Tudor. Since she was at court, she had ample opportunity to intercede for her son, and during the last years of the reign it looked as though her efforts might be rewarded. Only recently evidence has been discovered which shows just how near she came to reconciling the régime to 'the only imp now left of King Henry VI's blood.' The new evidence also refutes Polydore Vergil's assumption that Edward 'lived, as it were, in perpetual fear' of Henry Tudor.[5]

On 3 June 1482 a deed drawn up at Westminster in King Edward's presence gave permission for Henry to inherit lands worth £400 a year from his grandmother's estate, on condition that he came back to England 'to be in the grace and favour of the King's Highness.' In the same deed Lord Stanley promised that he would not ask for any changes to his wife's marriage settlement. As a result his stepson had every prospect of one day becoming a great landed magnate. We also know (from the *Calendar of Papal Registers*) that Stanley and Margaret had discussed with King Edward and Bishop Morton the possibility of a marriage between Henry and the King's eldest daughter, Elizabeth of York. The draft of a royal pardon for Henry survives, written on the back of the patent that had created his father Earl of Richmond.

There is therefore ample proof that Henry Tudor had been seriously considered as a candidate for the hand of Elizabeth long before the events of 1483 and the disappearance of her brothers. It explains why Dr Morton, the Queen Dowager and the Duke of Buckingham accepted Henry as the obvious suitor for the heiress of Edward IV, tacitly recognizing his claim to the throne – which was why they followed Margaret's lead in plotting against Richard from such an early stage. Richard's habitual absence from court indicates that he had known nothing of the proposed marriage and accounts for why he at first failed to identify Henry Tudor as his principal rival.

Because Edward Hall wrote sixty years later, obviously to flatter the Tudor dynasty in general and Henry VIII in particular, his *Union of the Two Illustre Families of York and Lancaster* is treated with considerable reserve by modern historians. They suspect him of trying to please King Henry by exaggerating the roles played by his father and his grandmother during the Wars. Yet Hall could well have had access to sources of information which have since disappeared. He gives a more than plausible account of an unpremeditated meeting between Margaret and the Duke of Buckingham which he says took place during the latter half of July 1483, just after Richard's coronation.

According to Hall, after attending the coronation, the Duke had suddenly grown disillusioned with King Richard and contemplated seizing the Crown for himself. On his way to Shrewsbury, quite by chance he encountered Lady Margaret Beaufort on the road between Worcester and Bridgnorth. She was making a pilgrimage to the shrine of the Blessed Virgin at Worcester. (As Henry Stafford's widow she was the Duke's aunt, so presumably they were on familiar terms and accustomed to speaking frankly to each other.) Margaret asked him to intercede with Richard to allow her son Henry Tudor to return to England and marry one of Edward IV's daughters 'without anything to be taken or demanded for the same espousals but only the king's favour.'[6]

What makes it so likely that this conversation really did occur are the negotiations which we now know to have taken place before Richard became King. Moreover, as Hall makes abundantly clear, the discussion between Buckingham and his aunt prepared the ground for the subtle arguments of Dr Morton.

After his arrest during the June coup, John Morton had been kept in close confinement at the Tower of London, although he was by now a venerable old man in his sixties. King Richard must have been very much aware of his reputation for unshakeable fidelity, how he had stayed loyal to the House of Lancaster throughout its darkest years. Nor can the King have forgotten that Edward IV had appointed Morton one of the executors of his will – which had mysteriously disappeared. In addition, so Mancini had heard, he was widely reputed to be 'of great resource and daring.' He was popular too, in certain quarters – the University of Oxford petitioned for his release from imprisonment, describing the Bishop of Ely as her dearest son. In response, he was placed in the custody of the Duke of Buckingham, under what would now be called house arrest at 'Brecknock' Castle on the Welsh border, which was the Duke's principal stronghold. (Today only fragments of it remain in the grounds of the Castle Hotel at Brecon.) There were many opportunities for the wily doctor to hold a private conversation with Buckingham.

Combining what he had gleaned from survivors of King Richard's council, from a manuscript copy of Polydore Vergil's history, and perhaps from the aged Morton himself, Sir Thomas More recreated the discussions between Morton and the Duke. When the latter began by praising King Richard, the Bishop answered frankly that he would have preferred to have seen Henry VI's son on the throne of England but, since the boy was dead, he had changed sides. 'So was I to King Edward faithful chaplain and glad would have been if his child had succeeded him.' Frustratingly, More's account is unfinished, but he makes it clear that in his opinion Morton's fluently expressed arguments persuaded the Duke of Buckingham to lead a rebellion.

The early Tudor historians admitted that they were puzzled by the Duke's volte-face since he had been Richard's main ally in seizing the throne. Vergil thought that it was either because the King refused to let him have all the old Bohun lands of his ancestors or else because he was genuinely sorry for what he had done. However, there is a much simpler if more cynical explanation – Buckingham was so shaken by the evidence of widespread hostility to Richard III that he realized that such an unpopular régime could not hope to survive for very long.

According to Vergil, the Duke proposed to Dr Morton that Henry Tudor

Brecon Castle, a stronghold of the Duke of Buckingham, where Dr Morton was confined by Richard III in 1483.

should become King, with Elizabeth of York for his consort. The Croyland chronicler on the other hand was convinced that the Bishop put the idea into Buckingham's head. 'We shall find Dr Morton his *Caput Argol*, or the malignant Planet of his Fortune,' the seventeenth-century historian George Buck says of the Bishop, 'who by his Politick Drifts and Pride, advanced himself and brought the Duke to his Ruin.'[7] Some modern historians suspect that Buckingham may have planned to make himself King instead of Henry. Had that been the case, however, the Duke would surely have opposed Henry's marriage with Edward IV's daughter.[8]

The same solution had already occurred to Margaret Beaufort. 'And she, being a wise woman, after the slaughter of King Edward's children was known, began to hope well of her son's fortune' is Vergil's comment. She used her personal physician, Dr Lewis Caerleon – 'a grave man and of no small experience' – to sound out the dowager Queen, whom he was also attending in a personal capacity. From the sanctuary in Westminster Abbey, Elizabeth Woodville answered that she would do everything in her power to persuade Edward IV's former

friends to support Henry Tudor, if he would marry her daughter Elizabeth when
he had gained the Crown.

Dr Morton sent a message to Margaret, informing her that the Duke of
Buckingham was ready to lead the rising. In response she dispatched her receiver-
general, Reginald Bray, to Brecon. (Bray was the household man to whom Henry
Stafford had left his grizzled old horse.) A gifted organizer, Bray recruited a large
number of conspirators, including many of the Queen Dowager's friends; each
man swore an oath of secrecy. At the same time Margaret sent her servant Hugh
Conway 'with a good great sum of money' to Henry Tudor in Brittany, advising
him to land in Wales where supporters would be waiting for him. Another messenger came to Henry from the gentlemen of Kent.

Reading Vergil's account, one has very much the impression of a grand conspiracy. It involved several distinct groups: old, unreconciled Lancastrians, former
servants of Edward IV, the Woodvilles, with all their connections, and anyone
else who simply could not stomach the usurpation. Many of the plotters were
men of substance with everything to lose, important landowners who had been
sheriffs of their counties or Members of Parliament, but there were also plenty
of lesser gentry and yeomen among them. Vergil singles out Dr Morton as the
chief recruiting agent, though Margaret Beaufort and Reginald Bray seem to have
been no less active in gathering supporters.

However, if this was a grand conspiracy, it was restricted to southern England,
the West Country and Wales. Moreover, it lacked proper co-ordination.
Inexperienced as a soldier, the Duke of Buckingham was no leader; his Welsh
affinity and tenants disliked the Duke as 'a sore and hard-dealing man' and followed him only with the greatest reluctance. Most ominous of all, Margaret's
husband, Lord Stanley, would not join the plot – he disliked Buckingham because
of territorial rivalry in North Wales. Other than the Duke and Henry Tudor, the
only other peer actively involved was the Marquess of Dorset, who was still in
hiding.

Richard III was famed for his watchfulness and swift reactions, 'a man much
to be feared for circumspection and celerity', as Vergil says. The King knew that
he must expect trouble, and expect it fairly soon. So many sympathizers were
trying to visit the Queen Dowager in Westminster Abbey that the guard round
the sanctuary had to be increased more than once. By early August he had discovered that a rising was imminent but could not ascertain any details. Vergil tells
us that Richard suspected the Duke of Buckingham and summoned him to court.

The Duke made excuses, 'alleging infirmity of stomach.'

At least the rebels' strategy was on a grand scale. Who planned it is unknown. There were to be separate risings all over the south-east on 18 October (St Luke's Day), together with a mock attack on London by the Kentishmen. The object was to keep the King busy while the Duke of Buckingham brought his Welshmen across the River Severn to link up with the West Country forces, and then meet Henry Tudor, who would land in Devon with 5,000 Bretons. The plan was far too elaborate.

Everything went wrong for the rebels from the start. Spies succeeded in learning their entire plan of campaign and warned Richard at the beginning of October. Knowing that the main threat was Buckingham, he ordered his supporters on the Welsh border to delay the Duke's advance. Identifying the West Country as the most dangerous sector, on 23 October the King sent instructions to the Sheriff of Devon to issue a proclamation denouncing supporters of 'the great rebel, the late duke of Buckingham.'

What made the proclamation so extraordinary was its heading, 'Proclamation for the Reform of Morals'. First among those to be denounced was 'Thomas Dorset, late marquess of Dorset, who holds the shameful and mischievous woman called Shore in adultery.' In addition, the Marquess 'hath many and sundry maids, widows and wives damnably and without shame devoured, deflowered and defiled', while all the rebels were guilty of 'the damnable maintenance of vices and sin as they had in times past, as to the great displeasure of God and evil example of all Christian people.'[9] Professor Ross comments that the proclamation reads more like a tract against sexual licence than a condemnation of armed treason.[10]

On St Luke's Day, as planned, there were risings against Richard III in Kent, Berkshire, Wiltshire, Devon and Brecon, which began well enough. However, there was no need for the King's supporters to impede the march of the Duke of Buckingham's Welshmen into England; a torrential downpour set in for ten days, rivers bursting their banks and roads turning into quagmires. Half drowned, the Duke's unwilling army disintegrated. Disguised as a labourer, he went into hiding in Shropshire near the house of one of his own men – who promptly betrayed him. He was taken to Salisbury and beheaded in the marketplace there on 2 November. Margaret had lost yet another kinsman.

The rebellion collapsed, no one daring to wait and defy the infuriated King, who occupied Exeter without having to exchange a blow. Henry Tudor's little fleet was scattered by storms on its way over from Brittany. With two ships he anchored off Plymouth, sending a boat to investigate when he saw troops. From the shore they shouted that they were the Duke of Buckingham's men, but Henry was much too wary to be caught and made his way back to Brittany.

Lady Margaret Beaufort had everything to fear from King Richard since, so Vergil tells us, she 'was commonly called the head of that conspiracy.'

37

Mrs Shore Marries Again, 1483

JANE SHORE

T H E appearance of 'the shameful and mischievous woman called Shore' in Richard's proclamation of 23 October announced that Jane was in trouble again. Rearrested, she had been sent back to Ludgate gaol, almost certainly for sheltering the Marquess of Dorset. No details are recorded of Dorset's movements between his flight from sanctuary at Westminster in June 1483 and his arrival in Brittany towards the end of the year, but the wording of the proclamation ('*holds* in adultery') indicates that he had been living with Mrs Shore very recently indeed. Then, suddenly, Jane found a new protector in the person of her interrogator – the King's solicitor, Mr Thomas Lynom.

Some time in the 1490s a man called Edward Drury copied out a register of royal grants and writs, most of them dating from Richard III's reign. On the very last page of the collection there is a letter from the King himself to his Lord Chancellor, Bishop Russell. It concerns Jane and was apparently written during the last months of 1483:

> By the king. Right reverend father in God, &c. Signifying unto you that it is showed unto us that our servant and solicitor, Thomas Lynom, marvellously blinded and abused with the late [wife] of William Shore, now being in Ludgate by our commandment, hath made contract of matrimony with her, as it is said, and intendeth, to our full great marvel, to proceed to effect the same. We for many causes would be sorry that he should be so disposed. Pray you, therefore, to send for him, and in that ye goodly may, exhort and stir him to the contrary; and if ye find him utterly set for to marry her and none otherwise will be advertised, then, if it may stand with the Law of the

Church, we be content, the time of the marriage deferred to our coming next to London, that upon sufficient surety found of her good bearing, ye do send for her keeper and discharge him of Our said commandment, by warrant of these committing her to the rule and guiding of her father or any other by your direction in the mean season. Given &c.

(It seems that Mr Lambert was also known to King Richard.)

A member of the King's council, Mr Thomas Lynom styled himself 'gentil-man' and, while working in London, appears to have had a home at Sutton-on-Derwent. A northerner, he belonged to a new breed of specialist bureaucrat which entered the royal service during the Yorkist period, with offices in the City or at Westminster. In some ways he resembled the sort of industrious, ambitious high-flier who today finds a niche in the Cabinet Office or on the staff of the White House.[1]

Since the 1470s he had been doing legal work for Richard in Yorkshire. Working for Gloucester was no sinecure as he was the most legally minded magnate of his time. Constantly selling land in southern England to buy more in the north kept his staff extremely busy; they were always renegotiating leases, altering rents or trying to extract larger fees from his official posts. He seems to have employed a full-scale team of legal researchers, while he himself possessed an excellent knowledge of Common Law; his cartulary from his ducal days has survived and is the reference file of a man obsessed with litigation. His counsel were never out of court and he was not above cowing juries. Clearly he found Thomas Lynom a satisfactory servant. In 1482 Lynom and Richard Pottyer – the Mores' cynical friend – were rewarded with the goods and chattels in Hampshire of Sir Thomas Greenfield. (They cannot have amounted to much since Sir Thomas was an almsknight of Windsor.)

It was no small compliment to Mr Lynom's professional abilities that Richard should have appointed him King's Solicitor in August 1483, an office that had first emerged about 1460 and was the precursor of that of today's Solicitor General. He was made escheator of Essex and Hertford in November. An escheator collected lands and property due to the Crown by reversion and for-feiture, so understandably he was very busy with this type of work after the Duke of Buckingham's rebellion. A member of a commission investigating treasonable persons in Essex, he received the Bedfordshire manor of Colmeworth in March 1484 as a reward for his services. He sat on many commissions; for example, in June 1484, with Lord Lovell, William Catesby and others he was entrusted with seeing that Lord Grey of Powys took 1,000 archers from Southampton to

Brittany, while later that year he received the commissions of array to raise troops in Essex and Bedfordshire. He was also a tax expert and involved in extracting the loans that the King demanded from his wealthier subjects during 1485. However, his main duties appear to have been organizing the collection of revenue from the Crown lands.[2]

Disregarding his employer's objections, the highly respectable Mr Thomas Lynom married 'Shore's wife', undeniably an odd choice of husband for someone with quite such a colourful past. It has been ungallantly suggested that he was after her money, but this had all gone by now. The King may have been justified in describing Thomas as 'marvellously blinded.' Perhaps he persuaded her to take him by offering to arrange her release from Ludgate gaol. Quite soon – certainly by 1487 – Mrs Lynom gave birth to a daughter whom they christened Julyan.

There are good reasons for supposing that Jane's parents were delighted by their daughter's sensible marrige. Mr Lynom was clearly a man of considerable influence, very well thought of by the King. They cannot have been happy when she was consorting with the régime's enemies – indeed, they must have been horrified. Henry Tudor's accession to the throne might all too easily mean the loss of John Lambert's West Country estates, which had once belonged to the Courtenays. The present head of that family, Edward Courtenay – heir to the attainted Earls of Devon – had played a leading role in Buckingham's rebellion and was now in exile with Henry in Brittany.

Apparently Mr Lambert had for some time been involved in litigation with a certain 'Alexander Verney, Esquire', over the possession of his Somerset proper-ties. However, at the end of November 1484 Verney formally recognized his ownership of the manor of Puriton, together with that of other lands in the county, in two deeds. Among those who witnessed the documents was John Kendall, King Richard's secretary.[3] It is not too fanciful to suppose that Thomas Lynom had intervened in the case in his father-in-law's interest. The Lamberts had become part of the Ricardian establishment.

Even if Jane had lost her own money, her father was richer than ever. According to a seventeenth-century antiquary, Sir Henry Chauncey, Mr Lambert bought the valuable manor of Pulters at Hinxworth in Hertfordshire from Sir John Ward, Mayor of London, in 1484 – 'the 2 Richard III in which year three Lord Mayors, and three Sheriffs of London dy'd of a Sweating Sickness.'[5] The village of Hinxworth is in the extreme north of the county, pleasantly situated on rising ground amid rich agricultural land on the flat borders of Bedfordshire and Cambridgeshire.

There is a well-attested tradition in the area (recorded in the *Victoria County History*) that Pulters Manor is in fact Hinxworth Place, a cheerful, rambling old house built of local 'clunch' – hard chalk – which was begun about 1460 and enlarged during the next century.[6] If so, this must be where John Lambert spent his last days. Locals say that it is haunted. Another building in the village which Jane would still recognize is the parish church, barely a mile away from Hinxworth Place, with a great square tower. It is reached from the house along a path through the fields, no doubt the same path trodden by Jane when she followed her father's funeral.

Her ex-husband returned to the City in the summer of 1484, with a letter for King Richard from the Governor of the Merchant Adventurers, Mr John Wendy, about problems of trade in Flanders. Apparently William Shore had prospered, acquiring property at Middleburg in Zealand, with business interests as far afield as Iceland. During the next reign he was to be appointed a Collector of Customs in Yarmouth and Ipswich, and then in London – a sure sign of wealth. In 1487 he would make a formal gift of all his goods and chattels to three trusted friends, one of them being the printer William Caxton. (The 'gift' was a legal fiction, cancelled by a second document and used to avoid taxes.) He died in 1495, during a visit to his brother-in-law, John Agard, at Scropton in Derbyshire, where he is buried. There is no reason to suppose that he had ever met his former wife again – there is no mention of her in his will.[7]

The first years of Mrs Lynom's second marriage must have been overshadowed, not so much by the burden of an unaccustomed respectability as by the problems of her husband's employer. According to the early Tudor historians, the King spent the entire twenty-six months of his reign in a state of permanent paranoia, constantly expecting an invasion or a plot to assassinate him. Although the Duke of Buckingham's rebellion had been crushed with little difficulty, Vergil says that 'King Richard, as yet more doubting than trusting in his own cause, was vexed, wrested and tormented in mind with fear almost perpetually of th'Earl Henry and his confederates' return; wherefore he had a miserable life . . .'

Sir Thomas More's description of the King is even grimmer. 'When he went abroad, his eyes whirled about, his body secretly armoured, his hand ever on his dagger.'

Even so, during Richard's reign the antiquary John Rous recorded how the King was 'full commendably punishing offenders of the laws, especially oppressors of the Commons . . .' Cynics have suspected him of trying to win support by good government. In a proclamation issued after Buckingham's rebellion, he asked that everyone who might

Hinxworth Place, Hinxworth, Herts – the Lamberts' country house.

find himself grieved, oppressed or unlawfully wronged do make a bill of his complaint, and put it to his highness, and he shall be heard and without delay have such convenient remedy as shall accord with his laws. For his grace is utterly determined all his true subjects shall live in rest and quiet, and peaceably enjoy their lands, livelihoods and goods according to the laws of this his land . . .

The Parliament of 1484 saw some sensible legislation, such as that preventing an accused person's goods being forfeit before they were convicted (too late for poor Jane) and prohibiting the benevolences introduced by Edward IV. But it did little for the King's popularity – if one may credit Vergil, many people even blamed him for any bad weather.

He took stringent precautions against invasion. Not only were the approaches from Brittany and France constantly patrolled by English ships, but there was also an early-warning system. This was a species of 'pony express' with riders stationed along all the main roads from the coast, poised to bring news of any enemy landing.

Nevertheless, it has to be said that Professor Ross discerns 'no hint in the administrative records of the reign of the nervous agonies or political palsy attributed to him by some of the chronicles.' Ross does, however, admit that Richard spent far more time in Nottingham – the strategic centre of the kingdom – than in London because of his need to strike as fast as possible at any invasion force.[8] By any reckoning, Richard III's régime was insecure.

There were compensations for men like Thomas Lynom. As a Yorkshireman, he must surely have welcomed the irruption of so many northerners into the administration; by 1484 at least two-thirds of sheriffs in the counties south of the Rivers Thames and Severn came from the north. Richard did not trust southerners. At the same time, there was plenty of work for Mr Lynom, who was kept busy extracting loans from the rich to augment insufficient revenues. Because of his excessive expenditure on precautions against invasion, the King had begun to find himself increasingly short of money, and had started using benevolences again, despite having made them illegal during the recent Parliament.[9]

It was an odd irony that Jane's future prosperity should depend on the survival of Richard III. For her husband's career was based on the King's continuing patronage. The Lynoms would have been less than human if they had not worried about a change of régime – one which they knew might take place at any moment, accompanied by much bloodshed.

38

'Mother to the king's great rebel and traitor', 1484

MARGARET BEAUFORT

As Polydore Vergil makes plain, Margaret Beaufort was generally thought to have been the brains behind the Duke of Buckingham's revolt.[1] In his flowery way, Kendall calls her 'the Athena of the rebellion', Athena being the Greek goddess of war. Richard recognized her as a most dangerous enemy.

When Parliament assembled in January 1484, there followed a savage proscription of every identifiable opponent of any importance, over a hundred bills of attainder being passed to confirm forfeiture of life and land. The King gave the confiscated estates almost indiscriminately to men who had served him in the north; borrowing More's words, 'with large gifts he gat him unsteadfast friendship.' There was a special Act of attainder for John, Bishop of Ely, together with two other prelates who had played a prominent role in the rising – Lionel Woodville of Salisbury and Piers Courtenay of Exeter. As clerics, they lost their possessions but not their lives.

There was also a special attainder against Lady Margaret Beaufort, which indicates the very wide extent of her involvement.

> For as much as Margaret, countess of Richmond, mother to the king's great rebel and traitor Henry, earl of Richmond, hath of late conspired, confeder[at]ed and committed high treason against our sovereign Lord King Richard III . . . in sending messages, writings and tokens to the said Henry, desiring, procuring and stirring him by the same to come into this realm and make war against our sovereign lord . . . Also the said countess made

chevisance of great sums, as well within the City of London, as in other places in this realm.[2]

Making 'chevisances' was raising loans. Clearly, Margaret had played a major part in financing the rebellion.

However, in view of the many excellent services performed by her husband Thomas, Lord Stanley, the King 'will forbear the great punishment of attainder of the said countess' for his sake. Nevertheless, all her estates and income were confiscated; they were given to Stanley, though only for his lifetime, after which they must pass to the Crown. In addition, Margaret's husband was ordered to keep her isolated, in some secret place without servants or company, so that she would be unable to communicate with Henry Tudor or his friends.

Polydore Vergil comments patronizingly that she escaped much worse punishment because 'the working of a woman's wit was thought of small account'. She was fortunate in that, unlike the Tudors, Yorkist kings did not send women to the headsman's block. Even so, a future member of her household, Henry Parker, Lord Morley, observed revealingly that 'in King Richard's days she was oft in jeopardy of her life, yet she bore patiently all trouble in such wise that it is wonder to think of it.'[3]

Meanwhile, although the Duke of Buckingham's rebellion had ended in abject failure, it had nonetheless proved to be a huge step forward for the cause of Henry Tudor. Even the elimination of the arrogant, ambitious Harry Buckingham from the political scene was a blessing. Henry had become generally accepted as the only hope for those who opposed King Richard. From being a solitary, isolated fugitive, friendless save for his uncle and his far-away mother, he now possessed his own court in exile. Most of the defeated rebels who escaped from Richard fled across the sea to join him in Brittany, while others who were disaffected would continue to do so. They included some genuinely distinguished figures: the Marquess of Dorset and the Bishops of Salisbury and Exeter, together with a large group of influential landowners; the latter, determined to regain their estates, had friends and relations who were secret supporters.

The exiles would have been greeted by a tall, slender and impressive young man in his mid-twenties, with small blue eyes and noticeably bad teeth in a long, sallow face beneath very fair hair. Amiable and high-spirited, Henry Tudor was friendly if dignified in manner, while it was clear to everyone that he was extremely intelligent. His definitive biographer, Professor Chrimes, credits him

– even before he had become King – with possessing 'a high degree of personal magnetism, ability to inspire confidence, and a growing reputation for shrewd decisiveness.'[4] On the debit side, he may have looked a little delicate – he had poor health – while despite his obvious ability, so far he had had no experience of warfare and as yet there was no military leader of repute among his followers. Nevertheless, it is obvious that he had no trouble in presenting himself as a serious rival to King Richard.

In any case, the rebellion of October 1483 had transformed Henry's position. The hitherto almost unknown 'imp' had by now become the acknowledged Lancastrian pretender who, it was widely known, had pledged himself to marry the heiress of York and was therefore an acceptable pretender to disaffected Yorkists as well. On Christmas Day 1483, in the cathedral at Rennes, the exiles knelt at Henry Tudor's feet and swore homage to him as though he were already King of England.

Needless to say, Margaret did not stop corresponding with her son. Lord Stanley appears to have turned a blind eye, though he took care to keep on good terms with Richard. There was no reason to prevent so pious a lady from being visited by her confessor. This was Dr Christopher Urswick, rector of Puttenham in Hertfordshire and a chaplain of the collegiate church at Manchester, whom she may have met in the north while staying on her husband's estates. He had entered her service in 1482. A lawyer like Morton, he was a man of great subtlety and courage who would one day become a distinguished diplomat. During 1484 he made more than one secret journey to Brittany.

Margaret Beaufort had shown that it was possible for a woman to play a key role in fifteenth-century politics. 'If Margaret's efforts on her son's behalf had an heroic quality, they were not forged out of a blind adherence to a dynastic loyalty but the ruthless practice of realpolitik' is the verdict of her most recent biographers. 'Her calculating temperament and natural astuteness allowed the organisation of an alliance with the Woodvilles in the autumn of 1483.' The part she played immeasurably strengthened her links with her beloved son. She was in truth 'Mother to the king's great rebel and traitor'.

39

Dr Morton Visits Rome, 1484–85

JOHN MORTON

Iɴ Professor Ross's opinion, 'the master-mind behind the entire plan may well have been the wily John Morton, bishop of Ely.'[1] Undoubtedly he was responsible for a good deal of it. Although Richard could not catch him, the King did his best to destroy the reputation of that elusive divine. One of the Acts of attainder included the name of Thomas Nandyke, 'necromancer', whom it alleged to have been at Brecon Castle with Morton. Sir George Buck states that during the 1484 Parliament 'there was accused and attainted of sorcery and other such devilish practices, Doctor Lewis, Doctor Morton, William Knevitt of Buckingham, the Countess of Richmond, Thomas Nandick, of Cambridge, conjurer, with others . . .' Admittedly Morton was not branded as a warlock in the Act which attainted him, but he may have been so in a speech in Parliament. Buck adds that Dr Morton was reported to have poisoned Edward IV. Richard's régime was far from averse to smear tactics.[2]

What is beyond question is that John Morton had escaped. As soon as he saw that the Duke of Buckingham's rebellion was collapsing, the Bishop made his way in disguise to an unknown refuge somewhere in his diocese of Ely. There were plenty of suitable hiding places amid the Fens. Moreover, from the lonely and sparsely populated East Anglian coastline nearby, it was very easy for him to cross discreetly to the Low Countries at whatever moment he chose. He may not have left England until the beginning of 1484 when the authorities started to relax their vigilance.

Exactly where Dr Morton spent his exile in Flanders is unknown. It may have been Bruges, though here he would have been in danger from agents of the dowager Duchess of Burgundy, Margaret of York. As a port where news of

THE REIGN OF RICHARD III, 1483–85

England could be had from the merchant community, Antwerp is more probable, but here there was a possibility of kidnap by Richard's spies.

On the other hand, Antwerp was a good place from which to watch the relations between France and Brittany, relations that were starting to have alarming implications for Henry Tudor. The Regent of France, Anne de Beaujeu, was threatened by the Duke of Orleans and Maximilian of Austria, Duke of Burgundy, who hoped to bring in the Duke of Brittany on their side. Francis II was mentally unstable, leaving his treasurer, Pierre Landois, to manage affairs of state. Landois favoured Orleans and Maximilian and in consequence sought an alliance with England to defend the Duchy against the French.

Meanwhile, from Morton's point of view, the situation in England was not unpromising. Richard III might have won a crushing victory yet, perversely, it only increased opposition to his rule. The southerners disliked being colonized by the northern squires who took over the confiscated manor houses; they wanted their old masters back instead of being bullied by these alien newcomers, the Croyland chronicler tells us. Another rising was only just forestalled at the end of 1484, while the long-expected invasion would come in 1485. There is evidence too that members of Richard's own household were plotting against him throughout his reign.

The King was obsessed by Henry Tudor. However thin his Plantagenet blood might be, however tenuous his claim to the throne, Richard now took him very seriously indeed as a rival. He worked feverishly to persuade the Bretons to eliminate Henry and the exiles. In June 1484 he signed a treaty with the Duke – inspired by Pierre Landois – in which he promised to lend the Bretons a thousand English archers if the French attacked them. At the same time he stipulated that Henry must be placed in close confinement.

It is likely that Lord Stanley heard of the agreement during a meeting of the council, and then told Margaret, who dispatched a fast messenger to Dr Morton in Flanders. The news reached Morton some time in September 1484. He at once sent Christopher Urswick – who happened to be visiting him at the time – to tell Henry that he must leave Brittany.[3] Having delivered the warning, Dr Urswick hurried to the French court where he obtained a safe conduct for him to enter France. Leaving all his followers behind at Vannes, Henry fled with five servants – exchanging clothes with one of them – and rode hard along unfrequented roads to the Breton border, sometimes changing direction in order to confuse his pursuers, stopping only to feed and water his horses. Even so, he crossed the border

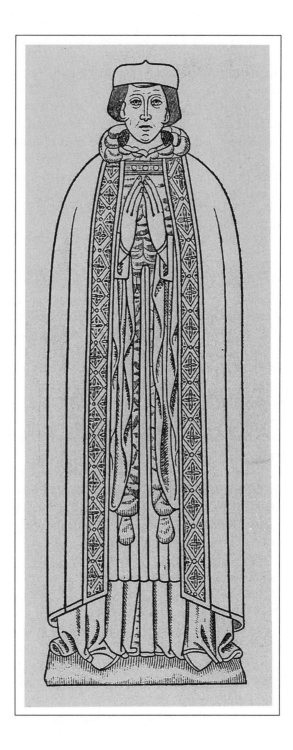

into Anjou a bare hour ahead of the pursuing men-at-arms.

Pierre Landois had owed his dominance to the temporary incapacity of Francis II. Suddenly the Duke recovered his wits and was enraged when he learnt how his treasurer had treated Henry. He gave Sir Edward Woodville and Edward Poynings permission to take their friends to Henry in France, providing them with money for the journey. The Tudor court in exile – the first Tudor court – was re-established at Montargis in the Loire Valley, attaching itself to that of Charles VIII of France. Even when at Vannes it had grown to 300, its chief luminaries besides Uncle Jasper and the Marquess of Dorset being Woodville and Poynings. It continued to grow steadily, especially after following the French King to Paris. Refugees from England went on flocking to it while young English students in Paris began to join, such as Richard Fox, a future Bishop of Winchester.

The French were far from convinced that the Hundred Years' War was over. They were fearful that Richard III might suddenly invade France through Brittany, seeing the thousand archers who had recently arrived in the Duchy as an advance guard. They welcomed Henry Tudor and gave him 3,000 livres to arm his men. Some urged Anne de Beaujeu to provide him with assistance for an expedition against Richard.

The exiled court's most important recruit was undoubtedly the Earl of Oxford, who arrived when it was still at Montargis. Vergil may well be quoting an eyewitness in saying, 'When Henry saw th'earl, he was ravished with joy incredible.' Oxford was one of the greatest noblemen in England and certainly the most distinguished soldier who had so far joined him; he was also a symbol of Lancastrian loyalty to all those who mourned for Henry VI. And he brought more than himself.

Lord Oxford had not only persuaded James Blount, the Captain of Hammes Castle, to let him escape but to come with him, accompanied by Sir John Fortescue – 'gentleman porter of Calais'. They had left Mrs Blount in charge of the garrison, which had also changed sides. Soon she sent word that Hammes

Dr Christopher Urswick, Margaret Beaufort's confessor, who in 1484 warned Henry Tudor that the Bretons were planning to sell him to King Richard. From a brass of 1523 at Hackney.

was being besieged by a large force of Richard's men from Calais. Oxford went to its relief with a band of exiles, attacking the besiegers from the rear, while Thomas Brandon led thirty others into the castle by a secret path through the adjoining marsh. King Richard did not recover Hammes until the end of January 1485, and then only by giving the garrison a free pardon together with leave to depart 'bag and baggage.' Mrs Blount and her soldiers went off to Paris.

Unlike most of the anti-Ricardian exiles, Dr Morton did not go to Paris but preferred to stay in Flanders, though keeping in close touch with Henry Tudor. After his days at Koeur-la-Petite, he had had quite enough of exiled courts. In the Low Countries he was able to receive news from England much more quickly, brought by alert friends who slipped over the sea unobserved in one of the many merchant vessels plying between East Anglia and Flanders – by contrast, the less-frequented sea-lanes to Brittany were being closely patrolled by Richard's ships.

Apparently aware of his unpopularity, Richard III was by now issuing pardons right and left in an attempt to buy support. Several went to gentlemen from the southern counties who had been involved in Buckingham's rebellion. One was given to Sir John Fogge, a connection of the Woodvilles. Richard had already pardoned Fogge in June 1483 after the coup, publicly shaking his hand when he emerged from sanctuary at Westminster – which had not stopped him from joining in the Duke's rising that autumn. Now Sir John received a second pardon, together with a grant of his former estates in Kent. Still more unexpected was a general pardon issued on 11 December 1484 to John Morton, Bishop of Ely – which was ignored by the doctor.

The King had serious dynastic problems. His only legitimate son had died in April 1484, a loss that might have been seen as divine retribution by fifteenth-century men, not least by Richard. Save for the King himself, the sole remaining male Plantagenet was Clarence's son, the nine-year-old Earl of Warwick. The boy made a far from suitable heir to the throne; besides being too young, the king had in any case declared his father to have been a bastard. Eventually Richard chose his nephew John de la Pole, Earl of Lincoln, as heir presumptive.

However, Richard's queen died in March 1485, leaving him free to remarry. His eye lit upon his niece, Elizabeth of York, who had obvious advantages as a consort; she was recognized by his opponents as the heiress of Edward IV and to marry her would effectively block Henry Tudor's dynastic aspirations in that direction, while by all accounts she was very attractive. As for the disadvantage of her being within the forbidden degree of consanguinity, the Church might be prevailed on to provide a dispensation for reasons of state.

During the seventeenth century Sir George Buck claimed to have seen a letter (now lost) from Elizabeth to the Duke of Norfolk in which the Princess expressed enthusiasm for Richard's proposal even before the Queen had died. Vergil, on the other hand, insists that Elizabeth 'abhored' the prospect. Nonetheless, her mother, the Queen Dowager – who, together with her daughters, had left sanctuary in the spring of 1484 – may well have welcomed Richard as a prospective son-in-law. Indeed, so eloquently did she urge her brother, the Marquess of Dorset, to leave Henry Tudor and make his peace with the King that he had to be forcibly prevented from returning to England. Rumours of such a marriage, Vergil informs us, 'pinched Henry by the very stomach.' If it took place, he might well lose all his Yorkist supporters.

The fifteenth-century English did not care for incest. Even that brutal ruffian and alleged rapist Sir Thomas Malory tells us, in *Le Morte d'Arthur*, how when Sir Mordred wanted to marry Queen Guenever, who was his aunt, the Archbishop of Canterbury cursed him with bell, book and candle for making 'a foul work in this land.'

Finally, his chief advisers, 'Mr Ratcliffe and Mr Catesby', warned the King that if he proceeded with the marriage then even his trusted northerners would rise in rebellion against him. At their advice he then submitted to one of the greatest public humiliations suffered by any English king. The records of the Mercers' Company recount how on 30 March the Mayor and citizens of London were summoned to the hall of the Knights of St John at Clerkenwell to hear King Richard complain of rumours that the Queen had been poisoned in order that he might marry Elizabeth. He denied that he had been glad of his wife's death or that he had ever meant to marry his niece. (Clearly some mercers must have been present at Clerkenwell to hear this sensational speech – no doubt Mr Lambert was among them, as a Freeman of the City of London and as the proud father-in-law of the King's Solicitor.)

Meanwhile, from France Henry was sending letters to as many important Englishmen as possible. Naturally most of such dangerous communications were destroyed, for reasons of self-preservation, but a single example has survived. 'Right trusty, worshipful and honourable good friends, I greet you well,' begins Henry, who assumes that he is going to have the recipients' support in 'the just depriving of that homicide and unnatural tyrant which now unjustly bears dominion over you.' As soon as they will inform 'your poor exiled friend' when they are ready to fight for him and how many men they can bring with them, he is prepared to invade England. If he is successful, then 'I shall ever be most forward to remember and wholly to requite this your great and most loving kindness in my just quarrel.' He signs himself 'H.R.' – *Henricus Rex*.

In June 1485 Richard responded with a characteristic proclamation against 'Piers [Courtenay], bishop of Exeter, Jasper Tudor, son of Owen Tudor calling himself earl of Pembroke, John, late earl of Oxon and Sir Richard Woodville with other divers rebels and traitors . . . of whom many be known for open murderers, adulterers and extortioners.' They have chosen for their captain

> one Henry Tydder, son of Edmond Tydder, son of Owen Tydder, which of his ambitiousness and insatiable covetise encroacheth and usurpeth upon him the name and title of royal estate of this realm of England, whereunto he has no manner interest, right, title or colour, as every man well knoweth. For he is descended of bastard blood, both of father side and of mother side, for the said Owen the grandfather was bastard born; and his mother was daughter unto John, duke of Somerset, son unto John, earl of Somerset, son unto Dame Katherine Swynford, and of their double adultery gotten . . .

Henry and his followers were planning 'to do the most cruel murders, slaughters and robberies and disherisons that ever were seen in any Christian realm.' Fortunately for England, however, 'our said sovereign lord, as a well-willed, diligent and courageous prince will put his most royal person to all labour and pain necessary . . . for the resistance and subduing of his said enemies, rebels and traitors, to the most comfort, weal and surety of all his true and faithful liegemen and subjects.'

The Bishop of Ely was not among the rebels listed in the proclamation. It seems that despite Dr Morton having ignored a royal pardon, Richard still hoped to win him over from Henry Tudor. The King may have been encouraged by the knowledge that the Bishop had not yet joined his rival's court in Paris.

In Vergil's phrase, King Richard 'was overwhelmed by pinching cares on every hand.' Almost each week, some gentleman of standing was reported to have gone to France to join Henry; the fugitives included Margaret Beaufort's half-brother John, Lord Welles. And it was painfully clear to the King that his rival must have many more secret supporters who had stayed behind. Among these, according to Vergil, were the Stanleys. Although Richard did not know their 'inward mind', he trusted none of them, 'and Thomas Stanley least of all because he had in marriage Henry's mother.' But the King dared not crush Thomas out of hand since he was one of the key magnates who formed his régime's perilously narrow power-base.

Dr Morton was far from being overwhelmed by pinching cares. He had so few that during the winter of 1484–85 he made a pilgrimage to Rome, accompanied by his nephew Robert (whom Richard had dismissed from his post as Master of the Rolls) and Dr Oliver King. The latter was another senior Yorkist official who had chosen not to serve Richard III; formerly secretary to Edward IV and Edward V, one day he would be secretary to Henry VII. Just how three supposedly penniless refugees were able to find the money for their trip remains a mystery – during the fifteenth century a pilgrimage to Rome was an expensive business. However, on 31 January 1485 John Morton became a member of the Fraternity of the Holy Spirit in Rome, signing its register.[4] So far as politics were concerned, he was prepared to wait on events. He did not have to wait very long.

40

Lord Oxford Wins a Battle, 1485

THE EARL OF OXFORD

NIGHT and day, Henry Tudor pestered the French Regent, Anne de Beaujeu, for funds to finance his expedition against Richard III of England. Finally she offered to lend him 'a slender supply', amounting to 40,000 livres. This was supplemented by various loans from 'other private friends'; presumably these were some of the secret supporters who had stayed in England, including his mother. As sureties for the Regent's money, Henry agreed to leave behind him the Marquess of Dorset – seriously out of favour for having tried to return and make his peace with Richard – and John Bourchier, who were both to remain in French custody until the money was repaid.

As the only exile with any first-hand experience of high command, Lord Oxford must have played a vital part in organizing and equipping the invasion force. (No doubt the money borrowed by Henry paid for the Earl's own armour and weapons, very expensive items.) The force was composed of about 500 English exiles, 1500 French troops under Philippe de Crevecoeur, several hundred Breton soldiers of fortune, and a contingent of Scots mercenaries commanded by Bernard Stewart, Seigneur d'Aubigny. Both Crevecoeur and d'Aubigny were gifted commanders, future marshals of France. Fortunately Oxford was well used to dealing with opinionated foreigners such as the Scots, having visited their country on more than one occasion.

Carrying about 3,000 fighting men at most, the little invasion fleet left Rouen 'with a soft southern wind' on 1 August 1485, sailing down the River Seine and out into the Channel. After a smooth voyage it put into Milford Haven six days later, disembarking at a secluded cove on St Anne's Head which was well away from prying eyes. Henry had landed here deliberately.

For not only was Pembrokeshire his uncle Jasper Tudor's old territory but one of the major landowners in the adjoining county of Caermarthenshire, Rhys ap Thomas of Dinefwr, had sent an encouraging message of support, promising that he would join; Rhys had been recruited by his former tutor, Dr Lewis Caerleon, who was none other than Margaret Beaufort's conniving physician. Margaret's steward, Reginald Bray (still at liberty despite his part in Buckingham's rising), had also advised Henry to land in Wales, adding that he had collected a substantial sum of money with which to pay his troops.[1]

First marching northward, 'through ragged and indirect tracts', according to the Croyland chronicler, Henry and his army then turned east into Powys and then into Shropshire. There was no sign yet of Rhys ap Thomas; 'very much a Welshman on the make' (to borrow Professor Ross's elegant description), understandably Rhys was extremely nervous about committing himself. Ross thinks that Henry hoped that he would be joined by the Stanleys, who owned estates not too far away in North Wales; on the other hand, given Lord Stanley's well-earned reputation for trimming, it was not at all impossible that he might decide to attack his stepson.

Only when the Tudor army reached Shropshire did supporters begin to join it, including – at last – Rhys ap Thomas. Sir Gilbert Talbot joined Henry in Staffordshire, though with a mere 500 men. They were still hopelessly outnumbered. Everything depended on the Stanleys.

From Shropshire Henry had sent messages to his mother and to the Stanleys, saying that he intended to march on London. No doubt Margaret Beaufort tried hard to convince her husband of the advantages of being stepfather to a new King of England. However, Thomas Stanley had survived the Wars of the Roses and profited by his shrewdness in identifying and then backing the more powerful side. While Richard III might well be too unpopular to have very much hope of long-term survival, in the short term he was looking alarmingly formidable – seemingly in complete control of the present situation.

Richard had not expected his enemies to land in Wales, but 'on hearing of their arrival, the king rejoiced or at least appeared to rejoice,' says the Croyland chronicler, who may have been present when the news reached him. Calmly, Richard summoned his own troops to meet him at Nottingham. A message from Lord Stanley was received; he had the sweating sickness and could not come.

As has been seen, the King always suspected Thomas Stanley. When he had recently left court to visit his estates, Richard insisted that he leave his son, Lord

Strange, behind. Just after the letter arrived, Strange tried to desert but was caught 'by stratagem', the Croyland chronicler relates. Questioned – no doubt tortured – he revealed that, together with his uncle, Sir William Stanley, and Sir John Savage, he had been planning to go over to Henry. However, he was adamant that his father was still faithful to the King. Richard kept Lord Strange a prisoner under close guard, his life depending on his father's satisfactory behaviour. William Stanley and John Savage were proclaimed traitors.

Henry knew that everything depended on Thomas Stanley, though he would certainly have been reminded of his stepfather's treacherous behaviour in 1470–71 by Lord Oxford. On the other hand Thomas had married Henry's persuasive mother, which may explain why her son took the highly dangerous risk of visiting Thomas and William Stanley secretly in the former's camp at Atherstone. Here, if Vergil is to be believed, they discussed how their troops should be deployed during the coming battle. The meeting has been questioned by historians, partly because Lord Stanley later stated he had known Henry 'well' from a date two days after the battle – yet he could scarcely say that he had known him *well* at this stage. Nevertheless, it is unlikely that, as Vergil claims, they were 'moved to great joy.' All three were men of the utmost cynicism. Whatever Vergil may claim, Henry still had everything to fear from the coming battle, knowing that the Stanleys were never men of their word.

Like Napoleon, Richard understood that the way to win a battle was to get there quickest with the most men. He had to wait at Nottingham for his troops to assemble, but when they came they were all mounted, archers as well as men-at-arms, composing an army of between 10,000 and 15,000 strong – two or three times as large as any force his opponent could muster. His cannon were serpentines, light guns that could be moved quickly in fast carts. When Henry reached the Midlands the King rode out to do battle with impressive pomp, wearing a crown on his gold-plated helmet – not the crown that he wore on state occasions, but a jewelled coronet valued at £20,000 in the period's money. He was escorted by John Howard, Duke of Norfolk, and by Henry Percy, Earl of Northumberland, together with half a dozen lesser peers. 'None evil captain was he in the war, as to which his disposition was more meetly than for peace,' More says of Richard. 'Sundry victories had he, and sometimes overthrows, but never in default as for his own person.' All contemporary sources testify to the King's reputation as an extremely capable soldier. Had his lavishly equipped troops and their commanders been loyal,

Henry Tudor could never have hoped to defeat him.

On the night of 21 August the royal army encamped a mile or two south of Market Bosworth, ready to intercept Henry on the following day. Yet for all his overwhelming superiority in men and weapons, not all was well with Richard III. Clearly he realized that there was some sort of treachery in the wind. Ominously, despite having been proclaimed a traitor, Sir William Stanley was still with his brother. Could the King rely on Lord Stanley, who was at the head of 3,000 men? And what about the other magnates? Richard must have sensed their own profound uneasiness, but he does not appear to have guessed that Northumberland was secretly in touch with his enemy and planning his destruction. While his troops were asleep, someone posted a note on the tent of his staunchest supporter, Norfolk, containing a couplet which later became famous.

> Jockey of Norfolk, be not too bold
> For Dickon thy master is bought and sold

When dawn came, the King made a ferocious speech to his assembled army in which he swore to be avenged not only on his enemies but on those who had failed to come and fight by his side. He wore a noticeably haggard look. If he had not dreamed of his murders, as Shakespeare would have us believe, he may well have been kept awake by worries about betrayal.

King Richard positioned his troops in echelon on the eastern ridge of Ambion Hill, close to Bosworth and looking down on to a marsh at the foot. (Ironically, it was land that had belonged to the late Lord Hastings.) In the very front stood a formidable contingent of dismounted archers commanded by the Duke of Norfolk. Behind them was the vanguard, its flanks protected by cannon that were linked together by chains to stop cavalry riding through them – the guns consisting of nearly 150 heavy bombards and the same number of light serpentines. There were so many troops in the vanguard, horse and foot, that Vergil (who had obviously spoken to survivors) records that 'to the beholders afar off, it gave a terror for the multitude.' Richard was behind it with a force of picked men-at-arms which included his knights and squires of the Body, and behind the King was the Earl of Northumberland with 3,000 northerners.

At most the opposing army numbered 5,000, with no proper artillery. Henry – who had never seen a battle before – commanded the reserve, a mere troop of men-at-arms and a few archers and billmen. Lord Oxford, who led the vanguard, was the Lancastrians' real commander. Vergil tells us that Henry was 'no little vexed and began to be somewhat appalled.' So too, no doubt, did his entire army.

His stepfather did not respond to desperate appeals.

With the same number of troops as Northumberland, Lord Stanley took up a position between the two armies, declining requests from both Henry and Richard to join them. When, after threatening to execute Lord Strange, the King received a message to the effect that Lord Stanley had plenty of other sons, he ordered the young man's immediate beheading. (The order was ignored.) Richard's worst suspicions were more or less confirmed. Even so, the odds remained very much in his favour.

Looking up, Henry Tudor and his men, who knew nothing of King Richard's difficulties, saw doom poised above them. A ballad called 'The Song of the Lady Bessy', almost certainly written by someone who was at Bosworth, says that the King 'hoveth upon the mountain' – meaning that his troops suddenly came into view on top of Ambion Hill. Then Oxford realized that Richard's narrow front might prevent him from making full use of his numbers, while it was difficult for fifteenth-century cannon to shoot down. Oxford decided that the only chance was to attack uphill; although many of his troops were second-rate, there were experienced soldiers among the exiles who composed their officers. Oxford led them round the marsh and up the slope, straight at Richard's archers, who fired down. Then the Duke of Norfolk charged them. Although in his mid-sixties, this veteran of Towton was still a most dangerous opponent. He intended to smash the Lancastrians before they could deploy and launch a proper attack.

The Earl ordered his men to group round their officers' banners, those of the exiled gentlemen – 'no soldier should go above ten foot from the standards' – and formed them into a triangle, after which he counter-charged Norfolk, uphill. According to a legend that is probably well founded, Oxford and the Duke met in personal combat. Norfolk is said to have wounded the Earl, but then Oxford knocked off his chin-guard, and a moment later the Duke fell down dead with a stray arrow through his exposed throat.[3]

Indirectly, Oxford's unexpectedly successful counter-attack was to save the day for Henry Tudor. Taken aback by Norfolk's failure to rout such puny opposition, and by now fully aware that the Stanleys were preparing to betray him, King Richard ordered the Earl of Northumberland to place his troops between the Stanleys and the Lancastrians. Northumberland refused. Alarmed, the King knew that he must act very quickly if he was to save the situation. Suddenly he recognized Henry and a small escort, beneath the banner of the Red Dragon of Wales, riding across the field below Ambion Hill. In desperation, he was going to throw himself on his stepfather's mercy.

'All inflamed with ire', the King at once led the knights, squires and yeomen of his household out from among the ranks of his army, and then in a furious charge downhill and over the field. He killed Henry's banner-bearer with his lance, knocked another man out of the saddle with his battle-axe and slew others. He may even have exchanged blows with his rival. Richard was 'making way with weapon on every side', and Henry's men 'were now almost out of hope of victory.'

The combat was taking place in full view of the Stanley brothers, only half a mile away. If Henry died, they would probably die too – soon after the battle. But here was the moment to decide it in their own favour. Sir William at their head, the 3,000 red-jerkined horsemen of the Stanley affinity – mindful of 'good lordship' – charged to rescue their good lord's stepson. Within a matter of a very few minutes all the royal household men were dead or in full flight.

King Richard, 'who was not ignorant that the people hated him, out of hope to have any better hap afterward', refused to leave the battlefield, 'such great fierceness and such huge force of mind he had,' we are told by Polydore Vergil. 'I will die King of England,' he insisted. 'I will not budge a foot.' After his horse was killed under him, he continued fighting on foot, shouting 'Treason! Treason!'

Vergil (who may have obtained his information from Lord Oxford) agrees with the generally well-informed Croyland chronicler and John Rous – no less hostile – that the last Plantagenet king died a hero's death. He fought on alone till he fell 'in the thickest press of his enemy.' Richard III preferred such an end, Vergil believed, rather than 'by foul flight to prolong his life, uncertain what death perchance soon after by sickness or other violence to suffer.'

How Henry Tudor was crowned on Bosworth Field by his stepfather has become part of the national myth, even though some historians may question his account.

> The soldiers cried 'God save King Henry! God save King Henry!' and with heart and hand uttered all the show of joy that might be, which when Thomas Stanley did see he set anon King Richard's crown, which was found among the spoil in the field, on his head as though he had been already by commandment of the people proclaimed king after the manner of his ancestors, and that was the first sign of prosperity.[4]

Meanwhile, the late King's mangled body, stripped naked – 'nought being left about him so much as would cover his privy member' – covered in blood and mud, was slung over a horse and taken back to Leicester for public display and then a pauper's burial.

Yet if the Earl of Oxford had not driven back the Duke of Norfolk's archers with quite such skill, the Stanley brothers would never have had their chance to intervene and win the battle for Henry Tudor.

THE END OF THE WARS,
1485–99

41

The Last Battle – Stoke, 1487

MARGARET BEAUFORT · JOHN MORTON
LORD OXFORD

On 30 October 1485 Margaret Beaufort attended the coronation of Henry VII in Westminster Abbey. In his *Morning Remembrance*, Cardinal Fisher tells us that 'when the king her son was crowned in all that triumph and glory, she wept marvellously.'[1] It was only two years since Margaret had watched King Richard's crowning and she knew very well that Henry was far from secure. However, he strengthened his position steadily, marrying Elizabeth of York in January 1486 – as soon as Parliament had removed the stigma of bastardy fastened upon her by her uncle.

'His appearance was remarkably attractive and his face was cheerful, particularly when speaking,' Polydore Vergil records of Henry Tudor. He was impressive, not at all the Welsh adventurer of popular legend but half Beaufort and a quarter Valois. (The painting in the National Portrait Gallery dates from 1505 when the King's face had been distorted by years of ill-health.) At the same time he was deeply suspicious, with reason. There were to be armed risings throughout the 1480s and 1490s while plots continued until the end of his reign. Henry never quite managed to lay the ghost of the White Rose.

Spectacular rewards went to his uncle, Jasper Tudor. Born a poverty-stricken Welsh squire, because of his Valois mother Jasper had known a very brief period of prosperity as Earl of Pembroke during the 1450s before entering on a quarter of a century's hazardous adversity. Fleeing from Mortimer's Cross, hunted over the Welsh mountains more than once, several times taking refuge overseas and for a time sharing the same Breton prisons as his nephew, his survival verged on the miraculous. He had sailed with Henry to Milford Haven, where his contacts among the local Welshry had proved invaluable, and had ridden with him to Bosworth Field. By now an old man of fifty-four, this once penniless fugitive was transformed into one of the greatest magnates in the whole realm. In October 1485 he was created Duke of Bedford and in 1486 he was appointed Lieutenant of Calais. Later he would be made Lord-Lieutenant of Ireland and Earl Marshal of England. He had never married, and in 1491 a bride was to be found for him in the person of the Duke of Buckingham's widow, Catherine Woodville. Jasper would die full of years and honour in 1495.

It was probably Jasper (though no doubt with his sister-in-law Margaret's approval) who was responsible for placing a very fine brass of his long-dead brother, Edmund Tudor, Earl of Richmond, over the latter's tomb in the church of the Greyfriars at Caermarthen. Edmund wears the armour fashionable forty years after his death, while his epitaph proclaims proudly that he had been 'father and brother of kings' – neatly emphasizing the dynastic link between Henry VI and Henry VII and the fact that the Lancastrian succession was invested in the Tudors. After being moved with the tomb to St David's Cathedral at the Dissolution of the Monasteries, and then damaged by Roundhead vandals during the seventeenth century, the brass was heavily restored in Victorian times. However, it is said to be a good likeness of the original.

Although Henry VII did not base his claim to the throne on his Beaufort descent, he was nonetheless eager to remind all his subjects that he had royal blood,[2] and the statute of 1397 which had legitimized the Beaufort family was re-enacted. Not only was the attainder against 'My lady the King's mother' reversed by Parliament, so that she regained all her former estates, but she was given many new lands and houses in addition. By the 'great grant' from Henry of March 1487 she acquired properties worth well over £1,000 a year in the Midlands, in Wales and in the West Country – where she received Corfe Castle and the town of Poole in Dorset. Eventually her annual income would amount to the enormous sum of £3,000.[3]

Her husband and her servants profited too. Lord Stanley, now 'the king's right entirely beloved father', was made Earl of Derby, Constable of England and chief steward of the Duchy of Lancaster, being given other valuable offices and rich estates as well. The earldom of Derby was almost royal, a title that had been borne by Henry IV, first of the Lancastrian kings, before he took the throne. In symbolic recognition of the new Earl's crucial role at Bosworth, he was allowed to keep the hangings from King Richard's tent, which remained on display at the Stanley house of Knowsley until the seventeenth century.

Dr Urswick became principal chaplain to the King and royal almoner, besides being appointed Dean of York and Master of King's Hall, Cambridge. Later, after declining a bishopric, he was to be Dean of Windsor – the most prestigious of all English deaneries. Reginald Bray was made Chancellor of the Duchy of Lancaster and, having done King Henry outstanding services as a financier and an administrator, Margaret's receiver-general would be created a Knight of the Garter.

From the very beginning of his reign Henry VII placed the fullest confidence in his mother. Immediately after Bosworth, before leaving Leicester, he had sent troops to Sheriff Hutton to secure possession of his principal rival for the throne, the ten-year-old Earl of Warwick, Clarence's son – the last male Plantagenet. He then entrusted the boy to Margaret, who kept him safely in her household for several months until he was moved to the Tower of London, which he was destined never to leave. As Lady Margaret's biographers comment, 'in the first year of his reign [she] acted as a jailer on behalf of her son.'[4] Henry could not have paid her a greater compliment.

'He fled the realm, went to Rome, never minding more to meddle with the world till the noble prince King Henry the Seventh gat him home again' is More's polite summary of Dr Morton's recent adventures. He was most welcome in the new England, one of the bishops who officiated at Henry's coronation. On 6 March 1486 he became Lord Chancellor, Dr Urswick being present at the ceremony when the King delivered the great seal into his hands. Cardinal Bourchier dying the same year, Morton succeeded him at Canterbury. Thomas More says of Archbishop Morton (in *Utopia*) that King Henry 'depended much on his counsels and the government seemed chiefly to be supported by him.'

John's nephew, Robert Morton, restored to his post as Master of the Rolls, was consecrated Bishop of Worcester early in 1487.

The third of the three exiles who had been on pilgrimage to Rome together, Dr Oliver King, returned to his former office as secretary to the monarch, ending his days as Bishop of Bath and Wells.

John de Vere, Earl of Oxford, received back all his estates and was at last recognized as hereditary Great Chamberlain of England, in which capacity he officiated triumphantly at the coronation banquet. In addition he was made Lord High Admiral of England, Constable of the Tower, and a Knight of the Garter – ironically, he was installed in the late Duke of Norfolk's stall at St George's Chapel. Despite his long and miserable imprisonment, he was magnanimous towards defeated enemies.

After Bosworth the captured Earl of Surrey (Norfolk's son) and his wife were placed in Lord Oxford's custody. Surrey was the former Sir Thomas Howard, one of King Richard's most brutal partisans, the man who had been in charge of William Hastings' arrest and murder, and who had dragged Jane Shore off to prison. 'I have found mine lord of Oxenford singular very good and kind lord to mine lord and me, and steadfast in his promise, whereby he hath won mine lord's service as long as he liveth and me to be his true beadswoman,' wrote a relieved Lady Surrey to John Paston, six weeks after the battle. 'For him I dreaded most and yet, as hitherto, I find him best.'[5]

He was now one of the three most powerful magnates in England, the others being Jasper Tudor and the Earl of Derby. When the Queen gave birth to a son, Prince Arthur, in 1486, Oxford and Derby were made godfathers. He gave as christening presents a massive silver gilt standing cup and two great silver basins.

Although Lord Oxford was reunited with his countess, seemingly none the worse for her privations under the Yorkists, the couple remained childless. At least there was an heir to the earldom, the son of his brother, George de Vere. When another old Lancastrian comrade from the Battle of Barnet and the siege of St Michael's Mount, Lord Beaumont – whose lands had also been restored – went mad in 1487, the Oxfords took Beaumont and his wife to live with them at Hedingham. During an age when lunatics were generally regarded as being possessed by the Devil, chained up and left to rot in cellars, the Earl showed himself to be surprisingly compassionate towards madmen. One can see this from a carefully phrased letter which he wrote one midsummer some years later to the Sir John Paston of the day about his brother, William Paston, who, while serving as a household man in the Oxfords' London house, had been afflicted by what was apparently a form of manic depression. William, according to the earl, was 'so troubled with sickness and crazed in his mind that I may not keep him about me, wherefore I am right sorry, and at this time send him to you, praying especially that he may be kept surely and tenderly with you, to such time as God fortune him to be better assured of himself . . .'[6]

Clearly Oxford wanted to think that the sickness was no more than 'midsummer madness'. One begins to understand why Lady Surrey liked him so much.

Lord Beaumont was lucky to have such friends. He may well have been sent off his head by rumours of yet more war impending. For the Earl of Oxford had another supreme service to perform for Henry VII. He was going to command the King's vanguard in the ultimate battle of the Wars of the Roses.

In recounting how Lady Margaret had wept at her son's coronation, Fisher makes it clear that she did so from foreboding rather than joy. Many people in the north and in Wales, who had done very well under Richard, disliked the new régime. So did the English-speaking Irish of the Pale, traditionally loyal to the House of York. In the Low Countries the late King's sister, Margaret of York – 'mine old lady of Burgundy' – was ready to welcome any of his former supporters who were in need of a refuge or who required a base from which to launch an invasion of England.

During April 1486 Sir Humphrey Stafford tried to raise his native Worcestershire against Henry VII while Lord Lovell, once King Richard's Lord Chamberlain ('Lovell our Dog'), attempted a rebellion in the North Riding. However, their candidate for the throne, the Earl of Warwick – Clarence's son – was a prisoner in the hands of Margaret Beaufort, and they failed to win any significant support. Sir Humphrey Stafford was dragged out of sanctuary and beheaded, though Lovell got away.

On 19 May Lady Oxford wrote to her husband's old ally, John Paston, in his capacity as Sheriff of Norfolk and Suffolk.

> I am credibly informed that Francis, late Lord Lovell is now of late resorted to the Isle of Ely to the intent, by all likelihood, to get him shipping and passage in your coasts, or else to resort again to sanctuary if he may. I therefore heartily desire . . . that ye in all goodly haste endeavour yourself that such watch or other means be used and had in the ports and creeks . . . to the taking of the same late Lord Lovell. And what pleasure ye may do to the King's Grace in this matter I am sure is not to you unknown.

The Countess had good reason to dislike Yorkists, but despite all her precautions Lovell succeeded in escaping to Burgundy.

Early in the spring of 1487 a priest brought an Oxford organ-builder's son called Lambert Simnel to Dublin, pretending that the boy was the Earl of Warwick. Lambert was immediately hailed as king by the Irish Chancellor, Sir

Thomas FitzGerald of Lackagh, a brother of the Earl of Kildare who was the most powerful man in Ireland. The FitzGeralds quickly contacted the Yorkist dissidents who had taken refuge in Flanders. Their leaders were Lord Lovell and John de la Pole, Earl of Lincoln, whom Richard III had recognized as his heir presumptive. The Yorkists and the FitzGeralds agreed that they should invade England together as soon as possible. They were warmly encouraged by Margaret of York who, according to Vergil, 'pursued Henry [VII] with insatiable hatred and with fiery wrath never desisted from every scheme which might harm him.' She gave them money and troops.

On Whit Sunday 1487 (24 May) Lambert, after having been recognized formally as its sovereign by the Irish Parliament, was crowned and anointed as 'King Edward VI' by the Archbishop of Dublin in Christchurch Cathedral. No proper crown was available so a diadem was borrowed from a statue of the Virgin. Another important Irish prelate, the Dominican Bishop of Meath, preached the coronation sermon.

Always on the alert, despite conflicting information from his many spies, Henry VII had already begun to suspect that a Yorkist invasion was imminent. His first concern was for the safety of the Queen and his mother. 'We pray you that, giving your attendance upon our said dearest wife and lady mother, ye come with them to us', he wrote urgently to the Queen's chamberlain, the Earl of Ormonde.[7] On 13 May the King summoned Lord Oxford to Kenilworth Castle, to discuss how they should prepare for the looming campaign.

By that time Lord Lovell and the Earl of Lincoln had landed at Dublin with a band of Yorkist diehards. They were accompanied by 2,000 Swiss and German mercenaries under the renowned Colonel Martin Schwarz (once an Augsburg cobbler), who had been hired by 'mine old lady of Burgundy'. Reinforced by the FitzGeralds, they sailed across to Lancashire, landing on the Furness peninsula, not far from Lancaster, on 4 June.

The Yorkist strategy seems to have been to march as far south as possible after crossing the Pennines before giving battle. Although the citizens of York failed to respond to a letter sent to them from Masham by 'Edward VI', and beat off an attempt to occupy their city by the two Lord Scropes, the Earl of Lincoln was surprisingly confident. Probably he was counting not only on the excellent quality of his troops but on the intervention of secret allies as at Bosworth once the two armies were engaged. Nothing else can explain his extraordinary optimism. Vergil was convinced that Lincoln (who may have planted Lambert Simnel on the Irish) was planning to seize the throne for himself as soon as Henry VII had been defeated. But Lambert was far too unconvincing a pretender to win much support, and no more than a score of knights and squires joined the Yorkists. Moreover, as a commander Lincoln was scarcely in the same league as the Earl of Oxford.

Christopher Urswick brought King Henry the news that the Yorkist expedition had landed in Lancashire. Although no overall figures are available, it is clear that the King had sufficient support from his magnates to be able to assemble an impressively large army. Vergil names more than sixty gentlemen of substance who served in it, and afterwards an unprecedented number of knights were created. It included 6,000 men provided by the Stanleys alone, the King's stepfather sending every retainer and well-wisher he could muster under his son, Lord Strange. Among the other peers who rallied to the King was William Hastings' son Edward, who had been restored to his father's barony and estates. Archbishop Morton, accompanied by his nephew, the Bishop of Worcester, brought a substantial force of retainers and of tenants from his wide estates. So did the Courtenay Bishop of Winchester.

The Archbishop of Canterbury and the Bishops of Worcester and Winchester were the first prelates to bring troops to a battle during the Wars of the Roses. However, it will be remembered that Dr Morton was no stranger to battlefields and might even be described as a veteran campaigner. He had been present at the second St Albans and Towton, had been besieged in the grim Northumbrian sieges of the 1460s, had been taken prisoner at Tewkesbury, and had been amid the collapse of the Duke of Buckingham's disastrous rebellion four years before. Although nearly seventy by now, John Morton was leaving nothing to chance – he did not underestimate the danger from the Yorkists. He rode with his troops as far as Loughborough in Leicestershire before handing over command to his nephew, Robert. They were going to fight in the front ranks, in Lord Oxford's contingent.

As Professor Ross stresses, the battle about to take place could have gone either way.[8] Treachery might have lost it for Henry VII just as treachery had lost Bosworth for Richard III. Obviously the King suspected some sort of plot. There can be no other explanation for his ordering Oxford to place the Marquess of Dorset under arrest before he could join the royal army.

Despite being outnumbered, Lord Lincoln, the enemy commander, was only too eager to give battle. At 9 a.m. on 16 June the Yorkists, about 9,000 strong, engaged the royal army which was in three columns drawn up in echelon (one behind the other) outside the village of Stoke, a few miles from Newark. Schwarz's *landsknechts* were obviously professionals to their fingertips, while Lincoln's followers and the Irish gentlemen were well armed. However, the barefooted, saffron-shirted Irish kern who formed the bulk of their force were a different matter, being without any form of armour and equipped merely with axes, long knives and javelins.

The Earl of Oxford commanded the King's vanguard or front column, which alone engaged the enemy. Clearly Lincoln's men fought with great courage, but the unarmoured Irish suffered appalling casualties, one report saying that 4,000 of them were killed. Eventually Oxford won the day with a final determined charge. Schwarz's men fought to the death by the side of their colonel. Among the many other casualties were Lincoln and Sir Thomas FitzGerald. Lord Lovell – King Richard's old friend – was last seen swimming his horse across the River Trent.

The Yorkist diehards would never again dare to challenge the Tudors in armed confrontation, and they went underground. Yet their cause was far from dead. Nor had Henry's victory been a foregone conclusion. Northern noblemen had joined the rebellion, such as the two Lord Scropes, while the Bishop of St Asaph, Dr Richard Redmayne, was suspected of involvement. Significantly, when a mistaken rumour that Henry had been defeated reached London, riots broke out in favour of the Earl of Warwick. A City chronicler tells of 'false Englishmen . . . which untrue persons said that the king was lost and the field was lost.' Yorkists emerged from their sanctuaries to attack royal officials, shouting that Warwick was King. If the Earl had been old enough and of the same calibre as his uncles, he could have escaped from the Tower of London, and there might easily have been another Yorkist restoration.

The climax of this nervous year of 1487 was the coronation of the Queen, Elizabeth of York, on St Catherine's Day (25 November) in Westminster Abbey. During the ceremony the office of High Steward of England was shared by the men who had become the three most powerful magnates in the kingdom – Jasper Tudor, Duke of Bedford, Thomas Stanley, Earl of Derby, and John de Vere, Earl of Oxford. On the Friday before, Margaret accompanied Elizabeth in her gilded barge as she was rowed up the Thames from the Palace of Greenwich to the Tower. On the day itself, attended by 'a goodly sight of ladies and gentlewomen', she watched from a stand between the pulpit and the high altar as Archbishop Morton placed the crown upon her daughter-in-law's head. She also attended Elizabeth's coronation banquet.

Someone who was conspicuously absent from both ceremonies was Elizabeth's mother, the Queen Dowager Elizabeth Woodville. At first King

Henry had treated her very well, restoring property that had been taken from her by King Richard – there was talk of marrying her to the widowed James III of Scotland. But early in 1487 Henry confiscated her widow's jointure and sent her into retirement with the nuns of Bermondsey, where she died in 1492. It is not known why the King suddenly turned against his mother-in-law. Vergil thought it was because of Henry's lasting resentment at her having reconciled herself to King Richard, after he had murdered her children, but it is much more likely that she had been suspected of intriguing with Lambert Simnel's Yorkist supporters, as had her son Dorset. There is some evidence that she was again on good terms with Henry by early 1488. No doubt, like Dorset, Elizabeth Woodville succeeded in proving her innocence, though she never recovered her jointure or emerged from the convent at Bermondsey.

Margaret Beaufort occupied a far more prominent role in public life than any queen mother. When she gave a gift of 20s to the heralds at Greenwich during the Christmas festivities of 1487, they cried in their archaic Norman French, 'Largesse from the high, puissant and excellent princess, mother of the king our sovereign lord, the countess of Richmond.'[9] On the twelfth day of Christmas the courtiers noticed that she was wearing exactly the same clothes as the Queen, her daughter-in-law, even the same coronet. Soon she began to sign herself 'Margaret R', which might be read either as 'Margaret Richmond' or as 'Margaret Regina'.[10] In many ways she was the first of the Tudor dynasty.

42

Perkin Warbeck, 1491–99

LORD OXFORD

THE Tudor régime's obvious insecurity gave it good cause to value very highly indeed the steadfast loyalty and the proven military abilities of John, Earl of Oxford. Although we now know with hindsight that his victory over Lincoln at Stoke in 1487 had been the last pitched battle of the Wars of the Roses, for many years there seemed to be every reason why Henry VII should never for one moment relax his vigilance against Yorkist plots or rebellions. This is why Sir Francis Bacon claims (in his history of Henry's reign) that Lord Oxford was the King's 'principal servant both for war and peace'. Oxford was generally acknowledged to be the finest soldier in the land, a man who, as Bacon says, was 'well famed and loved among the people', and the firmest guarantee of the régime's survival.[1]

King Henry lived in constant fear of the White Rose. When in April 1489 a mob lynched the Earl of Northumberland near Topcliffe in Yorkshire during a protest against new taxation to pay for a war in Brittany, and a riot ensued in which the rebels seized York, the King at once suspected that behind the rising there lay a dangerous plot to overthrow him. Certainly, the anonymous author of the *Great Chronicle of London* thought that the Earl of Northumberland had been killed because the Yorkshiremen bore him 'deadly malice for the disappointing of King Richard at Bosworth Field', while some among the handful of gentry who joined the rising (such as Sir John Egremont) were former servants of the late King. Henry hastily assembled an army and marched north as quickly as he could, half a dozen East Anglian knights being summoned by the Earl of Oxford 'to meet with my lord at Cambridge with 30 men a-piece of them', according to Sir John Paston. However, the rebels had fled before the royal army even reached

York. Despite its unmistakeably Yorkist undertones – Egremont took refuge with Margaret of York in Flanders – the King realized that the revolt really had been no more than an unusually murderous protest against high taxation. Nevertheless, he was very much aware that he could not afford to take any chances.[2]

Henry had enemies in the most unlikely places, even in the cloisters. At the end of December 1489 the Abbot of Abingdon, John Sant, and others were found guilty of conspiring to overthrow him. In the spring of 1486 the Abbot had given sanctuary to a Yorkist fugitive, Sir Humphrey Stafford, at one of his abbey's dependent houses, Culham Priory. In January 1487 he had sent money 'to the help and aid of John, then earl of Lincoln'. At the beginning of December 1489, the Abbot had plotted to secure the release of the Earl of Warwick, 'and to have levied war against the king our said sovereign lord to th'entent to have destroyed his most royal person, and intending to put this whole realm into confusion.' Abingdon was one of the richest Benedictine abbeys in England, and its extremely influential abbot had a seat in the House of Lords. At least one other Abingdon monk was involved in the plot, together with a handful of townsmen and a priest from London. The group were not hardline Yorkists who had lost office and favour but ordinary honest men who were outraged at the way in which the last male member of the ancient ruling family of Plantagenet had been set aside and deprived of the throne. Many others must have thought like them.[3] The townsmen seem to have been hanged but, as a cleric Abbot Sant escaped the gallows. He was pardoned in 1493 on condition that, as long as he lived, he should say Mass daily for the King's well being. Henry had a sense of humour.

The Earl of Oxford was wholly successful in restoring the former influence of the de Vere family throughout East Anglia, presumably with the King's full approval. (As the region nearest Flanders it was an area where Yorkist agents might be expected to land.) There is a pleasant letter sent by the bailiffs of Yarmouth to Sir John Paston in the autumn of 1491 in which they ask him to put in a kind word for them with 'our old special good lord of Oxford', to whom they have sent a porpoise – 'and if we had any other dainties to do him a pleasure, we would, that knoweth God.'[4]

In October 1492 Oxford accompanied King Henry to Calais. He commanded the English army's vanguard during a campaign in Picardy which lasted only a few days and was present at a very brief siege of the port of Boulogne. Both campaign and siege were speedily terminated by the French promising to pay Henry a pension of the sort it had paid to Edward IV, the Earl being among the signatories of the treaty.

Then, in Bacon's words, Henry VII 'began again to be haunted with spirits by the magic and curious arts of the lady Margaret [of] York, who raised up the ghost of Richard, duke of York, second son to King Edward the Fourth, to walk and vex the king.' The ghost was Perkin Warbeck, whose impersonation of the younger of the Princes in the Tower attracted Yorkist support for some years and posed a serious threat. Frequently there were rumours of invasion. These invariably concerned Oxford who, as Admiral of England, was responsible for guarding the entire coastline, and not merely that of East Anglia.

'Pierrequin Werbecque' was born in Tournai in about 1474, the son of a boatman. He arrived in Ireland in 1491 as the servant of a Breton silk merchant and, while walking through the streets of Cork dressed in his master's splendid clothes, was taken for a member of the Yorkist royal family. Some English Yorkists in Cork made him pretend to be the Duke of York, teaching him English; he claimed that he had been spared by his 'brother' Edward V's murderer, on condition he lived abroad without revealing his name. In 1492 he went to France to seek help but had to leave in November after Charles VIII's treaty with England.[5]

Accompanied by Sir George Nevill and other Yorkist diehards, Perkin moved to Flanders. Here Margaret of York welcomed him as her nephew, acclaiming him as the 'White Rose'. It was now that he became a real threat to King Henry. He travelled to Vienna where King Maximilian recognized him as 'Richard IV'. Margaret and Maximilian supplied money for an invasion, an extremely dangerous plot being mounted against Henry in England. Among the conspirators were Lord Fitzwalter, the Prior of St John's, the Deans of York and St Paul's, and several rich knights – including Sir William Stanley who, after leading that decisive charge at Bosworth, had been made royal chamberlain but had grown dissatisfied. (It is highly significant that so experienced a politician as William Stanley should think that Perkin had a good chance of toppling the Tudor King.)

Henry VII defused the plot by bribing one of the Yorkists in Flanders, Sir Robert Clifford, with a pardon and £500. Clifford returned to England and revealed the names of those involved; most of them were executed, including Stanley. Perkin's invasion was postponed until July 1495.

Sir John Paston, working closely with Lord Oxford, was informed on 11 July that the 'Admiral's Deputy' had intercepted a Burgundian vessel off the Norman coast carrying horses, though eight or nine Englishmen on board had fled in the ship's boat. 'And as for the ships with the king's rebels, they be forth out of Camber [in Sussex] westward'. The next day 300 men landed at Deal but were quickly killed or rounded up by the Kentishmen. Perkin lost his nerve, sailing to Ireland instead. After failing to capture Waterford, he sailed on to Scotland where James IV gave him a royal welcome as 'Prince Richard of England' and married him to his cousin, Katherine Gordon. But all that came of Perkin's time with the Scots was a puny raid on Northumberland in September 1496.

Perkin was not the only danger. In the summer of 1497 Cornwall rebelled against King Henry's taxes. A Cornish army marched up to London, meeting no resistance on the way, and threatened the City. The Earl of Oxford was commander-in-chief of the three royal forces that routed the rebels at Blackheath just outside, killing a thousand Cornishmen. It was to be his last battle.[6]

Perkin finally left Scotland in the autumn of 1497, sailing to Ireland. Here he found only hostility, the FitzGeralds having at last made peace with King Henry. He made his final throw in September, landing in Cornwall with 300 men. A rabble joined him, Cornishmen still smarting over their defeat at Blackheath. After two unsuccessful attacks on Exeter, he marched as far as Taunton but, learning that a royal army was only twenty miles away, he abandoned his men and fled to the Abbey of Beaulieu in Hampshire where he took sanctuary.

He soon surrendered to Henry on being promised both life and liberty. After being paraded through the streets and making a full confession, he was treated surprisingly well, almost as a member of the court. Foolishly, he attempted to escape from London in June 1498 but was quickly recaptured. He was placed in the stocks on a scaffold at Westminster, racked, and then thrown into a windowless cell in the Tower. The Spanish ambassador, who met Perkin two months later, thought him 'so much changed that I, and all other persons here, believe that his life will be very short.'

The régime could never relax its guard against Yorkist plots. During the spring of 1499 yet another false Earl of Warwick appeared, this time on Lord Oxford's doorstep, on the borders of Norfolk and Suffolk. Apprehended, he was brought before the Earl and questioned. According to the *Great Chronicle of London*, the young man's real name was Ralph Wulford or Wilford, the son of a London shoemaker 'dwelling at the Black Bull in Bishopsgate'. He confessed that while studying at Cambridge he had dreamt that if he called himself the Duke of Clarence's son he would become King – 'after which confession he was sent up to the king and from him to prison, and upon that arraigned and convicted of treason, and finally upon Shrove Tuesday hanged at St Thomas Watering in his shirt . . .'[7]

Ralph Wulford was plainly insane, but he demonstrated just how widely Warwick's right to the throne was recognized by the country at large. Between them, Wulford and Perkin destroyed the Earl of Warwick – it 'was ordained that this winding-ivy of a Plantagenet should kill the true tree itself,' observes Bacon. For Henry VII could see only one solution. Lord Oxford was entrusted with Warwick's legal murder and appointed Lord High Steward of England so that he could preside over his trial. Poor Warwick, who may have been mentally defective, had almost certainly been tricked into plotting with Perkin, although the latter was by now a broken man. The Earl and Perkin were accused of plotting to break out of the Tower by bribing their keepers and killing the Lieutenant, with the intention of escaping abroad and overthrowing King Henry. On 27 November 1499 Warwick appeared before the court of the Lord High Steward in Westminster Hall, to be informed by Lord Oxford that it had considered the findings of a grand jury and found him guilty of treason, which the Earl admitted. Early in October Warwick was beheaded on Tower Hill.

Bacon believed that Henry VII had had the Earl of Warwick executed because Ferdinand of Spain had told him that while a last male Plantagenet remained alive, the Tudors had no guarantee of surviving on the throne of England, and that in such circumstances he could not possibly let his daughter, Catherine of Aragon, marry Henry's son.[8]

Perkin Warbeck had been tried on 16 November, found guilty and hanged a fortnight later. He was spared disembowlment and quartering, to avoid upsetting the London mob. 'This was the end of this little cockatrice of a [pretended] King' is Bacon's comment. He thought that Perkin had been very dangerous indeed, and that the story might well have had another ending if he had not been faced by such a tough opponent as Henry VII.

Even after the elimination of Warbeck and Warwick there were other Yorkist pretenders. Earlier that year, 1499, Edmund de la Pole, Earl of Lincoln – a younger brother of the Earl of Lincoln whom Richard III recognized as his heir and who fell at Stoke – had fled from England. Correctly, it was at once feared that Edmund was going to claim the throne. In August Lord Oxford wrote to one of the Pastons, telling him to try to find out who had accompanied the Earl abroad and what his intentions were. He also instructed Paston to keep a watch for 'any suspect person nigh unto the sea-coasts which shall seem unto you to be of the same affinity . . .' Edmund de la Pole would be a serious nuisance for some years to come.

Yet though a 'White Rose' faction would continue to scheme and plot until long after Henry VII's death, the King had learnt how to control the English magnates – by suspended threats of attainder or ruinous fines, and by restricting their recruitment of retainers. When he died in 1509 he had laid the foundation of the mighty Tudor monarchy. The Wars of the Roses were over.

Epilogue:
The Four Survivors

MARGARET BEAUFORT • JOHN MORTON
THE EARL OF OXFORD • JANE SHORE

MARGARET BEAUFORT

After 1485 and for the rest of her life, Lady Margaret's London residence was Coldharbour, that vast stone-built 'inn' on the north bank of the Thames which in her youth had belonged to the Duke of Exeter. Here she had a 'summer parlour' looking out on to the river, and an arbour where she took her meals in good weather. Everybody travelling along the river could see, from their wherries or their barges, the full Beaufort achievement of arms set prominently in its stained-glass windows. They could also hear impressive music coming from her chapel. She kept an entire *schola cantorum* with a dozen boys and four gentlemen singers who were directed by a 'master of the children of the chapel'. While she still stayed at her husband's houses, she felt increasingly the need for a country home of her own.

Nothing was allowed to fetter that independent spirit, not even marriage. When Parliament had reversed Richard III's attainder in 1485, it had also declared her a *'femme sole'*, giving her the right to hold property in her name and sue in the courts, regardless of her husband. Obviously this was her own idea. No other married noblewoman had ever done such a thing, nor would any of them have been allowed to do so. Because of her unique legal status, she possessed complete control over her estates, which she ran with ruthless efficiency, choosing able administrators. (John Oldham, receiver for her West Country manors, ended his career as Bishop of Exeter.)

She could even dress differently from other great ladies, if Edward IV's sumptuary law of 1483 was enforced. It ordered that 'no manner person of what[ever] estate, degree or condition he be, [to] wear any cloth of gold or silk of purple colour, but only the king, queen, my lady the king's mother, the king's childer . . . upon pain to forfeit, for every default, twenty pounds.'

In July 1498 a Spanish envoy reported to King Ferdinand and Queen Isabella that among the persons of greatest influence in England the first was the King's mother. (The second was Dr Morton.) The envoy also wrote that Queen Elizabeth was kept in subjection by the mother of the King. Another Spanish envoy, Pedro de Ayala, corroborates this. 'The king is much influenced by his mother . . . The queen, as is generally the case, does not like it.'[1] But, gentle and sweet-natured, Elizabeth of York gave her mother-in-law little trouble.

Undoubtedly Margaret interfered in the education of her grandchildren. During the negotiations for Margaret Tudor's marriage to James IV of Scotland, she insisted that it must be postponed until the little girl was much older. She remembered how her own marriage had been consummated too soon.

Her steely quality is evident in a letter of 1497, in which she thanks the Queen's chamberlain, the Earl of Ormonde, for sending her a pair of gloves from Burgundy. 'My lord chamberlain, I thank you heartily that ye list so soon remember me with my gloves, the which were right good save that they were much too big for my hand. I think the ladies of those parts be great ladies all, and according to their great estate they have great personages.'

This was a jibe at her family's ancient enemy, the dowager Duchess of Burgundy – Margaret of York. Reverting to her role of sweet old lady, she continues more amiably:

> As for news, I am sure ye shall have more surety than I can send you. Blessed be God, the king, the queen and all our sweet children be in good health. The queen hath be[en] a little crazed but now she is well, God be thanked. Her sickness is [not] so good as I would but, I trust, hastily it shall [be] with God's grace, whom I pray give you good speed in your great matters and bring you well and soon home.[2]

Sadly, her optimism about her family's health was unjustified. No British dynasty has been sicklier than the Tudors. Elizabeth of York bore eight children but only the future Henry VIII and two daughters reached maturity. The death of Arthur, Prince of Wales, in 1501 was a shattering blow for King Henry, who was still more grief-stricken at that of his queen two years later – he 'privily departed to a

A letter of 1497 from Margaret Beaufort to the Earl of Ormonde.

solitary place and would no man should resort to him.'[3] The loss of his children endangered the succession, encouraging further Yorkist plotting, as Margaret must have been well aware.

She was remarkably close to her son, despite having seen so little of him before 1485. 'There was an heroic quality to the relationship, rightly perceived by the Tudor poet Bernard André', Jones and Underwood observe. André was a blind old Frenchman, an Augustinian friar, with whom they both seem to have discussed their past perils during the Wars of the Roses – judging from some highly dramatic incidents which he recounts in his Latin life of King Henry. He describes Margaret begging her brother-in-law Jasper Tudor to take Henry with him into exile in 1471, though at the time she was in Surrey and Jasper was in Wales. (André also includes a speech supposedly made by Lord Oxford on his knees to Henry before they sailed from France in 1485, which contains a most unlikely reference to Julius Caesar at the Battle of Pharsalia.) However much the garrulous old friar may have exaggerated or invented, he genuinely admired Margaret whose courage he rightly calls *'firmus et constans'*.

Mother and son were frequently in each other's company. She rode with King Henry on those formal progresses that were really tours of inspection. And she was constantly at court, whether at Westminster, Greenwich, Sheen or Windsor.

The King knew how to make use of his mother's avarice and litigiousness. He entrusted her with extracting the ransom of the Duke of Orleans, captured at Agincourt in 1422, of which the balance had been owing since 1440, and offered her a share of the proceeds. Anyone else would have written the ransom off as a bad debt. 'It will be right hard to recover it without it be driven by compulsion and force', Henry wrote to her in 1504, admitting that while England was at peace with France there was little to bargain with. Yet it was worth persevering. 'For such a chance may fall that this your grant might stand in great stead for the recovery of our right . . .' Margaret bombarded the French with demands for payment, drafted by the King's French secretary and delivered by his heralds. Her grandson finally secured the money in 1514.

Sometimes she disagreed with the son whom she addressed in her letters as 'My King' or 'My good King'. When in 1502 the widowed Cecily of York, Henry's sister-in-law, married a humble squire, Thomas Kyme, without asking for the royal permission, Cecily was banished from court and her estates were confiscated, reducing her to beggary. Her first husband had been Margaret's half-brother, Lord Welles, and Margaret defended her, inviting Cecily and Mr Kyme to stay at Collyweston while she negotiated on their behalf. After nearly a year, Henry agreed to the marriage and returned most of Cecily's property.

The manor of Collyweston in Northamptonshire became her real home, where she led a life that in many respects was that of a nun. In 1499, with her husband's agreement, she took a vow of chastity. Her spiritual adviser, the future Cardinal Fisher, tells us that she confessed not less than twice a week and damaged her back badly from kneeling in prayer.[4] She fasted rigorously, taking only one meal a day in Lent, and wore a hair shirt. There were always twelve paupers in the almshouse at Collyweston, whom she insisted on nursing personally when they were ill or dying.

Lady Margaret first met Dr Fisher at Greenwich Palace in 1494 or 1495, when he was Master of Michael House (now Trinity College), Cambridge. He became her chaplain in 1502 and, despite being made Bishop of Rochester two years later, continued to be her confessor and remained the closest friend of her old age. An awesomely austere figure who had a skull placed on the altar whenever he said

Mass and on the dining table during meals, he was the greatest preacher in England, renowned for his majestic sermons on the seven penitential psalms. Nevertheless, Fisher wrote long afterwards that he had learnt more from her spiritually than anything he could teach. He was also full of praise for her hospitality:

> For the strangers, O marvellous God, what pain, what labour, she of her very gentleness would take with them to bear them manner and company, and entreat every person and entertain them . . . that nothing should lack that might be convenient for them, wherein she had a wonderfully ready remembrance and perfect knowledge.[5]

Fisher persuaded her to found and endow professorships at both Oxford and Cambridge in 1496–97, the Lady Margaret professorships which still exist. Her monuments at Cambridge are the beautiful gatehouses of two of the colleges: Christchurch, which she refounded in 1505, and St John's, which she founded in 1509. Both are adorned by her arms with the Beaufort supporters, two 'yales' – mythical beasts with multicoloured spots and revolving horns. St John's owns a sixteenth-century copy of a lost portrait of her, a nun-like figure in a white coif who kneels in prayer.

She was the patron of the pioneer printer, William Caxton. In 1488 he flattered her pride of birth by addressing her incorrectly as 'My Lady Margaret, Duchess of Somerset', in the dedication to *Blanchardin and Eglantine*, which he had translated at her request. He says in the *Fifteen Oes*, a prayerbook he produced in 1491, that it has been printed by command of the Queen and the Queen Mother, implying subtly that she told her daughter-in-law what to do. Wynkyn de Worde, who took over Caxton's business, printed several devotional works for her, including one she herself translated from the French, *The Mirroure of Golde for the sinful soule*. In 1509 Wynkyn proudly styled himself 'Printer unto the most excellent Princess My Lady the King's Mother'.

Her affection for her 'good and precious prince, king and only son' was obsessive, even neurotic. One letter from her to him begins, 'My own sweet and most dear king and all my worldly joy', while another starts, 'My dearest and only desired joy in this world'.[6] To some extent her affection was returned. In a long letter of July 1503, written in his own hand to 'Madam my most entirely well beloved lady and mother', Henry acknowledges 'the great and singular motherly love and affection that it hath pleased you at all times to bear me.' He apologizes for writing so seldom, explaining that it is due to his poor eyesight, because of

Bishop John Fisher preaching a sermon in memory of Margaret Beaufort in July 1509, a month after her death. Printed by Wynkyn de Worde during the same year.

which it has taken him three days to write the letter. (Her own eyes had grown weak – we know that she wore gold-rimmed spectacles.)

She was unlucky enough to outlive him. King Henry VII died at Richmond Palace on 21 April 1509, and during his last illness she visited him every day, rowed up the Thames from Coldharbour. Fisher tells us that 'by the space of twenty-seven hours together, so long I understand, he lay continually abiding the sharp assaults of death.' His mother asked Fisher to preach a funeral sermon at St Paul's, which pleased her so much that afterwards it was printed at her request

by Wynkyn de Worde. The chief executor of the King's will was 'his dearest and
most entirely beloved mother, Margaret, countess of Richmond.'

King Henry's obsequies were suitably magnificent. Ten thousand tapers lit
Westminster Abbey where his effigy lay in state, wearing the crown of St Edward,
with an armed knight guarding each corner of his catafalque. Three great
requiems were sung in the Abbey, the last by the Archbishop of Canterbury.
There is a late legend – probably fanciful, though one would like to believe it –
that Jane Shore came and strewed flowers around the catafalque, the tribute due
to a victor.

'My lady the king's grandam' – as she was now officially known – told her
grandson, the eighteen-year-old Henry VIII, whom to choose for his council.
She also gave instructions for his marriage to Catherine of Aragon and for his
coronation. Too frail to attend either ceremony, she watched the coronation procession go by from the window of a house in Cheapside. Though she rejoiced
that her grandchild was going to be crowned King of England, 'yet she let not to
say that some adversity would follow', Cardinal Fisher remembered. She had
never lost that sense of deep foreboding from which, understandably, she seems
to have suffered throughout her eventful life.

Her last weeks were spent in a house within the precincts of Westminster
Abbey where she died on 29 June 1509. One report says that her final illness was
brought on by eating a cygnet. In the sermon he gave a month after her death,
Fisher says that she had a difficult passing, crying out at the pain. He adds that
her entire household was grief-stricken:

> When they saw the death so haste upon her, and that she must needs depart
> from them and they should forgo so gentle a mistress, so tender a lady, then
> wept they marvellously, wept her ladies and kinswomen to whom she was
> full kind, wept her poor gentlewomen whom she loved tenderly before,
> wept her chamberers to whom she was full dear, wept her chaplains and
> priests, wept her other true and faithful servants.[7]

She left the staggering sum of £15,000, together with a hoard of jewels, most of

---

'Thomas Fowler, Sqwyer and Gentilman Ussher of the Chambre unto the famous
King Edward the iiij & Edyth his wyfe and of late gentilwoman unto the Right
Excellent Princesse Margaret Countesse of Richmount' Edith, in charge of her
mistress's almswomen and of her jewels, was bequeathed a pension of £10 per
annum. From a brass of c 1510 at Christ's College, Cambridge.

which was bequeathed to her grandson, though there were substantial legacies to members of her household.

Margaret was buried in the awe-inspiring chapel which her son had been building at Westminster Abbey for many years, and which would not be completed for many more. The bronze effigy that Pietro Torrigiano cast in about 1514 may still be seen on her tomb. The austere face, handsome and commanding – modelled from a death-mask – is truly regal and worthy of a woman who founded one of the greatest dynasties in English history.

JOHN MORTON

Margaret had had a very high opinion of John Morton. In a letter to her son, written just before Morton's death, she refers to 'the cardinal which, as I understand, is your faithful true and loving servant.'[8] During his twilight years he was heaped with honours. In 1493, at King Henry's request, Pope Alexander VI (Borgia) created him cardinal priest of St Anastasia. In 1495 the University of Oxford insisted on making him its chancellor, despite the weary old man's warning that he would never have enough time to perform the duties.

Henry VII found the Cardinal's advice indispensable, and until his death he was present at almost every meeting of the council of which records survive. As Thomas More comments, Morton was someone who 'had gotten by great experience (the very mother and mistress of wisdom), a deep insight in politic, worldly drifts.' More also tells us that while 'the king put much trust in his counsel, the weal public also in a manner leaned unto him.' Undoubtedly, the Cardinal Archbishop of Canterbury commanded enormous authority. His speeches as Lord Chancellor at the opening of each parliament have been compared to a present-day monarch's speech from the throne – they were an accurate statement of the government's intentions.

Unfairly, he has been accused of inventing the approach to taxation known as 'Morton's Fork', which was used in 1491 when King Henry was extorting benevolences to raise money for an expedition to France. People who had paid already were told that they were obviously rich and could pay much more; those who pleaded poverty were told they were hiding their wealth. But the Cardinal was not responsible for raising taxes. The 'fork' has been attributed to Bishop Fox, who was keeper of the Privy Seal, but it really dates from Edward IV's reign.

Thomas More entered Cardinal Morton's household as a boy, becoming a page in order to further his education, and struck up a firm friendship with the old man. Morton took a great liking to him, fascinated by his intelligence. 'This child here, waiting at the table, whomsoever shall live to see it, will prove a marvellous

'Morton's Tower' at Lambeth, which he began to build about 1490 when he had
become Archbishop of Canterbury.

man,' he would often tell his guests. 'He was of a mean stature, and though
stricken in age, yet bare he his body upright' is how More remembered the
Cardinal during the 1490s. 'In his face did shine such an amiable reverence, as
was pleasant to behold, gentle in communication, yet earnest and sage.'

He had the misfortune of living too long. His nephew Robert, Bishop of
Worcester, died in 1497, prematurely ending a promising career. The Cardinal's
successor as Master of the Rolls and his fellow pilgrim to Rome, Robert had
clearly been close to him. There is no evidence of any affectionate relationship
with his other nephew and heir, Thomas Morton of Cirencester, though at least
Thomas was a man of some standing as High Sheriff for Gloucestershire and an
MP.

His passion for building never left him. As Archbishop of Canterbury his principal country palace was Knole in Kent, but the late Cardinal Bourchier had completed it and there was nothing he could add. His final architectural triumph was
in London. 'Morton's Tower', built in his customary red brick and begun in about

1490, is the majestic gatehouse that still guards the entrance to Lambeth Palace. He used the rooms over it as his personal apartments.

Like Lady Margaret he patronized printers, a superb *Missale* being printed for him in 1500 by Richard Pynson.

'Thus, living many days in as much honour as one man might well wish, ended them so godly that his death, with God's mercy, well changed his life' is More's valediction. The Cardinal died of the quartan ague – probably during one of the paroxysms that accompany that type of fever – on 15 September 1500. He was eighty, a remarkable age for his time. His clergy buried him in the tomb that he had prepared for himself in the crypt of Canterbury Cathedral. Over the years it split open and gradually his bones were stolen, the antiquarian Ralph Sheldon obtaining the skull, which was all that was left of them by 1670.[9] (It is now at Stoneyhurst, the Jesuit college in Lancashire.)

Unlike Cardinal Wolsey, Cardinal Morton has never caught the imagination of historians. There is no definitive study of him. This may be due to the lack of a gifted contemporary biographer such as Wolsey had, yet Morton is no less important as a statesman, while his career was even more dramatic. As a human being he was far more likeable, with none of Wolsey's puffed-up arrogance – we have Thomas More's testimony.

LORD OXFORD

In legal documents John de Vere styled himself proudly 'earl of Oxford, Viscount Bulbeck and Lord Scales, great chamberlain and admiral of England'. In addition, he was Admiral of Ireland and of Aquitaine, High Steward of the Duchy of Lancaster south of the River Trent, steward of the forests of Essex, and Constable of the Tower of London, where he had apartments and was keeper of the lions and leopards. His income from his offices and his estates came to nearly £2,000 a year. The stately old warrior must have cut a fine figure at court, with his admiral's badge of a mariner's whistle ('of ivory garnished with gold') hanging from the heavy gold chain around his neck.

During the Parliament of 1495 he petitioned the Lord Chancellor, Morton, to annul his mother's surrender of her lands in 1472. The petition says that the old Countess of Oxford had done so because she was 'menaced, put in fear of her life, and imprisoned by King Richard III, late in deed but not of right king of England, whilst he was duke of Gloucester', who had been angered by her steadfast loyalty to the 'most blessed prince King Henry [VI]'. Oxford recovered all his mother's property which till then had still been in other hands. It included Wivenhoe in Essex, a house where he must have spent much of his boyhood.[11]

The Earl translated a *Life of Robert Earl of Oxford* from the French – probably the Robert de Vere who witnessed Magna Carta. No copy survives, though he had it printed by William Caxton, who refers to him as 'my singular and especial lord'. Caxton had reason to do so. Not only did Lord Oxford commission another book in 1488, the *Four Sons of Aymon* (the story of four brothers and their magic horse who fought against Charlemagne), but he introduced the printer to Henry VII. The King asked Caxton to produce an English version of a French treatise on war, the *Faytes of Arms*. In its colophon or tail-piece Caxton gives a tantalizing glimpse of Oxford in attendance on Henry, relating how at the Palace of Westminster in January 1489 the King had entrusted the manuscript to him, 'that every gentleman born to arms and all manner men of war, captains, soldiers, victuallers and all others should have knowledge how to behave them[selves] in the feats of war and of battles and so delivered me the said book, then my lord the earl of Oxford awaiting on his said grace.'[12]

In August 1498 Henry VII visited the Earl at his grim family seat, Castle Hedingham, staying for almost a week. Francis Bacon relates how despite being sumptuously entertained Henry was so angry at seeing gentlemen and yeomen wearing Oxford livery – who at the King's departure 'stood in a seemly manner, in their livery coats with cognisances, ranged on both sides and made the king a lane' – that he fined him 15,000 marks – £10,000. Bacon's story of the fine is improbable. Although there was a law against livery and retaining, there is no documentary evidence for the story, and it seems most unlikely that Henry would have risked alienating the Earl.[13]

The visit may have been to celebrate the refurbishment of Castle Hedingham, which had fallen into decay during the Earl's absence at the Wars. Since 1485 he had added a chapel, a new great hall and other rooms. About 1540 the topographer John Leland recorded how 'afore the old earl of Oxford's time, that came in with King Henry the VII, the castle of Hedingham was in much ruin and [what] is now there was in a manner of this old earl's building except the gatehouse and the great donjon tower.' However, all Lord Oxford's rebuilding vanished long ago and only the donjon survives. Some of his badges, moved from the castle walls during the seventeenth century, can be seen on Hedingham church tower and over the church's west window.

He kept 120 servants, his senior household men being 'mine old friend Sir Thomas Lovell, Knight', 'my cousin John Vere', Sir William Waldegrave and Mr Burton, all of whom had their own chambers at Castle Hedingham. Clearly it was a household designed to give its master pleasure as well as to inspire respect; besides 'old Jegon the parker', who looked after the hunting, he employed a 'dissembler' (a master of the revels). More soberly, the Earl maintained a large choir, with two gentlemen singers, twelve singing boys and a master – a complete *schola cantorum* – accompanied by two organs. The choir served two chapels in the castle (one in the donjon, another in the Earl's closet) and a church in the court-yard, besides a chapel at Wivenhoe. Nevertheless, reading the inventory of his household goods, one has a distinct impression of shabbiness, apart from the splendid gold and silver plate; carpets and cushions are frequently described as 'old' or 'sore worn', even in 'my lord's chamber' or the 'inner chamber of my lady'.[14] In addition to Castle Hedingham and Wivenhoe, the Earl had apartments in Colchester Abbey, in Colne Priory, and 'at Sudbury in the Friars'.

Lady Oxford, Warwick the kingmaker's sister Margaret, died at the end of 1506. Lord Beaumont, the Earl's old friend and house guest who had lived with him since losing his wits in 1487, went the year after, and in 1508 Oxford married his widow, the former Elizabeth Scrope. Somewhat pathetically, although such an old man and although his new bride must have been nearly forty, he still seems to have hoped for a son and heir. In the will that he made on 10 April 1509, he says, 'I will that if I have issue male of my body lawfully begotten that then my same issue male shall have the goods and jewels ensuing . . .'[15] However, there would be neither sons nor daughters and, while Elizabeth – 'my most loving wife' – would live on until 1537, it was not to be a very long marriage.

In the year before King Henry VII's death, the Flemish ambassadors reported that the Earl of Oxford was 'the principal personage in this realm', which was what he remained for as long as he lived. A few weeks before his coronation, the young Henry VIII confirmed the grant of the castle and town of Colchester, which the Empress Matilda (William the Conqueror's granddaughter) had made to the first Earl of Oxford. It was a graceful, neatly contrived compliment which publicly acknowledged the antiquity of the oldest peerage in England.

During the coronation in June 1509 Lord Oxford officiated once again as Great Chamberlain of England. Fortunately, his duties were scarcely onerous for by then he was sixty-five years old. They consisted of seeing to the King's robing on the morning before the crowning, and then offering him water in which to wash his hands at the beginning and at the end of the banquet in Westminster

---

The Earl of Oxford's second wife, Elizabeth Scrope, widow of his friend Lord Beaumont, whom he married in 1508. She survived him by nearly thirty years. From a brass of 1537 at Wivenhoe, Essex.

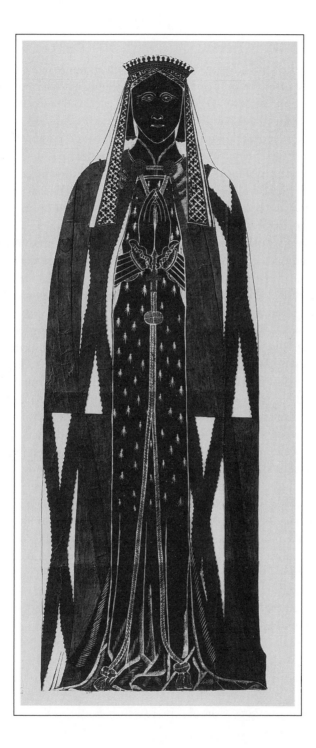

Hall. For this he received forty yards of crimson velvet, the royal bed, bedding, apparel and all the furniture of the room in which the King had slept the night before the coronation, together with the two silver gilt basins that had held the water.

He died at Castle Hedingham on 10 March 1513. His will begins, 'I, John de Vere, earl of Oxenford, being in good health and perfect mind, not grieved, vexed, troubled, nor diseased with any bodily sickness, knowing and considering well the uncertainty and unstableness of this wretched life.' The last words can be read as conventional piety, yet they also reflect the nagging insecurity of the early Tudor régime. Besides land in eleven counties, he bequeathed a great treasure of gold, silver gilt or silver plate, jewellery, tapestry and church vestments.

As a good Catholic, he first left a jewel to the shrine of Our Lady of Walsingham – 'a splayed eagle of gold with an angel face, with six diamonds and eleven pearls with four rubies', valued at £30. There were three gold salts, a tall silver gilt standing cup with a flower in the bottom, weighing twenty ounces – 'which is my daily cup' – and countless other vessels of silver gilt or silver. Among them were a salt of beryl (green crystal) resting on a silver gilt blackamoor, and an ostrich-egg cup mounted in silver gilt. Another salt, 'of silver and gilt with a pearl in the top', went to his old friend Sir Thomas Lovell. Personal jewellery included four gold chains, one of 121 links, worth £243, and a gold belt of tiny chairs set in gems – emblems of his office as Great Chamberlain. Four tapestries told the story of Porsenna and Cloelia; others bore whistles and chairs. Curiously, there was no suit of steel plate in the Earl's armoury, only sallets and brigandines with armour for his legs and arms.

Lord Oxford directed that he be buried 'in a tomb which I have made and ordained for me and Margaret [Nevill] my late wife' before the high altar of the Lady Chapel at Colne Priory, 'which house is of the foundation of me and mine ancestors.' Sadly, the couple's alabaster sepulchre was destroyed in Hanoverian times. However, a more enduring monument to the Earls of Oxford (who died out during the seventeenth century) is the sign of the blue boar hanging outside so many public houses in East Anglia. Wherever you see the crest of the de Veres, you may be sure that the Earls were once paramount in the neighbourhood.

'A significant number of families chose to support the cause of Lancaster to the bitter end at the cost of life, forfeiture and the ruin of their families', writes Charles Ross. 'The Wars of the Roses provide plenty of examples of rampant self-interest, of treachery and of cynical changes of side. The contrasting examples of stubborn loyalty to a cause have perhaps not received as much emphasis as they should. The English aristocracy during the fifteenth century was by no means uniformly selfish or politically cynical.'[15] The finest example of such loyalty is certainly John de Vere, Earl of Oxford.

JANE SHORE

Mrs Lynom – Jane Shore – lost her father in October 1487. Two years before, he had received a crushing blow, as heavy as the loss of his aldermanship. Henry Tudor's triumph at Bosworth had been followed by the restoration of Sir Edward Courtenay to the earldom of Devon in October 1485. All the Courtenay lands went with it, including Puriton and the other West Country manors that Edward IV had given to John Lambert in 1470.[17] However, John remained a landowner in Hertfordshire. Aware of King Richard's unpopularity, it is possible that he bought Hinxworth in anticipation of just such a disaster, and to ensure that whatever happened his son would be a gentleman. The story of John and his Devon and Somerset manors shows how the Wars of the Roses could affect the fortunes of the merchant class even though they might not fight in them.

Mr Lambert made his will on 24 September, only a month before he died, so he had probably known that death was approaching. He calls himself 'citizen and mercer of London, of the parish of St Olav in Silver Street.' The bulk of his property goes to his son John, while the furnishings of his chapel go to the priest son, 'Sir' William Lambert, parson of St Leonard's in Foster Lane. Jane is left 'a bed of arras with the velours tester and curtains, [and] a stained cloth of Mary Magdalen and Martha.' (Did John have his tongue in his cheek, leaving his daughter a marital bed with a picture of the repentant Magdalen?) Thomas Lynom, who was one of the executors, receives 20s and his granddaughter 40s. Despite losing his aldermanship and West Country estates, John Lambert had had a prosperous career.[18]

Over his tomb, in the middle of the chancel floor of the church of St Nicholas at Hinxworth, John had placed a magnificent brass, nearly four feet long and of superlative quality. It showed Mr and Mrs Lambert, with their four sons and two daughters below them. A scroll issued from John's mouth with the words, 'Lord, into thy hand I commend my spirit'; that from Amy's said, 'I know that I shall see the good Lord in the land of the living.' He wore a mercer's gown, turned back to reveal its rich fur lining, while at his belt hung a capacious purse and a rosary. The Latin inscription beneath described him as 'citizen, mercer and alderman of London' – he had never forgotten his lost dignity. The eldest son was dressed as a priest and Jane, the elder daughter, as a most respectable young matron. The brass may still be seen at Hinxworth, though it has been moved from the floor to the north wall of the chancel and the inscription is missing.

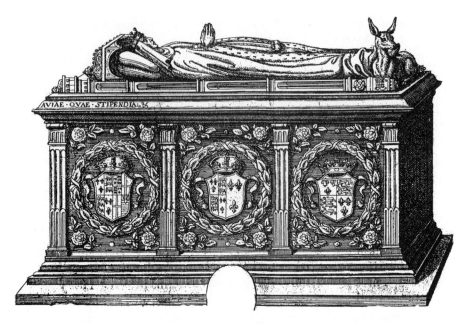

Margaret Beaufort's tomb at Westminster Abbey. From a seventeenth
century sketch.

Like the majority of Richard III's officials, Thomas Lynom had soon managed
to make his peace with the new régime, securing a general pardon on 26
September 1485. During the following year he was entrusted with granting
pardons and receiving former rebels into allegiance in Yorkshire. Although he
seems to have lost his post as King's Solicitor, he continued to be a royal bureaucrat for many years, and is probably the Thomas Lynom who was replaced as
escheator of Essex in 1498.

No chronicler mentions a Mrs Shore or a Mrs Lynom after 1483, and, until
More's wonderfully vivid account, all trace of Jane vanishes after her mother
Amy's will of 1488. (Mrs Lambert left her property to be divided equally between
her children.) We are not even sure when Thomas Lynom died, but if he was the
man from Sutton-on-Derwent, then he was dead by 1518.

Having lost Mr Lynom, she found herself an old woman, ugly and penniless,
no longer capable of attracting protectors. More, writing not earlier than 1518,
paints a harrowing picture of Jane as she had become by then – 'lean, withered

and dried up, nothing left but ravelled skin and hard bone.' He comments, 'I doubt not some shall think this woman too slight a thing to be written of and set among the remembrance of great matters . . . how much she is now in the more beggarly condition, unfriended and worn out of acquaintance.' More reminds his readers how her kind deeds, her interceding with King Edward, had all been forgotten – 'whoso doth us a good turn, we write it in dust, which is not worst proved by her, for at this day she beggeth of many at this day living, that at this day had begged if she had not been.'

It has been suggested, very unconvincingly, that Thomas More's description of Jane as a beggar need not be taken too literally, that she may have supported herself by begging letters.[19] But in the Latin version of his *History of King Richard the Third* he simply uses the word '*mendicando*', begging, and says nothing about writing letters.[20] The bleakest interpretation is probably closest to the truth. She begged her bread miserably through the streets of London.

In the earliest printed version of Sir Thomas More's history, Jane Shore is said to have died in the eighteenth year of King Henry VIII, which means at some time between April 1526 and April 1527. By then she must have been well into her seventies, since a copy of More's manuscript written not later than 1521 refers to her as '*septuagenaria*'. During her last wretched days the pitiful old woman must have seemed like some fantastic figure from legend.

The legend was a very bloody one indeed. Long before Shakespeare, Tudor England, scarcely squeamish, was horrified by memories of the Wars of the Roses. Even if they were over, the White Rose was far from dead. For most of his reign Henry VIII lived in fear of Yorkist rivals – and not without reason.

Notes

1. INTRODUCTION

1. The detail that Richard III was killed by a Welshman with a halberd is given only by Jean Molinet, a contemporary but admittedly sometimes unreliable French chronicler. J. Molinet, *Chroniques*, ed. S. A. Buchon, Paris 1827–28.

2. *The Waning of the Middle Ages*, London, 1924. Modern historians, such as J. R. Lander (in *Conflict and Stability in Fifteenth-Century England*), dismiss Huizinga's 'morphology of decay'. Yet the fifteenth century was that of the *danse macabre* and of flagellantism, a climate in which skulls and skeletons inspired countless painters and sculptors throughout northern Europe.

3. 'to leve right wisley and never to take the state of Baron upon them if they may leye it from them nor to desire to be grete about princes, for it is daungeros.' *Complete Peerage*, IX, p. 338. Lord Mountjoy (one of William Hastings' 'affinity') was only thirty-five when he died – his father had been treasurer to Edward IV while his elder brother had been killed at Barnet.

4. For landowners' incomes, H. L. Gray, 'Incomes from land in England in 1436', in *English Historical Review* XLIX (1934), and T. B. Pugh, 'The magnates, knights and gentry', in *Fifteenth-Century England*.

5. *The travels of Leo of Rozmital, 1465–67*, ed. M. Letts, Hakluyt Society, Second Series 108, Cambridge, 1957.

6. In 1460 commissions were issued to arrest 'certain persons of Sussex wandering about the country, spoiling, beating, maiming and slaying'. M. Clough, 'The Book of Bartholomew Bolney', in *Sussex Record Society* 67 (1964), p. xxvi.

7. 'The Sussex Colepeppers', in *Sussex Archaeological Collections*, Vol. xlvii, pp. 59–60. (The account of the girls' abduction comes from Early Chancery Proceedings, Bundle 27, No. 218, and Bundle 31, No. 281.)

2. THE FIVE

1. Jane Shore was not identified as Elizabeth Lambert until Nicholas Barker did so in 1972. N. Barker and Sir R. Birley, 'The Story of Jane Shore', in *Etoniana*.

3. JACK CADE'S REVOLT, 1450

1. 'Standards of Comfort' and 'Symbolic Elements in Standards of Living', in S. Thrupp, *The Merchant Class of Medieval London*, pp. 130–4 and 143–54.

2. For Jack Cade's revolt. R. L. Storey, *The End of the House of Lancaster*, and 'Parliamentary opposition and popular risings, 1449–50', in B. Wolffe, *Henry VI*.

4. LADY MARGARET BEAUFORT IS MARRIED, 1455

1. For Margaret Beaufort, M. K. Jones and M. G. Underwood,' *The King's Mother.*
2. For rumours of the Duke of Somerset's suicide, *Historiae Croylandensis Continuatio*, in *Rerum Scriptores Veterum*, p. 519.
3. 'a mornynge remembraunce had at the moneth mynde of the noble prynces Margarete countesse of Rychemonde & Darbye moder unto kynge Henry the vii . . .', in *The English Works of John Fisher, Bishop of Rochester*, p. 292.

5. THE EARL OF OXFORD IS LATE AT ST ALBANS, 1455

1. The account (which has not been translated) is in *Registrum Abbatiae Johannis Whethamstede, Abbatis Monasterii Sancti Albani*, I, 88. 166–78.
2. For the list of casualties, *Paston Letters*, 111, p. 29.

6. THE LOVEDAY AT ST PAUL'S, 1458

1. 'It was a time of rumour and innuendo worthy of Renaissance Italy . . .' R. A. Grifiths, *The Reign of King Henry VI*, p. 685.
2. Richard Grafton in *Grafton's Chronicle or History of England*. London 1809.
3. *Acts of Court of the Mercers' Company, 1453–1529*, p. 47, and *Calendar of the Patent Rolls, Henry VI, 1452–61*, VI, p. 339.
4. Rawcliffe, *The Staffords, Earls of Stafford and Dukes of Buckingham, 1395–1521.*

7. DR MORTON AND THE PARLIAMENT OF DEVILS, 1459

1. For Morton's career, A. B. Emden, *A Biographical Register of the University of Oxford to AD 1500*, Oxford, 1957–59. For his ancestry and relations, J. and J. B. Burke, 'Morton', in *Extinct and Dormant Baronetcies*, London, 1844.
2. For King Réné, R. A. Lecoy de la Marche, *Le Roi Réné*, Paris, 1875.
3. K. B. McFarlane, 'Bastard Feudalism', in *Bulletin of the Institute of Historical Research* XX (1945), pp. 161–80; and M. Hicks, 'Bastard Feudalism: Society and Politics in Fifteenth Century England', in *Parliamentary History* iii (1984).
4. The Act is in *Rotuli Parliamentorum* V, pp. 346–9.

8. THEY THAT WERE IN THE TOWER CAST WILDFIRE INTO THE CITY, 1460

1. Beaven, *Aldermen of the City of London*, Vol. 1, pp. 146, 416.
2. Ibid, Vol. 2, pp. 12, 14; *Acts of Court of the Mercers' Company*, p. 53.
3. Whethamstede, op. cit., 1, p. 400.

9. THE SQUIRE OF BURTON HASTINGS GOES TO WAR, 1461

1. When his father died on 30 October 1455, William Hastings was '*etatis viginti et quatuor annorum et amplius*', CP VI, p. 370.
2. For Hastings' ancestry, relatives and family, Dugdale's *Baronage* I, p. 580; and Wedgwood, p. 433.
3. For William Hastings' likely education, H. G. Richardson, 'Business Training in Medieval Oxford', in *American Historical Review* xlvi (1940–41).

4. 'The fifteenth-century retinue served as protection in a land otherwise ineffectively policed . . .' says Professor Lander, *Crown and Nobility*, p. 32.

5. Hastings does not appear in William Worcestre's list of 'Gentlemen who were with King Edward IV at the Battle of Mortimer's Cross' (*Itineraries*, ed. J. H. Harvey, Oxford, 1969, p. 204) but Worcestre was not present himself. Dugdale, however, was convinced that Hastings had fought in it, referring to 'signal adventures in divers Battels . . . against Jasper, Earl of Pembroke, James, Earl of Wiltshire' (*Baronage*, p. 581). Dugdale's source appears to be the patent that created Hastings a peer, printed in *Complete Peerage* VI, p. 371.

10. DR MORTON SEES A BATTLE – TOWTON, 1461

1. For Waurin's account, *Recueil des Croniques* V, pp. 339–42.

2. Whethamstede writes scornfully of 'those Northern rascals' – '*bobinantes Boreales*', op. cit. I, p. 410.

3. For a comparison of figures given for those killed at Towton, Goodman, *Wars of the Roses*, p. 244 (n. 78).

4. 'treatyse concerning the fruytful saynges of Dauid . . .', in *The English Works of John Fisher*, p. 239.

11. THE CORONATION OF KING EDWARD IV, 1461

1. Sylvia Thrupp quotes an anonymous fifteenth-century writer – 'many be dysseyved for be cause they take her wives at xii yere age or ther a boute'. *The Merchant Class of Medieval London*, p. 196.

2. For Sir Thomas More's daughters, *Aubrey's Brief Lives*, London, 1972, p. 375.

3. For Mr Shore's early years, A. F. Sutton, 'William Shore, Merchant of London and Derby', in *Derbyshire Archaeological Journal*, Vol. 106 (1986).

4. Thomas More, *History of King Richard the Third*, p. 56.

5. For Mr Lambert's appointment as a Collector of the Customs, together with a London tailor, Thomas Gay, *Patent Rolls, 1461–67*, p. 345.

6. *Rotuli Parliamentorum* V, pp. 462–3.

12. LORD HASTINGS OF HASTINGS, 1461

1. For Hastings' rewards, *Complete Peerage* VI, p. 371.

2. For Hastings' affinity, William H. Dunham, 'Lord Hastings' Indentured Retainers'; but also M. Hicks, 'Lord Hastings' Indentured Retainers', in *Richard III and his Rivals*.

3. For Lord Grey of Codnor and Roger Vernon's murder, *Annales [Rerum Anglicarum]*, pp. 788–9 – '*factum est horribile murdrum in quadam parte iuxta Derby*'. Also S. M. Wright, 'The Derbyshire Gentry in the Fifteenth Century', Derbyshire Record Society Vol. 8 (1983).

4. Robert Russell, *The Boke of Nurture folowyng Englond's gise . . .*', ed. F. J. Furnivall, London, 1868.

5. Ross, *Edward IV*, p. 317.

6. Hugh Bryce (or Brice) and his son James had worked with Hastings since 1462, when they had been entrusted with the post of 'usher of the King's Exchange within the Tower of London'. According to the Close Rolls, in 1469 Bryce was appointed 'deputy to William Lord Hastings in his office of master and worker of the King's moneys of gold and silver and keeper of the mints and exchanges in the Tower of London, the realm of England and the town of Calais.' Very rich, a banker who helped to finance Margaret of York's marriage settlement, he was

greatly respected; when an Act of 1478 gave Irishmen in England the choice of going home or of paying a tax for maintaining law and order in Ireland, he was specifically exempted. Bryce survived Lord Hastings, becoming Mayor of London and being knighted by Henry VII.

7. For the recoinage of 1464, Sir J. Craig, *The Mint: A History of the London Mint from AD 287 to 1948*, Cambridge, 1953.

8. There were never more than thirty to forty Knights and Esquires of the Body.

9. For Ralph's post at the Tower, *Patent Rolls, 1461–67*, p. 14.

10. 'The great majority of contemporary Englishmen regarded Wales with fear and suspicion.' R. A. Griffiths, 'Wales and the Marches', in *Fifteenth Century England*.

11. For John Donne's background, McFarlane, *Hans Memling*.

13. THE ADVENTURES OF DR MORTON, 1462–63

1. For William Hastings' letter to Lannoy, Scofield, *Life and Reign of Edward IV* II, pp. 461–2.

2. Clinker-built, about 50 tons and with 25 oars a side, the ballinger was not unlike the Mediterranean galley, but better suited for northern waters. Besides a crew of forty, they usually carried ten men-at-arms and ten archers. These may have been 'King's Ships' of the Scots Crown.

3. For Morton's loss of the archdeaconry of Norwich on 20 March 1464, *Patent Rolls, 1461–67*, p. 436.

14. THE LORD CHAMBERLAIN AND THE UNWELCOME GUEST, 1463

1. For this episode, Scofield, 'Henry, Duke of Somerset and Edward IV', in *English Historical Review* 21 (1906).

2. 'King Edward held him very dear' – '*valde carum*', *Annales [rerum Anglicarum]*, p. 781.

3. For Somerset, M. Hicks, 'Edward IV, the Duke of Somerset and Lancastrian Loyalism in the North', in *Northern History* XX (1984).

15. KING EDWARD FINDS A QUEEN, 1464

1. For Lencastre, C. Schofield, 'An Engagement of Service to Warwick the Kingmaker', in *English Historical Review* XXIX (1914).

2. For witchcraft, H. A. Kelly, 'English Kings and the Fear of Sorcery', in *Medieval Studies* 39 (1977).

3. More, *History of King Richard the Third*, p. 64.

4. For the Woodvilles, Lander, 'The Changing Role of the Wydevilles in Yorkist Politics to 1483', in *Patronage, Pedigree and Power in Later Medieval England*; and Lander, 'Marriage and politics in the fifteenth century; the Nevilles and the Wydevilles', in *Crown and Nobility*.

5. For Elizabeth and Hastings, Lander, *Crown and Nobility*, p. 107.

16. DR MORTON IN EXILE, 1464

1. [Queen] 'Margaret's diplomacy was singularly ineffective – until, that is, extraneous factors gave her and her son a certain importance in international affairs.' Griffiths, *Henry VI*. But Fortescue 'showed an increasing sense of *realpolitik*', according to A. Gross, 'Lancaster in Exile', in *History Today* 42 (August 1992).

17. LADY MARGARET ENTERTAINS KING EDWARD, 1468

1. For Old Woking, D. J. Haggard, 'The ruins of Old Woking Palace', in *Surrey Archaeological Collections* 55 (1958); also R. A. C. Goodwin-Austen, 'Woking Manor', in ibid 7 (1874).
2. Jones and Underwood, *The King's Mother*, p. 252.
3. For the Stafford–Woodville links, Rawcliffe, *The Staffords*; and Hicks, *False, fleeting, perjur'd Clarence*, p. 35.
4. Jones and Underwood, pp. 140–1.

18. 'MY LORD OF OXFORD IS COMMIT TO THE TOWER', 1468

1. Waurin, V, p. 363.
2. Schofield, 'The Early Life of John de Vere, thirteenth Earl of Oxford', in *English Historical Review* xxix (1914).
3. For Cook, M. Hicks, 'The Case of Sir Thomas Cook 1468', in *English Historical Review* xc (1978).
4. For Oxford's arrest, *Plumpton Correspondence*, pp. 19–20.
5. Dr Hicks believes so: 'Warwick had obtained the restoration of John de Vere to the earldom of Oxford and had married him to his sister Margaret.' *False, fleeting, perjur'd Clarence*, p. 45.

19. 'ROBIN OF REDESDALE' INVADES THE SOUTH COUNTRY, 1469

1. The best account of these months is in Hicks, op. cit.
2. Their letter and Robin's manifesto are printed in the notes to Warkworth's *Chronicle* (ed. Halliwell), pp. 46–51.
3. For an officially inspired account of these events, *Chronicle of the Rebellion in Lincolnshire, 1470.*

20. 'ELEVEN DAYS', 1470

1. For Edward IV's grant of lands to John Lambert, *Patent Rolls, 1467–77*, pp. 186–7. Nicholas Barker, 'The Real Jane Shore', overlooked the grant by confusing John with another John Lambert who was active in the West Country during Edward IV's reign.
2. 'The Manner and Guiding of the Earl of Warwick at Angers', in Ellis, *Original Letters*, Series II, I.
3. For John Lambert's 'exoneration' from his aldermanry, Corporation of London Records Office, Journal of Common Council, 7, f. 221.

21. THE 'READEPTION', 1470–71

1. For Clarence's dangerously threatened position, see Hicks, op. cit., pp. 96–100.
2. For Oxford's occupation of Lord Hastings' London house, *The Great Chronicle of London*, p. 212; for his condemning to death the Earl of Worcester, *Warkworth*, p. 13.
3. For Henry Spelman (or Spilman), MP, Wedgwood, *Biographies*.

22. WILLIAM HASTINGS IN EXILE, 1470–71

1. For the identification, Pamela Tudor-Craig, *Richard III* (National Portrait Gallery catalogue) 1973, p. 39.
2. For John Donne's triptych, McFarlane, *Hans Memling*.

3. D. H. Turner, *The Hastings Hours*, London, 1983.

23. WHO WILL WIN?, 1471

1. Sir Richard Corbet of Morton Corbet, b. 1448, was Lord Ferrers' son-in-law. Wedgwood, *Biographies*, p. 222.
2. Jones and Underwood, p. 49.
3. Ibid., p. 55.

24. LORD OXFORD LOSES A BATTLE – BARNET, 1471

1. For the authorship of the *Arrivall*, see L. Visser-Fuchs, 'Nicholas Harpisfield, Clerk of the Signet, Author and Murderer', in *The Ricardian*, June 1994.
2. According to Warkworth, 'one of the Erle [of] Oxenfordes brother with the comons of the cuntre arose up togedere, and put hym abake to the see ageyne.' *Chronicle*, p. 13.
3. For Lord Oxford's letter to his wife after the battle of Barnet, *Paston Letters* V, pp. 101–2.

25. DR MORTON TURNS YORKIST – TEWKESBURY, 1471

1. For Lancastrian optimism, *Paston Letters* V, p. 103.
2. At the time of writing, a housing estate is about to be built on the site of the battlefield.
3. Warkworth says enigmatically, 'And ther was slayne in the felde, Prynce Edwarde, which cryede for socoure to his brother-in-lawe the Duke of Clarence'. *Chronicle*, p. 18.
4. 'if the Bastard's attack on London had not come too late, things might have been very different'. Ross, *Edward IV*, p. 176.

26. WILLIAM HASTINGS, LIEUTENANT OF CALAIS, 1471

1. Appointed a Knight of the Body in 1471, Ralph was Captain of Guisnes 1474–83 and 1484–85. Wedgwood, *Biographies*, p. 433. For Richard Hastings, Lord Welles, *Complete Peerage* XII, pp. 445–8.
2. Scofield, *Life and Reign of Edward IV* II, pp. 36–37.
3. For Lord Hastings' trading activities, Scofield, op. cit., II, pp. 420, 454, 457.
4. For Kirby, A. H. Hamilton Thompson, 'The building accounts of Kirby Muxloe, 1480–1484', in *Transactions of the Leicestershire Archaeological Society* II, Pts 7 and 8 (1919–20); for Ashby, K. Hiller, 'William Lord Hastings and Ashby-de-la-Zouch', in *The Ricardian*, Vol. 8 (1988).
5. For this story, Dugdale, *Baronage*, p. 582, quoting J. Leland, *Collectanea* I (ed. T. Hearn), London, 1770, p. 144.
6. For Sir James Harrington, Wedgwood, *Biographies*, pp. 423–4; and Ross, *Edward IV*, pp. 408–9.
7. For the Garter ceremonies, Sir E. Ashmole, *The History of the Most Noble Order of the Garter*, London, 1672; and G. F. Beltz, *Memorials of the Most Noble Order of the Garter*, London, 1841.
8. For the reburial of the Duke of York, P. W. Hammond, A. F. Sutton and L. Visser-Fuchs in *The Ricardian*, Vol. 10 (December 1994).
9. 'Caxton's amusingly and unashamedly incompetent woodcuts are the first printed illustrations in any English book; perhaps this was the special feature which attracted the patronage of Bryce and Hastings.' G. D. Painter, *William Caxton*, London, 1976, p. 110.
10. Yet Cora Scofield, a most knowledgeable historian of the period, thought that 'Lord Hastings

. . . was neither a wise man nor a good.' *Life and Reign of Edward IV* II, p. 3.

27. LADY MARGARET BEAUFORT'S FOURTH HUSBAND, 1472

1. Jones and Underwood, pp. 58–59, 97.

28. LORD OXFORD TURNS PIRATE, 1473

1. For the monks' plot and Lord Oxford, *Paston Letters* V, p. 186.
2. For Lord Oxford in Cornwall, A. L. Rowse, 'The Turbulent Career of Sir Henry Bodrugan', in *History* xxix (1944), pp. 17–26.
3. For Clarence's dangerous boasting, *Paston Letters* V, p. 195.
4. For the naval blockade of Lord Oxford on St Michael's Mount, Scofield, *Life and Reign of Edward IV* II, p. 87.
5. For the Duke of Gloucester's persecution of old Lady Oxford, M. Hicks, 'The Last Days of Elizabeth, Countess of Oxford', in *English Historical Review* C (1988).

29. EDWARD IV INVADES FRANCE, 1475

1. For the speech to the House of Commons about the general suffering brought by the Wars of the Roses, *Literae Cantuarienses* III, ed. J. B. Sheppard (Rolls Series, London, 1889), No. 1079, pp. 274ff.
2. For the English invasion of France, F. P. Barnard, *Edward IV's French Expedition of 1475, the Leaders and Their Badges* (College of Arms MS 2 M 16), Oxford, 1925; and Lander, 'The Hundred Years' War and Edward IV's 1475 campaign in France', in *Crown and Nobility*, pp. 91–93.
3. For Edward IV and the Duke of Exeter's drowning, *The New Chronicles of England and France*, p. 663; and also *Calendar of State Papers . . . Milan* I, p. 220.

30. MRS SHORE'S DIVORCE, 1476

1. For Edward IV's love of Jane, Thomas More, *The History of King Richard the Third*, p. 57.
2. For the slandering of Mr Lambert as a traitor to Henry VI, *Calendars of Plea and Memoranda Rolls, 1458–82*, pp. 57–64.
3. For the Goldsmiths' law-suit against John Lambert, *Goldsmiths' Company Minute Book* A, pp. 170–2.
4. For John Agard of Foston, A. Sutton, 'William Shore, Merchant of London and Derby, vol 106 (1986) pp. 130–6.
5. For the 'gift', *Calendar of the Close Rolls, 1468–71*, No. 1147.
6. For Mr Shore's shortcomings, *Calendar of Entries in the Papal Registers . . .', XIII pt 2*, Vol. XIII, pp. 487–8 – '*quia tamen idem Wilhelmus idem adeo frigidus et impotens existit quod eandem Elizabeth interim carnaliter cognoscere non potuerat neque poterat, eadem Elizabeth que mater esse et prolem procreare desiderabat . . .*'
7. For Dr Thomas Millyngton, DNB.
8. For the career of Jane's ex-husband, A. F. Sutton, 'William Shore, Merchant of London and Derby', in *Derbyshire Archaeological Journal*, Vol. 106 (1986), pp. 127–39.
9. 'Jane Shore and Eton', in *Etoniana*, December 1972, pp. 408–10.

31. LORD OXFORD TRIES TO DROWN HIMSELF, 1478

1. For Sir John's view of the situation, *Paston Letters* V, p. 270.
2. For Louis XI's scheming, Ross, *Edward IV*, p. 240; and Scofield, *Life and Reign of Edward IV* II, p. 188.
3. For Edmund Bedingfeld's 'tidings' from Calais, *Paston Letters* V, pp. 296–7.
4. Hicks suggests that Gloucester may at least have participated in his brother's trial in some way or other. *False, Fleeting, Perjur'd Clarence*, p. 181.
5. For Lord Oxford's attempted suicide, *Paston Letters* VI, p. 2.

32. DR JOHN MORTON, BISHOP OF ELY, 1478

1. Schofield, *Life and Reign of Edward IV* II, pp. 246–8.
2. For Robert Morton, DNB.
3. *Calendar of Patent Rolls, 1476–85*, p. 215.

33. HASTINGS 'HIGHLY IN THE KING'S INDIGNATION', 1482–83

1. Lyell and Watney, *Acts of Court of the Mercers' Company*, p. 125.
2. For King Edward's hunting party, Sir Thomas More, *History of King Richard the Third*, p. 6.
3. *The Great Chronicle of London*, pp. 228–9. (More says the party was at Windsor)
4. For Mancini's characterization of Lord Hastings, *De Occupatione Regni Anglie*, pp. 67–8.
5. For the accusations made by Hastings and Rivers about each other, Mancini, *De Occupatione Regni Anglie*, pp. 68–9; and Gairdner, *History of the Life and Reign of Richard the Third*, pp. 338–9.
6. For Bartholomew Reed replacing Lord Hastings as master of the mint, *Calendar of Patent Rolls, 1476–85*, p. 343.
7. For Hastings' conversation with Tiger [or 'Hastings'] Pursuivant, Sir Thomas More, *History of King Richard the Third*, p. 52.
8. For the king's fury on hearing of the Treaty of Arras, Schofield, *Life and Reign of Edward IV* II, pp. 356–7; and Ross, *Edward IV*, p. 292.
9. For the funeral of King Edward, Scofield, *Life and Reign of Edward IV*, pp. 366–8.

34. THE END OF WILLIAM HASTINGS, 1483

1. Hicks believes that Gloucester had no intention of usurping the throne until after the death of Edward IV. 'Richard III as Duke of Gloucester: A Study in Character', in *Borthwick Papers* 70 (1986), p. 249.
2. For the threat to Richard's estates which resulted from George Nevill's death, Hicks, 'Richard III as Duke of Gloucester'.
3. For Buckingham, Rawcliffe, *The Staffords*, pp. 28–35.
4. For the Queen's foreboding, Sir Thomas More, *History of King Richard the Third*, p. 22.
5. 'The evidence for any conspiracy between Hastings and the Woodvilles, especially with Mistress Shore – the former mistress of Edward IV and now the mistress of Lord Hastings – as go-between, is slight indeed, and rests entirely on Richard's own allegations.' Ross, *Richard III*, p. 81.
6. For Catesby, 'William Catesby, Counsellor to Richard III', in *Bulletin of the John Rylands Library*, Vol. 42 (1959).

7. For More's account of Gloucester's coup, *History of King Richard the Third*, pp. 47–52.
8. For Vergil's account of the coup, *Three Books of Polydore Vergil's English History*, pp. 179–82.
9. For Lord Hastings' will, PCC 10 Logge, 1483, Public Record Office Prob. 11/7, f.10.
10. For Canon Stallworth's report, *The Stonor Letters* II, p. 161.
11. Not only did Richard reappoint Hastings' brother Ralph as Captain of Guisnes but he even made him a Knight of the Body.

35. MRS SHORE DOES PENANCE, 1483

1. 'Mastres Chore is in prisone: what schall happyne hyr I knowe nott' – in *The Stonor Letters* quoted above.
2. Mancini, *De Occupatione Regni Anglie*, pp. 90–1.
3. *The Great Chronicle of London*, p. 233.
4. For the theft of Jane's goods, Sir Thomas More, *The History of King Richard the Third*, p. 55.
5. We know that Jane was imprisoned in Ludgate gaol from the testimony of King Richard himself, in the letter he wrote to Dr Russell in October – reproduced at the beginning of Ch. 37.
6. The text of the Act *Titulus Regis* is in *Rotuli Parliamentorum* VI, pp. 240–2.
7. For More's account of Jane's penance, *History of King Richard the Third*, pp. 54–55.

36. LADY MARGARET BEAUFORT'S CONSPIRACY, 1483

1. A. F. Sutton and P. W. Hammond, *The Coronation of Richard III: The Extant Documents*, Gloucester, 1983, pp. 278–81.
2. 'This is the father's own figure, this his own countenance, the very print of his visage, the sure undoubted image, the plain express likeness of the noble duke', claimed Dr Shaa in his sermon at Paul's Cross. Sir Thomas More, *The History of King Richard the Third*, p. 68.
3. J. Stow, *Annales of England*, 1631, p. 459. But see M. Hicks, 'Unweaving the Web: the Plot of July 1483 against Richard III and its Wider Significance', in *The Ricardian* IX, September 1993.
4. Sir Thomas More, *History of King Richard the Third*, pp. 88–9.
5. Jones and Underwood, *The King's Mother*, pp. 60–1.
6. *Hall's Chronicle*, pp. 388–9.
7. Sir George Buck, *The History of King Richard III*, ed. A. N. Kincaid, Gloucester, 1979.
8. Rawcliffe, *The Staffords*, p. 29.
9. The proclamation is printed in Rymer, *Foedera* XI, pp. 204–5.
10. Ross, *Richard III*, p. 138.

37. MRS SHORE MARRIES AGAIN, 1483

1. For the nature of Mr Lynom's work, M. Hicks, 'The Cartulary of Richard III as Duke of Gloucester in British Library Manuscript Cotton Julius B XVIII', in *Richard III and his Rivals*.
2. For Lynom's career, Barker, 'The Real Jane Shore', op. cit., pp. 388–91.
3. For John Lambert's successful law-suit, *Close Rolls 1476–85*, pp. 395–6.
5. H. Chauncey, *The Historical Antiquities of Hertfordshire* II, London, 1700, p. 66.,
6. For the identification of Pulters with Hinxworth Place, *Victoria County History of Hertfordshire*, III 1912, p. 236.

7. For the later life of Jane's first husband, Sutton, 'William Shore, Merchant of London and Derby', op. cit., pp. 130–9.
8. Ross, *Richard III*, pp. 175–6.
9. A. J. Pollard, 'The Tyranny of Richard III', in *Journal of Medieval History*, 1977 (iii).

38. 'MOTHER TO THE KING'S GREAT REBEL AND TRAITOR', 1484

1. Margaret was 'commonly caulyd the head of that conspiracy'. Polydore Vergil, *English History*, p. 204.
2. For the sentence against Lady Margaret, *Rotuli Parliamentorum* VI, p. 250.
3. Quoted by Jones and Underwood, *The King's Mother*, p. 65.
4. Chrimes, *Henry VII*, p. 53.

39. DR MORTON VISITS ROME, 1484–85

1. Ross, *Richard III*, p. 113.
2. 'Richard III was the first English king to use character-assassination as a deliberate instrument of policy.' Ross, ibid, p. 138.
3. 'How it was that John Morton who had fled to Flanders got wind of this plot and was able to send warning to Henry remains a mystery, but this signal service, which must be understood as equivalent to saving Henry's life and all that depended thereon, was one that Henry could never forget . . .' Chrimes, op. cit., p. 29. Ross suggests Lord Stanley as the source. *Richard III* p. 199.
4. For Morton's entry into the confraternity at Rome in 1485, confirming his presence in the Eternal City, P. Egidi, *Fonti per la Storia d'Italia*, Institutia Storia Italia, 45 (1914).

40. LORD OXFORD WINS A BATTLE, 1485

1. As Margaret's steward, it was surely on her account that Bray had succeeded in collecting 'no small sum of money' for Henry. Vergil, *English History*, p. 559.
2. Recently the exact site of the battlefield has been disputed. An alternative site at least half a mile away to the south-west has been suggested, towards the village of Dadlington. However, the battle was certainly fought in the vicinity of Bosworth.
3. For Lord Oxford's counter-charge at Bosworth, Vergil, *English History*, pp. 563–4.
4. Part of the legend is that it was Margaret's steward, Reginald Bray, who found the crown. This detail first appears in W. Hutton, *The battle of Bosworth Field*, 1788.

41. THE LAST BATTLE – STOKE, 1487

1. 'Mornynge Remembraunce', p. 306.
2. In a petition of 1489 All Souls' College, Oxford referred tactfully to 'Youre dere Uncle of Noble Memorie Henry the Sexte' – *Rotuli Parliamentorum* VI, p. 436.
3. For the so-called 'great grant' to Margaret, Jones and Underwood, op. cit., p. 75.
4. Ibid, p. 100.
5. For Lady Surrey's good opinion of Lord Oxford, *Paston Letters* VI, pp. 87–8.
6. For Oxford on William Paston's madness, *Paston Letters* VI, p. 167.
7. For the King's letter to Lord Ormonde, Cooper, *Memoir of Margaret*, p. 38.
8. Ross, *The Wars of the Roses*, p. 105.

9. Cooper, op. cit., p. 40.
10. For Margaret's signature, Jones and Underwood, op. cit., p. 86.

42. PERKIN WARBECK, 1491–99

1. Bacon, *Henry VII*, p. 154.
2. For the implications of this revolt, M. Hicks, 'The Yorkist Rebellion of 1489 reconsidered', in *Northern History* xxii (1986).
3. For Abbot Sant's conspiracy, *Rotuli Parliamentorum* VI, pp. 436–7.
4. For the gift of the porpoise, *Paston Letters* VI, pp. 138–9.
5. The best account of Warbeck's career is I. Arthurson, *The Perkyn Warbeck Conspiracy 1491–1499*, Gloucester, 1994.
6. For the Battle of Blackheath, Busch, *England under the Tudors*, pp. 110–12.
7. For Ralph Wulford, *Great Chronicle of London*, p. 289.
8. 'Ferdinando had written to the King in plain terms, that he saw no assurance of his succession, so long as the earl of Warwick lived; and that he was loth to send his daughter to troubles and dangers.' Bacon, *Henry VII*, p. 179.

EPILOGUE: THE FOUR SURVIVORS

1. *Calendar of state papers, Spanish, I, Henry VII*, pp. 177–8.
2. The letter to Ormonde is in Cooper, *Memorial to Margaret*, pp. 48–9.
3. '*Vita Henrici Septimi*', in *Memorials of King Henry VII*, pp. 14–16.
4. 'Mornynge Remembraunce', p. 300.
5. Ibid, pp. 296–7.
6. These letters are in Cooper, *Memorial to Margaret*, p. 64 and pp. 91–4.
7. 'Mornynge Remembraunce', pp. 300–1.
8. Letter in Cooper, op. cit., p. 64.
9. For the Cardinal's skull, 'How posterity beheaded Morton: the case of the missing head', in *The Ricardian*, September 1992.
10. For Lord Oxford's expenditure, see M. J. Tucker, 'The Household Accounts, 1490–1491, of John de Vere' in *English Historical Review* 75 (1960).
11. For Oxford's petition to recover his mother's lands, stressing that Gloucester had made her hand them over 'by compulcion, cohercion and empresonment', *Rotuli Parliamentorum* VI, pp. 473–4.
12. For Oxford's patronage of Caxton, G. D. Painter, *William Caxton*, pp. 164–70.
13. For the King's visit to Lord Oxford, Bacon, *Henry VII*, p. 192.
14. For these details, Sir W. H. St John Hope, 'The Last Testament and Inventory of John de Veer, thirteenth Earl of Oxford', in *Archaeologia* LXVI (1915).
15. Ibid, p. 310.
16. Ross, *Wars of the Roses*, pp. 143–4.
17. For the return of Mr Lambert's West Country estates to the Courtenays, *Patent Rolls, Henry VII* I, pp. 28–9.
18. For Mr Lambert's will, Barker, 'The Real Jane Shore', p. 38.
19. Birley, 'Jane Shore in Literature', p. 407.
20. '*Miseram hodie vitam mendicando sustinet*'.

Select Bibliography

CONTEMPORARY

Acts of Court of the Mercers Company, 1453–1527, ed. L. Lyell and F. Watney, CUP, 1936.
ANDRÉ, B., *De vita atque gestis Henrici Septimi . . .*, in *Memorials of King Henry the Seventh*.
Annales [rerum anglicarum], in *Letters and Papers Illustrative of the Wars of the English in France*, Vol. II, Pt 2. London, 1869.
John Benet's Chronicle for the years 1400 to 1462, ed. G. L. Harriss and M. A. Harriss, in *Camden Miscellany*, Vol. XXIV, London, 1972.
A Brief Latin Chronicle, in *Three Fifteenth Century Chronicles*.
Brief Notes, in *Three Fifteenth Century Chronicles*.
Calendar of the Close Rolls: Henry VI, Vol. VI, 1454–61; Edward IV, Vols I–II, 1461–8, 1468–76; Edward IV – Edward V – Richard III, 1476–85; Henry VII, 1485–1500, London, 1949–67.
Calendar of Entries in Papal Registers Relating to Great Britain and Ireland Vol. XIII, pt 2 (1471–84), col. J. A. Twemlow, London, 1956.
Calendar of the Fine Rolls: XX (Edward IV, 1461–71); XXI (Edward IV – Edward V – Richard III, 1471–85), London, 1949 and 1961.
Calendarium Inquisitionum Post Mortem sive Exceatarum, ed. J. Cayley and J. Bayley (Record Commission), IV, London, 1828.
Calendar of the Patent Rolls: Henry VI, Vol. VI, 1452–61; Edward IV, Vols I–II, 1461–7, 1466–77; Edward IV – Edward V – Richard III, 1476–85, London, 1897–1901; and Henry VII, Vols I and II, London, 1956–63.
Calendar of Plea and Memoranda Rolls of the City of London, 1458–82, ed. P. E. Jones, CUP, 1961.
Calendar of State Papers and Manuscripts existing in the Archives and Collections of Milan, Vol. I (1385–1618), ed. A. B. Hinds, London, 1913.
Calendar of State Papers and Manuscripts, relating to English Affairs, existing in the Archives and Collections of Venice and in other Libraries of Northern Italy, ed. R. Brown, London, 1864.
CAXTON, W., *Prologues and Epilogues*, London, 1928.
——, *The Book of the Fayttes of Armes and of Chyualre*, London, 1937.
The Cely Letters, 1472–1488, ed. A. Hanham, London, 1975.
CHASTELLAIN, G., *Oeuvres*, ed. Kervyn de Lettenhove, Brussels, 1863–6.
The Chronicle of Calais, ed. J. G. Nichols, Camden Society, 1846.
Chronicle of the Rebellion in Lincolnshire, 1470, ed. J. G. Nichols, Camden Society, 1847.
Chronicles of London, ed. C. L. Kingsford, OUP, 1905.
COMMYNES, P. de, *Memoires*, ed. J. Calmette and G. Durville, Paris, 1924–5.

An English Chronicle of the reigns of Richard II, Henry IV, Henry V, and Henry VI, Camden Society, 1856.

Extracts from the Municipal Records of the City of York during the Reigns of Edward IV, Edward V and Richard III, ed. R. Davies, London, 1843.

FABYAN, R., *New Chronicles of England and France*, ed. H. Ellis, London, 1811.

FISHER, J., *The English Works of John Fisher*, ed. J. E. B. Mayor, Early English Text Society, 1876.

Foedera, Conventiones, ed. T. Rymer, The Hague, 1739–45.

FORTESCUE, SIR J., *De Laudibus Legum Angliae*, trans. F. Grigor, London, 1917.

—, *The Governance of England*, ed. C. Plummer, OUP, 1885.

—, *The Works of Sir John Fortescue, Knight, Chief Justice of England and Lord Chancellor to King Henry the Sixth*, ed. Lord Clermont, London, 1869.

GRAFTON, R., *Grafton's Chronicle, or History of England*, London, 1809.

—, *The Chronicle of John Hardyng . . . Together with the Continuation by R. Grafton*, ed. H. Ellis, London, 1812.

Grants etc. from the Crown during the Reign of Edward the Fifth, ed. J. G. Nichols, Camden Society, 1854.

The Great Chronicle of London, ed. A. H. Thomas and I. D. Thornley, London, 1938.

Gregory's Chronicle, in *The Historical Collections of a Citizen of London in the Fifteenth Century*, ed. J. Gairdner, Camden Society, London, 1876.

HALL, E., *Chronicle*, ed. H. Ellis, London, 1809.

Historiae Croylandensis Continuatio, in *Rerum Anglicarum Scriptores Veterum*, ed. W. Fulman, Oxford, 1684.

Historie of the Arrivall of Edward IV in England and the finall Recovery of his kingdomes from Henry VI, ed. J. A. Bruce, Camden Society, 1838.

Household Books of John, Duke of Norfolk, and Thomas, Earl of Surrey, ed. P. Collier, Roxburghe Club, 1844.

Ingulph's Chronicle of the Abbey of Croyland, trans. and ed. H. Riley, London, 1854.

Italian Relation: A Relation, or rather a True Account, of the Island of England, ed. C. A. Sneyd, Camden Society, 1847.

LELAND, J., *Itinerary in England and Wales*, London, 1964.

—, *Colectanea*, London, 1787.

Letters and Papers Illustrative of the Reigns of Richard III and Henry VII, ed. J. Gairdner, London, 1861–3

Letters and Papers Illustrative of the Wars of the English in France during the Reign of Henry the Sixth, ed. J. Stevenson, London, 1864.

MALORY, SIR T., *The Works of Sir Thomas Malory*, ed. E. Vinaver, OUP, 1973.

MANCINI, DOMINIC, *The Usurpation of Richard the Third*, trans. and ed. C. A. J. Armstrong, OUP, 1969.

Materials for a History of the Reign of Henry VII, ed. W. Campbell, London, 1873.

Memorials of King Henry the Seventh, ed. J. Gairdner, London, 1858.

MOLINET, J., *Chronique*, ed. G. Doutrepont and O. Jodogne, Brussels, 1935.

MORE, SIR T., *The History of King Richard III and Selections from the English and Latin Poems*, ed. R. S. Sylvester, Newhaven and London, 1963

—, *Utopia*, in Vol. 4 of the Yale edition of *The Complete Works of Sir Thomas More*, ed. E.

Surtz and J. H. Hexter, Newhaven and London, 1965.

Original Letters Illustrative of English History, ed. H. Ellis, London, 1824–46.

Paston Letters, 1422–1509, ed. J. Gairdner, London, 1904.

Plumpton Correspondence, ed. T. Stapleton, Camden Society, 1839.

Rotuli Parliamentorum, ed. J. Starchey and others, London, 1767–77.

ROUS, J., *Joannis Rossi Antiquarii Warwicensis Historia Regum Angliae*, ed. T. Hearne, Oxford, 1745.

—, *The Rous Roll*, ed. C. R. Ross, Gloucester, 1980.

Six Town Chronicles of England, ed. R. Flenley, OUP, 1911.

The Stonor Letters and Papers, 1290–1483, ed. C. L. Kingsford, Camden Series, 1919.

Three Fifteenth Century Chronicles, ed. J. Gairdner, Camden Society, 1880.

VERGIL, POLYDORE, *The Anglica Historia of Polydore Vergil, A.D. 1485–1537*, trans. D. Hay, Camden Series, 1950.

—, *Three Books of Polydore Vergil's English History . . . from an early translation*, ed. Sir H. Ellis, Camden Society, 1844.

WARKWORTH, JOHN, *A Chronicle of the First Thirteen Years of the Reign of King Edward the Fourth*, ed. J. O. Halliwell, Camden Society, 1839.

WAURIN, JEAN DE, *Recueil des Croniques et Anchiennes Istories de la Grant Bretagne, a present nomme Engleterre*, ed. Sir W. Hardy and E. L. C. P. Hardy, London, 1891.

WORCESTRE, WILLIAM, *Itineraries*, ed. J. H. Harvey, OUP, 1969.

LATER AND MODERN

ARTHURSON, I, The Perkyn Warbeck Conspiracy 1491–1499, Gloucester, 1994.

BACON, SIR F., *The History of the Reign of Henry VII*, Cambridge, 1888.

BEAVEN, A.B., *The Aldermen of the City of London*, London, 1908–13.

BUCK, SIR G., *The History of the Life and Reigne of Richard the Third*, London, 1646.

—, *The History of King Richard the Third*, ed. A. N. Kincaid, Gloucester, 1979.

BURNE, A.H., *Battlefields of England*, London, 1950.

—, *More Battlefields of England*, London, 1952.

BUSCH, W., *England under the Tudors, Henry VII*, New York, 1965.

CHRIMES, S. B., *Henry VII*, London, 1972.

—, *Lancastrians, Yorkists and Henry VII*, London, 1972.

Complete Peerage, ed. G. C. Cockayne and V. Gibbs, London, 1959.

COOPER, C. H., *The Lady Margaret: A Memoir of Margaret, Countess of Richmond and Derby*, Cambridge, 1874.

Dictionary of National Biography, passim.

DUGDALE, W., *The Baronage of England*, London, 1675.

DUNHAM, W. H., 'Lord Hastings' Indentured Retainers', in *Transactions of the Connecticut Academy of Arts and Sciences* (xxxix), New Haven, Connecticut, 1955.

EMDEN, A. B., *A Biographical Register of the University of Oxford to AD 1500*, Oxford, 1957–9.

—, *A Biographical Register of the University of Cambridge to 1500*, Cambridge, 1963.

Fifteenth Century England, 1399–1500: Studies in Politics and Society, ed. S. B. Chrimes, C. D. Ross and R. A. Griffiths, Manchester, 1972.

GAIRDNER, J., *History of the Life and Reign of Richard the Third*, Cambridge, 1898.

GILLINGHAM, J., *The Wars of the Roses*, London, 1981.

GOODMAN, A., *The Wars of the Roses*, London, 1981.

GREEN, V. H. H., *The Later Plantagenets*, London, 1955.

GRIFFITHS, R. A. (ed)., *The Crown and the Provinces in Later Medieval England*, Gloucester, 1980.

—, *The Reign of Henry VI*, London, 1981.

GRIFFITHS, R. A. and THOMAS, R. S., *The Making of the Tudor Dynasty*, Gloucester, 1985.

GRIFFITHS, R. A. and SHERBORNE, J. W. (eds), *Kings and Nobles 1377–1529*, Gloucester, 1986.

HABINGTON, W., *The Historie of Edward the Fourth*, London, 1640.

HAMMOND, P. W., *The Battles of Barnet and Tewkesbury*, Gloucester, 1990.

HAMPTON, W., *Memorials of the Wars of the Roses*, Upminster, 1979.

HANHAM, A., *Richard III and his Early Historians*, Oxford, 1975.

HARRISON, F. L., *Music in Medieval Britain*, London, 1958.

HARVEY, J. H., *Gothic England: A Survey of National Culture 1300–1550*, London, 1947.

HICKS, M. A., *False, Fleeting, Perjur'd Clarence*, Gloucester, 1980.

—, *Richard III and his Rivals*, London, 1991.

—, *Richard III: the Man behind the Myth*, London, 1991.

HOPE, SIR W. ST JOHN, *The Stall Plates of the Knights of the Garter*, London, 1901.

HORROX, R., *Richard III: A Study in Service*, Cambridge, 1989.

HOWARD, M., *The Early Tudor Country House*, London, 1987.

JACOB, E. F., *The Fifteenth Century 1399–1485*, Oxford, 1961.

JONES, M. K. and UNDERWOOD, M. G., *The King's Mother: Lady Margaret Beaufort, Countess of Richmond and Derby*, Cambridge, 1992.

KENDALL, P. M., *Richard III*, London, 1955.

LANDER, J. R., *Crown and Nobility 1450–1509*, London, 1976.

—, *Government and Community 1450–1509*, London, 1980.

LE NEVE, J., *Fasti Ecclesiae Anglicanae*, Oxford, 1851.

LEWIS, J., *Life of Dr John Fisher*, London, 1855.

LYELL, L. and WATNEY, F. D. (eds), *Acts of Court of the Mercers Company*, London, 1936.

MCFARLANE, K. B., *The Nobility of Later Medieval England*, Oxford, 1973.

—, *Lancastrian Kings and Lollard Knights*, Oxford, 1972.

—, *England in the Fifteenth Century*, London, 1981.

—, *Hans Memling*, Oxford, 1971.

MACKIE, J. D., *The Earlier Tudors*, Oxford, 1952.

MERTES, K., *The English Noble Household 1250–1600*, London, 1988.

METCALFE, W. C., *A Book of Knights*, London, 1885.

MUNRO, J. H. A., *Wool, Cloth and Gold: The Struggle for Bullion in Anglo-Burgundian Trade 1340–1478*, Toronto, 1972.

MYERS, A. R., *England in the Late Middle Ages*, London, 1952.

—, *The Black Book of the Household of Edward IV*, Manchester, 1959.

PAINTER, G. D., *William Caxton*, London, 1976.

POLLARD, A. J., *Richard III and the Princes*, Stroud, 1991.

POSTAN, M., *The medieval economy and society*, London, 1972.

POWER, E. and POSTAN, M. M, *Studies in English Trade in the Fifteenth Century*, Cambridge, 1951.

PUGH, T. B., *The Marcher Lordships of South Wales 1415–1536*, Cardiff, 1963.

RAWCLIFFE, C. W., *The Staffords, Earls of Stafford and Dukes of Buckingham, 1394–1521*, Cambridge, 1978.

ROSS, C. D, *Edward IV*, London, 1974.

—, *The Wars of the Roses*, London, 1976.

— (ed.), *Patronage, Pedigree and Power in Later Medieval England*, Gloucester, 1979.

—, *Richard III*, London, 1981.

SCOFIELD, C. L, *The Life and Reign of Edward IV*, London, 1923.

STOREY, R. L., *The End of the House of Lancaster*, London, 1966.

STOWE, J., *A Survey of London*, Oxford, 1908.

THOMSON, J. A. F., *The Transformation of Medieval England*, London, 1983.

THRUPP, S., *The Merchant Class of Medieval London*, Chicago, 1948.

TUDOR-CRAIG, P., *Richard III*, National Portrait Gallery, 1973.

WEDGWOOD, J. C., *History of Parliament: Biographies of Members of the Commons House 1437–1509*, London, 1936.

WOLFFE, B. P., *Henry VI*, London, 1981.

Note on brasses

The brasses are very much the stars of this book. A surprising number of people connected with the five personalities around whom this book is based are commemorated by examples which survive. Only one or two have ever been illustrated before, other than in specialist studies of brasses.

Book designers have ignored brasses, although they convey better than anything else how late medieval men and women liked to see themselves. To some extent I have pioneered their use as illustrations, in my *Hundred Year's War* (1978). I was also the first to identify the brass of Dr John Argentine (d. 1507) at King's College, Cambridge as that of the last man known to have seen alive the Princes in the Tower – reproduced in my *Richard III: England's Black Legend* (1983).

A monumental brass is generally an outline figure which has been engraved. The metal was manufactured abroad, in Germany, the Low Countries or France; known as 'latten', it was different from modern brass, an alloy of copper and calamine zinc produced in a crucible. However, the figure was shaped and engraved locally in England, fine quality brasses being specially commissinoned. When completed the figure was set in an indented stone slab, which was usually inserted into the floor of a church. The earliest English example to survive dates from 1279. Although popular in other European countries as well, more were laid down in England during the later Middle Ages than anywhere else. Many were destroyed during the Dissolution of the Monasteries, the Reformation or the Civil Wars – the metal often being melted down to make saucepans – but almost 4,000 remain.

The coats-of-arms which often accompany brasses were frequently enamelled and the unique series of medieval garter-plates – arms of Knights of the Garter – at St George's Chapel, Windsor are in fact brasses, though not generally acknowledged as such.

Incised slabs (such as William Shore's) are rare. They are very similar to brasses, etched on stone in much the same way that the latter were engraved on latten.

No period of English history is better illustrated by brasses than the Wars of the Roses, and not even the most beautiful illuminated manuscript conjures up its atmosphere more vividly – especially when the brass still lies in the ancient parish church where those whom it represents once prayed.

Index